Social Consciousness in Legal Decision Making

Social Consciousness in Legal Decision Making
Psychological Perspectives

Edited by

Richard L. Wiener
University of Nebraska-Lincoln
Lincoln, Nebraska, USA

Brian H. Bornstein
University of Nebraska-Lincoln
Lincoln, Nebraska, USA

Robert Schopp
University of Nebraska-Lincoln
Lincoln, Nebraska, USA

Steven L. Willborn
University of Nebraska-Lincoln
Lincoln, Nebraska, USA

 Springer

Richard L. Wiener
Dept. of Psychology
College of Law
University of Nebraska-Lincoln
338 Burnett Hall
Lincoln, NE 68588-0308

Robert Schopp
College of Law
University of Nebraska-Lincoln
1875 North 42nd Street
Lincoln, NE 68583-0902

Brian H. Bornstein
Dept. of Psychology
University of Nebraska-Lincoln
335 Burnett Hall
Lincoln, NE 68588-0308

Steven L. Willborn
College of Law
University of Nebraska-Lincoln
42nd and Fair Streets
Lincoln, NE 68502-0902

Library of Congress Control Number: 2006938537

ISBN-13: 978-0-387-46217-2   e-ISBN-13: 978-0-387-46218-9

Printed on acid-free paper.

9 8 7 6 5 4 3 2 1

springer.com

Contributors

Mccra Adya
Syracuse University
900 S. Crouse Avenue
Crouse-Hinds Hall, Suite 300
Syracuse, NY 13244-2130

Brian H. Bornstein
Dept. of Psychology
University of Nebraska-Lincoln
335 Burnett Hall
Lincoln, NE 68588-0308

Faye J. Crosby
Psychology Department
Social Sciences II 379
University of California
Santa Cruz, CA 95064

Samuel R. Gross
University of Michigan Law School
625 South State State Street
Ann Arbor, Michigan 48109

Barbara A. Gutek
McClelland Hall,
Eller College of Management
The University of Arizona

Jennifer S. Hunt
238 Burnett Hall
University of Nebraska, Lincoln

Mark R. Killenbeck
Wylie H. Davis Distinguished
   Professor of Law
228 Waterman Hall
University of Arkansas School of Law
Fayetteville, Arkansas 72701

Margaret Bull Kovera
John Jay College of Criminal Justice
445 W 59th Street
New York, NY 10019

Frederick M. Lawrence
Dean and Robert Kramer Research
   Professor of Law The George
Washington University Law
   School 2000 H Street, NW
   Suite E-200
Washington, DC 20052

Erin M. Richter
238 Burnett Hall
University of Nebraska, Lincoln

Amy E. Smith
Assistant Professor, Psychology
San Francisco State University
1600 Holloway Avenue
San Francisco, CA 94132

Tom R. Tyler
6 Washington Place,
New York University
New York, NY 10003

Richard L. Wiener
Dept. of Psychology
College of Law
University of Nebraska-Lincoln
338 Burnett Hall
Lincoln, NE 68588-0308

Steven L. Willborn
College of Law
University of Nebraska-Lincoln
42nd and Fair Streets
Lincoln, NE 68502-0902

Cynthia Willis-Esqueda
Dept. of Psychology
University of Nebraska-Lincoln
238 Burnett Hall
Lincoln, NE 68588-0308

Preface

Interdisciplinary scholarship in the area of Law and Psychology Law has grown in volume, variety, and sophistication in the last 10 years, so much so, that the area has become a mainstay of graduate training in the doctoral programs in psychology both in applied areas (clinical forensic psychology) and research based academics (experimental psychology and law). Researchers and commentators study and explore topics of risk assessment, psychopathy, forensic evaluation, children as witnesses, children as victims, jury decision making, eyewitness identification, and false confessions, just to name a few. There are regular meetings of the American Psychology-Law Society, the Law and Society Association, and the American Psychological Association that include dozens and dozens of papers, talks, posters, and symposia that explore many facets of these and other topics that examine the psychology of law, psychology in the law, and the law as a regulator of psychological practice.

This book is different! It is at least as much a Law and Psychology volume as it is a Psychology and Law volume. We apply the approach of Social Analytic Jurisprudence (see Chapter 1 this volume) to examine some current and controversial topics at the intersection of Law and Psychology. Social analytic jurisprudence begins with an analysis of legal doctrine, carefully looking for assumptions that the law makes about human behavior and proceeds with a psychological analysis of the law to identify theories, research results, and methodologies that are most suitable to address empirical issues in the law. Finally, researchers apply the powerful research methodologies of the social sciences to test theoretical answers to empirical questions. In this book, we use Social Analytic Jurisprudence to examine current legal doctrine in several areas of law that are controversial, timely, and that shape the decision-making of a diverse array of people in their everyday lives. The contents of this work hold important implications for judgments made by law enforcement officers, judges, attorneys, school officials, employers, workers, criminals, and litigants as they contribute (for better or worse) to social systems in which they (and all of us) function as we work, study, and engage in common social exchanges. After an introductory chapter, which frames the control of discrimination and prejudice as problems of legal decision-making, the book analyzes in four sections investigative profiling, affirmative action, workplace discrimination (sexual harassment), and hate motivated crime as examples of legal decision-making concerns. Each section contains a legal analysis of the problem followed by a description of the social science related to that area and finally a commentary on the integration of the two themes.

Following the social analytic framework, each of four units includes three chapters.[1] First is a chapter that explores the behavioral assumptions that make up an area of law analyzed from a policy and decision making perspective. Next, comes a chapter reviewing and evaluating current research in the area, carefully plotting the relationship between empirical results, human decision-making, and public policy. Rounding out each unit is an analysis and synthesis chapter in which commentators evaluate the main points made in the first two chapters and examine them in juxtaposition, pointing out areas of conflict and controversy and areas of agreement. In some cases, the commentaries spark additional theoretical analyses that contribute to a more through understanding of the area. The purpose of the analysis and synthesis chapters are to find areas in which the perspectives of the law and social science show significant unresolved tension, areas of agreement, and areas in which important issues are left unexamined. The final chapter in the book extends the earlier decision-making models that chapter 1 applies to profiling and affirmative action to workplace discrimination and ultimately hate crime.

The topics represent problems related to discrimination and prejudice that the law addresses by directly or indirectly guiding the decision making of professionals (judges, lawyers, police officers, employers, school officials) as well as, lay people engaging in the task of conducting their daily lives (students, employees, automobile travelers, and citizens in the community). The sections pertain to timely controversies in the ways in which we educate ourselves, earn our livelihoods, raise our families, and resolve our disagreements. These controversies arise out of tensions between our idiosyncratic values, beliefs, and attitudes about social reality and the legal principles and philosophies that shape law and legal process. In today's post 9/11 world, such conflicts are very difficult to resolve in a way that ensures, at the same time, the autonomy of the individual and the welfare of the community. The major premise of this volume is that the resolutions of these conflicts are powerful forces that shape the decisions that we make in our everyday lives. By examining these four current controversies in law and social life from the perspective of law, psychology, and models of human decision making, this volume develops a unique approach to understanding the role that law plays in the way we learn, work, socialize, and regulate ourselves.

Several people and institutions contributed greatly to this volume. The papers were the product of the 2005 Spring Program of Excellence Conference at the University of Nebraska at Lincoln. For this annual conference, the Law and Psychology Program, an interdisciplinary unit, which includes members of

---

[1] The section on workplace discrimination integrates the law and social science of sexual harassment research into three integrative chapters.

the Department of Psychology and the College of Law at the University of Nebraska at Lincoln, invites prominent legal and social science scholars to travel to Lincoln and interact over a 5 day period. The "think tank" begins with a two day symposium during which colleagues present papers, discuss the contents of the presentations, and debate in a conference format the ideas that they have been working on and for which they have gained national prominence. Following the two-day symposium are a series of less formal discussion sessions during which psychology faculty, graduate students, law professors and law students discuss, debate, and analyze the contents of the original papers and commentaries. This book is the result of the 2005 "think tank." Two other volumes will be forthcoming under the Springer label that will be the result of the 2006 and 2007 conferences.

Organizing and hosting a weeklong conference with invited guests from all over the country is a challenging enterprise by itself. This project was even more challenging because we pulled together 14 chapters based upon the contents of the meeting and organized them into this volume. The project was supported with a University of Nebraska Program of Excellence Grant awarded to the Law and Psychology Program. I am grateful and indebted to the Program of Excellence at the University whose trust and financial support was crucial to the completion of this project. I thank the committee and the University for its continued support of the Law and Psychology Program. The conference itself and this book required the dedicated work of a number of administrators, graduate students, and faculty members in both the Department of Psychology and the Law College at UNL. I thank all of them for their contributions to this project but I would especially like to acknowledge the assistance and cooperation of David Hanson (Chair of the Department of Psychology) and Steven Willborn (Dean of the College of Law). Most importantly I am grateful to Evelyn Maeder (graduate student at UNL) who made all the arrangements for the conference and who worked hard to assist in obtaining the final manuscripts for this book. Finally, the project was co-product of the four editors working diligently from the beginning to the completion of the effort. I am especially grateful to my co-editors and colleagues (Brian Bornstein, Bob Schopp, and Steve Willborn) for the time and effort that they put into this project. It has been a pleasure for me to work with all of them.

Richard L. Wiener
Law and Psychology Program
University of Nebraska-Lincoln
Lincoln, Nebraska

Contents

Introduction

1
Law and Everyday Decision Making: Rational, Descriptive, and Normative Models

Richard L. Wiener

This chapter, and indeed the entire book, focuses on some old topics, namely legal consciousness, legal decision making, and the interaction between the two. One can date the issue back at least to the ideas and writings of the famous (or infamous) psychologist Hugo Münsterberg (1908), who argued, perhaps somewhat unconvincingly at the time, that behavioral science, especially psychology, is relevant to law and legal analysis. Munsterberg was optimistic, and perhaps even prophetic, in his view that behavioral science and especially psychology would one day inform the courts on a number of critical issues. In the years following Munsterberg's attempt to infuse behavioral science into the law, there have been numerous scholarly efforts to study judicial decisions, legislative policy, jury decisions, decisions to litigate, outcomes of mediation, eyewitness judgments, and many other behaviors that are the outcome of decision-making processes in the service of the law. The current chapter and the specific theme of this book stem directly from a more recent scholarly debate. In 1985, the Nebraska Symposium on Motivation under the editorial directorship of Professor Gary Melton, at the time the director of the Law and Psychology program at UNL, took seriously the task of examining the intersection of everyday decision making and the law (c.f. Melton & Saks, 1985).

Melton and Saks (1985) broke from tradition to argue that the most important contribution that psychology could make to the law was not to be found in its contribution to civil or criminal litigation. Instead, they saw the greatest potential for the social sciences in investigating how the law influences, and is influenced by, everyday behavior of people in the environments (outside of court) in which they live, work, and play. In other words, Melton and Sacks argued that psychology can make its mark in the contexts in which law influences our everyday behavior, namely in the homes, schools, universities, businesses, and communities where people interact under the guidance (or perhaps misguidance) of the rules of law as they understand them to be.

The law in everyday life approach to psycholegal scholarship (Melton, 1988, 1990; Melton & Saks, 1985; Wiener, 1990, 1993; Wiener & Hurt, 1997, 1999,

2000) acknowledges the successes of psychologists in studying and sometimes even influencing the processes and procedures of the law. For example, psychologists have devoted considerable effort toward understanding how the police are able (or not able) to help witnesses identify guilty defendants at crime scenes. Indeed, they have been very successful at developing a viable theory of eyewitness identification from the encoding of information at the scene of the crime through selecting individuals from mug shots and lineups that the police construct on the scene or at the local police station. Indeed, in 1998 a lead journal in the field of psychology and law (*Law and Human Behavior*) published a "white paper" that made some helpful and very specific suggestions about how police should construct lineups to avoid biased results, especially type I errors (i.e., identifying innocent suspects as the perpetrators of criminal acts) (Wells et al., 1998). These recommendations flowed directly from years of empirical research carefully describing and explaining eyewitness behavior (Wells et al., 1998). It is a tribute to the success of experimental psychology that this "white paper" became the basis for a set of guidelines that the United States Department of Justice adopted in 1999 (Technical Working Group, 1999). The success of eyewitness researchers depended, and continues to depend heavily, on the use of simulation experiments to study the cognitive parameters of people as they encode, store, recognize, and recall the events to which they were exposed at simulated scenes of criminal or civil investigations.

Experimental psychologists have devoted an equal amount of effort to the study of how jurors and juries reach decisions of culpability and liability in criminal and civil trials. Early research focused on juror verdicts in criminal cases, emphasizing theoretical models of social and cognitive psychology (Devine, Clayton, Dunford, Seying, & Pryce, 2001). These methodologies sometimes paid little attention to the ecological structure of juries or jury trials. Instead, they focused on the decisions and judgment processes of individuals as they evaluated evidence of criminal charges (for the most part) and then reached attributions of responsibility and sometimes guilt. More recent investigators (c.f. Devine et al., 2001) have turned their attention to the processes and procedures of determining liability in civil cases (Bornstein, 2004; Bornstein, Rung, & Miller, 2002; Diamond, Saks, & Landsman, 1998; Hans, Hannaford, & Munsterman, 1999; Hastie, Schkade, & Payne, 1998; Kovera & Cass, 2002), sentencing in criminal cases (especially capital murder) (Lynch & Haney, 2000; Wiener et al., 1998; Wiener, Pritchard, & Weston, 1995; Wiener, Rogers, Winter, et al., 2004), and most recently to assessing damages in civil litigation (see Greene & Bornstein, 2003 for a review). There is an impressive body of work (although not always with consistent results) that litigators, trial consultants, and courts can rely on to estimate the effects of legal and extralegal factors on the outcomes of juror, if not jury, judgments and decisions. As in the case with eyewitness researchers, the success of experimental psychologists in the area of juror and jury decision-making relies on simulated mock jury paradigms to isolate the mechanisms that guide and eventually determine the judgments that people make when they are asked to evaluate trial-like evidence to reach culpability, sentencing, liability, and damage judgments.[1]

The purpose of this chapter and the book as a whole is to push the academic envelope to broaden the efforts of our admittedly post-positivist[2] approach to psycholegal investigation. The major thesis of this chapter is that we can use the post-postivist model of research and thinking about research to examine the effects of law in everyday behavior, and that the best way to do that is to adopt a model of legal decision-making that intertwines the law and behavioral science approach to legal analysis. While a decision-making approach makes use of simulated research as do its older cousins in eyewitness identification and jury research, it does so with an eye open to, and constrained by, the context in which people make legal decisions.

In some ways, the behavioral science and law program owes a great deal to the law and economics movement because the former often reacts, either explicitly or implicitly, to study chinks in the armor of the rational choice model, which is, of course, the central metaphor in the law and economics movement. It is not important whether law and social science as legislative fact, as empirical research, or as a more general theory of law sees itself as an alternative to the law and economics movement, or whether it plays a more complementary role, showing how psychology, sociology, and anthropology can go beyond describing and even explaining behavior "at the margins." What is important is that law and social

---

[1] Some of the most impressive accomplishments of the psychology and law movement concern the investigations of forensic assessment of legal competencies (c.f., Ackerson, Brodsky, & Zapf, 2005), risk assessment (c.f., Monahan et al., 2002; Slovic, Monahan, J., & MacGregor, 2000), psychopathy (Poythress, Edens, & Watkins, 2001; Edens, Petrila, & Buffington-Vollum, 2001; Porter, Birt, & Boer, 2001), and other issues related to psychological abnormalities. This chapter and the book do not focus on the accomplishments and the accompanying practice initiatives of clinical forensic psychologists in these areas because the topic of legal consciousness is more closely related to the content areas of social and cognitive psychology, broadly defined. These subdisciplines historically and pragmatically address the twin issues of legal decision making and legal consciousness.

[2] Our work more closely resembles a post-positivist paradigm than a traditional logical positivist approach because methodologies in the primary areas of empirical psychology and law typically rely on critical multiplism (Cook, 1985). First, constructs in legal decision-making studies are typically measured on multiple dimensions. For example, in eyewitness identification, research criteria usually include correct identifications, false identifications, correct rejections, hits, biases, and speed of responses. Similarly, in jury decision-making investigators are concerned with attributions of responsibility, guilt, credibility, liability, sentences, and ability of jurors to follow the law as given in jury charges. Second, research paradigms in psycholegal programs make use of multiple methodological approaches including archival investigations, laboratory experiments, field investigations, and large-scale survey studies. Third, most research in the field proceeds under the logic of a deductive model in which predictions are generated from law, psychological theory, or both and then are tested with the collection of empirical data. These approaches are very different from a more positivistic approach to social science in which single operationalizations of constructs prevail under rigid experimental designs from which researchers try to induce generalized laws of human conduct.

science as analytic tools can add significantly to the theory of rational choice, supplementing the tenets of the theory of the rational actor moving beyond formal rules of logic. While some psychology researchers challenge the adequacy of the "theory of rational choice" as the best descriptor of human decision-making in the law, they do not challenge the logic symmetry of the rational actor model. In other words, all decision makers who wish to maximize their own self-interest make judgments and decisions in accordance with the rules of formal logic and probability. Like those who have taken to task the rational choice model, we acknowledge its indisputable claim on how people can make decisions to maximize their gains and minimize their losses. That seems to be true by definition. However, we see another contribution and suggest that the theory of rational choice offers an important baseline for understanding both how people really do make legal decisions, and how the law would have them make those decisions. In the end, the rational choice model becomes a kind of decision baseline against which we can measure actual and normative decisions. We can learn a great deal by using the rational choice model to study the parameters of decisions that are, at least in part, determined from prohibitions, encouragements, and, in some cases, requirements in the law. We begin with a description of the law and economics approach, focusing on its central metaphor, the theory of rational action.

Law and Economics and the Rational Choice Model

Korobkin and Ulen (1998, 2000) identified as the chief tenets of the law and economics movement the principle that people respond to incentives and that skillful policy makers can use the law to encourage socially desirable conduct and discourage the undesirable. People acting under the boundaries and constraints of law weigh the costs and benefits of following the law against the same for not following the law. Further, the law encourages efficient use of social resources and discourages the wasteful use of those same resources. In the recent past, legal scholars used the efficiency principle to suggest that tort and other civil law claims achieve settlements that favor those for whom the gains are most valued, and against those who value the gains least (Landes & Posner, 1987). Landes and Posner (1987) illustrated and demonstrated (albeit without data) how the rule of incentives and the principle of efficiency justify existing common law rules. Law and economics authors use these basic principles to explain and justify areas of jurisprudence in both the criminal and civil law in accordance with accepted doctrine (Cooter & Ulen, 2004; Monahan & Walker, 2002, p. 26).

The driving force of the law and economics movement is "rational choice theory," borrowed from economics. According to decision theorists Hastie and Dawes (2001, p. 18), a rational choice must meet four criteria. First, a rational choice is based solely on a decision maker's assets at the time the decision is made, which include not only financial assets but also the nature of the decision maker's "physiological state, psychological capacities, social relationships, and feelings." The decision maker values these assets and acts in ways to increase or, at least, maintain them. Second, the rational decision maker takes into consideration the consequences of choices with respect to the status of the decision maker's extant assets (physical and psychological). Third, under conditions of uncertainty the rules of probability describe the way in which decision makers evaluate the likelihood of consequences that will influence the distribution of these assets. This is not to suggest that decision makers apply formal calculations to reach optimal outcomes. Instead, decision makers are intuitive statisticians whose subjective probability estimates are congruent with the basic and fundamental tenets of probability theory. Finally, the driving force in decision making is adaptation. Accordingly, decision makers reach decisions within the constraints of the probabilities of consequences and the values or satisfactions that stem from the possible outcomes of choice. In the language of Judge Posner, "man is a rational maximizer of his ends" (Posner, 1997, p. 24).

The expected utility model of rational choice puts more meat on the bare bones of the rational maximizer. Korobkin and Ulen (2000) write about a decision in which there are two choices, each with an uncertain probability, and the task for the decision maker is to select one choice over the other. Each choice leads to multiple possible outcomes and each of those outcomes is associated with a change in assets that is either valued or devalued. The choice would be simple if the consequences of the outcomes were certain, but in the real world, the consequences are usually uncertain, best described as probability statements associated with the outcomes and their consequences. According to decision analysts, the rational solution to selecting a choice is to estimate the expected utility of each choice and then select the choice with the highest expected utility. In other words, the adaptive approach is to conduct a cost–benefit analysis for each choice and then adopt the choice that maximizes the likelihood of a positive change in one's assets.

In the language of Korobin and Ulen (2000, p. 1051), "The actor will presumably attach a utility to each possible outcome U(O1), U(O2), and so forth, along with a probability of each outcome occurring p1, p2, and so on." The decision maker then calculates the simple utility for each outcome or consequence and aggregates the simple utilities to arrive an expected utility (EU) for each choice point, "EU (uncertain action) = $p1U(O1)^3$ + p2U(O2) . . .pnU(On)" and makes the choice associated with the greatest expected utility. Hastie and Dawes (2001) note that the utilities attached to each outcome are best conceptualized as "personal values." They reflect changes in assets that result from the choices and their outcomes or consequences.

To illustrate the application of the rational choice theory to a problem of legal decision-making, consider the decisions that police officers make when arresting speeders on our roads and highways with the aid of racial and ethnic profiles. Consider first the case of *State v. Soto* (1996) in which 17 African American

---

[3] The first term, p1U(O1), is not part of the Korobin and Ulen (2001) text because their configuration includes a certain cosequence in which p1 = 1, so that p1U(O1) reduces to U(O1).

defendants claimed that their arrests on the New Jersey turnpike resulted from discriminatory enforcement of New Jersey's traffic laws. The defendants claimed that the police stopped and subsequently arrested them for speeding on the turnpike, in part because of their African American ancestry. The defendants proffered data collected in a series of observational studies to support their discrimination claim. One research team working under the supervision of Dr. John Lamberth, a social psychology faculty member at Temple University, collected observational data of drivers during daylight hours on the New Jersey turnpike between the exits where the police had stopped the defendants. They found that 98% of all drivers were speeding on the road but found Black occupants in only 15% of these cars. Examining police stop data for the same stretch of road, Dr. Lamberth found African Americans in 46% of the cars that the police stopped.

The Soto Court ruled that the absolute discrepancy of 31% constituted evidence that the police were targeting minorities. Further, such a discrepancy between racial composition of the arrestees compared to the racial composition of the population (or at least those observed violating traffic laws) was so great that it was evidence of purposeful discrimination (citing *Wards Cove Packing Co. v. Atonio,* 1989). Because the defendants were able to show a prima facie case of selective discrimination and the state was unable to offer evidence to explain or disprove the disparity, the court found the police actions did constitute purposeful discrimination. Further, while the court recognized the state's interest in eliminating illegal drugs, it found that that interest did not offset the equal protection and due process rights of individual defendants (*State v. Soto,* 1996, p. 360). That is, stopping African American drivers because of heightened police suspicion of drug law violations triggered by race did not withstand the attack on the defendants' 14th Amendment rights to due process and equal protection. Finally, in *United States v. New Jersey* (1999), the federal government and the New Jersey police approved a Consent Decree in which the State of New Jersey agreed to amend its practices and procedures to eliminate discriminatory traffic stops based on racial background.

New Jersey police are not the only law enforcement officers who rely on racial profiling to select travelers for traffic stops, in part as a strategy to control illegal drug trafficking. In *Wilkins v. Maryland State Police* (1993) (cited in Gross & Barnes, 2002), the parties in a class action suit (i.e., the Maryland ACLU and the state of Maryland) reached a similar settlement agreement that required the state to collect detailed traffic stop, search, and arrest data to verify that the police did not use racial profiling to select motorists who were observed speeding (cited in Gross & Barnes, 2002). As in New Jersey, data collected in Maryland showed that during the period from May 1997 to April 2000 almost all drivers on the roads (regardless of race) violated some traffic law that would allow the police to make a stop and traffic arrest.

In general, we can translate the officer's decision, to stop a Black driver, a White driver, or no driver on the highway into an expected utility model that reflects the rational choice theory. Here, the consequences of the stops are (1) finding sizable amounts of illegal drugs, (2) finding smaller amounts of illegal drugs, (3) finding no illegal drugs, and (4) violating the due process and equal protection rights of the drivers. Hastie and Dawes (2001) propose that for consequences that are not readily quantifiable, it is possible to use a subjective scale in which -100 represents the worst outcome (negative change in assets) and 100 represents the best outcome (positive change in assets) to measure the utility or values of outcomes. Police officers finding illegal drugs of a sizable proportion (i.e., those that would support a charge of possession with the intent to distribute) in a driver's car would value greatly that outcome; say a utility value of 100. On the other hand, finding drugs of a smaller amount (i.e., enough to support only a possession charge) would represent an outcome of medium value, say a utility value of 50, and finding no illegal drugs would represent an outcome of neither positive or negative value, say 00 on the utility scale. Further, a stop that violated the rights of the driver would likely result in a dismissed charged, an outcome of negative valence (say -25) because that outcome would reduce the officer's psychological state (an asset) from a pre-stop reference point. A stop that did not violate the driver's rights would be an added asset and might receive 25 positive valence points.

Figure 1.1 uses a tree diagram (Hastie & Dawes, 2001) to illustrate a hypothetical officer's decision structure as that officer observes two speeding motorists, one of African American descent and one of White European descent. The squares on the chart represent choice points, and the circles uncertain outcomes of the choices, each associated with a simple utility or value as defined subjectively in that officer's mind. The probability assessments attached to each outcome are the likelihood that a specific consequence will result following an officer's choice. It is important to note that the valences and probabilities are subjective. In principle, at least, it is possible to collect objective data to estimate the utilities (in dollars or status points or advancement in the police force) for each of the consequences, and it is even equally feasible to collect objective data to estimate the probabilities of the consequences following an officer's decision. These are not the numbers entered in Figure 1.1. Instead, Figure 1.1 shows ostensible subjective utilities and probabilities intended to represent the decision field for one hypothetical officer.

If our hypothetical officer decides to stop and investigate a speeding Black driver, as compared to a White driver, this officer has greater expectations that the stop will produce larger quantities of drugs (perhaps supporting an arrest for possession with the intent to distribute).

However, that officer is taking a greater risk that the stop may violate the drivers' due process and equal protection rights. Calculating the EU (expected utility) for the three choices represented in the figure ($EU1_{Black} = 55.00.$, $EU1_{nostop} = 25.00$, $EU1_{White} = 35.00$) shows that under these conditions our hypothetical officer is most likely to stop the African American driver.

The strength of the rational choice model is that with estimates of a decision maker's subjective utilities and the subjective probabilities, it is easy enough to predict a rational decision. Further, individual differences in the subjective probability or utility estimates do not influence the predictions that the models

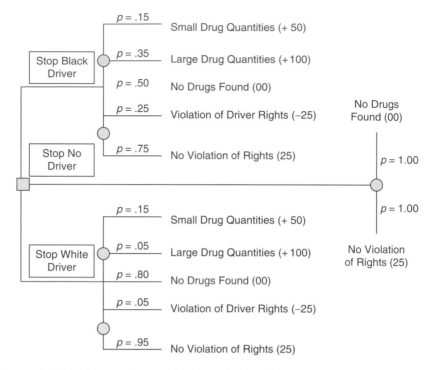

FIGURE 1.1. Decision tree diagram of a drug-related traffic stop. Squares represent decision points and circles represent outcomes.

make on the margins. Given randomly distributed individual differences and the principle of utility maximization (i.e., cost–benefit analysis), increasing the costs of outcomes and the likelihood of the occurrence of those costs will make the choice associated with those consequences less attractive. At the same time, increasing the benefits of consequences and the likelihood of the occurrence of those benefits will make the choice associated with these consequences more attractive. This is true regardless of the form or value of individual subjective probabilities or subjective utilities (Korobkin & Ulen, 2000). In other words, in cases such as *Wilkins v. Maryland State Police* (cited in Gross & Barnes, 2002), in which parties reached a settlement designed to reduce the effects of racial bias in traffic stops along the I-95 corridor, the law could alter the distribution of subjective probabilities and utilities to influence police decision-making. Simply put, increasing the likelihood that stopping a Black driver simply because of race would end in a rights violation would decrease the attractiveness of all officers' choices to stop a Black driver, as would decreasing the valence of violating a Black drivers' constitutional rights even more (i.e., creating a greater negative valence). In fact, this is what may have been the intended impact in 1997 when a settlement agreement was enforced so that the Maryland State Police were put under court order to collect data from each traffic stop and search, including the race of the driver and the type and amount of contraband discovered (Gross & Barnes, 2002). The mere act of collecting the data could increase the subjective probability that violating a Black driver's rights has the potential to become public and make traffic stops of Black or other minority drivers less attractive.

This picture is a great deal more complicated. Psychological research conducted in the last several decades under the rubric of behavioral decision theory (Fellner, 2005) has uncovered a number of systematic biases that influence the subjective probabilities and utilities of decision makers. A complete review of this well documented work is well beyond the scope or purpose of this chapter. However, research on cognitive heuristics such as representativeness, availability, anchoring, and adjustment (Hastie & Dawes, 2001; Tversky & Kahneman, 1974), counterfactual thinking (Roese & Olson, 1995), and framing (Hastie & Dawes, 2001; Kahneman & Miller, 1986; Kahneman & Tversky, 1979) demonstrates how situational factors as well as decision maker characteristics can alter the subjective probabilities and utilities in the rational actor model. Further, there is a widening literature that challenges the rational actor model and, indeed, the law and economics movement itself, based on investigations of these cognitive shortcuts using law and legal examples (Korobkin & Ulen, 1998, 2000; Suchman, 1997). More recent work examining the role of experienced (Loewenstein, Weber, Hsee, & Welch, 2001; Mellers, 2000; Mellers, Schwartz, Ho, & Ritov, 1997; Mellers, Schwartz, & Ritov, 1999) and anticipated emotion (Lerner, Gonzalez, Small, & Fischhoff, 2003; Lerner & Keltner, 2000, 2001; Tiedens & Linton, 2001), as well as implicit or automatic processes (Blair & Mahzarin, 1996; Dovidio, Kawakami, & Johnson, 1997; Fazio, 2001; Greenwald, Banaji, & Rudman, 2002; Rudman, 2004) demonstrate other systematic biases that alter subjective probabilities and utilities through mechanisms that are irrelevant to the choice, and that lie outside the control of the legal decision maker. In these ways, the rational choice model is limited in its ability to explain decision-making in the law. Indeed, while decision tree diagrams may be very helpful in describing the decision context and the parameters of making legal decisions, it is unlikely that people actually multiply probability weights by simple utilities to come up with expected utilities to guide their choices.

How Do People Really Make Decisions?

If one is interested in describing the ways in which decision makers actually make judgments and decisions, the lens model offers a generally accepted framework for capturing the values and weights that decision makers assign to informational inputs (Hastie & Dawes, 2001, p. 49). While there are a number of statistical procedures that researchers can and do use to measure the parameters that make up the lens model framework, the basic relationships that it describes between judgment inputs and outputs offered at a conceptual level go a long way to illustrate some of the mechanics of how people use environmental input to reach specific judgments and decisions.

Descriptive Models of Decision-Making

The lens model is a conceptual framework for describing the relationship between the information or cues in the external world and the judgments or decisions that people reach by considering those cues (Hammond, 2000a, 2000b; Hastie & Dawes, 2001). The name of the framework comes from the realization that people draw inferences about the external world, which they cannot really ever know, from imperfect sources of information. It is through this imperfect perceptual lens that decision makers ultimately make judgments and predictions. Figure 1.2 is a conceptual replication of the model, borrowed from Hastie and Dawes (2001) and others before them.

The model (Brunswick cited in Hastie & Dawes, 2001) shows that there is a relationship among informational cues that police officers gather from the environment as they try to judge the amount of illegal drugs that a traffic violator may possess. In other words, the information is redundant; each cue does not necessarily add more information to the judgment problem. The left side of the diagram shows the distal property in the environment that the officer seeks to estimate, and the right side of the diagram reflects the psychological processes that result in a final judgment about the amount of contraband in the driver's possession. There is some real amount of drugs, ranging from no drugs to some measurable amount (no drugs, small, medium, or large) that the driver possesses in the car and the

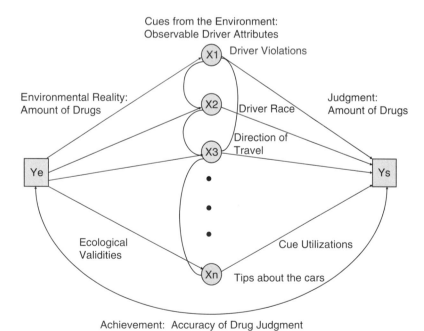

FIGURE 1.2. The lens model as a Description of Officers' Judgments of Drug Status of passing automobiles.

task for the officer is to determine that value and to decide whether to make the drug stop. Assume that the officer possesses some absolute cutoff above which it makes sense to stop the driver and initiate a search.[4] The officer must make this judgment based on the available information in the environment (cues from the environment), which in this case is limited to information directly observable (e.g., race of the driver, type of car, speed of the car, and direction of travel), or from tips that the officer might have learned about suspect cars from informants or other officers. The figure indicates that other cues may be available, and, in fact, one of the major problems for the decision analyst is determining the appropriate cues for any decision task.

The accuracy of the officer in estimating the amount of drugs and the subsequent decision about whether to stop any given driver depends on two important parameters in the model: the ecological validities (i.e., the relationship between the external reality and cues from the environment) and the cue utilization rates (i.e., the ability of the decision maker to review these cues and make judgments about the environmental reality). In the current case, the officer will be able to make an accurate assessment only if the evidence is accurate and the officer is able to weigh the evidence appropriately (according to the ecological validity associated with the cues) to reach an accurate judgment. The important questions are: What are the relationships between speeding, race of the driver, direction of the car, the accuracy of tips, and the amount of drugs in the car. Second, do the officers reliably use this information to assess accurately the drug status of the travelers as they encounter them on the roads and highways? There are several statistical approaches to estimating the ecological validities and cue utilization functions (including but not limited to regression analyses and linear modeling). All require researchers to collect data on a large number of incidents and estimate the relationships between the cues, external reality, and subjective judgments across an aggregate set of representative decisions. Regardless of the statistical technique used to estimate the weights and values in the lens model, they are only as good as the methodologies that estimated them in the first place.

Gross and Barnes (2002) studied in detail the judgment processes of the Maryland State Police in an effort to determine whether the officers engaged in racial profiling to determine which traffic violators to stop and ultimately search. The study took advantage of an unusual opportunity that resulted from a court order in Maryland in 1995, which resulted from the claim of an African American driver that the police had illegally detained him (cited in Gross & Barnes, 2002). African American Robert Wilkins was an assistant public defender traveling back to Washington, D.C. with his family from a funeral that they had attended in Chicago. Wilkins was speeding, driving 60 miles per hour in a 40-mile per hour zone when the police stopped him and asked him to consent to a search of his

---

[4] There is, of course, law that determines whether evidence is obtained in accordance with rules of search and seizure. The law on this issue is complex and represents another judgment that a police officer must make. However, a discussion of this area of law is beyond the scope of the current chapter.

automobile. Wilkins refused and the police produced a narcotics sniffing dog that found no evidence of any contraband from the outside of Wilkins' car. After waiting outside uncomfortably in the rain, Wilkins and his passengers were allowed to continue their trip.

Later in resolving Wilkins' claim, a Maryland court ordered the Maryland State Police to collect data on every traffic stop and to include "the race of the driver, the basis for the search, and the type and quantity of drugs recovered" (p. 659) (*Wilkins v. Maryland State Police*, No. CCB-93-468, 1993 as cited in Gross & Barnes, 2002). Further, in 1997, the court modified the order to include all stops in the I-95 corridor, regardless of whether the stop involved a search. Despite some serious limitations in these data (Gross & Barnes, 2002) the authors used the reports to examine what the lens model terms the ecological validity and cue utilization rates of the Maryland State Police as they made judgments about stops along the I-95 corridor, the area in which Mr. Wilkins was stopped and detained. The data analysis was based on more than 82,000 stops conducted on the I-95 corridor between 1997 and 2000.

With regard to the ecological and cue utilization validities, the authors report that almost all drivers of all races violated the traffic laws so that the decision of which driver to stop was almost completely up to the discretion of the Maryland State Police (Gross & Barnes, 2002, p. 666). Further, the police were almost twice as likely to stop Black drivers than White drivers. The data suggest that while race was associated with a rather high cue utilization rate, it was not a strong predictor of traffic violations and reasons to stop a driver. In other words, its ecological validity was rather low. Once Black drivers were stopped, the police were almost three times more likely to search them than to search White drivers and they were more than seven times more likely to search Hispanics than Whites. Of the cars stopped in Maryland, two thirds carry no drugs, and on the I-95 corridor, Black drivers were slightly less likely than were White drivers to possess drugs (3% less; p. 699). However, additional data showed a different result when considering the size of the contraband. The data for the I-95 corridor showed that Blacks and Hispanics who were searched and found to be in possession of drugs did have larger amounts of contraband (dealer portions as opposed to user proportions). Hispanic drivers were 3.5 times more likely to possess large enough amounts of illegal drugs to be classified as dealers, as compared to White drivers, and Hispanics were 1.8 times more likely to possess dealer levels of contraband (p. 703). Finally, direction of travel was related to the amount of drugs found. Among cars driving north that were searched, only 8% had quantities large enough to be considered dealers. Going south, 33% of searches produced dealer-sized quantities (p. 701). Putting these data together would suggest that the Maryland State Police hold subjective probabilities indicating that Black and Hispanic drivers heading south are the most likely to be dealers carrying large quantities of drugs, and the available data support this impression.

Applying the logic of the lens model to these informative and interesting data (Gross & Barnes, 2002) points out the difficulty in describing decision-making models in a legal context. While there is support for the discussion of ecological cue validities and cue utilizations described in the preceding text, some weakness remains in the main parameters of the lens model conceptualization. First, because the data pertain only to drivers who were, in fact, stopped and or searched, it is difficult to describe statistically the full relationship between the environmental cues and the external realities related to the drug contraband found among the drivers on the I-95 corridor. Needed are some control data regarding the race, driving behavior, and traveling direction of those whom the police did not stop or search. It is nearly impossible to collect these control data in a field setting like those in Maryland. Nonetheless, without data examining the characteristics of drivers who were not stopped and the cargo of their cars, it is very difficult to estimate with a high degree of accuracy either the ecological validities or the cue utilization rates of the Maryland State Police officers. While the data reported in Gross and Barnes (2002) are not a full description of the decision-making model that police officers used on the I-95 corridor, they are consistent with the conclusion that the officers relied heavily on the race of the driver to make traffic stops on the highway. Comparing these data to a normative version of the rational actor theory and to the conceptualization of the lens model place in perspective the contributions that these two approaches can make to understanding decision-making in a legal context.

A Normative Model

So far, we have discussed how to model legal decisions so that they meet the demands of the rational actor theory and how to describe the way in which actors actually make judgments and decisions. Next, we consider how decisions in the law ought to be made by distinguishing the rational actor and the descriptive models of judgment from a normative theory of decision making. Suchman (1997) separates rational from normative decisions, arguing that people make the latter through conscious and systematic deliberations, which arise from ingrained moral guidelines rather than from self-interest. In the case of decisions made in a legal context, a built in guideline controls how people ought to make decisions under a constrained set of situational contexts. Put very simply, the law is a set of enforceable guidelines that direct decision making, constricting and shaping the allowable subjective probabilities and subjective utilities. Rational actors will still act to maximize expected utilities, but will do so starting with subjective probabilities and simple utilities found in the law rather than in their own attitude, belief, and motivation systems. Further, if the law were effective in structuring decision making, one would expect to see its impact in the cue utilization coefficients in lens model descriptions of actual judgments. That is, even under conditions in which the ecological validities of the cues in a judgment task are weak (or strong), the law through its mandated requirements should influence cue utilization rates, making them strong (or weak) to reflect doctrinal commands. In other words, if the law is acting as a normative model of judgment, it should explain the cue utilizations independent of the ecological validities. When reality and the law clash, the law should win if it is a normative model of judgment and decision making. That is not to suggest that it is wise for the law to ignore social reality. To the contrary, we will argue later that one of the purposes of psychole-gal research is to help shape policy that is consistent with social reality, in other words, law that is at least congruent with the ecological validity of cues in the lens model.

In summary, it is helpful to think of decision-making in legal contexts on three separate but related levels. First, the rational actor model demonstrates how deci-sion makers act out of self-interest to maximize their personal utilities. Second, descriptive models allow for empirical estimation of ecological validities and cue utilization processes to represent the way decision makers actually reach conclu-sions. Finally, the law imposes normative rules, which direct and limit subjective probabilities, subjective utilities, and cue utilization processes. This chapter pro-poses that one can learn a great deal about the role of law in everyday decision making by comparing decision-making processes expected in the law to rational actor models (i.e., a decision tree analysis) and descriptive accounts (i.e., a lens model type of analysis).

What then does the law require of police officers deciding which drivers to stop and which to let go? It is not at all clear how the Equal Protection Clause should govern the conduct of police officer investigations. In *McClesky v. Kemp* (1987), the Supreme Court rejected even stronger statistical data of racial discrimination in a death penalty case. The Court held that a victim who is in violation of the Equal Protection Clause must show purposeful discrimination as determined in prior case law (i.e., *Washington v. Davis*, 1976) and that statistical evidence by itself is not enough to demonstrate purposeful discrimination. However, in *State v. Soto* (1996), a federal court did rely on statistical evidence to prove purposeful discrimination and the United States District Court of New Jersey (1999) approved a Consent Decree that prevents police officers from relying on race, eth-nic origin, or gender in deciding which cars to select for traffic stops. Further, the Maryland Court in Wilkins' case also enforced a settlement that, at the very least, focused attention on the decision processes of Maryland State Police with the intent to measure their use of racial and ethnicity in making traffic stops.

How can we use a comparison of decision-making models to answer questions about the policy implications of a rule that would use statistical evidence to pro-hibit the racial profiling? Once again, the signature of such a rule would appear in the rational and descriptive models of how police officers decide to make traf-fic stops. That is, a strict prohibition against racial profiling ought to alter the subjective probabilities of police officers, so that they expect higher probabilities of violation of individual rights after stops of minority members because of their race or ethnicity per se. In the end, the expected utility of such a stop would no longer be greater than the stop of a White driver. Theoretically, this would result from a theory of law that made it easier to demonstrate purposeful discrimination; that is, allowing statistical data as dispositive evidence of discrimination, pro-vided that the data could not be explained via an alternative justification for the suspected action. Such an approach would increase the subjective probability of violating the rights of drivers when the police followed their inclinations to arrest Black drivers in hopes of obtaining a big bust.

How would this norm be expressed in the decision models of everyday judgment? At the most general level, one would find its expression in the cue utilizations of police officers when they decide whom they would, in fact, stop for traffic violations. One would expect a more even distribution of stops by officers so that the rate of Black and Hispanic stops relative to White stops would not reflect the high disparities found in the Gross and Barnes (2002) data. If police officers abandoned their own self-interests and cognitive heuristic approaches in favor of the normative model endorsed in a broader purposeful discrimination theory (i.e., one that allowed statistical determination of purpose), then they would be less inclined to select Black and Hispanic drivers in hopes of making the big drug bust. On a more specific level, one could develop decision tree analyses for individual officers with estimates of the subjective probabilities for violating individual rights, and simple utilities for those violations, expecting higher values for the first and lower values for the second under a law that allowed statistical evidence of purposeful discrimination. In any event, our final point regarding this example is that a complete decision analysis of this problem would need to take into consideration all three levels of judgment models: a rational actor model, a descriptive model, and the normative model found in the law.

Rational, Descriptive, and Normative Models Applied to Affirmative Action in Education

We argue that this approach; comparing rational, descriptive, and normative models of legal decision making and judgment, can offer valuable insights about decision making under many areas of law, especially when the issues involve decisions that the law requires lay people to make under conditions of social sensitivity. To demonstrate the generality of the approach, we apply it to a second area of legal decision making that has taken on important social value, which recently was the focus of the highest Court, and that will likely continue to rise to the attention of appellate judges. Admissions officers at public institutions of higher education have come to recognize the value of a diverse student body. Educational research supports the value of diversity in the student population at the undergraduate, graduate, and professional levels of training (Antonio et al., 2004; Chang, 1999; Chang, Witt, Jones, & Hakuta, 2003; Gurin, 1999; Smith & Associates, 1997).

As a result, many admissions offices in public universities and colleges work hard to recruit diverse entering classes. At the same time, the ideal of recruiting underrepresented minorities in our public institutions is not always consistent with the Equal Protection Clause of the Fourteenth Amendment to United States Constitution. The resulting affirmative action recruitment plans have raised the ire of majority applicants denied entrance to public schools, when in fact their merit scores are similar to underrepresented students who have gained admission to these same institutions. A significant body of psychological research argues in favor of affirmative action plans in work and school environments, from both merit and diversity perspectives (Crosby, Iyer, & Downing, 2003). However, an equally impressive body of research points out the problems in using affirmative action plans to diversify work and school environments (Heilman & Alcott, 2001; Heilman, Battle, Keller, & Lee, 1998; Heilman & Blader, 2001; Heilman, Block, & Stathatos, 1997;). This was the general state of the field when the cases of *Gratz v. Bollinger* (2003) and *Grutter v. Bollinger* (2003) worked their ways up through the federal courts, ultimately landing at the United States Supreme Court.

In the case of *Gratz v. Bollinger*, the Supreme Court found that a mechanical admissions rule, which assigned automatic points to a minority (i.e., Hispanic, Black, or Native American) applicant was not narrowly tailored to the compelling state interest of diversity in education. The failing of such a rule was that it did not allow for the individual assessment of a wide range of diversity factors in making admissions decisions for the large number of undergraduate applications to the University of Michigan. However, in the companion case of *Grutter v. Bollinger* (2003), the Court not only recognized diversity as a compelling state interest, but it also ruled in a close 5 to 4 decision that the University of Michigan Law School's affirmative action plan was narrowly tailored to meet that school's diversity interest. The Law School examined each individual file and added a "plus" to each applicant that satisfied the school's broad definition of how students could make a diversity contribution to the class. The Law School admissions committee admitted enough students with such pluses to establish a "critical mass" of diverse students. The Court decided that the University of Michigan Law School's affirmative action program was not in violation of the Equal Protection Clause, in part, because it allowed for individualized assessments of the each student's file.

Consider the affirmative action plan for the University of Michigan Law School, in which admissions staff evaluate each applicant individually, examining all the information in each applicant's file. Evidence for admission includes the personal statement, letters of recommendation, a personal essay describing the student's likely contribution to diversity at the law school, undergraduate GPA, quality of the undergraduate college or university, and the student's choice of undergraduate coursework. The policy requires that the admissions officers look beyond undergraduate GPA and standardized test scores to consider the "applicant's likely contributions to the intellectual and social life of the institution" (*Grutter*, 2003, p. 315). The affirmative action policy recognizes diversity as a multifaceted social construct made up of a variety of exogenous factors including, but not limited to, race and ethnicity of the applicant. The plan goes beyond race to include other important diversity indicators such as an unusual knowledge of other cultures and language or residential status from an unusual geographical location, relative to the other members of the student body. Applying the law school plan, the admissions officers selected enough applicants from underrepresented ethnic and racial backgrounds to ensure that these students would be secure enough to make contributions to the law school and to assist that institution to develop a diverse educational cultural and climate (Grutter, 2003, p. 316).

On the other hand, the University of Michigan Office of Undergraduate Admissions (OUA) evolved an affirmative action plan that treated diversity in a much more limited manner.[5] In the plan that was in effect in 1998, 1999, and 2000, the OUA awarded points to applicants on a scale that ranged from 00 to 150 (as cited in *Gratz*, 2003, p. 255). This scale was referred to as the selection index. The OUA admitted students according to where they scored on the point scale.[6] Admissions officers assigned points based on high school GPA, standardized test scores, quality of high school attended, strength of the courses the student finished in high school, the student's in-state residency status, alumni relations of the student, the quality of the student's personal essay, and the student's leadership or personal achievement qualities (as cited in *Gratz*, 2003, p. 255). In addition, admission officers automatically assigned 20 points to the selection index for students who came from underrepresented racial or ethnic backgrounds. Further, starting in 1999, some students were "flagged" to receive additional consideration from an admissions review committee, but this added scrutiny was sought only for a subgroup of applicants (as cited in *Gratz*, 2003, p. 256).

Applying a rational actor model analysis to the diversity component of each of these University of Michigan admissions systems produces some very different results. Figure 1.3 represents the admissions policy regarding diversity for three hypothetical students. The backgrounds of the three students are modified from Justice Powell's hypothetical example in *Regents of University of California v. Bakke* (1978, p 323).[7] Student A is "the child of a successful Black physician in an academic community with promise of superior academic performance." Student B is a Black student "who grew up in an inner-city [ghetto] of semi-literate parents whose academic achievement was lower, but who demonstrated energy and leadership. . . ." Assume that the admissions committee *had* already accepted a good number of the student B type to the entering class. Finally, student C is "a White student with an extraordinary artistic talent. . . ." Also assume that all three students are beyond the minimum acceptability standards, that is, the "applicant's likely contributions to the intellectual and social life of the institution" (*Grutter*, 2003, p. 315) are above some absolute cutoff. However, assume that student A is slightly ahead of student B and student C on that measure. The decision tree diagram in Figure 1.3 reflects these sets of assumptions. It shows that the decision maker expects the White artistic student to contribute the most to the diversity of the incoming class, followed by the Black student with academic promise, followed by the Black student with a difficult background but strong leadership (several similar students having already been accepted).

---

[5] The OUA at U of M evolved a plan that started with the creation of different admissions formula for minority and majority students depending upon their state of residence and finished with a point system that added automatic credit to applicants who were Hispanic, African American, or Native American. The Supreme Court focused on the later formulation as does the treatment of the OUA plan in this chapter.

[6] The OUA admitted students who scored 100 to 150 points, admitted or postponed those between 95 and 99, postponed or admitted those between 90 and 94, delayed or postponed those between 75 and 89, and delayed or rejected those below 74.

[7] In the original example, student B was interested in Black power, a description that was much more apropos in 1978 than 2005.

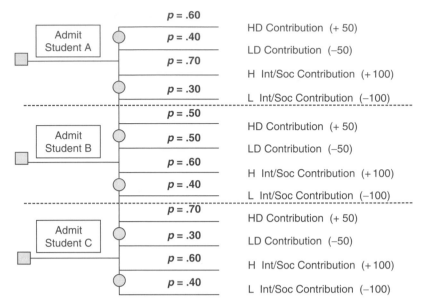

FIGURE 1.3. Decision tree diagram of an individualized affirmative action plan for student admissions favoring a Black applicant from a promising background and an artistic White student. Squares represent decision points and circles represent outcomes. Outcomes: HD = high diversity contribution; LD = low diversity contribution; H Int/Soc = high intellectual and social contribution; L Int/Soc = low intellectual and social contribution. Choices: student A: promising Black student who is a child of a successful physician; student B: Black student from a rough inner city background; student C: White student with extraordinary artistic talent.

Calculating the expected utilities for each choice shows that with this set of subjective probability and simple utility estimates reflecting the hypothetical problem posed by Justice Powell in *Bakke* as described in *Gratz* (2003), the admissions officer would select in order of preference student A (EU = 50), student C (EU = 40), followed by student B (EU = 20). That is, the minority student with a promise of academic success would be preferred to the minority student from the difficult background, as would the White student with artistic talent. In this model, the Black student with the difficult background would be least likely to receive an acceptance letter. Note that the preferences of the admissions officer are not fixed and could vary as a function of the beliefs of the officer, situational constraints of the decision, or the policy of the admissions office. Figure 1.4 represents a decision tree reflecting a policy in which the expectation that the Black applicant from the poor background with strong leadership skills is most likely to add to the diversity of the class, perhaps with fewer of these types of students already enrolled. Note that the preferences of this decision maker are very different because the EU for student B is now 70, making that student the first choice. The strength of the Law School model is that it allows for discretion in

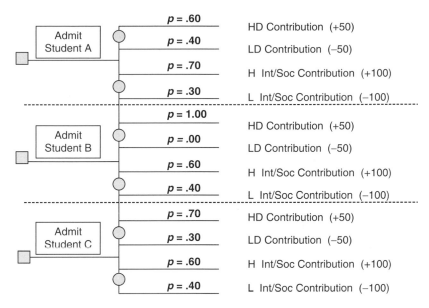

FIGURE 1.4. Decision tree diagram of an individualized affirmative action plan for student admissions favoring a Black applicant from a difficult background. Squares represent decision points and circles represent outcomes. Outcomes: HD = high diversity contribution; LD = low diversity contribution; H Int/Soc = high intellectual and social contribution; L Int/Soc = low intellectual and social contribution. Choices: student A: promising Black student who is a child of a successful physician; student B: Black student from a rough inner city background; student C: White student with extraordinary artistic talent.

the evaluation of diversity contribution, which can change according to the context of the judgment. In other words, because there is no automatic diversity advantage defined in the policy rules, individual consideration of each student could fluctuate as a function of the discretion of the admissions officer.

Now consider Figure 1.5, which represents a tree diagram for the same three hypothetical students applying a decision policy that fixes the subjective probabilities of admissions officers favoring the diversity contribution of any racial or ethnic minority student. Although the numbers do not show the full set of points in the OUA's selection index, they do reflect the decision policy of the OUA that limits allowance for diversity discretion.[8] Assume that all three students meet minimum requirements on the selection index. Applying a utility maximization rule produces EUs of 90, 70, −30 for student A, B, and C, respectively. Here the White student automatically fails the diversity hurdle without consideration of the diversity contribution that this student's uniqueness, unrelated to race or ethnicity, could add to the enrolling class. In other words, the OUA plan does not allow

---

[8] Remember that this system adds an automatic 20 points with complete certainty to the application of each and every minority candidate.

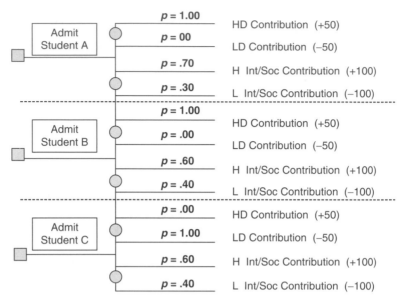

FIGURE 1.5. Decision tree diagram of a fixed point affirmative action plan for student admissions. Squares represent decision points and circles represent outcomes. Outcomes: HD = high diversity contribution; LD = low diversity contribution; H Int/Soc = high intellectual and social contribution; L Int/Soc = low intellectual and social contribution. Choices: student A: promising Black student who is a child of a successful physician; student B: Black student from a rough inner city background; student C: White student with extraordinary artistic talent.

for discretion in evaluating the diversity component, and therefore automatically removes the White student who is equivalent to the Black student from the poor background in terms of potential intellectual and social contributions.

Of course, the subjective probabilities and the simple utilities in this model were set by assumption, and not by any empirical estimation of how the admissions officers actually do weigh these pieces of information to reach final decisions. Any complete evaluation of the two different affirmative action plans would benefit from a lens model type of analysis as depicted in Figure 1.6. Using that approach researchers would collect large samples of admissions officer decisions and systematically measure the ecological validities (associations between GPA, test scores, letters of recommendation, . . . diversity contribution and the students' overall contributions to the class) and the cue utilizations (associations between the cues and the admission officers' evaluation of the students' overall performance in the class). In addition, a measure of overall judgment accuracy (i.e., the association between the students' contributions to the class and the admissions officers' predictions for the students) would be useful to estimate the accuracy of the admissions process. While it would be difficult to apply a descriptive model to this problem, its contribution would be invaluable to assessing the

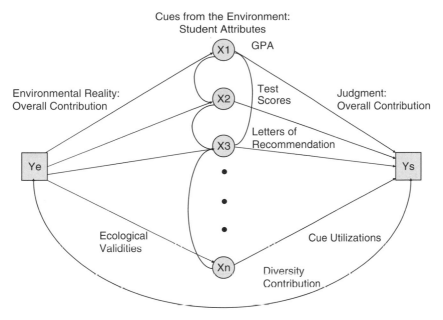

Cues from the Environment:
Student Attributes

X1   GPA

Environmental Reality:
Overall Contribution

X2   Test
     Scores

Judgment:
Overall Contribution

X3   Letters of
     Recommendation

Ye

Ys

Ecological
Validities

Cue Utilizations

Xn   Diversity
     Contribution

Achievement: Accuracy of Student Contribution

FIGURE 1.6. The lens model as a description of admission officers' judgments of student applications to the university.

reality of how the admissions procedures actually function under any of these or other models. The difficulties would arise in coming up with measures of the "softer" subjective cues (e.g., student statement and letters of recommendation) and the external measure of each student's contribution to the enrolled class. However, absent an empirical evaluation of the descriptive decision model, it is even more difficult to know how admissions officers actually weigh factors such as GPA, test scores, letters of recommendation, racial and ethnic contributions to diversity, and contributions to diversity from other sources. As the normative model analysis to follow shows, the distribution of weights for the racial/ethnic sources of diversity and the nonracial sources are critical to satisfying the law.

In *Gratz v. Bollinger* (2003, p. 252) and *Grutter v. Bollinger* (2003, p. 316), White plaintiffs denied admission to the University of Michigan's undergraduate college and law college filed separate class action suits in federal court against the state alleging that the affirmative action policies using race as a factor in admissions to a public institution were in violation of the Equal Protection Clause of the Fourteenth Amendment, Title VI of the Civil Rights Act of 1964, and 42 U.S.C. Sec. 1981, 1983, and 2000. Following the standards put forth in *Adarand Constructors, Inc. v. Pena* (1995), the Court adopted a strict scrutiny test for affirmative action plans in public institutions, but in accordance with Justice Powell's opinion in *Bakke* (1978), it held ". . .that student body diversity is a compelling state interest that can justify the use of race in university admissions" (*Grutter*, p. 325). The Court found the Law College's plan (outlined previously) was narrowly tailored to accomplish the diversity interest because it did not use a quota system (i.e., an approach that prevents applicants with certain desired characteristics from competing with other applicants with regard to other academic qualities), and instead allowed race or ethnicity to act as a "plus" in the applicant's file (*Bakke*, 1978, 315; *Grutter*, 2003, p. 334). The admissions committee must "consider all pertinent elements of diversity in light of the particular qualifications of each applicant" (*Bakke*, p. 317; *Grutter*, p. 334). "Universities can, however, consider race or ethnicity more flexibly as a 'plus' factor in the context of individualized consideration of each and every applicant" (*Grutter*, p. 334).

The Court went on to say that the law college's procedure of consulting daily records of the racial and ethnic composition of class admissions to ensure that it was developing a critical mass of underrepresented students did not a constitute a quota system. The law college did not automatically accept or reject students based on race or ethnicity, nor did it automatically or mechanically award bonuses to applicants according to race or ethnicity as a defining attribute (*Grutter*, 2003, pp. 336–337). Further, the Law School's admission policy considered many potential factors as contributions to the applicants' diversity including traveling abroad, overcoming personal adversity and hardships, community service accomplishments, careers in other fields, and underrepresented minority status (*Grutter*, p. 338). Finally, all applicants may submit their own personal statement to demonstrate the diverse nature of their backgrounds, accomplishments, and interests (p. 338). The Court made note of the fact that the law school weighed factors other than race and ethnicity in evaluating diversity, as evidenced by the fact that it "frequently accepts non-minority applicants with grades and test scores lower than underrepresented minority applicants (and other non-minority applicants) who are rejected" (*Grutter*, p. 338). In the language of decision theory, the Court supported affirmative action plans that allowed variability in the subjective probabilities tied to the utilities of diversity outcomes. This would be evidenced in descriptive models as variable weights assigned to such diversity factors as race, ethnicity, persistence in the face of adversity, unusual cultural experiences, and other individualized factors represented in an application. A normative model that lets admissions officers set the parameters for these factors on an individual basis appears to be pivotal in meeting the strict scrutiny test (see Figures 1.3 and 1.4).

On the other hand, while the Court accepted the diversity interest outlined in *Gratz*, it rejected the University of Michigan Office of Undergraduate Admissions (OUA)'s affirmative action policy based upon an inflexible point system (*Gratz*, 2003, p. 270). ". . .[T]he University's policy, which automatically distributes 20 points, or onefifth of the points needed to guarantee admission, to every single "underrepresented minority" applicant solely because of race, is not narrowly tailored to achieve the interest in educational diversity. . ." As the Court made clear in Grutter, such an automatic system that considers only race and ethnicity as measures of diversity is in violation of the Equal Protection Clause (*Gratz*, 2003, p. 275). (See Figure 1.5 for an example.) Further, the fact that an individualized system like the one used at the Law School is impractical with the large number of applicants that the OUA processes does not justify a violation of the Equal Protection Clause (*Gratz*, 2003, p. 275). These cases and the normative decision model that emerges appear to favor clinical or expert decision making as opposed to actuarial or statistical rules because the former allows for individualized treatment of diversity as opposed to fixed assessments of diversity as a function of race or ethnicity.

The findings in *Grutter* (2003) and *Gratz* (2003) are not in agreement with the literature on judgment and decisions making, which shows that in almost all situations actuarial approaches to decision making are superior (produce stronger achievement relationships between judgment and external measures of criterion) than are clinical or expert-based decision models (Hastie & Dawes, 2001; Meehl, 1954). The consistency and accuracy of actuarial models are found again and again to be superior to pure expert judgments such as the one that the Court adopted for a normative model of educational affirmative action in *Grutter* (2003) and *Gratz* (2003). In one review, Grove and Meehl (1996) concluded, "Empirical comparisons of the accuracy of the two methods (136 studies over a wide range of predictions) show that the mechanical method is almost invariably equal to or superior to the clinical method" (p. 293).

The task for researchers is to develop structured decision-making aids that are practical for large university admissions offices, but that take advantage of the strengths of the actuarial models, while at the same time not violating the normative model that features individualized attention to a variety of diversity factors among applications. We believe that such decision models can be developed using structural approaches that allow experts to combine statistical data with individualized assessments of diversity factors (including "soft" factors) that add to the applicants' potential contributions to the diversity of an incoming class at all levels of university education. In fact, forensic clinical psychologists already make use of similar hybrid models in assessing risk in offender populations for the courts (Borum, 1996; Dolan & Doyle, 2000; Green, Pedley, & Whittingham, 2004). Such models would need to allow a subjective and individualized assessment of diversity contributions for each applicant, but combine them in an algorithm with statistical and objective indicators of worthiness. Once researchers develop these models for affirmative action programs, they can test them by fitting them to decision tree analyses and descriptive models of admission officers' decision making.

The General Use of Rational, Descriptive, and Normative Models in Psychology and Law

We have tried to show with two examples how a comparison of rational actor, descriptive, and normative models of decision making can add useful insights to the analysis of legal decision-making problems. Especially useful are the discrepancies between the three types of models and the insights that those discrepancies hold for both law and social scientific analysis. In this final section of the chapter, we try to locate this approach within a more general method of studying law and psychology. In a series of articles, we have laid out a model of psycholegal analysis that is the product of an interdisciplinary methodology (Wiener, 1993, 1995; Wiener, Block-Lieb, Gross, & Baron-Donovan, 2005; Wiener & Hurt, 1997, 1999; Wiener et al., 2002; Wiener, Hurt, Russell, Mannen, & Gasper, 1997; Wiener, Watts, Goldkamp, & Gasper, 1995; Wiener, Winter, Rogers, & Arnot, 2004). We have termed the model "social analytic jurisprudence" because it combines empirical investigation of social and psychological reality with traditional legal analysis.[9] Our approach is to provide empirical knowledge to the legislative function of the courts and other lawmaking bodies. Social analytic jurisprudence makes three important assumptions about the role of psychology in law and public policy.

First, psychology as it relates to law is an empirical science (Wiener, 1993, 1995; Wiener & Hurt, 1997). That is, there exists a collection of psycholegal scientists who share a common commitment to a set of scientific beliefs and values and who agree on common problems and appropriate methodologies to study substantive and procedural issues that are relevant to the law (i.e., a research paradigm; Kuhn, 1996; Lachman, Lachman, & Butterfield, 1979). We believe it is appropriate to use the product of these scientists' efforts to influence judicial and legislative decision making. Second, the psycholegal scholar ought to contribute to the legal debate only by presenting the tested results of psychological research. The legitimacy with which psychological knowledge can be applied to issues of law is directly related to the psychological facts that are tested and accumulated. When psychologists base their arguments on a value consensus rather than a reliable database, they engage in value debate rather than scientific analysis. Finally, the proper role of scientific psychologists in policy debate and conflict resolution is that of consultant rather than advocate (Wrightsman, 1991). While advocates adopt confirming perspectives in which they search psychological knowledge for research results that support a chosen position, consultants adopt disconfirming points of view and search research results for evidence that can refute all plausible rival explanations including, and especially, their own.

Social analytic jurisprudence begins with an analysis of legal doctrine, carefully looking for assumptions that the law makes about human behavior (Wiener, 1993, 1995; Wiener & Hurt, 1997, 1997; Wiener et al., 2002, 2004a, 2004b, 2005). Psycholegal research that directly addresses questions of substantive law is most useful to the courts and legislatures. The language and concepts of the empirical investigation should match closely those that make up statutory and/or case law. In our current analysis, we treated the law as normative models of legal decision making in racial profiling and in affirmative action in education. While we ended with normative models, rather than beginning with them, they played the same role, that is, directing psycholegal analysis of public policy issues.

The second stage of social analytic jurisprudence is a psychological analysis of the law (Wiener, 1993, 1995; Wiener & Hurt, 1997; Wiener et al., 2005). Statutory

---

[9] Wiener & Hurt (1997) provide a detailed account of social analytic jurisprudence. The current description is a summary of the full argument.

and common law are comprised of legal tests that the courts apply to the social facts presented in specific cases. Legislatures and appellate level courts often frame the tests in language that stimulates social scientific and sometimes psychological investigations. Ultimately, social science findings can tip the scales in judicial decisions that require the courts to balance conflicting legal principles. Among the primary goals of psycholegal scholarship is to test assumptions and answer empirical questions in the law. To realize this objective, the psycholegal scholar reviews the psychological literature to identify theories, research results, and methodologies that are most suitable to address empirical issues in the law. The current approach treated rational action models, behavioral decision theory, and the lens model as psychological constructs that help define legal assumptions as hypotheses about decision making in profiling and affirmative action civil issues.

In the final stage of social analytic jurisprudence, researchers apply the powerful research methodologies of the social sciences to test intuitive answers to empirical questions. In this chapter, we merely suggested some ways in which additional empirical work could contribute to the issues that the law struggles with regarding racial profiling and affirmative action. While we stopped short of specifying research designs and protocols, we have identified a number of empirical questions that are answerable with additional policy-related research. Psycholegal scholarship should take advantage of the sophisticated quantitative and qualitative methodologies of the social sciences but it should do so in the context of the knowledge base of the social sciences (Wiener, 1993, 1995; Wiener & Hurt, 1997).

There are three ways in which social science can be brought to bear on the law and policy: it can assume an adjustment or assessment role, an implementation role, or an evaluative role. Law embodies normative theories of behavior in the statutes, court opinions, and administrative rules and regulations. In the current chapter, law gives rise to what we have termed normative models of legal decision making. Psychological research can and does study the actual conduct of people to measure the fit between everyday behavior and the law's regulatory scheme. In the context of the current chapter, empirical research has the ability to measure the fit between the normative decision models in the law and both the rational actor models (i.e., decision tree analyses of legal decisions) and lens model conceptualizations (i.e., empirical descriptions of ecological validity, cue utilizations, and accuracy between decision makers' outcomes and external realities). Researchers study the everyday behavior of people to offer suggestions of how to improve the fit between the normative model and the social milieu.

Second, psychology can and does assist with the implementation of procedural and substantive law. It is perhaps in this role that research psychology has had its most recognizable impact. Examples include the study of police decision making (Mann, Vrij, & Bull, 2004), jury decision making (Greene & Bornstein, 2003), judicial decision making (Krauss, 2004; Lurigio, Carroll, & Stalans, 1994; Wrightsman, 1999), eyewitness identification (Wells et al., 1998), and sentencing (Wiener, Pritchard, & Weston, 1995; Wiener et al., 1998, 2004). It is not a coincidence that each of these areas focuses on the judgment capability of significant actors in the legal process, because the implementation of law is closely tied to making decisions under the constraint of legal rules. The purpose of our current work is not only to improve the quality of the legal process but also to apply our knowledge of social and cognitive behavior to understand how people make decisions in their roles as university administrators, police, lawyers, jurors, judges, administrators, legislators, and so on.

Finally, the evaluative function of social science is to measure the impact of the law on the everyday lives of citizens. Psychological research can either test how legislation or judicial holdings affect those citizens who are consumers of the law, or it can examine how different formulations of law influence the social and cognitive behavior of those citizens. In the current chapter, we examined the role of law in shaping the way in which police make traffic stop decisions and the way in which school admissions teams select applicants for university programs.

We believe that the current application of social analytic jurisprudence to problems in legal decision making offers useful insights about the structure and actualization of legal decisions that people make in their everyday environments. Applying these models to judgments in socially sensitive areas will allow a subtle but legally relevant analysis of the everyday judgments that the law requires of all of us. In the end, such an analysis will help us describe the social consciousness of deliberate decision strategies that are so important in shaping our lives. We offer this approach as one way to encourage analysis, research, and debate in the psychological analysis of social issues.

References

Ackerson, K. S., Brodsky, S. L., & Zapf, P. A. (2005). Judges' and psychologists' assessments of legal and clinical factors in competence for execution. *Psychology, Public Policy, & Law. 11*(1), 164–193.

Antonio, A. L., Chang, M., Hakuta, K., Kenny, D. A., Leven, S., & Milem, J. F. (2004). Effects of racial diversity on complex thinking in college students. *Psychological Science, 15*(8), 507–510.

Blair, I. V., & Mahzarin R. (1996). Automatic and controlled processes in stereotype priming. *Journal of Personality and Social Psychology, 70,* 1142–1163.

Bornstein, B. (2004). The impact of different types of expert scientific testimony on mock jurors' liability verdicts. *Psychology, Crime & Law, 10*(4), 429–446.

Bornstein, B., Rung, L. M., & Miller, M. K. (2002). The effects of defendant remorse on mock juror decisions in a malpractice case. *Behavioral Sciences & the Law, 20*(4), 393–409.

Borum, R. (1996). Improving the clinical practice of violence risk assessment. Technology, guidelines, and training. *American Psychologist, 51,* 945–956.

Cooter, R., & Ulen, T. (2004). *Law and economics* (4th ed.). London: Addison-Wesley.

Chang, M. J. (1999). Does racial diversity matter?: The educational impact of a racially diverse undergraduate population. *Journal of College Student Development, 40,* 377–395.

Chang, M. J., Witt, D., Jones, J., & Hakuta, K. (Eds.). (2003). *Compelling interest: Examining the evidence on racial dynamics in higher education.* Stanford, CA: Stanford University Press.

Cook, T. D. (1985). Post-positivist critical multiplism. In R. L. Shotland & M. M. Mark (Eds.), *Social science and social policy* (pp. 21–62). Beverly Hills: SAGE.

Crosby, F. J., Iyer, A., & Downing, R. A. (2003). Affirmative action: Psychological data and the policy debates. *American Psychologist, 58*, 93–115.

Devine, D. J., Clayton, L. D., Dunford, B. B., Seying, R., & Pryce, J. (2001). Jury decision making: 45 years of empirical research on deliberating groups. *Psychology, Public Policy, and Law, 7*(3), 622–727.

Diamond, S. S., Saks, M. J., & Landsman, S. (1998). Juror judgments about liability and damages: Sources of variability and ways to increase consistency. *DePaul Law Review, 48*, 301–325.

Dolan, M., & Doyle, M. (2000). Violence risk prediction: Clinical and actuarial measures and the role of psychopathy. *British Journal of Psychiatry, 177*, 303–311.

Dovidio, J. F., Kawakami, K., & Johnson, C. (1997). On the nature of prejudice: Automatic and controlled processes. *Journal of Experimental Social Psychology, 33*, 510–540.

Edens, J. F., Petrila, J., & Buffington-Vollum, J. K. (2001). Psychopathy and the death penalty: Can the psychopathy checklist-revised identify offenders who represent "a continuing threat to society?" *Journal of Psychiatry and Law, 29*(4), 433–481.

Fazio, R. H. (2001). On the automatic activation of associated evaluations: An overview. *Cognition & Emotion, 15*, 115–141.

Fellner, G. (2005). The psychology of economic decisions. Vol. I: Rationality and well-being. *Journal of Economic Psychology, 26*(1), 151–154.

Green, B., Pedley, R., & Whittingham, D. (2004). A structured clinical model for violence risk intervention. *International Journal of Law & Psychiatry, 27*(4), 349–359.

Greene, E., & Bornstein, B. (2003). *Determining damages: The psychology of jury awards.* Washington, DC: American Psychological Association.

Greenwald, A. G., Banaji, M. R., & Rudman, L. A. (2002). A unified theory of implicit attitudes, stereotypes, self-esteem, and self-concept. *Psychological Review, 109*, 3–25.

Gross, S. R., & Barnes, K. Y. (2002). Road work: Racial profiling and drug interdiction on the highway. *Michigan Law Review, 101*, 651–751.

Grove, W. M., & Meehl, P. E. (1966). Comparative efficiency of informal (subjective, impressionistic) and formal (mechanical, algorithmic) prediction procedures: The clinical-statistical controversy. *Psychology, Public Policy, and Law, 2*, 293–323.

Gurin, P. (1999). The compelling need for diversity in higher education: Expert testimony in *Gratz, et al. v. Bellinger, et al. Michigan Journal of Race and Law, 5*, 363–425.

Hammond, K. R. (2000a). *Judgments under stress.* Oxford: Oxford University Press.

Hammond, K. R. (2000b). Coherence and correspondence theories in judgment and decision making. In T. Connolly, H. R. Arkes, & K. R. Hammond (Eds.), *Judgment and decision making: An interdisciplinary reader* (pp. 53–65). New York: Cambridge University Press.

Hans, V. P., Hannaford, P. L., & Munsterman, G. T. (1999). The Arizona jury reform permitting civil jury trial discussions: The views of trial participants, judges, and jurors. *University of Michigan Journal of Law Reform, 32*, 349–377.

Hastie, R., & Dawes, R. M. (2001). Rational choice in an uncertain world. Thousand Oaks, CA: SAGE.

Hastie, R., Schkade, D. A., & Payne, J. W. (1998). A study of juror and jury judgments in civil cases: Deciding liability for punitive damages. *Law and Human Behavior, 22*, 287–314.

Heilman, M. E., & Alcott, V. B. (2001). What I think you think of me: Women's reactions to being viewed as beneficiaries of preferential selection. *Journal of Applied Social Psychology, 86*, 574–582.

Heilman, M. E., Battle, W. S., Keller, C. E., & Lee, R. A. (1998). Type of affirmative action policy: A determinant of reactions to sex-based preferential selection? *Journal of Applied Social Psychology, 86*, 190–205.

Heilman, M. E., & Blader, S. L. (2001). Assuming preferential selection when the admissions policy is unknown: The effects of gender rarity. *Journal of Applied Social Psychology, 86,* 188–193.

Heilman, M. E., Block, C. J., & Stathatos, P. (1997). The affirmative action stigma of incompetence: Effects performance information ambiguity. *Academy of Management Journal, 40,* 603–625.

Kahneman, D., & Miller, D. (1986a). Comparing reality to its alternatives. *Psychological Review, 153*(93), 136–153.

Kahneman, D., & Tversky, A. (1979). Prospect theory: an analysis of decision under risk. *Econometrica, 47,* 263–291.

Korokbin, R. B., & Ulen, T. S. (1998). Efficiency and equity: What can be gained by combining Coase and Rawls? *Washington Law Review, 73,* 329–347.

Korobkin, R. B., & Ulen, T. S. (2000). Law and behavioral science: Removing the rationality assumption from law and economics. *California Law Review, 88,* 1051–1144.

Kovera, M. B., & Cass, S. A. (2002). Compelled mental health examinations, liability decisions, and damage awards in sexual harassment cases: Issues for jury research. *Psychology, Public Policy, & Law, 8*(1), 96–114.

Krauss, D. A. (2004). Adjusting Risk of Recidivism: Do Judicial Departures Worsen or Improve Recidivism Prediction Under the Federal Sentencing Guidelines? *Behavioral Sciences & the Law, 22*(6), 731–750.

Kuhn, T. S. (1996). *The structure of scientific revolutions* (3rd ed.). Chicago, IL: University of Chicago Press.

Landes, W., & Posner, R. (1987). *Economic structure of tort law.* Cambridge, MA: Harvard University Press.

Lachman, R., Lachman, T., & Butterfield, S. (1979). *Cognitive psychology and information processing.* Orlando, FL: Academic Press.

Lerner, J. S., Gonzalez, R. M., Small, D. A., & Fischhoff, B. (2003). Effects of fear and anger on perceived risks of terrorism: A national field experiment. *Psychological Science, 14,* 144–150.

Lerner, J. S., & Keltner, D. (2000). Beyond valence: Toward a model of emotion-specific influences on judgement and choice. *Cognition & Emotion, 14,* Special issue: Emotion, cognition, and decision making, 473–493.

Lerner, J. S., & Keltner, D. (2001). Fear, anger, and risk. *Journal of Personality & Social Psychology, 81,* 146–159.

Loewenstein, G. F., Weber, E. U., Hsee, C. K., & Welch, N. (2001). Risk as feelings. *Psychological Bulletin, 127,* 267–286.

Lurigio, A. J., Carroll, J. S., & Stalans, L. J. (1994). Understanding judges' sentencing decisions: Attribution of responsibility and story construction. In L. Heath (Ed.). *Applications of heuristics and biases to social issues: Social psychology applications to social issues.* New York: Plenum Press.

Lynch, M., & Haney, C. (2000). Discrimination and instructional comprehension: Guided discretion, racial bias, and the death penalty. *Law and Human Behavior, 24,* 337–358.

Mann, S., Vrij, A., & Bull, R. (2004). Detecting true lies: Police officers' ability to detect deceit. *Journal of Applied Psychology, 89,* 137–149.

Meehl, P. E. (1954). *Clinical vs. statistical prediction: A theoretical analysis and a review of the evidence.* Minneapolis: University of Minnesota Press.

Mellers, B. A. (2000). Choice and the relative pleasure of consequences. *Psychological Bulletin, 126,* 910–924.

Mellers, B. A., Schwartz, A., Ho, K., & Ritov, I. (1997). Decision affect theory: Emotional reactions to the outcomes of risky options. *Psychological Science, 8,* 423–429.

Mellers, B. A., Schwartz, A., & Ritov, I. (1999). Emotion-based choice. *Journal of Experimental Psychology: General, 128*, 332–345.

Melton, G. B. (1988). The significance of law in the everyday lives of children and families. *Georgia Law Review, 22*, 851–895.

Melton, G. B. (1990). Law, science, humanity: The normative foundation of social science in law. *Law and Human Behavior, 14*, 315–332.

Melton, G. B., & Saks, M. J. (1985). The law as an instrument of socialization and social structure. In G. B. Melton (Ed.), *The law as a behavioral instrument: Nebraska Symposium on Motivation* (pp. 235–277). Lincoln NE: University of Nebraska Press.

Monahan, J., Heilbrum, K., Silver, E., Nabors, E., Bone, J., & Slovic, P. (2002). Communicating violence risk: Frequency formats, vivid outcomes, and forensic settings. *International Journal of Forensic Mental Health, 1*(2), 121–126.

Monahan, J., & Walker, L. (2002). *Social science in law: Cases and materials.* Mineola, NY: Foundation Press.

Münsterberg, H. (1908/1976). *On the witness stand.* New York: AMS Press.

Porter, S., Birt, A., & Boer, D. P. (2001). Investigation of the criminal and conditional release profiles of Canadian federal offenders as a function of psychopathy and age. *Law and Human Behavior, 25*(6), 647–661.

Posner, R. (1997). Are we one self or multiple selves? Implications for Law and Public Policy, *Legal Theory, 3*, 23–39.

Poythress, N. G., Edens, J. F., & Watkins, M. M. (2001). The relationship between psychopathic personality features and malingering symptoms of major mental illness. *Law and Human Behavior, 25*(6), 567–582.

Roese, N. J., & Olson J. M. (Eds.) (1995). *What might have been: The social psychology of counterfactual thinking.* Hillsdale, NJ: Erlbaum.

Rudman, L. A. (2004). Sources of implicit attitudes. *Current Directions in Psychological Science, 13*(2), 79–82.

Slovic, P., Monahan, J., & MacGregor, D. G. (2000). Violence risk assessment and risk communication: The effects of using actual cases, providing instruction, and employing probability versus frequency formats. *Law & Human Behavior, 24*(3), 271–296.

Smith, D. G., & Associates. (1997). *Diversity works: The emerging picture of how students benefit.* Washington, DC: Association of American Colleges and Universities.

Suchman, M. C. (1997). On beyond interest: Rational, normative, and cognitive perspectives in the social scientific study of law. *Wisconsin Law Review, 1997*, 475–501.

Technical Working Group on Eyewitness Evidence (1999). *Eyewitness evidence: A guide for law enforcement.* Washington, D.C.: U.S. Department of Justice.

Tiedens, L. Z., & Linton, S. (2001). Judgment under emotional certainty and uncertainty: The effects of specific emotions on information processing. *Journal of Personality and Social Psychology, 81*, 973–988.

Tversky, A., & Kahneman, D. (1974). Judgments under uncertainty: Heuristics and biases. *Science, 185*, 1124–1131.

Wells, G. L., Small, M., Penrod, S., Malpass, R., Fulero, S. M., Brimacombe, C. A. (1998). Eyewitness identification procedures: Recommendations for lineups and photospreads. *Law & Human Behavior, 22*(6), 603–647.

Wiener, R. L. (1990). A psycholegal and empirical approach to the medical standard of care. *Nebraska Law Review, 69*, 112–157.

Wiener, R. L. (1993). Social Analytic Jurisprudence and Tort Law: Social Cognition Goes to Court. *Saint Louis University Law Journal, 37*(3), 503–551.

Wiener, R. L. (1995) Social analytic jurisprudence in sexual harassment litigation: The role of social framework and social fact. *Journal of Social Issues, 51*, 167–180.

Wiener, R. L., Block-Lieb, S., Gross, K., & Baron-Donovan, C. (2005). Unwrapping assumptions: Applying social analytic jurisprudence to consumer bankruptcy law and policy. *American Bankruptcy Law Journal, 79,* 453–483.

Wiener, R. L., Hackney, A., Kadela, K., Rauch, S., Seib, H., Warren, L., & Hurt, L. E. (2002). The fit and implementation of sexual harassment law to workplace evaluations. *Journal of Applied Psychology, 87,* 747–764.

Wiener, R. L., & Hurt, L. E. (1997). Social sexual conduct at work: How do workers know when it is harassment and when it is not? *California Western Law Review, 34*(1), 53–99.

Wiener, R. L., & Hurt, L. E. (1999). An interdisciplinary approach to understanding social sexual conduct at work. In R. Wiener & B. Gutek (Eds.), *Advances in sexual harassment research, theory, and policy. Psychology, Public Policy, and Law, 5,* 556–595.

Wiener, R. L., & Hurt, L. E. (2000). How do people evaluate social-sexual conduct: A psycholegal model. *Journal of Applied Psychology, 85,* 75–85.

Wiener, R. L., Hurt, L. E., Russell, B., Mannen, K., & Gasper, C. (1997). Perceptions of sexual harassment: The effects of gender, legal standard, and ambivalent sexism. *Law and Human Behavior, 24,* 71–93.

Wiener, R. L., Hurt, L. E., Thomas, S. L., Sadler, M. S., Bauer, C. A., & Sargent, T. M. (1998). The role of declarative and procedural knowledge in capital murder sentencing. *Journal of Applied Social Psychology, 28*(2), 124–144.

Wiener, R. L., Pritchard, C. C., & Weston, M. (1995). Comprehensibility of approved jury instructions in capital murder cases. *Journal of Applied Psychology, 80*(4), 455–467.

Wiener, R. L., Rogers, M., Winter, R., Hurt, L. E., Hackney, A., Kadela, K., Seib, H., Rauch, S., Warren, L., & Morasco, B. (2004a). Guided jury discretion in capital murder cases: The role of declarative and procedural knowledge. *Psychology, Public Policy, and Law, 10*(4), 516–576.

Wiener, R. L., Watts, B. A., Goldkamp, K. H., & Gasper, C. (1995). Social analytic investigation of hostile work environments: A test of the reasonable woman standard. *Law and Human Behavior, 19,* 263–281.

Wiener, R. L., Winter, R., Rogers, M., & Arnot, L. (2004b). The effects of prior workplace behavior on subsequent sexual harassment judgments. *Law and Human Behavior, 28*(1), 47–67.

Wrightsman, L. S. (1991). *Psychology and the legal system.* Pacific Grove, CA: Brooks/Cole.

Wrightsman, L. S. (1999). *Judicial decision making: Is psychology relevant?* Dordrecht: Kluwer Academic.

Legal Citations

Adarand Constructors, Inc. v. Pena, 515 U.S. 200 (1995).

Gratz v. Bollinger, 539 U.S. 244 (2003).

Grutter v. Bollinger, 539 U.S. 306 (2003).

McCleskey v. Kemp, 107 S. Ct. 1756 (1987).

Regents of University of California v. Bakke, 438 U.S. 265 (1978).

State v. Soto, 734 A.2d 350, (N.J. Super. 1996).

United States v. New Jersey, Civil No. 99-5970(MLC) (U.S. District Court N.J. 1999).

Wards Cove Packing Co. v. Atonio, 490 U.S. 642, (1989).

Wilkins v. Maryland State Police, No. CCB-93-468 (D. Md. 1993).

Unit I
Investigative Profiling: Legal Developments and Empirical Research

2
The Rhetoric of Racial Profiling

Samuel R. Gross

In 1988 few of us, if any, had heard the term "racial profiling." A dozen years later, everybody knew about racial profiling and almost everybody agreed that it's bad. That remains the case. There is nearly universal agreement that racial profiling is bad and illegal. This is a singular turn of events for a phrase that is simply shorthand for a claim of racial discrimination in the administration of criminal justice. In this chapter, I try to track that development.

The Beginning

If you search the Lexis database for the earliest reported American court decisions to use the phrase "racial profiling," one of the first cases you'll run into is *United States v. Miller*,[1] which was decided by the United States Court of Appeal for the Eleventh Circuit in June of 1987. Here are the critical facts, as described by the court:

The appellant, Miller, was driving northbound on Interstate 95 near Orlando, Florida, on June 18, 1985. Florida Highway Patrol Trooper Robert Vogel was parked perpendicular to the northbound lanes, with his headlights illuminating passing vehicles and their occupants. Miller drove by Trooper Vogel at approximately 9:40 p.m. Based on the facts that Miller was driving just below the posted speed limit of 55 miles per hour, Miller was driving a car with out-of-state license plates, and Miller did not turn his head to look into the headlights of Trooper Vogel's parked car, Trooper Vogel decided to pursue Miller's car in order to stop and search the car for drugs.[2]

Trooper Vogel then followed Mr. Miller until Miller "allowed his right wheels to cross over the White painted lane marker about four inches, in violation of Florida traffic laws,"[3] and then stopped Miller—officially because of this technical violation of the traffic rules, but actually, as Trooper Vogel admitted, to search for drugs.[4]

---

[1] United States v. Miller, 821 F.2d 546 (11th Cir. 1987).
[2] Id. at 547.
[3] Id.
[4] Id. at 459.

All of this may sound familiar if you have read other descriptions of racial profiling on the highway. But there's a problem. The term "racial profiling" does not appear anywhere in the court's opinion, nor does any similar term, nor the word "race" or any related word, nor any specific racial or ethnic reference such as "Black," "White," or "Hispanic." The reason this case shows up in a Lexis search is that "racial profiling" is mentioned, apparently inexplicably, in the "overview" of the case that was written by the Lexis staff: "The court held that the initial stop was illegal and violated the U.S. Const. amend. IV because the trooper had engaged in racial profiling."[5]

Literally, this description of the Eleventh Circuit's 1987 opinion is flat wrong. Racial profiling is not mentioned by the court. But in another sense, the Lexis editors may have gotten it right, even if that's clear only in revisionist retrospect. What Trooper Vogel did may well have been "racial profiling," as we now use the term—and if so, it did violate the constitution, although probably not the Fourth Amendment as we now understand it. In any event, the case did explicitly involve "profiling," if not racial. Before there was "racial profiling" there was "profiling" generally, and specifically "drug courier profiling." That is what the *Miller* opinion, as originally written, was about. In the late 1980s and 1990s "drug courier profiling" morphed into "racial profiling," and the officer who stopped Mr. Miller, Trooper Robert L. Vogel, was a central actor in that drama.

"Profiling" is used by law enforcement officers to help them find needles in haystacks—to identify the few bad guys hiding in plain view among the mass of ordinary people. The idea is to use visible cues to narrow the field of possible suspects to a manageable scope, and then focus attention on that smaller group. For the process to work, the cues that are used in the profile must in fact correlate with the misbehavior at issue. I have my doubts about the actual value of the profiles I've read and heard about, but that issue is beyond the scope of this chapter.

The earliest investigative "profiles" that went by that name were the "hijacker profiles" that were used in American airports in the late 1960s and early 1970s.[6] From our blood-soaked vantage point in the early twenty-first century, there is a quaint innocence to that period: Hijackers mostly flew planes to Cuba (not counting the cult-figure hijacker "D.B. Cooper," who collected $200,000 in ransom and parachuted into the Oregon night[7]), and usually they merely threatened violence. In that context, hijacker profiles were used for a purpose that has long since become obsolete: to decide *which* passengers and bags to scan for weapons. The earliest mention of profiling of any sort in Lexis is this abbreviated abstract of a story from September 1972:

---

[5] United States v. Miller, 1987 U.S. App. LEXIS 8112, at *1 (11th Cir 1987).

[6] David A. Harris, PROFILES IN INJUSTICE at 17 (The New Press: New York, 2002).

[7] Douglas Pasternak, *Skyjacker at Large, Florida Widow Thinks She Has Found Him*, US News & World Report, 7/24/00, available at: http://www.usnews.com/usnews/doubleissue/mysteries/cooper.htm

FAA repts on Sept 6 that its hijacker behavioral profile has led to discovery of small arsenal hidden in violin case at Cleveland Airport; say J Jeusnik, owner of cache, was asked to open case after his actions matched those in behavioral profile; attempted to board Amer Airlines flight to Tucson with weapons.[8]

Four months later, in January 1973, the Federal Aviation Administration (FAA) adopted an early version of the current practice, requiring *all* passengers to pass through metal detectors and to have all carry-on luggage X-rayed.[9]

The next stop on the line was "drug courier profiling," also typically practiced in airports. Maybe it was a coincidence; may be the earlier practice of hijacker profiling at airports morphed into this new form. In any event, starting in the mid-1970s federal Drug Enforcement Agency (DEA) agents began to use behavioral and demographic profiles to try to identify air travelers who were transporting drugs.[10]

The practice mushroomed. Between 1976 and 1986 more than 140 reported federal cases involved airport stops by DEA agents based on a "drug courier profile,"[11] plus an unknown number of unreported court cases—which, of course, is only the tip of an iceberg. It's anybody's guess how many suspects were found with drugs and pled guilty with no court decision on the legality of the search, or how many innocent travelers were stopped or searched but never charged.

The DEA has never published an official description of the drug courier profiles it has used. That would defeat their purpose. However, DEA agents have testified to some of the components in court cases over the years. The net effect is a bad joke. The tell-tale signs of a drug courier include: buying a one-way ticket or buying a round-trip ticket; paying in large denomination bills or paying in small denomination bills; walking quickly through the terminal, or walking slowly through the terminal; being one of the first passengers to deplane, or the last passenger to deplane, or deplaning in the middle of the crowd; traveling with a companion or traveling alone; carrying no luggage, a small tote bag, or a medium-size bag, or taking a lot of luggage; behaving nervously, or appearing calm and cool.[12] The common denominator, of course, is that the defendant before the court did or had whatever it took to fit the profile de jour.

The DEA agents who testified about drug courier profiles of the 1970s and 1980s sometimes admitted that they took into account racial characteristics. For example, in a case in 1978 an agent said that "a Black [man] arriving from a

---

[8] Lexis, Information Bank Abstracts, NEW YORK TIMES, September 7, 1972, Thursday, Page 85, Column 8 (AP).

[9] Judy Rumerman, *Aviation Security*, available at the U.S. Centennial of Flight Commission Web site, at: http://www.centennialofflight.gov/essay/Government_Role/security/POL18.htm

[10] Harris, supra note 6 at 19–21.

[11] Charles L. Becton, *The Drug Courier Profile: "All Seems Infected That Th' Infected Spy, as All Looks Yellow to the Jaundic'd Eye,"* 65 N.C. L. Rev. 417 (1987).

[12] Id. at 438–54, 474–80; see also David Cole, NO EQUAL JUSTICE at 47–52 (The New Press: New York, 1999).

major heroin distribution point"[13] was singled out for attention. In a different case, in 1977, a DEA agent testified that "[i]n the majority of cases the courier has been a Black female."[14] And in another case, in 1979, an agent testified that "the fact that a person is of Spanish descent would ... make us more aware of them."[15] Until the 1990s, however, courts simply reported these admissions that race was used in deciding who to stop and search without suggesting that they raised any special legal concerns.[16]

The final step in the evolution of the modern practice that became known as "racial profiling" was to apply the logic of drug courier profiling to the highway. Which brings us back to Trooper Robert L. Vogel. In the early 1980s, American law enforcement agencies became concerned about large drug shipments that were believed to arrive in Florida by water from Latin America, and to be distributed from there across the United States by land. Vogel, who had joined the Florida Highway Patrol in 1972,[17] focused on the second part of this operation, drug distribution over the highways. By his own account, he had a natural talent for spotting drug dealers.[18] That may be true, but Vogel's lasting contribution to the enterprise was less idiosyncratic. He invented two investigative techniques that have been widely emulated.

First, Vogel developed a highway drug courier profile that was similar in kind to those used in airports, but different in content. Suspicious factors included a car not registered to the driver, driving in the early morning hours, objects out of place (e.g., a spare tire in the back seat), a male driver, and occupants who avoided eye contact with the trooper.[19]

---

[13] United States v. Coleman, 450 F. Supp. 433, 439 n. 7 (E.D. Mich. 1978).

[14] United States v. McClain, 452 F. Supp. 195, 199 (E.D. Mich. 1977).

[15] United States v. Vasquez, 612 F.2d 1338, 1353 n. 10 (2d Cir. 1979).

[16] Charles L. Becton, then a judge on the North Carolina Court of Appeals, is a telling example. In 1987 Judge Becton published an excellent article describing and criticizing the DEA's drug courier profiles in great detail. See Becton, supra note 11. Judge Becton described how DEA agents testified to explicit reliance on racial factors, but attached no special significance to this use of race, noting only, as with other factors, that the agents were inconsistent and wedded to the wisdom of hindsight.

One of the first courts to focus on the use of race in police profiles was the United States Court of Appeals for the Sixth Circuit. In 1988, a single judge of that court wrote in a concurring opinion "we do not . . . express any view on the constitutional permissibility of basing stops and/or arrests on "profiles" containing racial characteristics." United States v. Pino, 855 F.2d 357 (6th Cir. 1988) (Jones, J., concurring). Four years later the court commented ambiguously that the inclusion of racial components in a drug courier profile raised "due process and equal protection implications," United States v. Taylor, 956 F.2d 572, 589 (6th Cir. 1992), and in an unpublished opinion the next year that court said that it would be unconstitutional for an officer "to approach ... a person of color *solely* because of that person's color, absent a compelling justification," but that there was no proof that the DEA agents had done so in that particular case. United States v. Jennings, 1993 U.S. App. LEXIS 926, *11 (6th Cir. 1993) (emphasis added); see also United States v. Travis, 62 F.3d 170 (6th Cir. 1995), United States v. Avery, 137 F.3d 343 (6th Cir. 1997).

[17] Harris, supra note 6 at 21–23.

[18] Gary Webb, *DWB**, Esquire, April 1999, pp. 118–127 at p. 122.

[19] Harris, supra note 6 at 22.

This profile alone, however, wouldn't do the trick. In an airport, an officer can approach a suspect on foot and in the course of what is classified by courts as a voluntary interaction ask questions, observe the person up close, gather additional information that might justify a detention or a search of the suspect, or perhaps ask for "voluntary" consent to search the suspect's bags. Invariably, in this and every other context, almost all suspects do "consent" to searches when asked by police officers, probably because it never occurs to them that they have a choice.[20] On the highway, however, the very first step is an *involuntary* stop. The suspect's car has to be pulled over—which is classified as a coercive seizure—before the officer can get close enough to ask any questions or see the interior of the car. Under the Fourth Amendment, that means that the officer must have a "particularized" suspicion about that car—"probable cause" to believe that a crime is afoot, or at least a "reasonable suspicion" based on specific "articulable facts,"[21] before he turns on his flashing lights.

The limited information that Trooper Vogel could gather through the windows of his cruiser usually did not satisfy the courts. In *United States v. Smith*,[22] for example, "Trooper Vogel stopped a car because two young men were traveling at 3:00 a.m. in an out-of-state car being driven in accordance with all traffic regulations." The Eleventh Circuit condemned Vogel's "profile" as "a classic example of those 'inarticulate hunches' that are insufficient to justify a seizure under the fourth amendment."[23] In other words, because Vogel didn't have the required "reasonable suspicion" based on "articulable facts," the evidence found in a search of the car–including a kilogram of cocaine–could not be used in court.

Second, Vogel also pioneered the classic solution to the legal problem posed by the limited informational value of his highway drug courier profile: the pretextual stop. As every driver knows, there are hundreds of technical violations for which a car may be stopped, most of which are rarely enforced—"burned-out license plate lights, out-of-kilter headlights, obscured tags, and windshield cracks"[24]— not to mention speeding (which is nearly universal) and straying over a white line, one of Vogel's favorites. If he observed any of these things, Vogel could stop the car for that traffic or equipment violation, however trivial, and then, as in an airport, look carefully at the car and its occupants, ask questions, gather additional information that might justify further action, and perhaps ask for (and routinely get) consent to conduct a search. Defendants who were prosecuted on the basis of the searches that followed some of these stops objected. They argued that the arresting officers used trivial traffic violations as pretexts to circumvent the "particularized suspicion" requirements of the Fourth Amendment, and they

---

[20] See Samuel R. Gross & Katherine Y. Barnes, Road Work: Racial Profiling and Drug Interdiction on the Highway, 101 Mich. L. Rev 651, 675–77 (2002).

[21] Terry v. Ohio, 392 U.S. 1, 26–27 (1967).

[22] 799 F.2d 704, 707 (11th Cir. 1986).

[23] Id. See also State v. Johnson, 561 So. 2d 1139 (Fla. 1990).

[24] Webb, supra note 18 at 123.

sometimes won. It was the pretextual nature of the stop (rather than "racial pro-filing," as Lexis decided years later) that troubled the Eleventh Circuit in *United States v. Miller,*[25] the 1987 case with which we began:

[T]he record reveals that Trooper Vogel made the stop because of his hope to catch a courier, and not because the appellant strayed over the white line a few inches for a few seconds. Based on the record, we hold that a reasonable officer would not have stopped Miller absent some other motive. Thus ... we hold that the initial stop of Miller's car was not legitimate.

As a result, the court suppressed cocaine that Vogel found in a consensual search following this pretextual stop.

Nine years later, in 1996, the Supreme Court overruled *Miller* and other lower court cases that prohibited pretextual traffic stops. In *Whren v. United States*[26] the Court held that: "[T]he constitutional reasonableness of traffic stops [does not] depend[] on the actual motivations of the individual officers involved ... . Subjective intentions play no role in ordinary ... Fourth Amendment analysis."

Whren authorizes police officers to conduct pretextual stops with impunity, but such stops were also common before *Whren*, and rarely disapproved. Some courts rejected the legal argument against pretextual stops years before the Supreme Court reached the issue.[27] Other courts rejected similar claims for lack of proof. The problem was the difficulty of showing the officer's pretextual purpose in making the stop if he didn't happen to admit it. Consider *Esteen v. State*, a Florida state court decision, also from 1987:

Trooper Robert Vogel was in his marked vehicle parked on the median of I-95. Parked alongside him in another patrol car was Trooper Collins and his narcotics dog, Dixie. Vogel observed a northbound car traveling at about 45 MPH and driving in an erratic fash-ion, which he described as "weaving within the right lane ... ."[28]

This sounds like the prologue to another drug stop, but this time, rather than admitting it as he did in *Miller*, Vogel testified that he did not have any suspicion that the driver was transporting drugs and that he stopped the car only because of his concern that the driver was drunk or asleep, or because the vehicle might be having some mechanical difficulty.[29]

Therefore, the court concluded, "the record supports the trial court's finding that Vogel was justified in making the stop."[30]

---

[25] 821 F.2d 546, 549 (11th Cir. 1987).

[26] Whren v. United States, 517 U.S. 806, 813(1996).

[27] See, e.g., State v. Irvin, 483 So. 2d 461, 462 (Fl. App. 5th Dist. 1986) ("[T]hat the police may have wished or even intended to detain a suspect for another reason does not invali-date an apprehension which follows the commission of a traffic or other offense which would subject any member of the public to a similar detention.")

[28] Esteen v. State, 503 So. 2d 356 (Fl. App. 5th Dist. 1987).

[29] Id. at 358.

[30] Id.

The Middle

Trooper Vogel attracted attention. He was honored repeatedly by law enforcement organizations, and in 1987 was the subject of a flattering profile on *60 Minutes*. In 1988 Vogel was elected Sheriff of Volusia County, Florida. One of his first official acts was to set up a "Selective Enforcement Team" of deputies trained in his own techniques of highway drug profiling.[31] By then his fame had spread beyond Florida to Washington, where the DEA was developing a nationwide program of highway drug interdiction, Operation Pipeline.

Law enforcement in the United States is notoriously fragmented. If the French Ministry of the Interior were to develop a national plan for drug interdiction it would implement that plan directly, through the French National Police and the national Gendarmerie, the two agencies responsible for law enforcement in urban and rural areas, respectively.[32] In the United States there are approximately 18,000 separate police agencies.[33] The great majority of law enforcement is carried out by local police forces, typically sheriffs' departments with elected sheriffs in command (for example, Robert Vogel in Volusia County, Florida, as of 1988), or municipal police forces under the command of police chiefs chosen by local elected officials. To create a national program in the United States, the DEA had to recruit the voluntary participation of hundreds if not thousands of these state and local police forces, and construct a framework in which they could work as independent agencies.

The core of Operation Pipeline was training: "Each year, the [DEA], with the assistance of state and local highway officer, conduct[ed] dozens of training schools across the country, attended by other state and local highway officers." In addition, DEA resources made it possible for "state and local agencies ... to share real-time information with other agencies," and to "immediately obtain the results of their record checks and receive detailed analysis of drug seizures."[34] The DEA's official history of Operation Pipeline says that "the success of [unrelated] highway interdiction programs [in the early 1980s] in New Mexico and New Jersey eventually led to the creation of Operation Pipeline in 1984."[35] That may be, but both by his own account[36] and that of Operation Pipeline instructors,[37] the training

---

[31] Webb, supra note 18 at 123.

[32] Ministère de l'Intérieur, *The General Directorate of the National Police,* available at: http://www.interieur.gouv.fr/rubriques/divers/anglais/dgpn; Ministère de l'Intérieur, *The General Directorate of the National Gendarmerie*, available at: http://www.interieur. gouv.fr/rubriques/divers/anglais/gendarmerie

[33] U.S. Department of Justice, Office of Justice Programs, Bureau of Justice Statistics, *Law Enforcement Statistics*, available at: http://www.ojp.usdoj.gov/bjs/lawenf.htm

[34] U.S. Drug Enforcement Agency, *Operations Pipeline and Convoy* , available at: http://www. usdoj.gov/dea/ programs/pipecon.htm

[35] Id.

[36] Harris, supra note 6 at 22.

[37] Webb, supra note 18 at 123.

program they used was a direct application of the profiling techniques developed by Robert Vogel. Ultimately, some 27,000 officers across the country received such training.[38]

It's easy to see how this program might have been sold to state and local police officials. The key argument would have been that participation in Operation Pipeline would not cost their agencies a dime. They could do it in the interstices of their existing operations, as they went about their other work, as a form of law enforcement multitasking.

The most important duties of highway patrol officers are infrequent events: They must respond to periodic accidents and other emergencies, police extreme violations of traffic regulations (drivers who do 130 miles an hour, or drag race in traffic), and handle occasional nontraffic crimes on the highway. In between times they may deter routine traffic violations to some extent by sporadic enforcement of speed limits and other official rules, but their most important jobs are to be available and to be visible. As long as all they need to do, most of the time, is be there and give out some tickets, why not troll for drugs along the way? After all, the officers have virtually unlimited discretion in choosing which few cars to stop, and are at least as visible as otherwise when they question a drug suspect by the side of the road or conduct a search for drugs. Of course, the state and local officers who do this need training, backup, coordination—the very items that Operation Pipeline was happy to provide.

In reality, no major operational program is cost free. Training and coordination take time, processing drug arrests takes time, and focusing attention on drugs takes time and attention from other law enforcement activities. In a 1998 pamphlet extolling Operation Pipeline, the California Highway Patrol emphasized how well it fit with their other duties:

What the Department has learned from Operation Pipeline training is that an enthusiastic traffic officer with training who vigorously works the roads for speeders, drunk drivers, car thieves, safety belt violators and unregistered vehicles is also the most likely to catch drug couriers.[39]

The truth was less of a win–win proposition. By 1996, the California Highway Patrol had organized special drug interdiction units whose "primary objective" was "highway drug interdiction ... to apprehend drug traffickers and confiscate illegal drugs." The officers involved were told, in so many words, that traffic safety was not their concern: "Continue to concentrate on drug enforcement duties" wrote one supervisor, "and let the field officers handle the traffic problems."[40]

---

[38] Id.

[39] California Highway Patrol, *Operation Pipeline Training Targets Drugs*, (1998), available at: http://www.chp.ca.gov/pdf/per98-12.pdf

[40] Cal. State Assembly Democratic Caucus Task Force on Gov't Oversight, Operation Pipeline: California Joint Legislative Task Force Report (Sept. 29, 1999), available at http://www.aclunc.org/discrimination/webb-report.html (hereinafter "Pipeline Report").

The costs of participation in Operation Pipeline, however, were opportunity costs. Traffic and law enforcement may have suffered in other respects,[41] but there was little or no drain on the budgets of the agencies involved. The benefits, on the other hand, were visible and substantial. Then as now, traffic enforcement is boring, but a big drug bust is a catch—$10,000 worth of cocaine seized, two bad guys put away. It's a satisfying, attention grabbing, career-building success; it generates headlines and trophies. And it also probably generates cash. In the mid-1980s, almost simultaneously with the beginning of Operation Pipeline, there was another major development in the War on Drugs: a dramatic increase in the seizure and forfeiture of the assets of drug suspects, and in the use of those forfeited assets to fund local police forces.

Forfeiture is an old practice. The common type—"civil forfeiture"—is described legally as a proceeding against an asset, the thing itself rather than its owner, because it is of a type that is defined as forfeited to the government. Under federal law that includes illegal drugs, any equipment and materials used in their manufacture and distribution, all vehicles or weapons or other equipment used to transport or distribute such drugs, any real estate used to violate drug laws, and any money, negotiable instruments, securities, or other things of value obtained as the proceeds of illegal drug transactions or intended for use in such transactions.[42] The procedure for civil forfeiture is attractively simple, from the point of view of the government. The asset in question may be seized if there is probable cause to believe that it is forfeitable.[43] No criminal charges are necessary; the government merely takes possession of property that is presumably its own. A "claimant"—that is, the owner or a co-owner—may contest the seizure, but in such a proceeding, once the government has presented enough evidence to show probable cause to believe that the asset is forfeitable, the claimant has the burden of proving by a preponderance of the evidence that the forfeiture is improper.[44]

Until 1984, the proceeds of federal forfeitures were deposited in the general fund of the United States Treasury. In 1984, Congress created two special forfeiture funds earmarked for law enforcement, in the Department of Justice and in the United States Customs Service,[45] and amended governing law to permit the federal government to "transfer the [forfeited] property to any Federal agency or to any State or local law enforcement agency which participated directly in the seizure or forfeiture of the property."[46] This change coincided with a huge increase in drug-related forfeitures. The amount deposited in the Justice Department's

---

[41] Donald J. Boudreaux & A.C. Pritchard, *Civil Forfeiture and the War on Drugs: Lessons from Economics and History*, 33 San Diego L. Rev. 79 (1996); Bruce L. Benson et al., *Police Bureaucracies, Their Incentives, and the War on Drugs*, 83 Pub. Choice 21 (1995).

[42] 21 USC §881.

[43] 18 USCS §981(b)(2).

[44] 19 USCS §1615, 18 USC §981(d).

[45] GAO, Asset Forfeiture: Historical Perspective on Asset Forfeiture Issues (March 19, 1996), p. 3.

[46] 21 USCS §881(e)(1)(A).

Asset Forfeiture Fund (including criminal as well as civil forfeitures) grew from $27 million in 1985 to $556 million in 1993.[47] The amount that was transferred to state and local police agencies grew in parallel, from $23 million in 1986 to $283 million in 1991.[48]

Forfeiture is also available under many state laws, although the terms are not always as appealing to law enforcement. In Missouri, for example, proceeds of forfeitures are earmarked for education.[49] But if the forfeiture is part of a program with federal participation—for example, Operation Pipeline—state or local officers can seize assets, turn them over to the feds, and get most of the proceeds back directly from the Department of Justice. This is a particularly desirable form of funding because it is independent of local taxpayers and local elected officials. A report prepared for the Department of Justice in 1993 describes an extreme version of this incentive, and its implications for the "multijurisdictional drug task forces" the DEA was busy setting up around the country:

Asset seizures play an important role in the operation of [multijurisdictional drug] task forces. One "big bust" can provide a task force with the resources to become financially independent. Once financially independent, a task force can choose to operate without Federal or state assistance.[50]

In other words, if a police commander wins big in this lottery he can become a politically independent, self-financing bounty hunter.

But how to do it? To win you have to find drugs, in quantity, and that turns out to be quite hard. Many Operation Pipeline officers did not share Robert Vogel's record of success, or perhaps they were less comfortable than Vogel with a high rate of failure. Sometimes they complained about their failures, and were told to persevere. "Keep up your enthusiasm. I know that it seems that seizures can be few and far between," a California Highway Patrol supervisor wrote to a Pipeline officer who over a 9-month period had stopped more than 1200 cars, searched 163, and found drugs only 18 times.[51] As best we can tell, the overall record in California is comparable: fewer than 10% of highway drug searches, and a tiny fraction of highway drug *stops*, produced any contraband drugs.[52] In New Jersey, a report by the state Attorney General's Office found that only 19% of highway searches produced an arrest or a seizure, and a much smaller fraction of all drug stops.[53]

---

[47] CIVIL ASSET REFORM ACT, Report 106-192, Committee on the Judiciary, House of Representatives (Rep. Hyde Chair), 106th Congress, 1st sess., June 18, 1999, p. 4.
[48] Annual Report of the Dept. of Justice Asset Forfeiture Program, Fiscal Year 1996, p. 3.
[49] Eric Blumenson & Eva Nilsen, *Policing for Profit: The Drug War's Hidden Economic Agenda*, 65 U. Chi. L. Rev 35, 52–53, n. 66 (1998).
[50] Justice Research and Statistics Association, Multijurisdictional Drug Control Task Forces: A Five-Year Review 1988–1992, p. 9 (Oct 1993), quoted in Blumenson & Nilsen, supra note 49, at 35.
[51] Pipeline Report, supra note 40 at 19.
[52] Id. at 20.
[53] Peter Verniero & Paul H. Zouber, Attorney Gen. of N.J., Interim Report of the State Police Review Team Regarding Allegations of Racial Profiling 28 (1999).

Unfortunately, the problem is built into the plan. The reason highway patrol officers can do this sort of drug interdiction in the first place is that they have the discretion to stop virtually any one of the thousands of drivers who speed by them. By the same token, however, they must make their initial choices on the basis of very limited information: what they can see at high speed, from a distance. As a result, they rarely find what they are looking for. Not surprisingly, the officers use any clue that might improve their odds, and race is a clue that is always available and widely believed to be associated with drug trafficking.

A DEA web site states: "Although Operation Pipeline relies in part on training officers to use characteristics to determine potential drug traffickers, it is important to understand that the program does not advocate such profiling by race or ethnic background."[54] The accuracy of this statement depends on what the meaning of the word "advocate" is. The DEA and other federal drug control agencies certainly provided detailed, specific information that could be read as instructions on how (and why) to conduct racial profiling, if a police force happened to be interested. For example, in 1999 the web site of the Office of National Drug Control Policy told visitors that in Trenton, New Jersey, "crack dealers are predominantly African-American males," powder cocaine dealers are "predominantly Latino," heroin traffickers are "mostly Latinos," and the marijuana market is "controlled by Jamaicans."[55] As recently as 2001 that office reported that "New York City-based Dominican DTOs [Drug Trafficking Organizations] are prominently mentioned as having an ever-increasing role in supplying heroin and cocaine to DTOs" in the Washington/Baltimore area, while "Jamaican DTOs continue their marijuana distribution activities" in that area.[56] This is not the slightest bit surprising. The original, airport-based, drug courier profiles on the 1970 and early 1980s frequently included race or ethnicity as a factor—as we have seen—but at that time the racial aspect of those profiles received little attention.

Robert Vogel himself has denied that race was ever an element of the drug courier profiles he taught. Lou Garcia, a canine-unit deputy who worked in Vogel's Selective Enforcement Team in Volusia County, remembers things differently. In an interview for a 1999 article, Garcia described a meeting on the

---

[54] U.S. Drug Enforcement Administration, *Operations Pipeline and Convoy*, available at: http://www.dea.gov/programs/pipecon.htm

[55] C. J. Chivers, *Ex-Police Leader's Claim of Bias Attacked*, N.Y. Times, Oct. 4, 1999, at B4.

[56] Office of Nat'l Drug Control Policy, National Drug Control Strategy, The High Intensity Drug Trafficking Area Program: 2000, at 164–65 (2001). See also, e.g., Nat'l Narcotics Intelligence Consumers Comm. ("NNICC"), The NNICC Report 1997: The Supply of Illicit Drugs to the United States (1998):

Colombia-based traffickers continued to control wholesale level cocaine distribution throughout the heavily populated northeastern United States ... often employing Dominican criminals as subordinates ... . In major U.S. cities, organized criminal groups of Cuban, Jamaican, and Mexican nationals, as well as African-American and ethnic Dominican gangs, dominated the retail market.

median strip of highway I-95 at which Vogel told his Selective Enforcement deputies to focus on Black and Hispanic drivers. Garcia thought the injunction was superfluous: "I knew who they were stopping. I saw the people. It was Blacks, mostly, and they were all being pulled over for weaving. The Black race was the only race I knew that wasn't able to stay in the lane."[57]

There's a name for this race-specific traffic violation: Driving While Black.[58]

The End

On Sunday, February 28, 1999, the Newark *Star Ledger* published a lengthy interview with Colonel Carl Williams of the New Jersey State Police on the subject of drug interdiction. Williams explained: "Today with this drug problem, the drug problem is cocaine or marijuana. It is most likely a minority group that's involved with that … ." Williams condemned racial profiling—"As far as racial profiling is concerned, that is absolutely not right. It never has been condoned in the State Police and it never will be condoned in the State Police"—but he said that the illegal drug trade is ethnically balkanized: "If you're looking at the methamphetamine market, that seems to be controlled by motorcycle gangs, which are basically predominantly White. If you're looking at heroin and stuff like that, your involvement there is more or less Jamaicans." Hours later, still on Sunday, New Jersey Governor Christie Whitman fired him from his job as superintendent of the New Jersey State Police because "his comments today are inconsistent with our efforts to enhance public confidence in the State Police."[59] Six months later Colonel Williams sued the state for damages, pointing out that he had said nothing that couldn't be found on federal government web sites.[60]

On April 20, 1999, the Attorney General of New Jersey—after years of defending the New Jersey State Police in court and in public—switched sides. He dropped an appeal of a trial-court decision condemning highway stops on the New Jersey Turnpike, and simultaneously issued his own report that racial profiling by the State Police was "real."[61]

What happened?

---

[57] Webb, supra note 18 at 125.

[58] "Driving While Black" appears to be an older term than "racial profiling." There are news stories that refer to it in the early 1990s as a concept that was well known in the Black community. For example, a story from 1990 quotes a Black teenager from Teaneck, NJ: "We get arrested for D.W.B. … You know, driving while Black." Tim Golden, *Residents and Police Share Lingering Doubts in Teaneck*, New York Times, 5/21/1990, p. B1.

[59] Kathy Barrett Carter & Ron Marisco, *Whitman Fires Chief of State Police,* Star Ledger (New Jersey), Mar. 1, 1999, at 1A.

[60] See notes 55 and 56 supra, and accompanying text.

[61] Peter Verniero, Att'y Gen. of N.J., *Interim Report of the State Police Review Team Regarding Allegations of Racial Profiling* (1999).

Colonel Williams' comments require some unpacking. He says that racial profiling is "absolutely not right" and that his troopers have never done it, but he goes on to give a detailed racial description of drug crimes. What should we make of this?

At first blush, Williams seems to have done no more than restate the common law enforcement position that minority groups dominate major drug trafficking in the United States. Supporters have described him as an honest cop who was fired for telling the unpleasant, non-PC truth.[62] In their view, he was saying: "We don't target by race, we just arrest those who should be arrested. Maybe it's unfortunate that most of them turn out to be Black and Hispanic, but that's not our fault." But Colonel Williams' comments could also be interpreted as a wink and a nod in defense of racial profiling: "Of course we stop and search motorists based on their race—because it works. The first rule of duck hunting is hunt where the ducks are. So cut us some slack." He didn't *say* that—the official line had to be the opposite—but didn't he imply it?

It is certainly not news, now or in 1999, that American police devote a disproportionate amount of their attention to racial and ethnic minorities, especially African Americans. They usually get away with it. If it's seen as a problem at all, they just deny that race had anything to do with their behavior, and that's the end of it. Official hypocrisy about race is hardly new. So why was Colonel Williams tossed overboard?

The short answer is that the type of highway drug interdiction that Operation Pipeline promoted was a dumb idea, and the racial profiling it incorporated was crude and obvious. Operation Pipeline put thousands of police officers out on the highway across the country in a competitive and potentially lucrative search for drugs and money. Their task: to spot drug couriers—who were described to them as Black and Hispanic—at a distance, among the huge anonymous stream of cars speeding by. Unsurprisingly, these officers concentrated heavily on Black and Hispanic drivers. With little else to go on, they did so in a transparent and indiscriminate manner, which provoked a powerful backlash. The cops were caught red handed.[63]

The legal issue at stake here is not difficult. The police may not target Blacks because they believe that Blacks as a group are likely to be criminals. That's racial profiling, and it is illegal. In *Whren v. United States*, the same opinion in which the Supreme Court held that it was constitutional to use traffic stops as a

---

[62] Heather MacDonald, *The Myth of Racial Profiling*, City Journal Vol. 11, No.2 (Spring 2001), available at http://www.city-journal.org/html/11_2_the_myth.html

[63] Operation Pipeline was a dumb idea in another respect as well: It had no major impact on the flow of illegal drugs. For example, drug interdiction by the Maryland State Police on I-95—described officially as one of the most successful programs of its kind—was designed to cut off the flow of drugs to from New York and New Jersey to the Washington/ Baltimore metropolitan area. Judging from official reports, however, from 1995 through 2000 the Maryland State Policed managed to seize less than half of 1% of the cocaine consumed in Washington and Baltimore. Gross & Barnes, supra note 20 at 750–53.

pretext for drug investigations,[64] the Court also reiterated that "the Constitution prohibits selective enforcement of the law based on considerations such as race."[65] The Court added that race-specific policing violates the equal protection clause of the Fourteenth Amendment and not the Fourth Amendment prohibition on unreasonable searches, but it's illegal all the same.

The factual question is much more of a problem. Did the cops target *Blacks*? Or did they just do their job and target *criminals*, most of whom happen to be Black? In most contexts it's very hard to tell.

Suppose that 80% of the young men who are stopped, questioned, and sometimes searched by police officers in a particular city are Black, even though 60% of the population is White. It might look like the cops are deliberately going after Blacks, but maybe they are just focusing on high-crime neighborhoods, and those are the areas where the pedestrians and the residents are overwhelmingly Black. In addition, the decision to stop a specific person might be based on a wide range of observations by an officer operating at close range. These observations may justify the officer's decision in non-racial terms: "there was a bulge in his pocket;" "when he saw me he attempted to conceal an object under his coat;" "he kept looking over his shoulder;" and so forth. In any event, the initial encounter between the officer and the suspect will probably be considered "consensual,"[66] and it may provide additional non-racial case-specific information—"he answered my questions evasively"—that could justify a more extensive and coercive intrusion, usually a detention or a pat-down search .

The police may do a passable job of honing in on young Black men on the street who are more likely than average to be involved in criminal activities. It's not obvious, but it's possible. Whether they do or not, they will probably be able to explain any particular encounter in race-neutral terms, and they will certainly be able to say that because each stop was based on unique observations, no overall racial motive can be inferred from the racial makeup of the suspects. Equally important, on the streets of a large city the cops know where to look for lower class young Black men, and can spot them at a distance. Black lawyers, grandmothers, teachers, and servicemen are unlikely to get caught in the net.

Highway stops, by contrast, are stylized. An officer in a cruiser pulls up behind a car and turns on his flashing light and perhaps his siren, ordering the driver to stop. In deciding to do so, he can only rely on the few things he can see: the license plate, model and appearance of the car; the speed and direction of travel; other traffic violations; and the appearance of the occupants, including, of course, race and gender. As a result, it is hard to narrow the field to a plausible set of suspects, and equally hard to argue that the officer made a plausible, legitimate, holistic nonracial judgment that this car might be dirty.

---

[64] 517 U.S. 806, 813 (1996). See supra note 26 and accompanying text.
[65] Id.
[66] See supra, note 20 and accompanying text.

Highways are also impersonal and democratic. Everybody in America drives; there are no ghettos or exclusive neighborhoods on the interstate. If you stop people by race on the highway, you're likely to get a reasonably representative cross section of that race, Hispanic teachers and Black civil servants, as well as jobless high school dropouts and undocumented aliens.

In short, racial profiling is a much riskier on the highway than on city streets. It's easier to spot, easier to prove, harder to defend, and more likely to victimize substantial law-abiding citizens. The backlash was not long in coming. I'll mention only a few highlights.

- In June, 1992, the *Orlando Sentinel* ran a series of articles collectively entitled "Tainted Cash or Easy Money?" The paper ultimately won a Pulitzer Prize for this series, "For exposing the unjust seizure of millions of dollars from motorists—most of them minorities—by a sheriff's drug squad." The subject of the series: Sheriff Bob Vogel of Volusia County and his Selective Enforcement Team. A look at some of the headlines gives an outline of the story:

> June 14: "Volusia Deputies Have Seized $8 Million From I-95 Motorists. The Trap Is for Drug Dealers, but Money Is the Object. Three of Every Four Drivers Were Never Charged."
> June 15: "Blacks, Hispanics Big Losers in Cash Seizures. A Review of Volusia Sheriff's Records Shows that Minorities Were the Targets in 90 Percent of Cash Seizures Without Arrests."
> June 16: "Confiscated Cash Bankrolls Fight Against Drugs. Critics Say the Seizure Law Encourages Police Agencies to Spend Time Looking for Drug Money Instead of Fighting Crime."
> June 17: "Videotape Gives a Look at Volusia Squad's Tactics. The Tape Reflects the Findings of a 'Sentinel' Investigation. In 31 Traffic Stops, 25 of the Drivers are Black or Hispanic."

As the *Sentinel* pointed out, the Selective Enforcement Team did occasionally seize large quantities of drugs, or hoards of cash that were obviously intended for criminal purposes. But their day-to-day business had sunk to the level of highway robbery. In one case, for example, a deputy sheriff stopped Joseph Kea, a Black Navy reservist from Savannah, Georgia, for driving 6 miles over the speed limit.[67] Kea was issued a warning, and consented to a search of his car. The deputy found his Navy uniform in the trunk, and a nylon bag with $3,989 in cash. The deputy decided that this meant that Kea was a drug trafficker and seized the money, but did not arrest Kea. Kea hired a lawyer who provided the sheriff's office with pay stubs to account for the cash. After eight months of bickering the sheriff's office agreed to a "settlement:" they returned $2,989 and kept $1,000. Kea's lawyer took another 25% of Kea's share of his own money, as a fee.

---

[67] Jeff Brazil & Steve Berry, *Tainted Cash or Easy Money?*, Orlando Sentinel, June 14, 1992, at A1.

- Early in the morning of May 8, 1992, a Maryland State Trooper stopped a car in which Robert Wilkins, an African American lawyer, was driving from Chicago to Washington, D.C. He was returning from the funeral his grandfather, a minister, with his aunt, uncle, and cousin, driving through the night to get to work that morning. The trooper asked for consent to search the car because they had "problems with rental cars coming up and down the highway with drugs." Mr. Wilkins was a deputy public defender in the Public Defender Service for the District of Columbia. Unlike almost all drivers who are asked, he refused to agree to the search. In response, the trooper had the family wait for over half an hour and then stand out in the rain while a German shepherd sniffed the car carefully but found nothing.[68] This stop got a lot of attention. Wilkins became the lead plaintiff in the first of two racial profiling class action lawsuits brought by the ACLU against the Maryland State Police, along with many other innocent Black motorists, from all walks of life, who had been stopped, sniffed, or searched.
- In 1993, the New Jersey Office of the Public Defender began a systematic effort to prove that the New Jersey State Police engaged in racial profiling.[69] They focused on the southern end of the New Jersey Turnpike, New Jersey's portion of I-95, which runs from Miami, Florida, to the Canadian border in Maine. The office hired Professor John Lamberth, chair of the psychology department at Temple University, who conducted two surveys of a sort that could never be done on city streets. First, he had fixed observers watch the cars passing by on the Turnpike and record the race of the drivers, between 8 a.m. and 8 p.m., in June of 1993; 13.5% of the cars had a Black occupant. Second, he had an observer drive the highway with cruise control set to the speed limit, and count the number of cars that passed him, the number he passed, and the race of the occupants. More than 98% of the cars passed the observer, and therefore could have been stopped for speeding; of these "violators," 15% were Black. On the other hand, official records showed that 46% of those stopped were Black, which means that Black speeders were about five times as likely to be stopped as nonblack speeders, even lumping drug stops together with ordinary traffic stops.
- In January 1995 the ACLU and the Maryland State Police agreed to a court-supervised settlement of the racial profiling suit that followed the May 1992 stop of Robert Wilkins and his family.[70] Under the settlement, the State Police—while continuing to deny that they engaged in racial profiling—agreed to maintain detailed information on car searches on I-95 in Maryland. In 1996, using the records collected as part of this settlement, Professor Lambert

---

[68] Angela J. Davis, Race, Cops, and Traffic Stops, 51 U. Miami L. Rev 425, 439–40 (1997).

[69] See State v. Soto, 324 N.J. Super. 66; 734 A.2d 350 (1996).

[70] Wilkins v. Maryland State Police. Civil Case No. CCB-93-468 (D. Md. 1993) (settlement agreement) (copy on file with authors).

conducted a traffic survey in Maryland similar to the one he had done in New Jersey, with similar findings.[71]

- Also in 1996, a Superior Court judge in New Jersey issued a detailed opinion condemning the New Jersey State Police and excluding drugs seized in 17 cases because of racial profiling on the New Jersey Turnpike.[72] By then, in addition to the statistical evidence, there was, among other items, testimony from former troopers that they had been "trained and coached to make race based profile stops."[73]

This last the decision was the ruling on racial profiling that the New Jersey Attorney General first appealed, in 1996, and then conceded in 1999. In between, the level of public exposure leaped ahead. For 1996, there are five news stories in the Lexis database that refer to "racial profiling" in the body of the story. For 1999 there are 2714 such stories,[74] including many attacks on the practice and a major detailed expose of Operation Pipeline.[75] Racial profiling had become a political liability to anybody who might be associated with it, so the Governor and the Attorney General of New Jersey threw in the towel.

Racial profiling in New Jersey drew more attention than in other states, so it makes sense to spot The End at this about-face by the state government of New Jersey. It's an arbitrary line. What's clear is that by the 2000 presidential campaign racial profiling was an identified public enemy. For example, on January 28, 2000, the *State Journal-Register* of Springfield, Illinois, ran a column that began:

In a year of presidential primaries that features some of the most boring and bland candidates in the last 20 years, there seems to be only one issue thus far that has created much excitement   racial profiling.

The three leading candidates—Democrats Al Gore and Bill Bradley and Republican George W. Bush—have all offered their views on the problem. They all agree that racial profiling is a disgrace and a social cancer that is eating away at our society.[76]

Less than a month later, in a debate between the main democratic candidates, Vice President Al Gore of Tennessee and Senator Bill Bradley of New Jersey, the first question was about racial profiling. They responded:

---

[71] Aff. of Dr. John Lamberth in Wilkins v. Maryland State Police, No. CCB-93-468 (D. Md. 1993) (filed November 14, 1996); Mem. in Support of Plaintiffs' Motion for Enforcement of Settlement Agreement and for Further Relief, Wilkins, Exhibit 11 (filed November 14, 1996) (copies on file with authors). For a detailed analysis of the data on racial profiling in Maryland, see Samuel R. Gross & Katherine Y. Barnes, Road Work: Racial Profiling and Drug Interdiction on the Highway, 101 Mich. L. Rev 651 (2002).

[72] State v. Soto, 324 N.J. Super. 66; 734 A.2d 350 (1996).

[73] Id. at 357.

[74] Since 2000, there have been more than 3000 such stories a year, the limit the search engine will count.

[75] Webb, supra note 18.

[76] Vibert White, *Make Racism, Hatred and Bigotry Historical Artifacts*, The State Journal-Register (Springfield, IL), January 28, 2000, p. 9.

BILL BRADLEY: Last month in the debate in Iowa, when Al said … that he would issue an executive order, I said, "why doesn't he walk down the hall now and have President Clinton issue an executive order?" (Applause)

AL GORE: First of all, President Clinton has issued a presidential directive under which the information is now being gathered that is necessary for an executive order. Look, we have taken action, but, you know, racial profiling practically began in New Jersey, Senator Bradley. (Cheers and applause)[77]

Epilogue

The End of course was not the end of racial profiling. It was just the end of the story of the rhetoric of racial profiling. We now know what racial profiling is. It's a Bad Thing.

In 1954, the year the Supreme Court decided *Brown v. Board of Education*,[78] racial segregation was the official policy of a dozen states and thousands of local governments. By 1980, if not earlier, no politician in either major party would defend segregation in public, but our schools and neighborhoods are as segregated as ever to this day. The form has changed and the content has changed, but segregation by race remains a major fact of American life. Racial profiling is more recent and it lost official favor almost as soon as it was named, but it has no more disappeared than segregation. In 1995, for example, Black motorists on I-95 in Maryland were 15 times more likely than Whites to be stopped and searched by Maryland State Troopers; in 2000 they were 6 times more likely to be stopped and searched[79]—an improvement but hardly a cure.

There was a spate of public support for racial profiling after the massive terrorist attacks on the World Trade Center and the Pentagon on September 11, 2001. For example, in the fall of 1999, 81% of respondents on a national poll said they disapproved of "racial profiling,"[80] and a few conservative commentators were the only people who publicly defended racial profiling on the practical ground that it helps catch bad guys.[81] But after 9/11, on September 14, 2001, a poll found that 58% of Americans favored "requiring Arabs, including those who are U.S. citizens, to undergo special, more intensive security checks before

---

[77] Online NewsHour, *Democratic Debates, Feb. 22, 2000*, available at: http://www.pbs.org/newshour/bb/politics/ jan-june00/dems_debate2-22.html

[78] 347 U.S. 483 (1954).

[79] Gross & Barnes, supra note 20 at 720.

[80] Gallup Poll, Sept. 24, 1999–Nov. 16, 1999, Public Opinion Online, The Roper Center at the University of Connecticut, available at LEXIS, News Library, Rpoll file [hereinafter Roper Data Base] (describing results from question 1, accession no. 0346115, and question 9, accession no. 0346123).

[81] See, e.g., John Derbyshire, *In Defense of Racial Profiling: Where Is Our Common Sense?*, Nat'l Rev., Feb. 19, 2001, at 38; Heather MacDonald, The Myth of Racial Profiling, City J., Spring 2001, at 14, 26.

boarding airplanes in the U.S.,"[82] and similar sentiments were heard from across the political spectrum.[83] For example, Floyd Abrams, the celebrated First Amendment lawyer, said that under the scary circumstances we now face, "it seems entirely appropriate to look harder at such people. Remember, Justice [Robert] Jackson said 'the Constitution is not a suicide pact.'"[84]

Public opinion on racial profiling remains split, depending on how the question is framed. If pollsters describe profiling as a tool in the "fight against terrorism" nearly half approve;[85] if they describe it as an aspect of law enforcement on the highways or in shopping malls, two-thirds or more say it's never justified.[86] But the revisionist rhetoric on racial profiling never stuck, not even right after 9/11. One reason is that by the fall of 2001 government officials up and down the country had just recently committed themselves in public to defeat the cancer of racial profiling, and they were in no position to say otherwise. Consider a bizarre example:

In November of 2001 the Department of Justice began a program of "voluntary" interviews with thousands foreigners residing in America, "the majority Middle Eastern men ages eighteen to thirty-three who came here within the last two years on nonimmigrant visas."[87] This certainly sounds like racial or ethnic profiling, but in testimony before the Senate Judiciary Committee, then Assistant Attorney General (later Secretary of Homeland Security) Michael Chertoff said No: "We have emphatically rejected ethnic profiling. What we have looked to are characteristics like country of issuance of passport … ."[88] He might as well have said: "We have emphatically rejected age discrimination. What we have looked to are characteristics like date of issuance of birth certificate."

---

[82] Roper Data Base, supra note 80 (describing results from question 1, accession no. 0387144, from the Sept. 14, 2001 Gallup Poll); see also David E. Rovella, *Pro-Police Opinions on the Rise, Poll Says Wiretaps, Profiling Gain Juror Support*, Nat'l L.J., Jan. 21, 2002, at A1 (finding that 59% of adults eligible for jury duty say that profiling is acceptable in certain circumstances).

[83] See, e.g., Stanley Crouch, *Drawing the Line on Racial Profiling*, N.Y. Daily News, Oct. 4, 2001, at 41; Editorial, Profiling Debate Resumes, Denver Post, Oct. 3, 2001, at B6; Michael Kinsley, *When Is Racial Profiling Okay?*, Wash. Post, Sept. 30, 2001, at B7; Stephen J. Singer, *Racial Profiling Also Has a Good Side*, Newsday, Sept. 25, 2001, at A38.

[84] Henry Weinstein et al., Racial *Profiling Gains Support as Search Tactic*, L.A. Times, Sept. 24, 2001, at A1.

[85] Opinion Dynamics poll, July 26, 2005 (42% approve, 49% disapprove), Roper Data Base, supra note 80 (describing results from question 82, accession no. 1630825).

[86] Gallup Poll, June 9, 2004 (67% say "never justified" on roads and highways, 72% say "never justified" in shopping malls and stores), Roper Data Base, supra note 80 (describing results from question 16, accession no. 0456354 and question 18, accession no. 0456356).

[87] Allan Lengel, *Arab Men in Detroit to Be Asked to See U.S. Attorney*, Wash. Post, Nov. 27, 2001, at A5.

[88] Michael Chertoff, Testimony Before the Senate Judiciary Committee Hearing on Preserving Freedoms While Defending Against Terrorism, Federal News Service, Nov. 28, 2001, available at LEXIS, News Library, News Group File, All.

Mr. Chertoff had little choice. Ten months earlier his boss, Attorney General John Ashcroft, had told the same committee "[t]here should be no loopholes or safe harbors for racial profiling. Official discrimination of this sort is wrong and unconstitutional no matter what the context."[89] If it's that bad the government Doesn't Do It—and whatever the government does do is, by definition, something else.

In this new atmosphere, the programs that were most conspicuously associated with the racial profiling as it burst in public awareness were in trouble. Some had been under attack for years, and not just from the ACLU and public defenders. Under the Clinton administration, the Civil Rights Division of the Department of Justice investigated some of the very same police forces that the DEA, another branch of the Justice Department, had worked with to develop the practices that caused the uproar. Specifically:

- Sheriff Vogel and his Selective Enforcement Team were investigated starting in 1993. Vogel narrowly escaped federal indictment in 1995, and the investigation was ultimately closed without charges in 1997.[90] Vogel—who considered himself vindicated—decided to retire from office in 2000.[91]

- In 1996 the Department of Justice began an investigation of the racial profiling on the New Jersey Turnpike. It ended on December 30, 1999, with a consent decree that includes provisions for training, supervising and disciplining troopers to prevent profiling in the future.[92] By the end of 2001, the Department had settled half a dozen similar racial profiling law suits against other police forces, and more were pending.[93]

- Operation Pipeline itself seems to have gone into a sort of bureaucratic hibernation. Its Web page still exists—and it still boasts about the program's successes—but the drug seizures it totals up are nearly five years out of date: "Jan. 1986-Dec. 2001."[94] After several calls to the DEA asking whether Operation Pipeline was still in existence, we were referred to a public information officer in the Detroit Field Office, who eventually responded by e-mail: "I have tried numerous times to get you the information you need to no avail so I am suggesting that you file a Freedom of Information (FOIA) Request with the DEA. … I wish I could have been of more assistance …"[95]

---

[89] Nomination of Senator John Ashcroft to the Office of Attorney General: Hearings Before the Senate Comm. on the Judiciary, 107th Cong. (Jan. 22, 2001) (answer from Senator Ashcroft, to written question submitted by Senator Russell D. Feingold), available at http://www.senate.gov/~leahy/press/200101/ashcroft.html

[90] Ludmilla Lelis, *Feds Had Evidence on Vogel; Prosecutor Didn't Think Case Was Strong Enough to Win*, Orlando Sentinel, Oct. 3, 1997, p. A1.

[91] Amy C. Ripel, *Sheriff Vogel: It's Time to Go; After Years of Success and Controversy, He Decided Not to Run for a Fourth Term in Volusia*, Orlando Sentinel, June 24, 2000, p. A1.

[92] United States V. State of New Jersey, Civil No. 99-5970(MLC) (D. NJ. 1999), Joint Application for Entry of Consent Decree, available at: http://www.usdoj.gov/crt/split/ documents/jerseysa.htm

[93] Gross & Barnes, supra note 20 at 728 n. 219.

[94] http://www.dea.gov/programs/pipeconp.htm

[95] The calls and e-mails to the DEA were done by Mr. Joel Flaxman, University of Michigan Law School, Class of 2007.

- Other federal drug programs have also changed their tune, in part. As we have seen, a 2001 national report from the Office of National Drug Control Policy described drug distribution in the Washington/Baltimore area as dominated by "Dominicans" (heroin and cocaine) and "Jamaicans" (marijuana).[96] The 2004 edition of the report describes those responsible for drug distribution in the same area as "Drug Trafficking Organizations" and "gangs;"[97] for the New York/New Jersey area there is no longer any description of the drug distributors whatever.[98] Nevertheless, the old versions survive in descriptions of drug trafficking in areas of the country that were not caught in the racial-profiling spotlight. The same 2004 report continues to discuss the dominance of "African American street gangs" in drug distribution in Wisconsin and Montana, and of "Jamaican" and "Hispanic" traffickers in Ohio.[99]

By now, half a dozen years after The End we may have reached at least a temporary equilibrium on racial profiling as a social issue. It has three components: (1) Racial profiling is broadly defined, far more so than when the term originated. (2) Racial profiling is actively condemned. (3) Racial profiling continues, if perhaps less frequently and certainly less conspicuously than before. I will discuss these elements in turn.

The Reach of the Term "Racial Profiling"

A question on a 1999 Gallup poll defined racial profiling as follows: "some police officers stop *motorists* of certain racial or ethnic groups because the officers believe that these groups are more likely than others to commit certain types of crimes."[100] By 2004 the same polling organization was asking about racial profiling at airports and shopping malls as well.[101] Airports, of course, are where "profiling" originated, but it only picked up the adjective "racial" after Driving While Black on interstate highways made profiling a major national issue. The shopping mall is a new context for "profiling," and not the only one.

In 2000 Kenneth Meeks, an African American journalist, published a book entitled *Driving While Black: What to do if You are a Victim of Racial Profiling*.[102] It includes a chapter on "Driving While Black" (subtitled "the New Jersey Turnpike")—and chapters on lots of other activities: "Riding the Train While Black," "Shopping Alone While Black," "Shopping in a Group While Black," "Flying While Black," "Living While Black." By 2000, it seems, racial profiling had escaped from the highway and spread across the land.

---

[96] See supra note 56 and accompanying text.

[97] Office of Nat'l Drug Control Policy, National Drug Control Strategy, The High Intensity Drug Trafficking Area Program: 2004, at 157–63 (2004).

[98] Id. at 97–101.

[99] Id. at 65, 102, 123.

[100] Gallup Poll, Sept. 24, 1999–Nov. 16, 1999, supra note 80 (emphasis added).

[101] See note 82 supra.

[102] Broadway Books (Random House), New York, 2000.

So far I haven't needed a general definition of racial profiling, but I do now:

Racial profiling" occurs whenever a law enforcement officer questions, stops, arrests, searches, or otherwise investigates a person because the officer believes that members of that person's racial or ethnic group are more likely than the population at large to commit the sort of crime the officer is investigating.[103]

Under this definition, racial profiling can and does occur on trains and planes, streets, and malls, as well as on I-95. By extension, it includes similar conduct by security officers as well as police, and seizures and deportations as well as investigations. The evacuation and internment of West Coast Japanese Americans during World War II was an outrageous case of mass racial profiling. Racial profiling has been a feature of police work in many settings for as long as we have had police, but that's not what we used to call it. Now anything within shouting distance is called racial profiling, and some beyond. I'll give three of many examples:

- In 1994, the New York City Police Department launched an aggressive anti-gun campaign that resulted in the stopping and frisking of tens of thousands of young Black and Hispanic men. In 1999, after a comprehensive study of this program by the New York State Attorney General, the United States Civil Rights Commission charged the Police Department with racial profiling. The Department replied that it deployed its officers in high-crime neighborhoods that are mostly minority dominated, and that the racial breakdown of those stopped corresponded to the racial makeup of those arrested or suspected of violent crimes.[104] The same dispute could have occurred ten years earlier, but the police practice would have been called something else—"racial discrimination" or perhaps "harassment."
- In 2004 the *Harvard Civil Rights-Civil Liberties Law Review* published an article entitled "The Law and Genetics of Racial Profiling in Medicine."[105] It's not about law enforcement. It's about racial discrimination in medical care—and in part about racial segregation and racial stereotyping. The authors, who never define racial profiling, seem to use the term synonymously with "racial discrimination,"[106] but apparently *The Law and Genetics of Racial Discrimination in Medicine* wouldn't ring the right bell.

---

[103] Samuel R. Gross & Debra Livingston, *Racial Profiling Under Attack*, 102 Columbia L. Rev. 1413, 1415 (2002).

[104] Id. at 1431–32.

[105] Erik Lillquist & Charles A. Sullivan, *The Law and Genetics of Racial Profiling in Medicine*, 39 Har. Civ. Rights-Civ. Liberties L. Rev. 391 (2004). This is not the only use of the concept of "racial profiling in medicine," but appears to be the main one in a legal journal.

[106] For example, the section entitled "The Legality of Racial Profiling in Medicine" begins: "From a legal standpoint, the constraints on *race discrimination* in general— let alone in health care—are more limited than might be expected given the strong national consensus against such discrimination." Id. at 442 (emphasis added).

- In February 2006 The Detroit News ran a column complaining that "abortion-ists disproportionately set up shop in predominately African-American neighborhoods." The headline for the column was *Stop Racial Profiling of Abortion Clinics.*[107]

It's easy to see why racial profiling became so popular a description after 1999. Like Simon Legree, it's now a well known and hated villain. There aren't many who fit that bill.

Racial discrimination in the operation of the criminal justice system is ancient and common, but for the most part nobody cares. It is notoriously hard to prove it in court, and equally hard to get politicians to pay attention. We are used to living in a country in which a third of young Black men are in custody or on probation or on parole. Whether it's due to discrimination or not, we assume that crime and punishment are much more common among those with dark skin. We're not surprised to hear that Blacks and Hispanic teenagers are harassed by the police, or that young Black men are nearly eight times as likely to be imprisoned as young White men.[108] We barely notice.

When *racial profiling* became commonplace—the phrase, not the practice—all of a sudden one form of racial discrimination by the police became a national crisis. Naturally, every complaint about racial or ethnic discrimination in law enforcement is now described as racial profiling, plus quite a few that have nothing to do with crime or justice. Some of these complaints clearly do involve racial profiling, strictly speaking, and some, whatever their merits on other grounds, are pretty far afield.

The Response to Racial Profiling

The Department of Justice web site lists dozens of publications on the subject of racial profiling, from short notices to long detailed studies. They are plainly intended for a variety of audiences. For the general public, the tone is set by a six-page "Fact Sheet" released on June 17, 2003, when the Department issued guidelines prohibiting racial profiling by federal agencies. The title (after strongly worded quotes from the President and the Attorney General) is unambiguous: *Racial Profiling Is Wrong and Will Not Be Tolerated.*[109] A different publication is aimed at police commanders: *How to Correctly Collect and Analyze Racial Profiling Data: Your Reputation Depends On It!*[110] This 150-page report begins by telling the reader that while a majority of the public believes that the police engage in racial profiling, most police chiefs do not, and that this difference in

---

[107] James B. Teela, *Stop Racial Profiling of Abortion Clinics*, The Detroit News, February 21, 2006, p. 9A.
[108] Paige M. Harrison & Allen J. Beck, *Prison and Jail Inmates at Midyear 2004*, U.S. Dept. of Justice, Bureau of Justice Statistics (2005), available at http://www.ojp.usdoj.gov/bjs/ pub/ pdf/pjim04.pdf
[109] http://www.usdoj.gov/opa/pr/2003/June/racial_profiling_fact_sheet.pdf
[110] http://www.cops.usdoj.gov/mime/open.pdf?Item=770

views poses a serious threat to law enforcement that should be addressed by careful study, training, and work with the affected communities.

The role of the Justice Department in educating local police forces on racial profiling should not be underestimated. It was certainly crucial in the uphill portion of the trip—when the practice was taking hold—and it may be influential now, on the downhill run. Still, after the firestorm in reaction to racial profiling in New Jersey and Maryland, I think the message would have gotten through on its own. In any event, many police departments have taken it to heart. Hundreds, if not thousands, of police forces across the country have issued rules prohibiting racial profiling,[111] or developed antiprofiling training programs,[112] or both.

Professor John Lamberth, who did the original studies for the New Jersey Public Defender and the Maryland ACLU that proved racial profiling on I-95, has organized an outfit called Lamberth Consulting. The web site tells us that it was "formed in 2000 in an effort to provide racial profiling assessment, training, and communication services to universities, states, counties, cities, civil rights groups, litigators, and communities."[113] Judging from the testimonials on the web site, his clients are mostly police departments.

Lamberth, of course, is not alone. The Racial Profiling Data Collection Resource Center at Northeastern University (which collaborates with Lamberth Consulting), maintains a web site that lists current news on racial profiling investigations in Iowa, Nevada, Missouri, and Rhode Island.[114] Even the most casual search on the Internet produces dozens of stories of racial profiling studies, regulations, and reports by police departments from Syracuse to Seattle—typically with the help of consultants. It's a budding new service industry.

The Practice of Racial Profiling

How far have these reforms penetrated? To what extent has the practice of racial profiling changed in the last decade? There is no way to tell.

In June 2002, 30% of respondents on a national poll of registered Black voters said that they had been subjected to racial profiling, and an additional 22% said it had happened to a family member or an acquaintance.[115] This is not a literal description of external reality. Some respondents who believed that they had been profiled may not have been. On the other hand, it's a good guess that Blacks who

---

[111] Lorie Fridell et al., *Racially-Biased Policing: A Principled Response* 24–26 (2001) (results of 2001 survey indicating 12% of law enforcement agencies had modified racial profiling policies and 19% had adopted new ones), available at http://www.cops. usdoj.gov/mime/open.pdf?Item=1598

[112] Id.

[113] http://www.lamberthconsulting.com/index.asp

[114] http://www.racialprofilinganalysis.neu.edu/

[115] Public Opinion Strategies poll, June 20, 2002, Roper Data Base, supra note 80 (describing results from question 63, accession no. 0412026).

are not registered to vote are considerably more likely to be victimized by racial profiling than the respondents on this survey. The clearest implication is that in 2002 racial profiling remained a huge issue for African Americans.

Most policing in America is done by local police departments—of which, as I've mentioned, there are thousands. It's all but impossible to get an overall picture of what happens across this deeply fragmented landscape. We do know one thing, however: Racial profiling has not been eradicated.

On May 9, 2005, the *Chicago Tribune* published a story under the headline "Shady Cash Fattens Towns' Coffers Along Drug Routes."[116] It's surprisingly familiar:

For years, this small town [Hogansville, Georgia] nestled in the pine forests off Interstate Highway 85 has struggled to keep its Police Department financially afloat. But the town is riding high these days on a $2.4 million windfall—thanks to drug dealers who happened to be passing through. ...

With the help of the federal Drug Enforcement Administration, small towns across the country are filling their coffers with drug money as a result of federal asset forfeiture laws that allow authorities to seize drug dealers' property, including cars, cash, and houses used to facilitate crime. ...

Law enforcement officials say the law is a powerful tool in the war against drugs. Opponents claim it encourages racial profiling. ...

While seized money cannot be used to hire personnel, it can be used for police training, equipment, vehicles and, in the case of Hogansville, a new police station, a walking trail and a hefty donation to a youth group.

"This has really changed things for us. We have the best equipment and the best-trained officers in this part of the state," said City Manager Randy Jordan. "What we do here is not a secret. People know if you come to Hogansville and commit a crime, you are going to jail." ...

Several police departments have been accused of targeting Hispanic and African-American drivers. ...

In Villa Rica, Ga., off Interstate Highway 20 about 30 miles west of Atlanta, police confiscated about $2 million from 1998 to 2003, enough to build a new police station. But the city curtailed its program after the Justice Department found that the officers had engaged in racial profiling. A federal report said officers would shine spotlights at oncoming cars to "determine the skin color of the occupants."

Has anything changed, or is the same old show just moving around, from one venue to another?

In October 1988 the *Los Angeles Times* ran a story titled "Police Adapt 'Profiling' Tactic to Grab Car Thieves."[117] The article does not criticize the police.

---

[116] Dahleen Glanton, *Shady Cash Fattens Towns' Coffers Along Drug Routes*, Chicago Tribune, May 9, 2005, p.1.
[117] Michael Connelly, *Police Adapt 'Profiling' Tactic to Grab Car Thieves*, Los Angeles Times, October 29, 1988, Metro p. 10.

Quite the opposite. It explains how a pioneering unit of the Los Angeles Police Department was applying techniques learned from drug interdiction to car theft, using a "profiling system" based on "such factors as a driver's age, race and behavior." The reporter describes with apparent approval how at one intersection on a particular evening "several Latino youths driving new Toyota pickups were pulled over by surveillance officers. All but one of the drivers were allowed to go on their way when they proved ownership of the vehicles they were driving."

In 2006 the Los Angeles Police Department is operating under a Federal Court consent decree based in part on charges of racial profiling.[118] We can be sure that the innovative 1988 experiment in car-theft policing has long since been officially abandoned—and equally sure that the same thing still happens in Los Angeles today. If nothing else, however, this behavior now has a name. In 2006 no cop in his right mind anywhere in the country would own up to racial profiling in a news interview, let alone with pride, and no major newspaper would publish that description without mentioning, in some form, that we all know that racial profiling is wrong. Along the way, it has probably also become less common.

---

[118] See http://www.usdoj.gov/crt/split/documents/laconsent.htm

3
Racial Profiling, Attributions of Motive, and the Acceptance of Social Authority

Tom R. Tyler

During the past several years, issues of racial profiling have been central to public discussions of police–community relations. Before the terrorist actions of September 11, a variety of politicians condemned the practice of racial profiling—actions that legal authorities may be taking, at least in part, based on the race of a person. President Bush has labeled racial profiling "wrong" and argued that "we must end it," while Congress and a number of states have considered or passed laws designed to lessen racial profiling. Further, more than 80% of Americans said in a poll that they "disapprove" of racial profiling (Gallup Poll, December, 1999). Racial profiling has been blamed for a variety of negative elements in policing, from increasing friction between the police and minority communities to overall decreased confidence in and cooperation with the police.

The issue of racial profiling can be considered from a number of perspectives. For example, legal scholars focus on whether and under what conditions profiling based on ascribed characteristics such as race, gender, or age is or ought to be illegal (Harris, 1999; Kadish, 1997; Knowles & Persico, 2001; Meeks, 2000; Thompson, 1999).

The discussion began with a focus on racial profiling of Blacks and/or Hispanics, but, after the terrorist attacks of September 11th, has more recently involved discussions of profiling based upon "Arabic" appearance or background (Gross and Livingston, 2002; Stuntz, 2002). The question these scholars are concerned with is when it should be legal for the police to stop someone not for actions they are engaged in, such as behaving suspiciously, but because they fit some demographic profile, such as "Driving while Black."

Criminologists have been interested in determining how often profiling based on ascribed characteristics actually occurs (Lamberth, 1998; Rudovsky, 2001). Through a variety of studies involving both the analysis of statistical information on arrests and the observation of police behavior, researchers have attempted to establish how frequently the police target people on the basis on race, rather than on whether they are engaging in potentially illegal behavior. Such studies look at the proportion of those stopped who are minorities in comparison to the proportion of those speeding who are minorities.

Police institutions have focused on profiling as a reflection of possible racism among legal authorities, attitudes that lead to "bias based" policing (Fridell, Lunney, Diamond, & Kubu, 2001). Such bias based policing is not confined to stops, but may also potentially involve decisions about whom to protect, whom to provide with services, and, conversely, whom to subject to verbal abuse, as well as the possible application of physical force. This focus tries to determine whether the police are prejudiced and when that prejudice, if it exists, shapes their actions.

Although each of the perspectives outlined differs in its specific focus, they all attempt to study the actual behavior of legal authorities. This analysis approaches profiling from a different perspective. It looks at the attributions that members of the public make when trying to explain what is causing the behavior of legal authorities. In other words, I treat profiling as something that an observer (a member of the public) infers that a legal authority (a police officer, a judge) is doing. For example, people could infer that the police stopped them because they were Black. This inference may or may not correspond to the actual motivations of the police.

The study of attributions develops from a central insight of social psychologists—that when people have an interaction with another person they ask themselves why events are occurring as they are. The classic discussion of this literature by Heider (1958) argues that people seek to identify the motivations that lead other people to behave as they do so that they will know how to react. For example, my reaction to this statement made by a police officer—"I stopped you because you resemble the description of a burglar working in this area"—would be completely different if I thought that his true motivation for stopping me was that I was a young person than it would be if I thought he actually had stopped me because I fit a description he had been given. So, our reactions to behavior depend on our inferences concerning what motivates that behavior, that is, why we think the behavior is occurring.

In considering attributions that people might make to explain why they have been stopped by the police, I distinguish between attributions of profiling, in which a person attributes the behavior of the police to the ascribed characteristics of the person with whom the authority is dealing, and behavioral attributions, in which a person attributes police behavior to actions of the person the police are dealing with. For example, someone might think that the police officer stopped her because she was speeding or driving erratically, reasons that link police action to her behavior. If I thought that I was being stopped because of what I was doing, my reaction would be completely different than it would be if I thought I was being stopped because of the type of person I was (young, Black, etc.).

In other words, the analysis I describe in this chapter focuses on the subjective experience of feeling or not feeling profiled, rather than the objective experience of the police actually profiling and stopping a citizen. It is concerned with why people think the police have stopped them. I make this distinction between different explanations that people might have for the behavior of the police because I believe that the experience of receiving police attention based upon one's race (profiling)—regardless of whether profiling has actually occurred—may be responsible for many of the negative effects associated with racial profiling.

Observational studies of the actual behavior of legal authorities suggest that those authorities seldom make overt statements that link their behavior to racial profiling. They do not say, for example, "I stopped you because you are Black (Sherman, 1999)." When authorities do provide reasons or explanations for their actions, those reasons legitimate their actions, as when the police say that the person "fits the description of someone who is wanted for a crime." Hence, a person stopped by the police must make an inference as to the reason that the police stopped him or her, often based on unclear, ambiguous cues.

From this perspective, we can view the subjective experience of being profiled as an aspect of people's more general desire to understand why undesirable events are happening to them. Inferences about observed behavior are central to the social psychology of attribution (Heider, 1958), which recognizes that a key task of social inference is the effort to infer the motivation underlying the observed behavior of others (Fiske & Taylor, 1991; Ross & Nisbett, 1991). People are constantly engaged in an effort to understand the social world by inferring the reasons underlying the actions of the others with whom they are dealing, and understanding the motives of legal authorities may be looked at as such a case.

A core distinction made by attribution theory is between causes that are "achieved," that is, that are due to the person's actions, and causes that result from "ascribed characteristics" of the person—his or her race, age, or gender. People have considerable control over their actions and therefore feel responsible and accountable for the behavior that they choose to engage in. On the other hand, ascribed characteristics are not generally the result of choice and are not under the person's control. Therefore, people do not feel responsible and accountable for those characteristics. Hence, people are typically more comfortable and accepting of being judged by others based on what they choose to do, that is, based on their volitional self, rather than on their race, gender, or age (Fiske & Taylor, 1991).

And, of course, the law takes a position that is consistent with this, encouraging the police to act based on "suspicious" or illegal behavior, and discouraging actions based on race. Early profiles developed to detect drug smugglers and airline hijackers (before the era of screening) were enjoined from including race as a criterion for decision making, irrespective of whether race had predictive power. In developing profiles, authorities were encouraged to focus on people's actions.

In an encounter with legal authorities, people might infer that their own actions have led to or caused the behavior of the authorities—"The police stopped me because I was speeding." This behavioral attribution for the actions of the police puts the causality for the police conduct in the actions of the person, in the things he or she was doing. Such an attribution leads to a focus on whether the behavior a person was engaged in does or does not violate the law and is or is not different from the behavior of others in a similar setting.

Conversely, people might infer that the actions of the authorities were the product of ascribed characteristics, that is, "The police stopped me because I am Black, a woman, a young person, etc." It is this judgment that the authorities are acting in reaction to ascribed characteristics that is the core of an attribution of profiling. Finally, people may also do a combination of the above, attributing police behavior to both their own behavior and their ascribed characteristics, such as, "I was speeding, but the police singled me out because I am Black, young, etc. . . ." Such an attribution focuses attention on issues related to prejudice and the application of stereotypes.

Examining people's opinions about the motives underlying police behavior allows us to investigate important questions left unaddressed by previous work on the topic. First, we can ask the question, "What are the consequences of a person making a profiling attribution for the behavior of the police"? Does this inference, independent of its validity, have negative organizational consequences for police institutions? Second, what are the factors that shape inferences of profiling? What variables are people relying on when they make judgments about the reasons for police behavior?

The importance of these questions becomes apparent when thinking of the best way to stop the problem of racial profiling. Obviously, ending its actual occurrence would have a tremendous impact, and this is the tack taken by legislative bodies that have created laws making racial profiling illegal.

The current approach, however, argues that if people feel that they are the subjects of racial profiling, it may not be sufficient to "actually" stop the profiling. If profiling inferences are responsible for negative consequences to the police, the police and other bodies of authority attempting to address the profiling problem must make sure that they do so in a way that they deal not only with actual profiling, but with the public's perception of profiling as well. It is easy to imagine a situation in which objective profiling ceases, but people still think that they are the subjects of police singling them out because of the social group to which they belong. Thus, knowledge of the factors that shape whether a person will make a profiling attribution or decision becomes crucial in that it is through addressing those factors that authorities influence the public's perception of events.

Consequences of Profiling Attributions

As mentioned in the preceding text, the public blames profiling for a variety of ills, and generally disapproves of it by a wide margin. I have tried to empirically examine the association between belief that the police engage in profiling and support for the police (Tyler & Wakslak, 2004). From a policing perspective, the public's support is critical, in that it predicts the public's cooperation with legal authorities (Sunshine & Tyler, 2003). That cooperation, in turn, is crucial for the police because they depend on voluntary deference to police decisions (Tyler & Huo, 2002); general everyday compliance with the law (Tyler, 2006); and active cooperation with police officers. All of these elements of public behavior are important in shaping the degree to which the police are able to control crime (Sunshine & Tyler, 2003). The argument I wish to make is that attributions of profiling are associated with decreased support for the police.

Antecedents of Profiling Attributions

What determines whether a person stopped by the police makes a profiling attribution? One suggestion is that people's belief in the fairness of the manner in which the police exercise their authority might prevent them from making profiling attributions, since a profiling attribution is a judgment that the police are in some way being unjust. But what determines whether people will find the police fair? The procedural justice model argues that people judge fairness based on several process-based criteria (Tyler & Huo, 2002; Tyler, Boeckmann, Smith, & Huo, 1997). In these articles, we argued that fair procedures consist of two primary categories: (1) quality of decision making—perceived neutrality and consistency—and (2) quality of treatment—being treated with dignity and respect, having one's rights acknowledged.

These two procedural elements can shape procedural justice judgments, as well as inferences about the trustworthiness of the authorities involved, a second inference about the police that also shapes reactions to them and to their actions (Tyler and Huo, 2002). Inferences about trustworthiness reflect assessments of the degree to which the police are concerned about the needs of the people whom they are dealing with, and consider their situation when deciding how to act.

This procedural justice perspective has been widely applied to the issue of regulation. The resulting model, the process based model of regulation (Tyler, 2003; Tyler & Huo, 2002), hypothesizes that people will evaluate the actions of the police against criteria of procedural justice (Tyler et al., 1997; Tyler & Smith, 1997). In particular, one of its arguments is that the exercise of legal authority via fair procedures minimizes inferences of bias (Tyler & Huo, 2002). Applied to the current discussion, the model implies that the way the police exercise their authority when they stop people—both in terms of quality of their decision making and the quality of their treatment of people—shapes the attributions those people make about whether they are being racially profiled.

Perhaps the most straightforward example is that of interpersonal style. If people experience themselves as not being listened to and/or as being treated in a disrespectful manner, that does not necessarily provide information about the motivations of the police officer. The officer may simply be acting on the precepts of a command and control approach to policing, which tells officers to take control of situations and people, to establish and maintain dominance. Yet the findings outlined argue that people will interpret these actions as reflecting on the motivations of the officer—as indicating disrespect for the person. And, when people are in groups about which prejudice exists, they may infer that it is prejudice that is motivating this disrespect.

Another model of justice, the instrumental model (Thibaut & Walker, 1975), makes a different argument. It argues that people make these kinds of decisions based on the outcomes of the interactions rather than on procedures, In other words, people evaluate their experience based on the fairness or the favorability of the outcomes they receive from the group and the desirability of those outcomes. The model argues that people evaluate the police based on issues related to their outcome, including both the favorability of outcomes and distributive fairness, and this evaluation affects the likelihood that they will believe that the police are engaging in racial profiling. This model suggests that people will infer that they are being profiled based on their age, race, and/or gender when they receive negative outcomes, such as a traffic ticket, especially when they believe that they do not deserve to receive the outcome because others in the same situation would receive more favorable treatment.

Many studies have found instrumental concerns to be important predictors of people's feelings of justice (Tyler, 2006; Tyler & Huo, 2002), although procedural justice factors are sometimes even more influential (Tyler et al., 1997). Thus, my second argument is that both instrumental factors and procedural justice will influence people's profiling attributions, but procedural justice factors will have a stronger influence. Thus, the more people feel that the police exercise their authority fairly, the less they will be likely to attribute police behavior to profiling.

Empirical Research on Profiling

I test these two hypotheses—(1) that inferences of profiling are associated with diminished support for the police and (2) that the police's exercise of authority via fair procedures, and to a lesser extent instrumental concerns, are associated with inferences of profiling—in a series of empirical studies of profiling (Tyler & Wakslak, 2004). In these studies members of the public were interviewed about either their personal experiences with the police or their views about how the police generally behaved. They were asked to infer motivation—that is, to indicate whether or how often the police were motivated by attitudes about people that were based on the groups to which they belonged. The studies then explore how those inferences shaped both behavioral reactions during personal experiences and general support for and deference to the law.

I focus here on the first two studies discussed in that article. Study One explored inferences of racial profiling during personal experiences involving stops by the police. It consisted of interviews with members of the public in Oakland and Los Angeles. The study found, first, that when people inferred that they were stopped because of ascribed characteristics (race, age, etc.), they were less willing to accept the decisions made by the authorities, and they expressed more anger toward those authorities.

When did people infer that the police selected them through profiling? As we might expect, members of potentially stigmatizable groups were more likely to infer that they were targets of police profiling. However, this effect was small (accounting for only about 2% of the variance in inferences). A much more important factor was the fairness of the procedures the police used. If the police exercised their authority fairly by making neutral, factual decisions, and by treating people with politeness and respect, respondents did not believe that they were selected through police profiling. In a second study of young people in the New York area, we similarly found that profiling attributions undermined support for the police. Again, the manner in which the police treated community residents when they dealt with them shaped whether they thought the police were profiling them.

These studies provide support for the argument that there is value in treating profiling as an attribution that can be understood from a psychological perspective. Moreover, as suggested earlier, there is value in treating these inferences distinct from the actual occurrence of profiling. While treating people politely and not subjecting them to profiling may be related, they are clearly distinguishable. We can imagine rude and abusive police who do not profile, and polite police who do profile. From a psychological perspective, the findings noted make clear that quality of treatment is a key issue. Poor quality of treatment leads to profiling attributions, resistance to the police, and less willingness to cooperate with them.

Overall Discussion

The results of the studies presented suggest that people react negatively to attributions of profiling, irrespective of whether they think that profiling occurs in their own personal experience or generally during policing activities in their neighborhood and city. These findings support the psychological argument by showing that people's inferences about the motives underlying police behavior shape their support for the police.

Since the question of profiling has had wide public exposure, has attracted considerable political attention, and is rated by police chiefs as one of the central issues in policing today (Fridell et al., 2001) these findings suggest the value of psychology as a framework within which to approach issues of policing and regulation. In many ways, it is the subjective experience of profiling—the first-person accounts of people's experiences of being stopped by the police—that has drawn so much attention to the issue of racial profiling.

As I have noted, these experiences of being of being the target of police profiling are not necessarily linked to actual profiling, so efforts to eliminate actual profiling may or may not resolve the issue of public feelings that the police profile members of the minority community. It is often extremely difficult to know objectively exactly what is going on inside a police officer's head at the exact moment of a stop. The current perspective argues that regardless of the objective truth, racial profiling is a serious issue. People certainly feel that profiling exists, and Tyler and Wakslak (2004) linked that feeling to a marked decrease in support for the police.

In addition, the results support the argument that the procedural justice framework in particular is valuable in understanding how to manage issues of profiling. The core conclusion of the studies is that when people indicate that they have experienced fair procedures when dealing with the police and/or when they indicate that the police generally use fair procedures when dealing with members of their community, they are less likely to infer that profiling occurs. Hence, the police can manage their relationships with members of the communities they serve through their behavior when dealing with members of the public. These findings, therefore, support the general argument about policing made by Tyler and Huo (2002)—that process-based regulation has important advantages for the police and for policing. Tyler and Huo (2002) argued that people's willingness to cooperate voluntarily with the police and the courts was based on the fairness of the procedures through which those legal authorities exercised their authority. And, that same procedural justice also shaped the impact of personal experiences on views about the legitimacy of legal authorities. Hence, by acting justly the police both facilitated immediate acceptance, and created the groundwork for later public cooperation.

The findings are especially striking given the unique nature of the situation we have been discussing, being stopped by the police. In addition to its being very subjective, with the choice of whom to stop being largely in the hands of the police and the criterion used unclear, it is a situation in which the person stopped has very little control over the situation. Both of these factors have been discussed as ones that may increase the level of identity threat experienced by minorities (Steele, Spencer, & Aronson, 2002), that is, factors that may make members of frequently stigmatized groups suspicious that a stereotype related to that aspect of their identity is relevant in a current situation. This, we would imagine, would make the judgment of profiling more likely. In other words, if a person is in a situation in which he or she is vulnerable to the application of stereotypes—for example, he or she is a member of a minority group—the person is more likely to infer that the actions of others are due to the application of such stereotypes—i.e. to be sensitive to race-based rejection (Mendoza-Denton, Downey, Purdie, Davis, & Pietrzak, 2002).

In addition, the media has publicized this interaction as one tinged with bias, so people presumably enter into the interaction with identity concerns highly salient. There has been much publicity in the past number of years about incidents of racial profiling in particular (Harris, 1999), and tension –riddled police–minority relations in general (Fridell et al., 2001). Thus, the simple fact that a police officer has stopped a member of a minority group may, in itself, be a cue that a negative stereotype about the person stopped may be relevant to the situation. Given the current dynamic between the police and minorities, we would imagine a profiling attribution is one that it is particularly easy for people in the minority community to make.

The fact that these three aspects of procedural fairness—quality of decision making, quality of treatment, and inferences about trustworthiness—were found to impact significantly the inferences people make about their interactions with the police are important for a variety of reasons. The finding that people are less likely to infer that they have been profiled when they are treated with politeness and respect by the police is especially striking. The quality of interpersonal treatment is not necessarily an indicator of the manner in which police make decisions. We can imagine an officer who *is not* a neutral decision maker, but still treats people *with* dignity and respect. At the same time, we can imagine an officer who *is* a neutral decision maker, but treats people *without* dignity and respect.

Yet, people do not treat these two issues as distinct, and are found to be drawing inferences about profiling from indicators of respect. It is therefore critical that police officers realize the messages that their method of interaction sends to the people with whom they are dealing. For the public to consider a police force to be fair, the police must make decisions in an objective, consistent manner, while also being careful to treat citizens with dignity and respect.

The final factor is trust. Of the three procedural justice issues, trust seemed the least connected to issues of profiling. In some studies, trust acted like the other procedural justice factors; in other studies it had no connection to profiling. It is hard to know why this is the case. It may be because quality of decision making and quality of interpersonal treatment, as more concrete judgments, are more central to the judgment about whether the police are profiling, while the more abstract judgment of trust is directly linked to the more general evaluation of the police. As we would expect from this perspective, trust does directly encourage institutional support (Tyler & Wakslak, 2004).

The process-based model of regulation (Tyler & Huo, 2002) advocates an environment of fairness that incorporates all of these objectives. Along this line of thinking, Stuntz (2002) argues that to deal effectively with racial distrust of the police in the minority community it is important to regulate not only the selection of the people whom the police stop, but also the manner in which they conduct stops as well. According to his argument, this perspective may also offer one way of dealing with the complex issue of profiling in a post-9/11 world. Many maintain that suddenly the normative question of profiling is much less clear (Gross & Livingston, 2002). Should all profiling, including that of potential terrorists, be disallowed?

Stuntz (2002) argues that in the type of situation faced post-9/11, in which it is unclear whether prohibiting profiling is an appropriate thing to do, we should focus on the manner in which people are stopped, which is a large cause of the harm associated with profiling. Regulating the manner of stops made by the police is a way to limit the harm associated with profiling independent of whether one believes in policy that prohibits all profiling in a post-9/11 world. Of course, we are not advocating that the police simply treat people fairly, and not take any actions to reduce profiling itself. Instead, my argument is that there are some situations, like combating terrorism, in which profiling may ultimately be found to be allowable under the law, and in which approaching the situation from a psychological perspective may be especially advantageous in reducing public dissatisfaction about profiling.

What specific implication for managing terrorism and those suspected of being terrorists can be drawn from this research. Probably the key issue is that of treatment with respect. Since, even among a potentially suspect group, such as Arab Americans, most of the people dealt with will not be involved in any illegal activity, the presumption should be that those being dealt with are entitled to respect and to treatment with dignity and politeness. Even with reference to "criminals," however, evidence suggests that this same type of treatment has the effect of lowering future law breaking and is, therefore, desirable on the part of the authorities. Further, it is important to make decisions about whom to stop, for example, using objective and transparent criteria that are explained to those being dealt with.

Does such an approach make sense from a law enforcement perspective? Tyler and Fagan (2006) used panel data based on interviews with the residents of New York City to demonstrate that those who personally deal with the police view them as more legitimate after their experience, if the police exercise their authority in ways that are viewed as fair. This is particularly true of those who receive negative outcomes. Hence, the police can engage in policing activities that involve stopping and questioning community residents and build their legitimacy, if they exercise their authority in fair ways.

Throughout this chapter, the main focus has been the benefits to the police of treating the people they deal with fairly. However, I wish to emphasize that a policing model focused on fairness is first and foremost beneficial to the community the police serve. The public gains from an increasingly neutral and respectful police force. In addition, process-based regulation creates an environment of fairness that fosters cooperation and a sense that the police are acting on behalf of the community. Increasing support for the police allows the police to function more effectively, better focusing their efforts on serving the community, a result that benefits both the police and the public.

Since there is a major ethnic group gap in trust and confidence in the law and the police (Skogan & Frydl, 2004), these findings have particular relevance to the task of managing the relationship between the police and the minority community. The procedural justice findings point to a clear strategy within which the police can work to create and sustain the trust and confidence of minority group members. While the findings outlined are not confined to minority group members, it is the members of that group that have been of greatest concern to legal authorities, since they have been consistently found to be the most disaffected and defiant members of our society. It is especially striking, therefore, that the findings outlined, as was true of the findings of Tyler and Huo (2002), are equally applicable to the majority and minority populations.

Because the focus of this chapter is on racial profiling, an issue that is important in the context of regulation (Tyler & Huo, 2002), the focus has been on the willingness of people to defer to legal authorities. We can expand this focus to general rule following as well as to cooperation with authorities. Results of studies of general rule following suggest that the overall fairness of group procedures also predicts general rule following (Tyler, 2006; Tyler & Blader, 2005). Similarly, results of studies of cooperation find that this, too, is linked to perceptions of procedural fairness (Sunshine & Tyler, 2003).

A broadened focus is important because authorities want more from the public than deference to laws and to the decisions of legal authorities. They also want proactive involvement. For example, studies of crime and urban disorder emphasize that the community must play an active role for the police to control crime effectively in their communities (Sampson & Bartusch, 1998; Sampson, Raudenbush, & Earls, 1997). Hence, the authorities also want to motivate proactive behavior on the part of those within their groups. A broader implication of these findings is that procedural fairness motivates proactive behavior on the part of group members. In this case, broader behavior involves cooperation with the police (see Sunshine & Tyler, 2003, for a discussion of the importance of cooperation with the police).

The issue of anti-terror profiling after the 9/11 terrorist attack on the World Trade Center illustrates what the police and community have to gain from treating people fairly and building their legitimacy within minority communities. While those of Middle Eastern appearance are the targets of profiling, anti-terror efforts depend on the cooperation of the members of the Arab community to identify and warn the authorities about terrorist activities. The key to successful terrorism is the ability to blend into the minority community without fear of detection. Just as with community cooperation in fighting everyday crime, community cooperation is important in fighting terrorism. Moreover, in both cases, cooperation flows from the belief that the police are legitimate social authorities.

The importance of cooperation from the public makes clear that our concern when dealing with minority group members is not just with encouraging their deference to authorities and institutions. I am more broadly interested in understanding how authorities and institutions can encourage the members of vulnerable minority groups to engage in society both behaviorally and psychologically. The willingness to work with others in one's community is one example of such engagement, as is achievement in school, integration into the workforce, and so forth. Consistent with the findings of Tyler and Wakslak (2004), research on this broader engagement process suggests that people in minority groups are more willing to involve themselves in groups when they experience those groups and their authorities as acting using fair procedures. Hence, more broadly, organizations that are characterized by procedural fairness are better able to gain the cooperation of minority group members.

Interestingly, some researchers have suggested that attributing a negative event to discrimination may, in fact, benefit members of stigmatized groups by protecting their self-esteem (Major and Crocker, 1993), an argument that is at odds with the claim that attributions to profiling are harmful for minority group members. Tyler and Wakslak (2004) examined this possibility using the data in their first study by looking at the relationship between attributions concerning the cause of a police stop and general measures of self-esteem and respect by others. In their study, they asked people who had dealt with the police about their self-esteem and their views about whether or not they were respected by others. This allowed them to determine whether one attribution produces more positive feelings of well-being. In the case of being stopped by the police it is not clear that feeling one has been stopped because of one's behavior ("I was breaking the law") has more positive implications than being stopped because of one's race. Consistent with this, they found no differential effects of attribution in Study One. In other words, being stopped by the police has small, but identifiable, negative effects on measures of self-worth. However, the magnitude of these effects was similar irrespective of which attribution was made about the cause of the event. Hence, when a person is stopped by the police, either explanation for why that stop occurred has a similarly small level of negative impact on well-being. It seems, therefore, that feeling one has been stopped because of one's race, as opposed to one's behavior, has similar negative implications for the self.

Another area for further work is an attempt to identify particular behaviors that would allow the police to tap into the general ideas outlined. It is nice to speak of "respect," "neutrality," and "fairness," but what seems to us to be a necessary next step is work that identifies exactly what those terms mean in the context of police–citizen interactions. This would allow us to develop specific training programs that could teach the police the most effective methods of interacting with the public, putting the theoretical ideas of process-based regulation into actual, on-the-street, practice.

As an example of the type of research that would be of value, police researchers often conduct "ride along" studies in which observers independently record the behavior of the police and those community residents with whom they interact. These types of records provide the potential for linking observable behaviors to the psychological experience of both the community resident and the officer. Analysis of such data can provide a specific set of guidelines concerning the types of police behaviors that are experienced by members of the community as being just (see McCluskey, 2003, for an example of this type of research). They can also help to identify behaviors that evoke the inference of profiling.

Another approach to this issue is to construct vignettes providing descriptions of various types of police interactions with community residents. Observers can then be asked to evaluate these descriptions and, through their evaluations, to provide guidance about police actions that lead to inferences that profiling is occurring. This approach can also, more generally, identify those behaviors by the police that are viewed by community residents as being just or unjust. Seron, Pereira, and Kovath (2004) have used this approach productively in their examination of public perceptions of police misconduct. In their case, they have further used this approach to compare public and police perceptions of particular forms of misconduct. That approach might also be productively used here to determine whether police officers have systematically different views about what the police would use as cues to indicate that profiling is occurring.

Irrespective of how such information is gathered, the key argument advanced here is that the police cannot assume that eliminating the reality of profiling will eliminate the perception of profiling. In recent decades, there have been advances in the quality of policing, including declines in the number of police abuse cases, but these improvements have not necessarily led to increases in trust and confidence in the police (Skogan & Frydl, 2004). Hence, recent discussions of policing emphasize treating trust and confidence as a separate issue from objective performance, to be studied distinctly. Similarly, I would argue, we need to study the experience of being profiled as a separate issue, and not treat it as a simple reflection of when profiling is actually found to occur. This study of the experience of being profiled presents an opportunity for psychologists to make a distinct contribution to the interface of law and psychology.

References

Fiske, S., & Taylor, S. E. (1991). *Social cognition*. New York: McGraw-Hill.

Fridell, L., Lunney, R., Diamond, D., & Kubu, B. (2001). *Racially biased policing: A principled response*. Washington, DC: Police executive research forum.

Gross, S. R., & Livingston, D. (2002). Racial profiling under attack. *Columbia Law Review, 102*, 1413–1438.

Harris, D. A. (1999). The stories, the statistics, and the law: Why "Driving While Black" matters. *Minnesota Law Review, 84*, 265–326.

Heider, F. (1958). *The psychology of interpersonal relations*. New York: John Wiley & Sons.

Kadish, M. J. (1997). The drug courier profile: In planes, trains, and automobiles; and now in the jury box. *American University Law Review, 46*, 747–791.

Knowles, J., & Persico, N. (2001). Racial bias in motor vehicles: Theory and evidence. *Journal of Political Economy, 109*, 203–229.

Lamberth, J. (1998, August 16). Driving while Black: A statistician proves that prejudice still rules the road. *The Washington Post*. C1.

Major, B., & Crocker, J. (1993). Social stigma: The affective consequences of attributional ambiguity. In D. M. Mackie and D. L. Hamilton (Eds.), *Affect, cognition, and stereo typing: Interactive processes intergroup perception* (pp. 345–370). New York: Academic Press.

Major, B., Quinton, W. J., & McCoy, S. K. (2002). Antecedents and consequences of attributions to discrimination: Theoretical and empirical advances. In M. Zanna (Ed.), *Advances in Experimental Social Psychology* (Vol. 34, pp. 251–330). New York: Academic Press.

McCluskey, J. D. (2003). Police requests for compliance: Coercive and procedurally just tactics. New York: LFB Scholarly Publishing.

Meeks, K. (2000). *Driving while Black: What to do if you are a victim of racial profiling*. New York: Broadway Books.

Mendoza-Denton, R., Downey, G., Purdie, V. J., Davis, A., & Pietrzak, J. (2002). Sensitivity to status-based rejection: Implications for African American students' college experience. *Journal of Personality and Social Psychology, 83*, 896–918.

Miller, C. T., & Myers, A. M. (1998). Compensating for prejudice: How overweight people (and others) control outcomes despite prejudice. In J. K. Swim & Stangor, C. (Eds.), *Prejudice: The target's perspective*. New York: Academic Press.

Paine, L. S. (1994). Managing for organizational integrity. *Harvard Business Review, 72*, 106–118.

Quinn, D. M., & Crocker, J. (1998). Vulnerability to the affective consequences of the stigma of overweight. In J. K. Swim & C. Stangor (Eds.), *Prejudice: The target's perspective*. New York: Academic Press.

Ross, L., & Nisbett, R. E. (1991). *The person and the situation*. New York: McGraw-Hill.

Rudovsky, D. (2001). Law enforcement by stereotypes and serendipity: Racial profiling and stops and searches without cause. *University of Pennsylvania Journal of Constitutional Law, 3*, 296–349.

Sampson, R. J., & Bartusch, D. J. (1998). Legal cynicism and (subcultural?) tolerance of deviance. *Law and Society Review, 32*, 777–804.

Sampson, R. J., Raudenbush, S. W., & Earls, F. (1997). Neighborhoods and violent crime. *Science, 277*, 918–924.

Seron, C., Pereira, J., & Kovath, J. (2004). Judging police misconduct: "Street-level" versus professional policing. *Law and Society Review, 38*, 665–710.

Sherman, L. W. (January 7, 1999). *Consent of the governed: Police, democracy, and diversity*. Conference in honor of Professor Menachem Amir. Institute of Criminology, Hebrew University of Jerusalem. Jerusalem, Israel.

Skogan, W., & Frydl, K. (2004). *Fairness and effectiveness in policing: The evidence*. Washington, DC: The National Academies Press.

Steele, C., Spencer, S., & Aronson, J. (2002). Contending with group image. In M. Zanna (Ed.), *Advances in Experimental Social Psychology* (Vol. 34, pp. 379–440). New York: Academic Press.

Stuntz, W. J. (2002). Local policing after the terror. *Yale Law Journal, 111*, 2137–2192.

Sunshine, J., & Tyler, T. R. (2003). The role of procedural justice and legitimacy in shaping public support to policing. *Law and Society Review, 37*, 555–589.

Swim, J. K., & Stangor, C. (1998). *Prejudice: The target's perspective*. New York: Academic Press.

Thompson, A. C. (1999). Stopping the usual suspects: Race and the fourth amendment. *New York University Law Review, 74*, 956–1013.

Thibaut, J., & Walker, L. (1975). *Procedural Justice*. Mahwah, NJ.: Erlbaum.

Tyler, T. R. (2000). Social justice: Outcome and procedure. *International Journal of Psychology, 35*, 117–125.

Tyler, T. R. (2003). Process based regulation: Procedural justice, legitimacy, and the effective rule of law. In M. Tonry (Ed.), *Crime and justice* (Vol. 30, pp. 431–505. Chicago: University of Chicago Press.

Tyler, T. R. (2006). *Why people obey the law*. Princeton, NJ: Princeton University Press.

Tyler, T. R., & Blader, S. L. (2000). *Cooperation in groups*. Philadelphia: Psychology Press.

Tyler, T. R., & Blader, S. L. (2003). Procedural justice, social identity, and cooperative behavior. *Personality and Social Psychology Review, 7*, 349–361.

Tyler, T. R., & Blader, S. L. (2005). Can businesses effectively regulate employee conduct? *Academy of Management Journal, 48*, 1143–1158.

Tyler, T. R., Boeckmann, R. J., Smith, H. J., & Huo, Y. J. (1997). *Social justice in a diverse society*. Boulder, CO: Westview.

Tyler, T. R., & Fagan, J. (2006). *Legitimacy and cooperation: Why do people help the police fight crime in their communities?* Unpublished manuscript, New York University.

Tyler, T. R., & Huo, Y. J. (2002). *Trust in the law: Encouraging public cooperation with the police and courts*. New York: Russell-Sage.

Tyler, T. R., & Lind, E. A. (1992). A relational model of authority in groups. In M. Zanna (Ed.), *Advances in experimental social psychology* (Vol. 25, pp. 115–191). New York: Academic Press.

Tyler, T. R., & Smith, H. J. (1997). Social justice and social movements. In D. Gilbert, S. Fiske, & G. Lindzey (Eds.), *Handbook of social psychology* (4th ed., Vol. 2., pp. 595–629). New York.: McGraw-Hill.

Tyler, T. R., & Wakslak, C. (2004). Profiling and the legitimacy of the police: Procedural justice, attributions of motive, and the acceptance of social authority. *Criminology, 42*, 13–42.

4
Racial Profiling as a Minority Issue

Cynthia Willis-Esqueda

> Blacks—in particular, Black men—swap their experiences of police encounters like war stories, and there are few who don't have more than one story to tell.
>
> —Gates, Jr. (1995)

On a recent airing of the Actor's Studio (May 21, 2006), James Lipton interviewed Don Cheadle about the movie *Crash* and his personal experiences as a Black man in Beverly Hills, California. Mr. Cheadle related that the police stopped him as he was walking down the street. "Did they give you a reason for why you were stopped?" asked James Lipton. "Oh yea, I fit the profile. You always fit the profile," replied Don Cheadle. This response brought a burst of laughter from the studio audience. Yet, the response and the laughter highlighted some noteworthy issues. First, the audience shared in the understanding that Black men in America can be stopped by police on any pretext, and this shared knowledge does not have to originate from direct experience with crime or with criminal suspects (Klein & Naccarato, 2003; Oliver, 1994; Prosise & Johnson, 2004; Weitzer & Tuch, 2005). We obtain the stereotyped link between race and crime from family, peers, media, film, and literature. Second, while we know racial profiling happens, we allow it to continue, and as a society, we may be motivated to do so (Wilson, Dunham, & Alpert, 2004). Racial profiling and its outcomes allows the dominant culture to maintain their status in the social hierarchy (Sidanius, Levin, & Pratto, 1998) and keeps minorities, mostly men of color, in a precarious psychological state.

By racial profiling, I mean the term as it is used to "identify law enforcement practices that use race to make discretionary judgments" (Aguirre, 2004, p. 929). I refer to the use of racial profiling as a means for law enforcement to wield power against individuals of color with irrelevant or no evidence for doing so. Racial profiling has received increased attention in the legal community (Banks, 2003; Gross & Barnes, 2002; Hickman, 2005; Johnson, 2003; *Traffic Stops Statistics Study Act*, 2001; Totman & Steward, 2006), in part owing to the number of personal testimonies and studies indicating its prevalence for people of color at the national, state, and local levels (*Black police executives*, 1999; *Indian drivers*, 2004; Kafka, 2000; Kocieniewski, 2002; Melton, 2002; *Missouri Vehicle Stops*, 2005; Novak, 2004; Parker, MacDonald, Alpert, Smith, & Piquero, 2004; Ramirez, McDevitt, & Farrell, 2000; Reitzel, Rice, & Piquero, 2004; Tomic & Hakes, 2004; Williams, 2002; Wolfson, 2005). Its significance as a human rights issue in the United States has been noted as well (Amnesty International, 2004).

We have garnered a clearer understanding of the legal issues that permeate racial profiling, particularly from the work of Gross (this volume; Gross and Barnes, 2002). We also have an understanding of the psychological processes involved in making judgments about whether racial profiling has occurred and whether it is accepted, most notably from the work of Tyler, who outlines these processes in Chapter 3 (this volume; Tyler, 2005). Although racial profiling has been noted in the psychological literature as an issue involving the intersection of race, psychology, and law (Barrett, 2005), we know little about the cognitive processes that are used to determine a racial category in a profiling situation. We know less about the short-term and long-term psychological ramifications of such profiling for its targets from an empirical standpoint.

Nevertheless, "Driving while Black," "Driving while Brown" (DWB), and "Driving while Indian" (DWI) are common occurrences for (and maybe offenses against) people of color in the United States, particularly for men, regardless of socioeconomic status (SES). In fact, while those in high SES categories may be less likely to experience racial profiling from law enforcement, high SES does not preclude men of color from experiencing racially motivated police stops, interrogations, and detainments (Becerra, 2001; *Black executives*, 1995; Johnson, 2000). In 2001, for example, an African American surgeon from Florida who taught at the University of Miami School of Medicine was en route to lecture at the UCLA Medical Center. The LAPD stopped him in his rental car, made him lie on the pavement, and detained him for 4 hours. His handcuffs were so tight that his wrists were injured and he could no longer perform surgery. He tried to show officers the rental car documents and information about his trip, but to no avail. It was later determined that the rental agency had placed the wrong plates on the rental car, and the stolen car was not the car the surgeon was driving. However, the LAPD had refused to call the rental agency to determine the status of the car. The case resulted in a jury award of $33 million to the plaintiff.

Historical Context

Although there is an increased interest in racial profiling, in part owing to cases like the one described in the preceding text, it has been a problem, both psychologically and legally for most people of color in the United States for hundreds of years. The significance of racial profiling as a legal and psychological issue makes it a rich area for research. Unfortunately, for those who are the usual targets of such profiling, it promises to remain an issue of concern and of research in the future. Racial profiling will remain an issue of concern because of its lengthy and powerful history in weaving and maintaining the fabric of United States social life. Racial profiling did not begin with a label arising out of the annals of U.S. jurisprudence. Rather, with or without a label, it has had real implications for the social, spiritual, and economic life of people of color since the beginning of America. For example, in colonial America, officials used such profiling to relocate American Indians to "praying towns" and to determine if Indians should be stopped and interrogated concerning their piety and commitment to Puritan rules and guidelines. Transgressions of such rules resulted in public displays of punishment.

The importance of and attention to racial profiling issues today does not surprise those who have historically come to expect some form of racial profiling during daily activities (Reitzel et al., 2004). For example, after the Civil War the enforcement of the Black Codes[1] was based on the use of race and the assumption that one's "racial" features signifying blackness were sufficient to warrant a stop and processing for appropriate papers and permission to live in certain areas, hold employment, maintain employment, and travel (Adamson, 1983). If a person was stopped, failure to provide documentation or to have left employment without permission resulted in significant punishment. Black people could lose a year's wages and be required to pay the persons who caught them and returned them to their employers. Moreover, anyone who helped a Black person would be guilty of a crime and punished as well (e.g., the Mississippi Black Codes of 1865). Such codes were in force in both the South and the North (e.g., Ohio Black Codes of 1804) and were the predecessor of the Jim Crow laws.

Legal authorities also subjected the indigenous ancestors of today's Mexican American and American Indian populations to racial profiling (Castro, 2001;

---

[1] For example, Sections 5 and 7 of the Mississippi Black Codes of 1865, read as follows: Section 5. Every freedman, free negro and mulatto shall, on the second Monday of January, one thousand eight hundred and sixty-six, and annually thereafter, have a lawful home or employment, and shall have written evidence thereof as follows, to wit: if living in any incorporated city, town, or village, a license from that mayor thereof; and if living outside of an incorporated city, town, or village, from the member of the board of police of his beat, authorizing him or her to dod irregular and job work; or a written contract, as provided in Section 6 in this act; which license may be revoked for cause at any time by the authority granting the same.
Section 7. Every civil officer shall, and every person may, arrest and carry back to his or her legal employer any freedman, free negro, or mulatto who shall have quit the service of his or her employer before the expiration of his or her term of service without good cause; and said officer and person shall be entitled to receive for arresting and carrying back every deserting employee aforesaid the sum of five dollars, and ten cents per mile from the place of arrest to the place of delivery; and the same shall be paid by the employer, and held as a set off for so much against the wages of said deserting employee: Provided, that said arrested party, after being so returned, may appeal to the justice of the peace or member of the board of police of the county, who, on notice to the alleged employer, shall try summarily whether said appellant is legally employed by the alleged employer, and has good cause to quit said employer. Either party shall have the right of appeal to the county court, pending which the alleged deserter shall be remanded to the alleged employer or otherwise disposed of, as shall be right and just; and the decision of the county court shall be final.

Valdez, 1998). In the Spanish colonial world, the establishment of missions and haciendas meant the enslavement of indigenous peoples, and racial profiling was used to determine who could be taken and used as slave labor (Castro, 2001; Valdez, 1998). If there were runaways, racial profiling was used to stop and forcibly return indigenous people to the mission or hacienda owners (Kehoe, 1992). Indeed, some have argued that the use of racial profiling for the forced submission of California's Indians in the establishment of the mission system meant their near destruction (Heizer, 1993), and it certainly was used to enforce California's anti-vagrancy laws like the "Greaser Act" of 1855, which targeted those of Mestizo and Indian descent (Takaki, 1993). It is no wonder that "passing" by people of color in the United States was a method of advancing one's social position well into the advent of the civil rights movement.

Recent Events

Racial profiling has been apparent in more recent times as well (Harris, Henderson, & Williams, 2005). In one of the more egregious instances of overt profiling, in 1986 Sheriff Harry Lee of Jefferson Parish, outside New Orleans, Louisiana, gave an order for all deputies to stop "Blacks" who traveled in "White" neighborhoods. Sheriff Lee later apologized for the order and rescinded it (*Louisiana sheriff apologizes*, 1986). However, this event did not cost Sheriff Lee his position or, apparently, his credibility. The people of Jefferson Parish, Louisiana have reelected Sheriff Lee to the position of Sheriff continuously since the incident occurred.

While academics have studied the problem of racial profiling for African Americans in some detail (Johnson, 2000; Johnson, 2001; Johnson, 2003), research and legal scholarship on such discrimination against other groups has been lacking, particularly for Mexican Americans (Luna, 2003). The issue of racial profiling may not be conceptually similar or experienced in the same way for African Americans and Latino/as (Higgins & Jordan, 2005). Today, Hispanics constitute the largest U.S. minority group, and Mexican Americans are the largest subgroup within the generic "Hispanic" label (United States Census Bureau, 2000). Thus, the scope and ramifications of racial profiling for this group is noteworthy. Certainly, Hispanics are more likely to believe that racial profiling occurs in their community and that they have been victims of such profiling, compared to non-Hispanics (Reitzel et al., 2004).

In addition, racial profiling of Mexican Americans occurs for possible immigration violations and illegal immigrant status, in addition to criminal acts (Johnson, 2000; in *United States v. Brigoni-Ponce*, 1975; *United States v. Montero-Camargo*, 2000). As with African Americans, high SES does not preclude racial profiling. Judges, mayors, and attorneys of Mexican descent and even those born in the United States have been targeted through racial profiling for stops and interrogations of immigrant status (Aguirre, 2004).

Indeed, Mexican Americans demonstrated the frequency of racial profiling in their social life by providing extensive testimony concerning the use of racial profiling within the legal system more than 30 years ago (U.S. Commission on Civil

Rights, 1970). Testimony to the United States Commission on Civil Rights in 1970 attested to the use of racial profiling against Mexican Americans across the southwestern United States during much of the last century. The use of profiling has been documented steadily since that time (Johnson, 2003). In 2006, a report on the use of discretionary stops by Texas police indicated that 30% of all stops were discretionary (i.e., not motivated by arrest warrants or probable cause for arrest) and that 62% of Texas police departments performed more such stops with Latinos compared to Anglos (Totman & Steward, 2006).

For Mexican Americans, case law exists that encompasses racial profiling outside of criminal activity, as well. Aguirre (2004) provided a sound review of such cases in his analysis of the psychological harm racial profiling has had on the social identity of Mexican Americans. One example of racial profiling that was unrelated to actual criminal behavior, but was merely an indicator of the possibility for such behavior, occurred in *City of Chicago v. Morales* (1999). Chicago had passed an anti-loitering law, which allowed police to disband gatherings of two or more persons if they were on a public street or in a park and the police suspected gang behavior. During the 3 years that the law was in effect, more than 40,000 arrests occurred, with the majority involving members of minority groups, including Latinos. The Supreme Court determined that "the ordinance violates due process in that it is impermissibly vague on its face and an arbitrary restriction on personal liberties," and overturned the statute.

However, government workers are not immune from the use of racial profiling as a means to "deter" crime. In 2000, the U.S. Forest Service distributed a memo that directed forest service officers to detain persons who were "Hispanics" and interrogate them for possible drug smuggling if they drove through a national forest (Aguirre, 2004). Apparently, no one questioned the practice until a newspaper printed the memo, and no court has declared the practice illegal.

Johnson (2003) contends that "Intellectually and practically, racial profiling in criminal law differs little in kind and substance from that employed in immigration enforcement" (p. 343). In both instances, agents of the government demonstrate their power of social control by relying on race to determine who has violated the law, and then detaining persons to determine if a law violation has occurred. And, this use of race for immigration enforcement continues to haunt Mexican Americans, because it is deemed appropriate to do so in light of concerns over illegal immigration and Mexican nationals. In fact, one of the by-products of the use of racial profiling in immigration law enforcement has been the development of Fourth Amendment requirements for valid search and seizures (Valencia et al., 2004).

For example, roving stops by border patrols were the issue in *U.S. v. Brignoni-Ponce* (1975). Roving stops occur when roving patrols of border agents stop and detain people along the U.S. border and interrogate them. The Supreme Court found that the use of race alone by the border patrols in roving stops was not constitutional, because it violated the Fourth Amendment's search and seizure requirements. However, race (or Mexican appearance) could be used as a relevant factor, along with other factors. Thus, border patrols can rely on race to make a roving stop, as long as they can articulate another factor for the stop. This finding is still good law, and race is one of the most important features border patrols consider.

In *United States v. Martinez-Fuerte* (1976) the Court considered the issue of the use of race at permanent border checkpoints. Often at such permanent checkpoints, after an initial stop to determine citizenship and residency status, authorities can single out cars for further interrogation of occupants and require the drivers to pull over and stop, before exiting the checkpoint. In *United States v. Martinez-Fuerte* the question arose over whether a second stop was legal if race alone was the motivation for the second stop, detainment, and interrogation. The Supreme Court found that a second stop could be required, even if police based such a stop on race or "apparent Mexican ancestry."

More recently, in *United States v. Montero-Camargo* (2000), the 9th Circuit Court of Appeals found that the use of "Hispanic" appearance for making immigration stops was no longer of value because of changing demographics in southwestern states. In fact, in some areas of the southwestern states, those of "Hispanic" appearance are the majority. Thus, the 9th Circuit found that physical appearance as "Hispanic" would not aid in the detection of illegal immigrants. The court in this case concluded that "at this point in our nation's history, and given the continuing changes in our ethnic and racial composition, Hispanic appearance is, in general, of such little probative value that it may not be considered as a relevant factor where particularized or individualized suspicion is required" (p. 1135).

Given the increased attention to illegal immigration in the United States today, the courts are sure to revisit the use of race and physical appearance in making immigration stops. And, currently, Mexican appearance or race and other suspect criteria, such as clothing and facial expression, can be used to forcibly stop and interrogate for immigration violations (Johnson, 2001). It remains to be seen which racial features (e.g., skin tone, hair color, eye color, nose structure, etc.) are used to determine possible illegal immigrant status. It is also unclear if all "Hispanic" groups (i.e., Cubans) are subject to racial profiling in immigration stops. Some research on how these cues are used in decisions to make stops would be useful.

Psychological Implications

There are psychological implications for racial profiling for both majority and minority group members. For majority group members, racial profiling means the use of race, as an indicator of who performs socially sanctioned behaviors, is intensified and implicitly associated with negative information. Psychologists have demonstrated this process in recent research on implicit processing of "racial" features with African American and European American targets. Correll, Park, Wittenbrink, and Judd (2002) studied reaction time data in a simulated shooting task and found the decision threshold for whether to shoot an armed target and not shoot an unarmed target was different, depending on whether the target was Black or White. Specifically, when the target was African American, the decision to shoot the armed target was faster, compared to when the target was White. When the target was unarmed, the decision not to shoot was faster for the White target compared to the African American one. This effect was the same for African American and White shooters. Apparently, both samples had learned the link between African Americans and the likelihood of criminal conduct independent of other actual evidence of illegal behavior.

In a series of studies, Eberhardt, Goff, Purdie, and Davies (2004) demonstrated that the visual processing link between African American faces and crime is real, reliable, and "bi-directional" (i.e., being primed with African American faces invokes crime schemata and crime schemata invokes African American faces). In terms of the significance of such findings for racial profiling, police officers were more likely to resonate with Black faces, compared to White faces, when primed with crime words. Moreover, the more stereotypically Black the faces were judged, the more frequently they were misidentified as the initial stimulus person by the officers, and the officers rated Black faces as being more "criminal," compared to White faces, as well. Thus, police officers have learned the cognitive link between "Blackness" and criminal schemata by demonstrating an implicit association and providing explicit responses that demonstrate the link.

Ruby and Brigham (1996) investigated racial and socioeconomic biases by police officers. Officers read crime vignettes that varied the race (Black or White or no race information) and SES (high, low, or none provided) of the suspect. No effects for SES on culpability measures were found. However, officers were biased against an African American suspect, compared to a White one, on culpability measures, including guilt and deceptiveness. Compared to laypersons, officers were also more likely to believe the typical burglar was Black, rather than White.

Taken together, this research serves as further evidence that the culturally held associations between race and sanctioned social behaviors influences the decision processes of police officers. For African Americans, these findings indicate that officer's over-reliance on socially learned crime stereotypes may influence their attention to and processing of crime-related behavior. Whether intended or not, the implicit stereotypical link between race and crime promotes racial profiling and inequitable enforcement of the law (Tomaskovic-Devey, Mason, & Zingraff, 2004).

Does this Occur for Mexican Americans?

Would this link between race and negative information for police officers also exist with Mexican Americans and Mexican nationals as the target race? We can assume that indigenous and/or stereotypical "Mexican" features would also invoke negative evaluations and make profiling more likely. Law enforcement has been known to use "indigenous" features in requests for an indictment. For example, during the grand jury hearing in the infamous 1943 Zoot Suit riots, a Los Angeles Sheriff's office witness proclaimed that ". . . because of their descent from Mayans, who practiced ritual murder, Mexicans were "biologically" predisposed to violence" (Valencia et al., 2004, p. 6). Moreover, research indicates that, as for African Americans, skin tone for Latinos is also associated with negative characteristics. For example, the more one "looks" Mexican, the more one is assumed to possess negative characteristics (Padilla, 2007). Weyant demonstrated the implicit linkage between being Hispanic and perceived low intelligence using a modified Implicit Association Test or IAT (Weyant, 2005). The link between Latinos and negative characteristics is invoked automatically during cognitive processing, as well. Uhlmann, Dasgupta, Elgueta, Greenwald, and Swanson (2002) provide evidence of a strong implicit preference for lighter skinned Latinos. They found that while American Hispanics showed no preference based on skin color (i.e., between light- and dark-skinned Latinos) at the explicit level, they did demonstrate a preference for light skin at the implicit level. It remains to be seen if the real, reliable, and bidirectional link between Mexican Americans and illegal activity exists to the same degree as it does for African Americans. Certainly, criminal and negative stereotypes exist for this group. Many in our culture attach a variety of negative features, such as being uneducated, poor, illegal aliens, innately criminal, lower class, and ambitionless (Berg, 1990; Bodenhausen, 1990; Cowan, Martinez, & Mendiola, 1997; Neimann, 2001; Willis Esqueda, 1997), to Mexican Americans. And, those with darker complexions and indigenous features suffer more from discrimination than their fair skinned, European-looking counterparts (Espino & Franz, 2002; Mason, 2004; Padilla, 2007).

If implicit stereotypes for the link between race and illegal activity exist, then law enforcement officers' subjective judgments concerning racial categories would tend to promote racial profiling. And, this may be the case. In providing race statistics for traffic stops, the U.S. Department of Justice reported, "Most agencies (27) relied on their officers' observation of the driver's race or ethnicity as the method of determining the race or ethnicity of the motorist. Officer observation was the exclusive method in 15 State agencies" (Hickman, 2005, p. 2). Thus, the use of physical characteristics to determine race leaves the link between race and other negative expectations in place and reinforces racial bias. Research on the implicit associations between African Americans and Hispanics and negative characteristics would seem to indicate a vulnerability to implicit racial profiling, if not explicit profiling, by law enforcement and immigration officials.

Mexican American Psychological Issues

For minority persons who are targets of racial profiling, everyday expectations of discrimination can affect their attitudes toward the majority group and the legal system. The review of research by Tyler includes an analysis of the decision-making process in identifying racial profiling and how such identification influences perceptions of law enforcement. Certainly, Mexican Americans possess negative attitudes concerning law enforcement in the southwest (Carter, 1983; Torres & Applewhite, 2004; U.S. Commission on Civil Rights, 1970; Valencia et al., 2004). And, in New York, Hispanics have reported their belief that they have been targets of racial profiling and that racial profiling is common (Reitzel et al., 2004). Mexican Americans are aware of the negative stereotypes that majority group members possess about them (Casas, Ponterotto, & Sweeney, 1987) and they may share in those stereotypes (Neimann, 2001). Thus, racial profiling may leave a vulnerable population even more at risk for mental health dysfunction. Aguirre (2004) argues that racial profiling of Mexican Americans goes to the very core of identity, both personal and social, and calls into question the place of Mexican Americans in a land their ancestors occupied before the Mayflower left English shores.

We know nothing about the increased stress, anger, and resentment that targets may experience because of racial profiling, particularly when we consider that it likely takes place over a lifetime of psychological vigilance. Minority group members who are targets of racial profiling may experience a plethora of psychological distress that we have yet to investigate. Regardless of the psychological ramifications of racial profiling, minority parents know that eventually they will have the obligatory "talk" with their children regarding the appropriate behavior to express around police, particularly when officers stop and question them.

Issues for Future Consideration

Commentators have made several arguments concerning the best approach to eliminating racial profiling. Some involve disentangling criminal profiles from racial profiles (Banks, 2003), so that effective law enforcement can proceed while ensuring racially impartial policing. Others maintain that reporting requirements that include race information lessens the number of stops based on race alone and without reasonable suspicion of wrong-doing (Totman & Steward, 2006). It highlights the use of race for law enforcement and ensures that factors other than race are considered. Still others maintain that, as a society, we need to eliminate the distortion of crime-related information that erroneously focuses on minorities as criminals who commit violent crime (Prosise & Johnson, 2004) so that the stereotypical link between minorities and crime will cease. There is a considerable body of research that addresses the means to reduce prejudice (Oskamp, 2000), and this method has been argued to be at the root of racial profiling and its acceptance at the societal level (Aguirre, 2004). All of these methods, alone or in combination, might reduce reliance on racial profiling as a means of law enforcement and social control. Research on any of these possible solutions would be noteworthy, as would continued work on the influence of racial profiling on the judgments and decisions of authorities as begun by Gross (this volume) and Tyler (this volume). We are particularly in need of studies of the use of race and ethnicity in decisions and judgments that involve Mexican Americans and others in the Latino/a community.

"How we choose to comprehend racial inequality has tremendous normative implications for how we shape our national identity" (Bracey, 2003, p. 914). If we intend to bring the national social life of U.S. ethnic groups to a place of equality, then the use of mere physical appearance to determine the administration of justice must end. As a matter of national conscience, we cannot continue to use the methods of the Black Codes or the colonial systems of social control with the use of physical appearance and demand equality before the law by other nations on the international scene. Indeed, the research that is dedicated to understanding such profiling, both legally and psychologically, may be our only hope of eliminating it.

References

Adamson, C. R. (1983). Punishment after slavery: Southern state penal systems, 1865–1890. *Social Problems, 30*, 555–569.

Aguirre, A. (2004). Profiling Mexican American identity. *American Behavioral Scientist, 47*, 928–942.

Amnesty International. (2004). *Threat and humiliation: Racial profiling, domestic security, and human rights in the United States.* Retrieved June 1, 2006 from http://www.amnestyusa.org/racial_profiling/index.do.

Banks, R. R. (2003). Beyond profiling: Race, policing, and the drug war. *Stanford Law Review, 56*, 571–603.

Barrett, K. H. (2005). Case examples: Addressing racism, discrimination, and cultural bias in the interface of psychology and law. In K. H. Barrett & W. H. George (Eds.), *Race, culture, psychology, and law* (pp. 19–30). Thousand Oaks, CA: Sage.

Becerra, H. (2001, March 29). LAPD blames car agency error in Black doctor's arrest. Los Angeles Times. Retrieved March 29, 2001 at http:www.latimes.com.

Berg, C. R. (1990). Stereotyping in films in general and of the Hispanic in particular. *The Howard Journal of Communications, 2*, 286–300.

Black executives still face prejudice despite success. (1995, June 25). Omaha World Herald, p. 1, 5.

Black police executives tackle racial profiling. (1999, December 4). Retrieved June 6, 2005 from http://www.aclu.org/racialjustice/racialprofiling/15936prs19991204.html.

Bodenhausen, G. V. (1990). Second-guessing the jury: Stereotypic and hindsight biases in perceptions of court cases. *Journal of Applied Social Psychology, 20*, 1112–1121.

Bracey, C. A. (2003). Thinking race, making nation. *Northwestern University Law Review, 97*, 911–940.

Carter, D. L. (1983). Hispanic interaction with the Criminal Justice System in Texas: Experiences, attitudes, and perceptions. *Journal of Criminal Justice, 11*, 213–227.

Casas, J. M., Ponterotto, J. G., & Sweeney, M. (1987). Stereotyping the stereotyper: A Mexican American perspective. *Journal of Cross-Cultural Psychology, 18*, 45–57.

Castro, R. F. (2001). Rescuing Catalina: Law, storytelling, and unearthing the hidden history of southwestern slavery. *La Raza Law Journal, 12*, 123–135.

Correll, J., Park, B., Wittenbrink, B., & Judd, C. M. (2002). The police officer's dilemma: Using ethnicity to disambiguate potentially threatening individuals. *Journal of Personality and Social Psychology, 83*, 1314–1329.

Cowan, G., Martinez, L., & Mendiola, S. (1997). Predictors of attitudes toward illegal Latino immigrants. *Hispanic Journal of Behavioral Sciences, 19*, 403–415.

Eberhardt, J. L., Goff, P. A., Purdie, V. J., & Davies, P. G. (2004). Seeing Black: Race, crime, and visual processing. *Journal of Personality and Social Psychology, 87*, 876–893.

Espino, R., & Franz, M. M. (2002). Latino phenotypic discrimination revisited: The impact of skin color on occupational status. *Social Science Quarterly, 83*, 612–623.

Gates, Jr. H. L. (1995, October 23). Thirteen ways of looking at a Black man. *The New Yorker.* pp. 56–65.

Gross, S. R., & Barnes, K. Y. (2002). Road work: Racial profiling and drug interdiction on the highway. *Michigan Law Review, 101*, 651–754.

Harris, A. G., Henderson, G. R., & Williams, J. D. (2005). Courting customers: Assessing consumer racial profiling and other marketplace discrimination. *Journal of Public Policy and Marketing, 24*, 163–171.

Heizer, R. (1974/1993). *The destruction of California Indians*. Lincoln, NE: University of Nebraska Press.

Hickman, M. J. (2005). *Traffic stop data collection: Policies for state police, 2004*. Department of Justice. Washington, DCL: NCJ 209156.

Higgins, G. E., & Jordan, K. L. (2005). Race and gender: An examination of the models that explain evaluations of the court system for differences. *Criminal Justice Studies, 18*, 81–97.

Indian drivers in Nebraska more likely to be searched. Retrieved April 2, 2004 from Indianz.com at http://www.indianz.com/News/2004/001200.asp.

Johnson, K. R. (2000). The case against racial profiling in immigration enforcement. *Washington University Law Quarterly, 78*, 675–736.

Johnson, K. R. (2001). Race profiling in immigration enforcement. American Bar Association. Retrieved May 30, 2006 from http://www.abanet.org/irr/hr/winter01/johnson.html.

Johnson, K. R. (2003). The case for African American and Latina/o cooperation in challenging racial profiling in law enforcement. *Florida Law Review, 55*, 341–363.

Kafka, J. (2000, May 30). *Wagner police chief says his office doesn't profile*. Retrieved May 30, 2002 from http://www.argusleader.com.

Kehoe, A. B. (1992). *North American Indians: A comprehensive account*. Upper Saddle River, NJ: Prentice Hall.

Klein, R. D., & Naccarato, S. (2003). Broadcast news portrayal of minorities. *American Behavioral Scientist, 46*, 1611–1616.

Kocieniewski, D. (2002, January 14). New Jersey troopers avoid jail in case that highlighted profiling. Retrieved January 15, 2002 from Jhttp://www.nytimes.com/2002/01/15/nyregion/ 15TROO.html?ex=1012120655&ei=1&en=009712e92e151f9d.

Louisiana sheriff apologizes, revokes order to stop blacks. (1986, December 4). Lawrence Journal World, p. 8C.

Luna, E. (2003). How the Black/White paradigm renders Mexicans/Mexican Americans and discrimination against them invisible. *Berkeley La Raza Law Journal, 14*, 225–253.

Mason, P. (2004). Annual income, hourly wages, and identity among Mexican-American and other Latinos. *Industrial Relations, 43*, 817–834.

Melton, J. H. (2002, January 11). Warner announces legislation on profiling in Virginia. Retrieved January 11, 2002 from http://www.washingtonpost.com/wp-dyn/articles/A31033-2002Jan11.html.

Mississippi Black Codes. (2006, May 24). Retrieved from http://afroamhistory.about.com/library/blmississippi_blackcodes.htm.

Missouri Vehicle Stops: 2004 Annual Report. (2005, May 31). Missouri Attorney General. Retrieved June 13, 2005 from http://www.ago.mo.gov/newsreleases/2005/053105.htm.

Neimann, Y. F. (2001). Stereotypes about Chicanas and Chicanos: Implications for counseling. *The Counseling Psychologist, 29*, 55–90.

Novak, K. J. (2004). Disparity and racial profiling in traffic enforcement. *Police Quarterly, 7*, 65–96.

Ohio Black Codes. (2006, May 24). Retrieved from http://afroamhistory.about.com/library/blohio_blacklaws.htm.

Oliver, M. B. (1994). Portrayals of crime, race, and aggression in "reality-based" police shows: A content analysis. *Journal of Broadcasting and Electronic Media, 38*, 179–192.

Oskamp, S. (2000). *Reducing prejudice and discrimination*. Mahwah, NJ: Lawrence Erlbaum.

Padilla, A. (2007). Social cognition, ethnic identity, and ethnic specific strategies for coping with threat due to prejudice and discrimination. In C. Willis Esqueda (Ed.), *Nebraska Symposium on Motivation: Vol. 53. Motivational aspects of prejudice and racism*. Springer.

Parker, K. F., MacDonald, J. M., Alpert, G. P., Smith, M. R., & Piquero, A. R. (2004). A contextual study of racial profiling. *American Behavioral Scientist, 47*, 943–962.

Prosise, T. O., & Johnson, A. (2004). Law enforcement and crime on Cops and World's Wildest Police Videos: Anecdotal form and the justification of racial profiling. *Western Journal of Communication, 68*, 72–91.

Ramirez, D., McDevitt, J., & Farrell, A. (2000). *A resource guide on racial profiling data collection systems: Promising practices and lessons learned*. Washington, DC: U.S. Department of Justice. NCJ 184768.

Reitzel, J. D., Rice, S. K., & Piquero, A. R. (2004). Lines and shadows: Perceptions of racial profiling and the Hispanic experience. *Journal of Criminal Justice, 32*, 607–616.

Ruby, C. L., & Brigham, J. C. (1996). A criminal schema: The role of chronicity, race, and socioeconomic status on law enforcement officials' perceptions of others. *Journal of Applied Social Psychology, 26*, 95–111.

Sidanius, J., Levin, S., & Pratto, F. (1998). Hierarchical group relations, institutional terror, and the dynamics of the criminal justice system. In J. L. Eberhardt & S. T. Fiske (Eds.), *Confronting racism: The problem and the response* (pp. 136–165). Thousand Oaks, CA: Sage.

Takaki, R. (1993). *A different mirror: A history of multicultural America*. New York: Little, Brown.

Tomaskovic-Devey, D., Mason, M., & Zingraff, M. (2004), Looking for the driving while black phenomena: Conceptualizing racial bias processes and their associated distributions. *Police Quarterly, 7*, 3–29.

Tomic, A., & Hakes, J. H. (2004). *Case dismissed: New evidence in racial profiling*. Retrieved November 15, 2004 from http://ssrn.com/abstract=618122.

Torres, C. C., & Applewhite, S. R. (2004). Mexican American attitudes towards crime: A border study. *Journal of Ethnicity in Criminal Justice, 2*, 47–65.

Totman, M., & Steward, D. (2006, February). *Searching for consent: An analysis of racial profiling data in Texas*. Austin, TX: Texas Criminal Justice Coalition.

Traffic Stops Statistics Study Act (2001). S. 19. Retrieved June 7, 2006 from http://www.thomas.loc.gov.

Tyler, T. R. (2005). Policing in Black and White: Ethnic differences in trust and confidence in police. *Police Quarterly, 8*, 322–342.

Uhlmann, E., Dasgupta, N., Elgueta, A., Greenwald, A. G., & Swanson, J. (2002). Subgroup prejudice based on skin color among Hispanics in the United States and Latin America. *Social Cognition, 20*, 198–225.

United States Census Bureau. (2000). *Hispanic population of the United States*. Retrieved on April 15, 2005, from http://www.census.gov/population/www/socdemo/hispanic.html.

United States Commission on Civil Rights. (1970). *Mexican Americans and the administration of justice in the southwest*. Washington, DC: U. S. Government Printing Office. Publication Number 365-265-0-70-8.

Valdez, N. (1998). Ethnicity, class, and the Indigenous struggle for land in Guerrero, Mexico. In J. R. Wunder & C. Willis Esqueda (Eds.), *Native Americans: Interdisciplinary Perspectives*. New York: Taylor and Francis.

Valencia, R. A., Garcia, S. R., Flores, H., & Juarez, Jr., J. R. (2004). *Mexican Americans and the Law*. Tucson, AZ: The University of Arizona Press.

Weitzer, R. & Tuch, S. A. (2005). Determinants of public satisfaction with police. *Police Quarterly, 8*, 279–297.

Weyant, J. M. (2005). Implicit stereotyping of Hispanics: Development and validity of a Hispanic version of the Implicit Association Test. *Hispanic Journal of Behavioral Sciences, 27*, 355–363.

Williams, L. (2002, March 3). *Racial profiling North Dakota style*. Retrieved March 4, 2002 from www.argusleader.com/news/Sundayfeature.shtml.

Willis Esqueda, C. (1997). European American students' perceptions of crimes committed by five racial groups. *Journal of Applied Social Psychology, 27*, 1406–1420.

Wilson, G., Dunham, R., & Alpert, G. (2004). Prejudice in police profiling: Assessing an overlooked aspect in prior research. *American Behavioral Scientist, 47*, 896–909.

Wolfson, S. R. (2005). *Racial profiling in Texas Department of Public Safety motor vehicle searches: Race aware or race benign?* University of Texas at Dallas. Unpublished manuscript.

Zingraff, M. T. (2003, November). Studying racial profiling in North Carolina. *NIJ Journal*, No. 250, 48–50.

Legal Citations

City of Chicago v. Morales, 119 S. Ct. 1849 (1999).
United States v. Brignoni-Ponce, 422 U.S. 873 (1975).
United States v. Martinez-Fuerte, 428 U.S. 543 (1976).
United States v. Montero-Camargo, 208 F. 3d 1122 (9th Cir. 2000).

Unit II
Affirmative Action: Legal
Developments and Empirical Research

5
Affirmative Action and the Courts: From *Plessy* to *Brown* to *Grutter*, and Back?[1]

Mark R. Killenbeck

Affirmative action is one of the most controversial and least understood facets of American life. Proponents speak eloquently of programs that are morally justified as appropriate responses to a history of repression that relegated certain groups to, at best, second-class status. Viewed in this manner, affirmative actions allow us to in some small way negate the effects of past discrimination by assisting individuals based on their status as members of previously disfavored groups. If, as was often the case, individuals were denied employment or education opportunities based on their race or gender, an affirmative regime takes that reality into account. Its goal, to use one hackneyed but illustrative turn of phrase, is to produce a workforce or a student body that "looks like America." And that objective is achieved by using membership in a favored group as a criterion, perhaps even as the determinative one, in the decision-making process.

Critics argue in turn that affirmative action violates core American values. This is, after all, a nation that believes (with at best slight apologies to the original draftsman and the original understanding) that "all persons are created equal." And it is one that has given legal force to that declaration of principle through the constitutional guarantee that each individual is entitled to "the equal protection of the laws." Once again, the essence of this claim is perhaps best seen in a phrase, in this instance one taken (ironically) from the first Justice Harlan's eloquent dissenting opinion in *Plessy v. Ferguson* (1896). "Our Constitution is color-blind, and neither knows nor tolerates classes among citizens. In respect of civil rights, all citizens are equal before the law" (*Plessy*, 163 U.S. at 559).

---

[1] Portions of this chapter have been taken from or are based on two prior works and are used here with the permission of the publishers. They are:

Killenbeck, M. R. (1999). Pushing things up to their first principles: Reflections on the values of affirmative action. *California Law Review, 87*(6), 1299–1407.

Killenbeck, M. R. (2004). *Affirmative action and diversity: The beginning of the end? Or the end of the beginning?* Princeton, NJ: Educational Testing Service.

The ETS publication was a volume in their series Policy Information Perspectives. It is no longer available in print, but may be accessed, read, and printed from the ETS Web site at: http://www.ets.org/Media/Research/pdf/PICAFFACTNDIVSTY.pdf

The debate is longstanding. It has also been appropriately described as "intractable" (Fisher & Devins, 1993, p. 283), "stalled" (Becker, 1993, p. 93), and "sterile" (Farber, 1994, p. 894). Indeed, there are any number of individuals who believe that it makes little or no sense to discuss these matters further. "All the relevant material is known to people of good will on both sides; continued discussion of it has very little practical effect beyond educating successive generations of adversaries" (Becker, 1993, p. 93).

The editors of this volume and the authors contributing to it obviously disagree. We believe that there are better ways to think about these matters, creative lines of inquiry that illuminate the values that should inform affirmative action, the manner in which the courts should assess it, and whether our society should accept or reject these programs. My task is then arguably a simple one, focusing on a small number of interrelated questions. What is the law of affirmative action, at least as matters stand today? What are the assumptions that the courts have made and should make when confronted with challenges to affirmative action measures? In particular, how should the equal protection guarantee be interpreted in a society within which justice and fair play have, in certain key instances, been the exception rather than the rule? And how should policy makers proceed in the light of what the courts have told us?

The questions are simple. But the answers are infinitely more complex. As matters now stand,[2] the law of affirmative action is controlled by a small number of decisions by the Supreme Court of the United States, in particular *Grutter v. Bollinger* (2003) and *Gratz v. Bollinger* (2003). Both involved policies and practices at the University of Michigan, which argued vigorously that a racially, ethnically, and socially diverse student body is the sine qua non of excellence, an essential means by which each participant in the educational process maximizes educational attainment and personal and social development.

The Court agreed. Writing for what was admittedly a bare majority in *Grutter*, which focused on the policy employed by the University's Law School, Justice Sandra Day O'Connor announced that the higher education community does indeed have "a compelling interest in attaining a diverse student body" (p. 329). The nation's colleges and universities, both public and private,[3] "may accordingly

---

[2] The qualification is an important one. The Supreme Court now has before it two cases involving the use of racial preferences in the assignment of students in K-12 public schools. They were argued together on December 4, 2006. The decisions will be announced before this book comes to print. Predictions in such matters are at best risky. But based on the questions asked during argument it seems highly unlikely that a majority of the Court will be inclined to extend the logic of *Grutter* and *Gratz* and sustain the programs at issue. More to the point, as I note later in this chapter, these and future cases will be decided by a Court that has changed in what will likely prove to be fundamental and important respects with the retirement of Justice Sandra Day O'Connor and her replacement by Justice Samuel Alito. And that Court remains free to change its mind.

[3] The Michigan cases obviously involved public institutions, and the legal focus was the Fourteenth Amendment, which governs only public actors. The Court made it clear, however, that the analysis is the same under Title VI of the Civil Rights Act, which does apply to private actors.

take the group identity of an individual into account when they make the decision to admit or reject an application, provided they undertake a highly individualized, holistic review of each file, giving serious consideration to all the ways an individual might contribute to a diverse educational environment" (p. 337). The importance of how that process operates was reaffirmed in *Gratz*, within which the Court considered, and rejected, a different policy employed by Michigan's College of Literature, Science, and the Arts.

So far so good. Given the importance of diversity as a social or educational goal, it now appears that the equal protection guarantee will occasionally yield in the face of an appropriately structured and properly implemented plan of affirmative action. The Constitution, it seems, is not in fact color or gender blind, and at least for some purposes truly equal treatment will not be the norm.

Unfortunately, there is a wide gap between the rhetoric and rulings of the Court majority, which track the views of affirmative action's champions, and the degree to which affirmative action has achieved public acceptance. The importance of diversity and the need for affirmative action is an article of faith in the higher education community and is widespread in business and industry. I, for example, have been unable to find any mainstream higher education institution or advocacy group that does not believe that diversity is a fundamental educational value. The president of the one possible exception, Texas A&M University, did declare in the wake of *Grutter* that "Students at Texas A&M should be admitted as individuals, on personal merit, and on no other basis" (Arnone, 2003, p. 17). However, even that supposed rejection of affirmative action was a qualified one, as it is quite clear that A&M embraces the diversity principle. For at the same time that A&M announced that it would not grant preferences it stressed that it would nevertheless "redouble" its efforts to "admit and enroll more minority students" (Arnone, 2003, p. 17).

The support for affirmative action and diversity is then widespread in certain quarters. But it is not by any means universal, even within higher education, where the enthusiasm for the concept has been most pronounced. Dr. Carl Cohen, a professor of philosophy at the University of Michigan, has, for example, argued vigorously and at length that affirmative action on the basis of race is wrong. He believes that the policies his institution has embraced are "ugly and unfair" and constitute a form of "well-meaning racism [that] is unhappily but widely ensconced" (Cohen, 2003, p. ix). Many have attacked Cohen and his views, as they have another individual who has tried to cast doubt on the efficacy of these programs, Professor Richard H. Sander of the UCLA School of Law.

Sander argues that "In the law school system as a whole, racial preferences no longer operate as a lifeline vital to preserve the tenuous foothold of Blacks in legal education. Quite the contrary: racial preferences have the systematic effect of corroding Black achievement and reducing the number of Black lawyers" (Sander, 2005, pp. 474–475). His analysis, as Professors Crosby and Smith (pp. 123–125) point out, was based on a set of assumptions he made as he analyzed the records of some 27,000 law students. It has also been subjected to extensive and occasionally harsh criticism, a level of response that did not follow in the wake of studies that spoke in favor of affirmative action and posited that diversity does have important, positive outcomes for students who are enrolled at institutions or in programs that have a diverse student body. The point here is not to take issue with Sander, or with his critics.[4] It is rather that the level of support for diversity within the higher education community is such that its opponents are few and far between.

The same cannot be said of the body politic. A nationwide poll conducted in January, 2006 asked, "What do you think should happen to affirmative action programs? Should they be ended now, should they be phased out over the next few years, or should affirmative action programs be continued for the foreseeable future?" Only 36% of those responding agreed that such programs should be continued, while 45% stated that they should be ended now (12%) or phased out (33%) (CBS News Poll, 2006). In a similar vein, a recent proposal by the American Bar Association (ABA) to change its accreditation standards for law schools and require that they document the steps they are taking to achieve a diverse student body has drawn harsh criticism.

Indeed, various individuals and groups argued that the ABA's position justified revoking its authority to serve as the accrediting body for legal education when its authorization as such was up for renewal in 2006 (Mangan, 2006). That did not happen. But the Department of Education did not grant the ABA the usual five year term. Rather, it extended its authority for only eighteen months, an action that observers have characterized as putting the ABA on a "short leash" with regard to matters of affirmative action and diversity.

Both of these examples are consistent with what generally happens when questions about affirmative action are referred to the electorate. In California and Washington State, for example, popular referenda have led to measures such as California's Proposition 209, a state constitutional amendment declaring that "The state shall not discriminate against, or grant preferential treatment to, any individual on the basis of race, sex, color, ethnicity, or national origin in the operation of public employment, public education, or public contracting" (Cal. Const. art. I, § 31(a)). Both are also in line with a parallel phenomenon, within which views shift in fundamental ways when the questions posed are altered. In California and Washington, the measures presented to the electorate paired affirmative action and discrimination in ways that conveyed the message that the two were inevitably the same. In 1997, however, voters in Houston rejected a measure that would have ended affirmative action programs. That initiative originally created the impression

---

[4] I did examine most of the studies then available in an earlier article and offered some thoughts on their strengths and weaknesses (Killenbeck, 1999, pp. 1323–1332). Time constraints did not allow me to repeat that process for this chapter. I am not accordingly in a position to assess whether Sander is right or wrong or whether, for that matter, the account of Professors Crosby and Smith of the current state of the evidence is, at least for me, convincing. I will note, however, that my sense is that the available evidence is more complex than diversity's advocates would lead us to believe. For example, as I stressed in my earlier article (Killenbeck, 1999, p. 1327), the picture that William Bowen and Derek Bok painted in their important study, *The Shape of the River* (1998), was not uniformly positive, a reality that is not apparent in virtually all of the discussions of that book that one finds in the diversity literature.

that affirmative action and discrimination were synonymous. But it was changed to eliminate that connection, a shift in emphasis that was a critical factor in a vote that "put a surprising brake on a national movement that has often seemed to have the momentum of an unstoppable freight train" (Verhovek, 1997, p. A1).

The most recent and by far most telling example of this phenomenon occurred in November 2006, when the voters of Michigan resoundingly approved an amendment to their state constitution that prohibits any preferences on the basis of race, color, ethnicity, national origin, or gender. The "Michigan Civil Rights Initiative" was the brainchild of one of affirmative action's most vehement and persistent foes, Ward Connerly. And the point-person for the organization that sought its approval was the lead plaintiff in one of the two University of Michigan cases, Jennifer Gratz (Schmidt, 2006). The University and its allies fought the initiative at every turn, investing substantial resources (by one account, some $4.6 million) and their arguably considerable prestige as affirmative action's most eloquent and successful champions. Their failure to persuade the citizens of their state that their cause was just was, by any reasonable standard, a stunning defeat. And the inability of these particular advocates to carry the day in an electoral referendum speaks volumes about the reluctance of the people themselves to embrace the cause of affirmative action and diversity.

What are we to make of this? I suspect that a significant part of the problem lies in the realities I noted at the outset of this chapter. Affirmative action is widely discussed but only imperfectly understood. More fundamentally, the debate about affirmative action poses a conflict between two fundamental American values. There is on the one hand the belief that the Constitution is, or at least in normal circumstances should be, color and gender blind. In particular, there is a deep and abiding commitment to individual merit, the notion that each person should be free to succeed or fail on the basis of his or her own abilities and skills. There is at the same time widespread acknowledgment that we do not live in a perfect society. We can agree to disagree about the extent to which invidious discrimination persists today. But it is undeniable that what the courts characterize as the "present effects of past discrimination" persist, the unfortunate consequences of regimes within which certain groups were relegated to the economic, social, and educational margins. In those instances, so the argument goes, it is both fair and appropriate to "level the playing field."

It is in this respect that I see the debate about affirmative action as a progression: from the separate but equal regime of *Plessy*, to the nondiscrimination principle in *Brown v. Board of Education of Topeka* (1954), to the embrace of diversity and, by necessary implication, the approval of a limited and arguably positive form of discrimination in *Grutter* and *Gratz*. Two threads, each of which sounds in both law and policy, run through this sequence of decisions. The first is the extent to which we should accept or reject the Harlan dissent in *Plessy*: In respect of civil rights are, or should, all citizens be equal before the law? The second explores whether the social sciences can help us as we decide these matters. For there is another telling progression in this sequence of cases, from the arguably total absence of social science data in *Plessy*, to the initial and at the time intensely controversial embrace of social science studies as a part of constitutional discourse in *Brown*, to the pervasive and, at least for some, the dispositive role that such materials played in *Grutter* and *Gratz*.

Definitions, and Their Significance

One of the central problems in this area is that our understanding of what affirmative action means has changed over time. And the nature of the change has a very great deal to do with how people react when they think about or are confronted with an affirmative action measure.

What we now know as affirmative action came into being in 1961,[5] when President John F. Kennedy issued Executive Order 10925, a measure that contained what one scholar has justifiably described as a "vague and almost casual reference to 'affirmative action'" (Graham, 1990, p. 41). Most observers understood that the Order was a modest, largely symbolic first step in the new administration's efforts to eventually outlaw discrimination. And they sensed that the phrase "affirmative action," to the extent they thought of it at all, was shorthand for procedural fairness. That is, it described a simple obligation to treat individuals appropriately by taking "affirmative action to ensure that applicants are employed, and that employees are treated during employment, without regard to their race, creed, color, or national origin" (Executive Order 10925, 1961, p. 1977). As the person who introduced the phrase into modern race and gender relations observed, "I put the word 'affirmative' in there because I was searching for something that would give a sense of positiveness to performance under that executive order" (Taylor, 1995, p. 36).

The assumption at the time was that an affirmative action program was a procedural measure, a means to open an application process and ensure that it recognized individual merit so that all qualified applicants could compete. The Executive Order mandating its adoption never defined the term affirmative action. Thoughtful contemporary observers speculated that it "Presumably . . . meant such things as advertising the fact, seeking out qualified applicants from sources where they might be found, and the like" (Glazer, 1975, p. 46). The major legislative and regulatory initiatives undertaken in its wake seemed to verify that this was what it intended. For example, Title VII of the Civil Rights Act of 1964 made it unlawful for any employer to discriminate on the basis of "race, color, religion,

---

[5] The term actually surfaced much earlier, in the National Labor Relations Act, which authorized the National Labor Relations Board to order an employer that committed an unfair labor practice "to take such affirmative action including reinstatement of employees with or without back pay, as will effectuate the policies" of the Act (National Labor Relations Act, 1935, § 10.) "Affirmative action" accordingly actually first became an important factor for the Court in decisions probing whether, for example, the Board had the authority to order reinstatement of individuals who had engaged in illegal conduct (*NLRB v. Fansteel Metallurgical Corp.*, 1939), or possessed "unlimited" authority to impose "punitive" measures (*Republic Steel Corp. v. NLRB,* 1940), both of which it answered in the negative.

sex, or national origin" and stated expressly it did not "require . . . preferential treatment" on the basis of race.

Thus, as one contemporary commentator stressed, "read together, the various measures 'indicate that the overarching policy . . . is to insure the neutrality of the . . . process' to insure that . . . decisions are made on *merit*, with neither positive nor negative reference to minority determinative characteristics" (*Harvard Law Review*, 1971, pp. 1300–1301). A university or employer might, for example, undertake aggressive recruitment efforts to document a good faith effort to end prior discriminatory practices. The decisions it made about applicants, however, and their subsequent treatment by the institution, would be governed by the traditional assumption that individual merit controlled. Indeed, during the early years of affirmative action many of its proponents maintained, vigorously, that "Any institution that gives preferences . . . on the basis of sex, race, or ethnic origin is violating the law" (Sandler, 1975, p. 402).

There were compelling reasons for embracing affirmative action as a matter of positive public policy. The persistent failure of equal opportunities to translate into equal actual participation led a number of individuals to argue that something more was needed (Edwards & Zaretsky, 1975; Hughes, 1968; Young, 1964). These claims often found a receptive audience, especially during the halcyon days of the Great Society. In a commencement address delivered at Howard University in 1965, President Lyndon B. Johnson declared that "We seek not just freedom but opportunity . . . not just legal equity but human ability, not just equality as a right and a theory but equality as a fact and equality as a result" (Johnson, 1966, p. 636) This pledge, "to frame a society within which equal opportunity is essential, but not enough, not enough" eventually became a regulatory reality with the promulgation of what became known as Revised Order No. 4. It required anyone who received federal funds provide "an evaluation of opportunities for the utilization of minority group personnel," including "specific steps" to guarantee equal opportunity and "when there are deficiencies . . . specific goals and timetables for the prompt achievement of full and equal employment opportunity" (Revised Order No. 4, Part 60-2).[6]

The transformation of affirmative action from a procedural mandate to a substantive goal was then the product of two complementary yet contradictory motives. One was the need to ensure that both the reality and effects of deliberate discrimination would end. This had an important practical dimension, since an affirmative action mandate that did not produce, or at least was not in some sense required to produce, actual, measurable results invited the accusation that it was a "sham effort" (Leonard, 1990, p. 49). A second, less commendable impulse was the need for organizations subject to an affirmative action mandate to demonstrate progress to both their government overseers and a skeptical public. The theory was quite simple: "Neutrality . . . [or] even the espousal of equal opportunity,

---

[6] The Order was a Nixon administration initiative and reflected the strange mixture of enlightened civil rights instincts and cynical political calculation that characterized Richard Nixon's record in these matters.

will not overcome the years of . . . discrimination to which minorities have been subjected. Where no affirmative action is taken . . . as was the prevailing situation prior to 1969, recruitment and upgrading of minority individuals proceeds at an extremely slow pace" (United States Commission on Civil Rights, 1970, p. 189).

As a result, numerical objectives became very specific performance criteria against which progress was measured. The goals themselves were not, in any meaningful legal sense, quotas. They tended, nevertheless, to operate inexorably in that manner when managers mistook mere statistical progress for appropriate accomplishment. As Lawrence Silberman, Undersecretary of Labor from 1970 to 1973, explained, "We wished to create a generalized, firm, but gentle pressure to balance the residue of discrimination. Our use of numerical standards in pursuit of equal opportunity . . . led ineluctably to the very quotas, guaranteeing equal results, we initially wished to avoid" (Silberman, 1977, p. 14).

The transition from procedure to substance was especially evident in higher education. Ironically, the initial commitment to procedural affirmative action seemed to be nothing more than an appropriate expression of the manner in which higher education had always operated. For example, in an early statement on affirmative action the American Association of University Professors stressed that the "first test of equal opportunity" is that there be "standards of competence and qualification . . . set independently of the actual choices made" (1984, p. 83). At least in theory then, any affirmative action that involved anything more than, for example, simply broadening the pool from which one selected the best qualified candidate should have been characterized as fundamentally at odds with both the academic ethic and higher education's understandings of its legal obligations. The assumption was that overt discrimination would be eliminated and, to the extent positive actions were called for, higher education would "correct" its past effects by simply "stimulating the hiring of minorities and women" (Steele & Green, 1976, p. 414).

Of course, most people understood that the realities of hiring and admissions were infinitely more complex. Some of the distinctions traditionally drawn were benign. Others were indefensible by any possible standard. The preference for admitting "legacies," that is, the children of often wealthy graduates, may deny opportunity to someone with arguably superior credentials. However, such plans are understandable institutional imperatives, especially for private universities that depend greatly on the generosity of their alumni. The naked desire to exclude women and African Americans, on the other hand, often based on spurious "scientific" evidence, reflected the worst impulses of the American people.

Many influential actors in academy argued accordingly for a different approach to hiring and admissions. In 1975, for example, the Carnegie Commission on Higher Education defined affirmative action as "actions to eliminate discrimination: creation of more adequate pools of talent, active searches for talent wherever it exists, revision of policies and practices that permitted or abetted discrimination, development of expectations for a staff whose composition does not reflect the impacts of discrimination, provision of judicial processes to hear complaints, and the making of decisions without improper regard for sex, race, or ethnic origin" (p. 2). This approach was arguably purely procedural. It spoke largely of how one treated individuals and the operational theory remained mere elimination of discrimination. But it is worth noting that the Commission condemned only the "improper" consideration of group identity, a formulation that left open ample channels for a program within which these traits became positive factors in the decision-making process.

In a similar vein, the AAUP "commended" plans "which are entirely affirmative, i.e., plans in which 'preference' and 'compensation' are words of positive connotation rather than words of condescension or *noblesse oblige*—preference for the more highly valued candidate and compensation for past failures to reach the actual market of intellectual resources available to higher education" (1984, p. 82). Indeed, it also took direct aim at the notion that there were any defined, or even definable, dimensions to merit, declaring that:

We cannot assume uncritically that present criteria of merit and procedures for their application have yielded the excellence intended; to the extent that the use of certain standards has resulted in the exclusion of women and minorities from professional positions in higher education, or their inclusion only in token proportions to their availability, the academy has denied itself access the critical mass of intellectual vitality represented by these groups. We believe that such criteria must be considered deficient on the very grounds of excellence itself. (AAUP, 1984, p. 83)

To their credit, many colleges and universities recognized and accounted for the fundamental contradiction in affirmative action: in order to "get beyond" race or gender, institutions otherwise dedicated to decisions purely on the merits needed to expressly take race or gender into account. As one individual observed, "Affirmative action can only have the effect that is hoped for (the effect that would justify it) if employers, boards of admissions, and the like are compelled (or compel themselves) to accept a significant proportion of applicants from minority groups—even if, after giving consideration to what would traditionally be regarded as their credentials, they must accept many whom they would otherwise have passed over" (Green, 1981, p. 14).

It is then one thing to assert that an institutional initiative simply levels the playing field so that all individuals may apply and be considered on an equal, nondiscriminatory basis. It is quite another to maintain that active consideration of race or gender in the admissions process is consistent with accepted norms designed to distinguish between applicants with similarly strong objective credentials. But that is precisely the distinction that arose when affirmative measures were transformed from a mandate for procedural fairness into some variation on what might properly be characterized as a substantive entitlement. Of course, all institutions, and virtually all proponents of affirmative action, deny vigorously that diversity initiatives do, or even should, create absolute preferences. The difficulty with these protestations is that actual practices often reveal that this is precisely the case, especially when tested in the unforgiving light of litigation. And it is these examples, more often than not, that have shaped much of both the public perception and judicial response to diversity initiatives.

In *Regents of the University of California v. Bakke* (1978), for example, the Court had before it an admissions policy adopted by the medical school at the

University of California, Davis. That program reserved, on what appeared to be an absolute basis, 16 of the 100 available slots for "disadvantaged" students, a term that became a proxy for racial minorities. The Court accepted the argument that it was constitutionally appropriate for a university to seek a diverse student body. It also found, quite properly, that the particular system at issue created a quota, admitting individuals on the basis of race rather than simply using racial identity as a possible "plus" factor in a truly individualized admissions process. I will discuss the details of the *Bakke* holding shortly. It is sufficient for current purposes to note that in the wake of that decision it seemed reasonable to assume that race could be taken into account as one factor in the admissions process, but that it could not become the driving force in such decisions.

Political and social pressures mounted and institutions found themselves pressed to attain diversity in the face of a dearth of otherwise qualified applicants. Those forces converged in *Hopwood v. Texas* (1996), in which the Court of Appeals for the Fifth Circuit was asked to hold that an admissions program employed by the University of Texas School of Law was consistent with *Bakke*. Unfortunately, the Texas program pursued a series of minority enrollment goals in ways that did not simply test the limits of the *Bakke* rationale, but actually embraced many of the characteristics the Court had expressly condemned. It created a two-track system within which the applications of non-minorities and those of the favored minorities, African Americans and Mexican Americans, were evaluated separately (*Hopwood*, p. 936). Its numerical screening device, the "Texas Index," which reflected a composite of the applicant's undergraduate grade point average and score on the Law School Admissions Test, used two standards, one for White applicants and another for minority candidates. The law school also routinely adjusted these numerical standards to produce an entering class that closely approximated its racial goals (*Hopwood*, p. 936).

Both the district court and the court of appeals had little difficulty rejecting an admissions program that the law school itself appeared to concede was indefensible by abandoning it prior to trial (Elliott, 1994, p. 10). The damage had nevertheless been done. The law school at a major university—indeed, one of the better law schools in the nation—had adopted and defended an affirmative admissions program that could not possibly be viewed as legal in the light of *Bakke*. In doing so, it gave a hostile court the opportunity to castigate the institution, reject diversity as a compelling educational goal, and argue that the fragmented nature of the *Bakke* Court meant that the Powell opinion was not in fact binding precedent. The stage was accordingly set for what would follow, a major national debate about affirmative action and diversity that would eventually find its way back to the Supreme Court.

The Michigan Approach

The policies under attack in *Grutter* and *Gratz* were premised on the assumption that for the purposes of fashioning a diverse student body, and making available the educational benefits that presumably inhere in such an environment, race matters. The university asserted that the diversity it sought is integral to its educational mission, within which diversity and excellence were inextricably linked. Moreover, it argued that it could not achieve meaningful diversity absent the active consideration of race in the admissions process.

At least as a legal matter, these assumptions appeared to violate what has been deemed by the Court—and in most instances by civil rights advocates—to be perhaps the most fundamental guarantee in our constitutional system: the Fourteenth Amendment's promise that each individual is entitled to "the equal protection of the laws." In particular, they seemed at fundamental odds with the premise that the color of one's skin simply cannot and should not matter when deciding how to allocate the benefits and burdens of daily life. The Constitution, the Court has emphasized, "protects persons, not groups" (*Adarand Constructors, Inc. v. Pena*, p. 227). This means that all "government action based on race—a group classification long recognized to be in most circumstances irrelevant and therefore prohibited—should" as a result "be subjected to detailed judicial inquiry to ensure that the personal right to equal protection of the laws has not been infringed" (*Adarand Constructors*, p. 227).

The Court has therefore insisted that we treat all racial classifications as constitutionally suspect and assesses them within the confines of its most rigorous analytic framework, strict scrutiny. This approach requires that the entity wishing to take race into account have a "compelling" reason for doing so and must employ the "least restrictive means," that is, demonstrate that there is simply no other way to attain that goal. This is an analytic regime whose demands—and the outcomes of virtually all of the cases within which it has been applied—have led some individuals to postulate that it is "strict in theory, fatal in fact." Indeed, the strictures imposed by this legal standard played an undeniably important role in what the Court did and did not hold the first time it assessed the constitutionality of affirmative action and diversity.

In the wake of *Bakke*, most educators assumed that race-based affirmative action admissions programs in higher education should be assessed within and generally were condoned by the analytic framework created by Justice Powell's opinion in that case. But the *Bakke* Court was deeply divided. Five different justices wrote opinions, within which a majority arguably agreed that the University of California, Davis Medical School had "a substantial interest that legitimately may be served by a properly devised admissions program involving the competitive consideration of race and ethnic origin" (*Bakke*, p. 320). A different group of five, however, found that the University had failed to establish that the particular approach it had adopted was "necessary to promote a substantial state interest" (*Bakke*, p. 320). The common link was Justice Powell, whose opinion came to be regarded as that of the Court.

The essential consideration for Justice Powell was his belief that universities had a compelling interest in pursuing what he characterized as "genuine" diversity. In a key passage, he declared:

It is not an interest in simple ethnic diversity, in which a specified percentage of the student body is in effect guaranteed to be members of selected ethnic groups, with the remaining percentage an undifferentiated aggregation of students. The diversity that furthers a compelling state interest encompasses a far broader array of qualifications and characteristics of which racial or ethnic origin is but a single though important element. Petitioner's special admissions program, focused solely on ethnic diversity, would hinder rather than further attainment of genuine diversity. (*Bakke*, p. 313)

The focal point was then the notion that the pursuit of a diverse student body was an appropriate and respected academic goal. Drawing on both the academic literature and the Court's own opinions, Justice Powell declared that "our tradition and experience lend support to the view that the contribution of diversity is substantial" (*Bakke*, pp. 316–317). And the linchpin in his analysis was an expectation that institutions opting to pursue diversity would in fact do so in the same way that Harvard College did, that is by simply "pay[ing] some attention to distribution among many types and categories of students" (*Bakke*, pp. 316–317).

Unfortunately, Justices Brennan and Marshall believed that the Davis program was appropriate. This disagreement with Justice Powell produced dissenting opinions that at least appeared to leave Justice Powell alone in his embrace of the diversity principle. As I have argued elsewhere, that was almost certainly not the case (Killenbeck, 1999). Nevertheless, the fragmented nature of the *Bakke* meant that it was subjected to sustained and increasing successful attacks in cases in which the various elements of the Powell opinion were debated. In each instance, the emphasis was on the threshold question: Is diversity a compelling interest?

Major decisions in the federal courts of appeals went both ways. Perhaps the most telling blow was struck in *Hopwood* when a panel of the Court of Appeals for the Fifth Circuit characterized Justice Powell's *Bakke* opinion as the work of a single Justice that did not command the support of a majority of the Court. Having freed itself from the strictures of *Bakke*, that panel then felt free to declare that "the use of race to achieve a diverse student body, whether as a proxy for permissible characteristics, simply cannot be a state interest compelling enough to meet the steep standard of strict scrutiny" (*Hopwood*, p. 948). A panel in the Eleventh Circuit seemed to agree in *Johnson v. Board of Regents of the University of Georgia* (2001), invalidating Georgia's program, albeit expressly declining to actually hold that diversity is, or is not, a compelling interest. But in *Smith v. University of Washington Law School* (2000), a panel in the Ninth Circuit did reach that question, relying on the Powell opinion as it held that "the attainment of a diverse student body 'is a constitutionally permissible goal for an institution of higher education'" (p. 1197, quoting *Bakke*) Then, in the decision ultimately reviewed by the Court, a narrow majority of the full Sixth Circuit, believing it was bound by *Bakke*, held that the University of Michigan "has a compelling state interest in achieving a diverse student body" (*Grutter*, 2002, p. 742).

The Court had previously refused to enter the lists, denying review in *Hopwood* and *Smith* when one or more of the parties in those cases asked that it exercise its discretion and hear the case. However, it did accept the Michigan cases, which were seen as ideal vehicles for a number of reasons.

One of those might have been one Justice O'Connor mentioned in *Grutter*: the need to resolve the conflict among the various federal courts of appeals created by divergent rulings that made such policies constitutional or unconstitutional depending not on their intrinsic legal merits, but rather on the location of the institution. But that rationale, while important, was almost certainly not determinative. Rather, I believe the critical consideration was the decision by the University of Michigan to defend its efforts vigorously and in a manner that set it apart from the other universities. For, more than any other institution, Michigan tried to make the debate about diversity a matter of both law and educational policy. As part of that effort it mobilized a broad cross section of the educational, professional, business, and military communities, all of whom asserted at length that diversity was an important principle. Michigan also argued that a combination of intuitive experience and extensive social science evidence supported the conclusion that, as a matter of constitutional law, the attainment of a diverse student body is a compelling education interest.

The catalyst for the decision to proceed in this manner may well have been a series of conferences sponsored by the Harvard Civil Rights Project. In particular, one held on May 9, 1997 brought together both leading social scientists and the attorneys who would represent Michigan in the lawsuits that were about to be filed. The focus at that and subsequent meetings, and in a series of studies and publications that followed, was narrow and specific: What is the evidence regarding the actual impact of diversity on student outcomes? And how might attorneys best employ it to frame the issues for a confrontation that seemed virtually certain to lead to a decision by the Supreme Court?

The Court's use of social science materials has a long, albeit occasionally controversial history. In *Brown*, for example, the Court stressed that "Whatever may have been the extent of psychological knowledge at the time of *Plessy v. Ferguson*," the conclusion that "segregation of White and colored children in public schools has a detrimental effect upon the colored children" is now "amply supported by modern authority" (p. 494, n. 11). Critics of Brown spoke out against a decision that was "based neither on the history of the [Fourteenth A]mendment nor on precise textual analysis but on" the "highly evanescent grounds" of "psychological knowledge" (Swisher, 1958, p. 158). Nevertheless, it is clear that the Court believed then, and continues to assume, that social science materials can play a role in its decision-making process. Indeed, this is an area where Judge Richard Posner's observations about the limitations of constitutional theory and the "need for empirical knowledge" are especially apt, for "[t]he big problem" surrounding the debate about diversity "is not lack of theory, but lack of knowledge—lack of the very knowledge that academic research, rather than the litigation process, is best designed to produce" (Posner, 1998, p. 3).

Michigan's decision to make social science materials a centerpiece in its defense of its policies was logical given the legal landscape it faced. The *Hopwood* panel had expressed its views regarding the continuing force of *Bakke*. But unless and until the Supreme Court itself repudiated that holding, it seemed appropriate to assume that it remained the law of the land and that diversity remained a compelling educational interest. Indeed, at least two members of the Court had indicated, in two different guises, that this was a safe bet.

In her concurring opinion in *Wygant v. Jackson Board of Education* (1986), Justice O'Connor spoke with approval of the "goal of promoting racial diversity among the faculty" and observed that "although its precise contours are uncertain, a state interest in the promotion of racial diversity has been found sufficiently 'compelling,' at least in the context of higher education, to support the use of racial considerations in furthering that interest" (p. 288). Assuming, as we must, that Justice O'Connor took some care when she wrote this, a statement simply describing one possible view expressed by a single member of the Court would have read quite differently. Indeed, it would certainly not have been followed by pointed speculation about whether "other governmental interests which have been relied upon in the lower courts but which have not been passed on here" would eventually be found "sufficiently 'important' or 'compelling' to sustain the use of affirmative action policies" (*Wygant*, p. 286).

Justice Scalia, in turn, had observed that Justice Powell's *Bakke* opinion is one that "we must work with as the law of the land" (Scalia, 1979, p. 148). Of course, he spoke at the time as then-Professor Scalia and he criticized the Powell opinion as "thoroughly unconvincing as an honest, hard-minded, reasoned analysis of an important provision of the Constitution" (p. 148). Nevertheless, his characterization of the Powell opinion as the law of the land was a common theme until *Hopwood* burst on the scene.

The other option available to Michigan was to argue that the admissions systems were justified within a line of cases, in particular *City of Richmond v. J. A. Croson Company* (1989) and *Adarand*, within which the Court accepted a compensatory or remedial purpose as a rationale for affirmative action. That is, the Court will occasionally allow an entity to adopt a preference under the theory that a group has been harmed in the past and it is appropriate to now favor them in an attempt to either make up for what had happened or to cure the problems caused. This rule is quite narrow, as the Court has also insisted that the institution adopting a plan of this sort must demonstrate that it itself discriminated against the groups now favored. And it has required that there be clear, present negative effects that arise from those past transgressions. That is, there must be a "strong basis in evidence for [the] conclusion that remedial action [is] necessary" (*Wygant*, p. 277). Indeed, "the mere recitation of a 'benign' or legitimate purpose for a racial classification is entitled to little or no weight. . . . Racial classifications are suspect, and that means that simple . . . assurances of good intention cannot suffice" (*Croson*, p. 500).

Michigan did not, for obvious reasons, want to argue that one of the reasons it now took race into account in its admissions policies was that it had itself discriminated on that basis in the past, and that as a result its campus remained a hostile or unwelcoming place. Indeed, the University vigorously opposed an attempt to intervene in the litigation by a group that wished to make precisely those claims and wanted to place before the various courts hearing the cases what it believed to be evidence of past discrimination and present effects.

An argument for diversity, bolstered by strong social science evidence, was accordingly the best line of defense, both as a matter of law and for a number of important instrumental reasons. It was certainly consistent with Judge Posner's preference for a court having the benefit of actual knowledge about the actual

effects of a diverse learning environment. More importantly, the Michigan litigation became the catalyst for an extensive series of studies and reports on both
sides of the debate. The information generated appears to have been of considerable value, a point Justice O'Connor stressed when she noted with approval "the
expert studies and reports entered into evidence at trial" and the "numerous
studies [that] show that student body diversity promotes learning outcomes, and
'better prepares students for an increasingly diverse workforce and society, and
better prepares them as professionals'" (*Grutter*, p. 330).

The studies accordingly arguably served certain important instrumental purposes. They freed the majority from the burden of making their acceptance of the
University's diversity rationale an exercise in pure deference.[7] As a result, they
made the case for diversity something more than a simple article of faith, one
otherwise skeptical Justices might have had difficulty accepting given higher
education's prior transgressions, in particular those documented in the *Bakke*
and *Hopwood* litigation. They also began a process that may ultimately be of
extraordinary importance, albeit one that may prove to be a double-edged sword,
by grounding the debate about the value of diversity in its actual impact on all
participants in the educational process, rather than admittedly important but
nevertheless elusive notions of equality or fairness.

The Michigan Decisions

The divisive nature of the diversity debate was on full display in *Grutter* and
Gratz. The majority opinion in *Grutter* commanded five votes: those of Justice
O'Connor, who wrote for the Court, and of Justices Stevens, Souter, Ginsburg,
and Breyer. Four members of the Court dissented: Chief Justice Rehnquist and
Justices Scalia, Kennedy, and Thomas. Consistent with prior decisions involving
questions about the constitutionality of using race as a decision-making or deci-
sion-influencing criterion, the majority answered two questions. Does the use of
race in postsecondary admissions constitute a compelling interest? And are the
means employed by the University of Michigan Law School narrowly tailored,
that is, has the Law School shown that the only way to achieve its arguably
compelling objectives is to take race into account?

The answer in each instance was yes.

The first question was clearly the most important. That does not mean that the
narrow tailoring inquiry is not also significant. Indeed, experience has shown that
it is actually the more difficult question as a practical matter, given the manner in
which so many colleges and universities have structured and implemented their
affirmative admissions programs. But if the Court had not held that the pursuit of

---

[7] Justice O'Connor did, in an unfortunate passage, note the extent to which the Court had
traditionally deferred to the professional judgment of educators. But, as I will stress
shortly, her opinion was more searching than this brief aside implied.

a diverse student body was a compelling constitutional interest, the active consideration of race in the admissions process would have been foreclosed in all but the most extreme circumstances, those instances in which a specific institution was acting to remedy the current effects of its own past, intentional discrimination. It is accordingly important to understand exactly why the Court held what it did regarding the importance of diversity.

The core of the *Grutter* opinion on this point is the majority's declaration that "we endorse Justice Powell's view that student body diversity is a compelling state interest that can justify the use of race in university admissions" (p. 325) That is, as Justice O'Connor emphasized, the majority accepted the "educational judgment" that "diversity will, in fact, yield educational benefits" (p. 328). Those benefits, the Court stressed, are both "real" and "substantial" (p. 330). Diversity "promotes 'cross-racial understanding,' helps to break down racial stereotypes, and 'enables [students] to better understand persons of different races'" (p. 330, quoting the District Court). These outcomes are in turn "'both important and laudable,' because 'classroom discussion is livelier, more spirited, and simply more enlightening and interesting' when the students have 'the greatest possible variety of backgrounds'" (p. 330). In particular, both social science evidence and the positions taken by a wide spectrum of business and military leaders made it clear that "These benefits are not theoretical, but real" (*Grutter*, p. 330).

Much of the emphasis in *Grutter* was then on a point I have already stressed. The Court was not simply taking at face value supposedly good faith assertions by the college and university community that diversity is important. Justice O'Connor did speak of an "educational judgment . . . to which we defer" (p. 328). But the very next sentence in her opinion made the immediate and important transition to what I suspect was, at least for her, the crucial consideration: the fact that the University's "assessment that diversity will, in fact, yield educational benefits is substantiated by [the University] and" by the parties supporting it before the Court (*Grutter*, p. 328). That is, the University and a wide spectrum of educational, political, business, military, and social groups offered what the majority believed to be compelling evidence demonstrating that the benefits associated with diversity actually occur in each of the many distinctive educational environments that comprise the spectrum of postsecondary education.

This is not, then, the sort of deference one finds in, for example, prison cases where claims implicating what would otherwise be deemed fundamental rights, are assessed under the relaxed standard articulated in *Turner v. Safley* (1987), within which the Court asks only if the contested policy is "reasonably related to "legitimate penological concerns" (p. 89). Nor, for that matter, is it the sort of deference the Court has granted to college and university faculty when they make academic judgments, consistent with its recognition in *Board of Curators of the University of Missouri v. Horowitz* (1978) that "A school is an academic institution, not a courtroom or administrative hearing room" (p. 88).

The dissenting Justices did not see it this way. Justice Thomas, for example, condemned what he characterized as the majority's "unprecedented deference to the Law School—a deference antithetical to strict scrutiny" (*Grutter*, p. 350). Some commentators have agreed. But it is difficult to see just what the majority could have done to satisfy these critics. Justice O'Connor's discussion of the issue was lengthy. Moreover, her conclusion that the benefits of diversity were "substantial . . . not theoretical but real" was supported not simply by the assurances of the University, but by a body of evidence. There is, at least for me, ample room to argue whether the studies in fact established all that their champions envisioned.[8] Nevertheless, their presence before the Court made gave the majority the opportunity to maintain that their conclusions were something much more than a matter of blind deference.[9]

Michigan also argued that the active consideration of race was in turn essential given its belief that it was important to enroll a "critical mass" of minority students. The assumption was that it was necessary to achieve numbers "such that underrepresented minority students do not feel isolated or like spokespersons for their race" (*Grutter*, p. 319). That could not be accomplished without making racial identity one factor in the admissions decision. In the case of the Law School, for example, the evidence established that "the race of the applicants [must be considered] because a critical mass of underrepresented minority students could not be enrolled if admissions decisions were based primarily on undergraduate GPAs and LSAT scores" (*Grutter*, p. 320). The University argued, accordingly, that without active consideration of race in the admissions process "most of this Nation's finest institutions [would be forced] to choose between dramatic resegregation and completely abandoning standards that have made American higher education the envy of the world" (University of Michigan, 2002, p. 13).

---

[8] Indeed, for reasons I cannot possibly explain in this brief chapter, they almost certainly did not, at least at the graduate and professional level.

[9] Steve Willborn (this volume) argues that the social science materials were "secondary" and that the key element of the O'Connor opinion was its deference to the University. I may well agree with him on the first of these points, depending on how one defines primary and secondary for these purposes. Let me be blunt. All knowledgeable observers suspected, to the point of virtual certainty, and long before the cases were argued, much less decided, that Justices White, Souter, Ginsburg, and Breyer would side with the University and that Chief Justice Rehnquist and Justices Scalia, Kennedy, and Thomas would vote against it. This made Justice O'Connor's vote the key. Whether or not the social science evidence tipped the scale for her is an interesting question. I suspect that it played at least an important role. If nothing else, it allowed her to frame the resolution of a divisive constitutional question in ways that made it at least appear that the Court was not simply imposing its own vision on a skeptical society. In that respect it tracked the manner in which the social science materials were used by the Warren Court in *Brown*. Is that a primary or secondary matter? Does it matter? Those are questions for another time and another place. In the interim, as I note in the conclusion to this chapter, those who argue that the social science materials were determinative had best be careful about what they wish for

As indicated, the conclusion that diversity is indeed a compelling educational interest provides only a necessary first step. It was also essential for Michigan to demonstrate that it had embraced a constitutionally appropriate means toward that end. That is, the University needed to prove that "the means chosen 'fit . . . the compelling goal so closely that there is little or no possibility that the motive for the classification was illegitimate racial prejudice or stereotypes'" (*Grutter*, p. 333, quoting *Croson*).

The majority believed that the Law School's approach was narrowly tailored within each of the four parameters deemed necessary. The first and arguably most important of these was that it treated each applicant as an individual. The Law School, Justice O'Connor stressed, took race into account "in a flexible, nonmechanical way" (*Grutter*, p. 334). It "engages in a highly individualized, holistic review of each applicant's file, giving serious consideration to all the ways an applicant might contribute to a diverse educational environment" (*Grutter*, p. 337). The Law School also met three additional requirements. It had considered and rejected various race-neutral alternatives, believing them inconsistent with its educational mission and institutional objectives. Since there was in fact an individual review of each applicant's file, the system did not impose an "undue" burden on those non-minority applicants who were denied admission. And the Law School recognized that the policy should be limited in duration and subject to periodic review, ensuring that this "deviation from the norm of equal treatment" would be "'a temporary matter, a measure taken in the service of the goal of equality itself'" (*Grutter*, p. 342, quoting *Croson*).

This contrasted sharply with the method employed by Michigan's College of Literature, Science, and the Arts, which used a point system to make virtually all of the critical decisions involved when it accepted or rejected an applicant. Writing for the majority in *Gratz*, Chief Justice Rehnquist declared that "the University's policy, which automatically distributes 20 points, or one-fifth of the points needed to guarantee admission, to every single 'under-represented minority' applicant solely because of race, is not narrowly tailored to achieve the interest in educational diversity that [the University] claims justifies its program" (p. 270). The sheer size of the point allocation was clearly important. The Chief Justice stressed that "even if [a student's] 'extraordinary artistic talent rivaled that of Monet or Picasso, the applicant would receive, at most, five points'" under the Michigan system, while "every single under represented minority applicant . . . would automatically receive 20 points [simply] for submitting an application" (*Gratz*, p. 273).

The critical flaw was not, however, the point system itself, but rather the mindset it represented. By relying on this mechanical screening device, and by loosening its strictures only in rare circumstances, Michigan created the impression that characteristics mattered more than the individual. It was accordingly the failure to provide meaningful individualized consideration that doomed the policy at issue in *Gratz*, an approach that stood in stark contrast to the one employed by the Law School.

Arguably, the victory for affirmative consideration of race in the pursuit of a diverse student body was complete. Unlike *Bakke*, a clear majority of the *Grutter* Court agreed on the core holdings, the presence of a compelling interest and the approval of at least one admissions policy that met the narrow tailoring requirement.

It is nevertheless important to recognize just how narrow the decision was. Depending on how one characterizes the views of Chief Justice Rehnquist and Justice Kennedy, the vote for diversity was either 5 to 4 or 6 to 2. The Chief's dissent focused on the narrow tailoring inquiry and is arguably silent on the diversity question. Justice Kennedy in turn seemed to accept the diversity rationale, but did so on the basis of "precedents" that allow for acceptance of "a university's considered judgment" and "empirical data known to us" (*Grutter*, p. 388). These strike me as slender reeds on which to hang the conclusion that Justice Kennedy accepts fully the diversity rationale, especially in the context of a dissent that treats strict scrutiny as a "unitary formulation" and then excoriates the majority for its handling of the narrow tailoring inquiry.

As a practical matter then, *Grutter* represents a triumph that could easily be reversed by the death of Chief Justice Rehnquist and the retirement of Justice O'Connor. Predictions in this regard are always risky. The conservative scorn for Justice Souter, for example, shows that assumptions about how an individual will vote when actually on the Court do not always bear out. The available evidence nevertheless suggests strongly that both Chief Justice John Roberts and Justice Samuel Alito will be at best hard sells. And while the Rehnquist for Roberts shift marks no real change in the balance of power, the transition from O'Connor to Alito does not bode well for diversity's advocates in two cases that the Court has now agreed to hear, both of which extend the rule and logic of *Grutter* by applying the principles articulated in that decision in the K–12 context.

These two decisions are *Parents Involved in Community Schools v. Seattle School District No. 1* (2005) and *Meredith v. Jefferson County Board of Education* (2005). In the first of these, race was used as the tiebreaker for assignment of students to oversubscribed high schools. In the second, a district's "managed choice plan" included "broad racial guidelines." Both plans were upheld in opinions that relied on *Grutter* and found that the districts had a compelling interest in using race as a criterion and that the plans themselves were narrowly tailored.

The Court could do any number of things when it decides these cases. It could, for example, simply distinguish *Grutter*, *Gratz*, and *Bakke*, holding that he diversity principle embraced in those cases applies only to the situations they presented, the admission of students to colleges and universities. It could also accept the argument that the diversity rationale is, if anything, even more compelling in K–12 education, where the students are younger and more impressionable (an argument the lower courts accepted). It could also overrule *Grutter*, *Gratz*, and *Bakke*, an option that one of the litigants posed in the questions presented that it framed for the Court.

Is such a result likely, or even possible? The Court does labor under its self-imposed doctrine of *stare decisis*, within which it deems an issue that has been litigated and resolved to be just that, an answered question. It has nevertheless made it clear on numerous occasions that this is at best a gentle rule of self-restraint, something it will cast aside if and when it chooses to do so. Indeed, in this respect the recent victory in *Lawrence v. Texas* (2003) by those devoted to civil liberties is worth noting. That was the case in which the Court struck down a Texas statute that made it "a crime for two persons of the same sex to engage in certain intimate sexual conduct" (p. 562). It was able to do so, however, only by discarding its own prior approval of such measures in *Bowers v. Hardwick* (1986), noting that while "The doctrine of *stare decisis* is essential to the judgments of the Court and to the stability of the law [i]t is not . . . an inexorable command" (*Lawrence*, p. 577).

Diversity's champions cannot, accordingly, rest on their laurels. The debate triggered by the two new cases will almost certainly be even more intense than that occasioned by *Grutter* and *Gratz*, as diversity's champions seek to preserve and expand those holdings and its opponents do all they can to seize the opportunities presented by a reconstituted Court.

Indeed, the degree of opposition to affirmative action plans and programs is such that litigation will likely continue regardless of the results. For example, the Center for Individual Rights, which has been perhaps the most active advocate against affirmative programs, and which represented the plaintiffs in the Michigan cases, has made it clear that it will monitor events at Michigan and elsewhere, testing both the continuing validity of the principles embraced in *Grutter* and the means employed to implement them. Some of these cases may well take the forms suggested by Justice Scalia in his *Grutter* dissent, where he offers a laundry list of potential claims, each of which, no matter how far-fetched, will likely materialize. Some will in turn focus on attempts to apply the logic of *Grutter* in other contexts, an expansion that has already begun by institutions using the diversity rationale as a predicate for scholarship programs and other initiatives outside the admissions process.

Contexts and Conundrums

Even if we assume that the legal principles established by the *Grutter* Court are safe, certain aspects of the decisions argue for caution. Perhaps the most important is one the majority stressed continuously: Context matters. The Court's holding is very specific and narrow. As things now stand, diversity is a compelling educational interest for the sole purpose of structuring admissions programs, specifically, for colleges and universities. Accordingly, unless and until the Court itself does so, these decisions do not offer a binding legal predicate for the affirmative use of race for any other purpose or in any other setting. Some observers disagree, finding in *Grutter* both "justification[s] for other types of race-conscious policies in higher education—such as recruitment and outreach, financial aid, and retention programs" and "a solid base on which to advance" a variety of diversity interests in areas other than higher education (Joint Statement, 2003, p. 17).

This may prove to be the case, although I am skeptical. It is always possible that *Grutter* will become to be another *Brown*. That opinion was on its face a holding limited to the problems posed by segregation in the nation's K–12 schools. But a Court firmly committed to the equality principle eventually used *Brown* as the predicate for a sweeping series of decisions that expanded and applied the anti-discrimination principle in a wide variety of settings and against a broad spectrum of actors. It is nevertheless important to recognize that this expansion ultimately required further action and affirmation by the Court itself. That, as I have already argued, may not be a result that is forthcoming from the current, significantly reconstituted Court.

The Supreme Court is not of course the only arena in which these matters are litigated, and there have been a small number of cases in which courts have accepted and applied the rule articulated in *Grutter* outside higher education. In *Petit v. City of Chicago* (2003), for example, the Court of Appeals for the Seventh Circuit held that "some rather modest affirmative action promotions were necessary for the effective operation of the police department" (p. 1114). Relying on *Grutter*, the opinion stressed "the compelling need for diversity in a large metropolitan police force charged with protecting a racially and ethnically divided major American city like Chicago" (*Petit v. City of Chicago*, p. 1114). This is certainly a positive result for those who value diversity, especially as the Supreme Court refused to hear the case when a petition for a writ of certiorari was filed.

However, it is important to recognize that the program in question was, as the court of appeals acknowledged, "modest." Moreover, the panel's willingness to accept both the diversity rationale and the means selected to attain it turned on the ability of the city to justify its efforts by identifying a particular problem and supporting the choices made with expert testimony. More tellingly, the city acknowledged that one of the major reasons for its actions was the need to adopt a remedy to alleviate the current effects of its own past discrimination (*Petit*, p. 1112). That concession may well have been critical. As I have already noted, there is a substantial difference between an affirmative action program undertaken by an entity that has itself violated the law and those that are adopted by entities that seek simply to "do what is right."

A second important aspect of *Grutter* and *Gratz* is the Court's insistence that any affirmative admissions program be narrowly tailored. An institution or entity wishing to take race into account must do so with care, mindful of each of the four hallmarks stressed by the Court. It cannot proceed in a thoughtless or mechanical fashion, a point driven home when the Court rejected the undergraduate admissions system at issue in *Gratz*. It must rather have what I have characterized elsewhere as the courage of its convictions, the willingness to expend the time, energy, and money necessary to create an admissions program within which consideration of race is simply one facet of a truly individualized decision (Killenbeck, 1999, 2004).

This will be especially important given the Court's acceptance of the critical mass principle, a holding that will almost certainly pose the temptation to engage in precisely the sorts of unconstitutional conduct that every member of the Court condemned. I am, for example, confident that the need for a critical mass will be used as the justification for fashioning a new generation of affirmative action policies within which bottom-line numbers will matter a very great deal. This poses a major problem given the comparatively small number of qualified minority applicants for whose affections an expanded universe of institutions will now compete. Diversity is after all an appropriate goal, and a critical mass is an appropriate component in that quest, only if each student admitted is in fact qualified. And provided further that the institution does not create the impression that its policy seeks the attainment of "some specified percentage of a particular group merely because of its race or ethnic origin," an approach that "would amount to outright racial balancing, which is patently unconstitutional" (*Grutter*, pp. 329–330).

The Court's emphasis on context raises an additional question. One of the hallmarks of the Michigan policies was that institution's determination to preserve its status as one of the nation's preeminent universities. The *Grutter* majority accepted the premise that active consideration of race in the admissions process was necessary not simply because diversity was important, but also because Michigan could not preserve its elite status any other way. This provoked both Justices Scalia and Thomas to argue vigorously in dissent that the real issue was not Michigan's quest for diversity, but rather its "interest in maintaining a 'prestige' law school whose normal admissions standards disproportionately exclude Blacks and other minorities" (*Grutter*, p. 347).

They were, of course, correct. Moreover, Justice O'Connor and her colleagues conceded as much when they accepted the argument that certain "race neutral" approaches were inappropriate in the specific context of institutions of this nature. "[T]hese alternatives," she wrote, "would require a dramatic sacrifice of diversity, the academic quality of all admitted students, or both" (*Grutter*, p. 340). In this respect, the situation Michigan faced was indeed one of its own making.

But is that really a problem, or at least one of constitutional dimensions? For example, if the only educational needs a public university can constitutionally serve are those of the citizens who pay the taxes that support it then it is entirely appropriate for Justice Thomas to compare Michigan to Wayne State and conclude that "The Law School's decision to be an elite institution does little to advance the welfare of the people of Michigan or any cognizable interest of the State of Michigan" (*Grutter*, p. 360).[10] I doubt, however, that this is the case. Every college and university, and virtually every degree program, serves a distinctive constituency and makes informed judgments regarding the characteristics required to successfully complete a course of studies. Indeed, we routinely find within a given state many public institutions that differ greatly in terms of their mission and structure: colleges, for example, that serve the distinct needs of the state that supports them, and research universities that see themselves as the equals of a Harvard or a Yale.

---

[10] Indeed, as the results of the November, 2006 election demonstrate, at least one aspect of that commitment to elite status, the embrace of diversity, was soundly rejected by the people of Michigan when they were given the chance to voice their opinion.

The pertinent legal question is not then whether the University of Michigan should be "elite." To the extent that this is an issue it is one for the people of Michigan. It is rather whether, having made that decision, an institution may take race into account when it admits students. That is certainly a proper concern for the Court, as it poses squarely the constitutionality of using a suspect characteristic as an admissions criterion. Whether or not it is proper for a university to aspire to elite status is, however, another matter entirely, and is at best a secondary consideration in the argument about affirmative action and diversity.

Another notable aspect of the decisions, less remarked on but potentially far more telling, is the Court's insistence that affirmative admissions programs be limited in duration. Assuming for the sake of argument that some critics are correct, and that much of what happened in the Michigan cases reflected the Court's willingness to treat higher education as special, Justice O'Connor nevertheless stressed that "We see no reason to exempt race-conscious admissions programs from the requirement that all governmental use of race must have a logical end point" (*Grutter*, p. 324). Noting that "It has been 25 years since Justice Powell first approved the use of race to further an interest in student body diversity" and that "[s]ince that time, the number of minority applicants with high grades and test scores has indeed increased," Justice O'Connor and her colleagues laid down the gauntlet: "We expect that 25 years from now, the use of racial preferences will no longer be necessary to further the interest approved today" (p. 343).

The full force of this passage is a matter of some dispute. For example, in an analysis published by the Harvard Civil Rights Project, a group of prominent constitutional law scholars maintained that it "should be construed as . . . expressing [the Court's] aspiration—and not its mandate—that there will be enough progress in equal educational opportunity that race-conscious policies will, at some point in the future, be unnecessary to ensure diversity" (Joint Statement, 2003, p. 11). There may be some force to this argument, at least to the extent that we can be certain that 25 years represents an absolute and inflexible deadline.

Nevertheless, there cannot and should not be any doubt about the underlying reality. Narrow tailoring clearly requires that "race-conscious admissions policies . . . be limited in time" (*Grutter*, p. 342). Indeed, in one of the decisions now before the Court, *Parents Involved in Community Schools*, the Court of Appeals for the Ninth Circuit accepted the principle that "A narrowly tailored plan must be limited not only in scope, but also in time" (p. 1192). The clock is then ticking. And the message it imparts is telling, given the continuing existence of achievement gaps, especially for African Americans, that are both substantial and persistent.

It is clear that *Grutter* and *Gratz* are important and that, if they remain in place, the consequences of these decisions could be profound. For example, if an organization wishes to rely on *Grutter* it must offer a compelling justification for achieving diversity that corresponds to its own mission and the realities that exist within it. That may, or may not, be an easy thing to do, even for a college or university, since the subset of the academy for which an affirmative program of the sort implemented by Michigan actually matters is arguably a small one, especially at the undergraduate level. As Bowen and Bok (1998) stressed in their extensive study, "Many people are unaware of how few colleges and universities have enough applicants to be able to pick and choose among them" (p. 15). Their work, and that of others who have examined the question, shows that "the vast majority of undergraduate institutions accept all qualified candidates and thus do not award special status to any group of applicants, defined by race or on the basis of any other criterion" (Bowen & Bok, p. 282; National Association, 2003, p. xi).

This changes at the graduate and professional level, especially for those programs most often associated with success, where all schools are at least arguably selective. But even there the statistics can be deceiving. For example, the only major study to examine the actual impact on admissions trends in law and medicine in the wake of *Bakke* found that "the decision largely served to institutionalize existing patterns and practices. The institutions that had large minority enrollments [before *Bakke*] also had them [after that decision]" (Welch & Gruhl, 1998, p. 131). In a similar vein, a number of studies and other reports have tended to show that minority enrollments in Texas and California, initially down in the wake of *Hopwood* and Proposition 209, have gradually but steadily increased back to the levels they were at before those bars on affirmative admissions schemes.

If then, as the *Grutter* majority stressed, context matters, it seems advisable for each individual institution to establish as a threshold matter that an affirmative regime is actually necessary in the light of its characteristics and the realities of that institution. Some have scoffed at this notion. But it is at the institutional level that litigation transpires, and individual institutions will have to defend what they have actually set out to do within the confines of strict scrutiny.

More tellingly, the ability of diversity's proponents to invoke the rule and logic of *Grutter* in other settings will almost certainly depend on the extent to which they can offer convincing evidence that diversity is important for them. As was the case in *Grutter*, that evidence must be something more than the assurances of the institution or organization that it believes that diversity matters. In law, as in life, faith matters. But the facts are more often dispositive, especially in an area where the conflicts are so fundamental.

A contextual reality that is a plus for diversity's supporters is that *Grutter* has in effect made an individual's racial or ethnic identity one important part of what it now means to be qualified for admission to a college or university. If, as Michigan argued and the Court accepted, diversity is an essential aspect of a complete education, then it is not simply permissible to take race into account; it is at least arguably essential to do so. The point here is not that a student cannot receive a quality education at an institution that is either not diverse or only minimally so, a judgment one might easily make given the import of so much of the pro-diversity rhetoric. It is rather that complete preparation for the experience of living in a complex and diverse society, which the Court characterized as an "increasingly global marketplace," requires that at some point one has the benefits of "exposure to widely diverse people, cultures, ideas, and viewpoints" (*Grutter*, p. 330).

Unfortunately, a parallel reality is that a substantial number of individuals from various identifiable groups do not have the grade-point averages and standardized test scores that would qualify them for admission to many colleges and universities, and in particular to the elite institutions for which affirmative action and diversity are so important. In *Grutter*, for example, the Court had before it data provided by the Association of American Law Schools indicating that in 2002 "there were only 75 Black applicants . . . to law schools whose LSAT score (165 or above) would have placed them above the 25th percentile of the entering class at the nation's most selective schools; by contrast, there were 5,990 White students who scored 165 or above" (Association of American Law Schools, 2002, p. 25). Does this necessarily mean, as the critics of diversity have argued, that a commitment to affirmative admissions inevitably means that standards must be compromised? I think not, but I also understand that considerable care must be exercised in making the argument.

A compelling case can be made that merit involves something more than objective qualifications. For example, as the philosopher George Sher has noted, there are both moral and nonmoral dimensions of merit (Sher, 1987, p. 109). The argument for admitting an individual based solely on objective criteria reflects a nonmoral claim, asking that we divorce that person's individual attainments from the circumstances within which he or she achieved them. The case for affirmative action, in turn, is premised on the assumption that context matters very much, both in terms of assessing individual worth and in assembling a group of individuals that reflects in an appropriate manner the full range of institutional objectives.

Universities, in particular the great universities, labor under the mandates imposed by two simultaneously contradictory yet complementary obligations. They must, on the one hand, articulate and adhere to standards appropriate to their professed mission. For the elite institutions, this inevitably involves the assumption that rigor must prevail. At the same time, these are the institutions where potential is realized and where individuals may well be able to succeed in spite of deficits imposed by inferior schools and by individual circumstances that thwart learning. Harvard, in this respect, will always remain Harvard, just as the University of Arkansas will always remain the University of Arkansas. However, assuming each institution's minimum thresholds are met, why should it be precluded from including within its student body individuals whose objective credentials belie their academic promise?

A final, cautionary note. Much of the discussion of affirmative action and diversity, both before and after these decisions, has tended to treat these matters as though we are talking only about the educational needs and prospects of this nation's African Americans. This reflects the perception in both the body politic and much of the higher education community that the need for affirmative admissions systems and the questions posed by them are invariably issues for which this is the only group that matters. Thus, when Justice O'Connor began her opinion for the Court in *Grutter* with the statement that "This case requires us to decide whether the use of race as a factor in student admissions by the University of Michigan Law School . . . is unlawful" (*Grutter*, 2003, p. 311), the assumption was that race in that instance means African American.

The policies at issue in the Michigan litigation were not, at least as written, that narrow. The Law School, for example, spoke of "many possible bases for diversity admissions," albeit with an emphasis on "one particular type of diversity," that is, "racial and ethnic diversity with special reference to the inclusion of students from groups which have been historically discriminated against, like African-Americans, Hispanics, and Native Americans, who without this commitment might not be represented in our student body in meaningful numbers" (*Grutter*, p. 316, quoting Law School admissions policy). These goals were entirely consistent with the diversity norm as properly understood, within which a potentially infinite range of personal characteristics factor into the quest to "achieve that diversity which has the potential to enrich everyone's education and thus make a . . . class stronger than the sum of its parts" (*Grutter*, p. 316).

This is as it should be, for, as I have made clear elsewhere when discussing what I characterize as "principled" affirmative action, a diversity policy cannot and should not focus on a single group, either in theory or practice (Killenbeck, 1999, 2004). The values associated with diversity are not confined to situations in which meaningful numbers of a given minority group gain admission to our colleges and universities or are hired by our businesses. This is a debate about educational opportunity for all individuals, and it is important to remember that the policies at issue are as much about the needs and interests of, for example, Latinos and Native Americans, as they are of African Americans. Indeed, the affirmative action debate is arguably even more so about the need to fashion an intellectually, philosophically, and politically diverse community, although such considerations are seldom if ever ones that are taken into consideration.

It is also worth recalling that in the not too distant past this was also a debate about the needs and aspirations of women. And it is telling that it may, ironically, soon mutate into a dialogue about the educational prospects of men. Justice Thomas noted at least one portion of this when he discussed the extent to which "Black men are 'underrepresented' at the Law School" and criticized the apparent failure of the Law School to take this into account (*Grutter*, 2003, p. 372). We have not yet reached the point where the argument about these matters has in effect come full circle. It is nevertheless quite possible that current concerns about the failure of men to seek a college or university degree may produce a new diversity debate about the extent to which student bodies reflect a gender imbalance (Tierney, 2006). If that happens, the irony posed by affirmative consideration of gender on behalf of White men will be profound—as will, I suspect, be the outrage expressed by some individuals at the very notion.

Conclusion

Having said all of this, I must confess that I remain deeply conflicted. Like my friend Kent Syverud, "I have come to believe that all law students receive an immeasurably better legal education, and become immeasurably better lawyers, in law schools and law school classes where the student body is racially heterogeneous" (Syverud, 1999). I know from personal experience that it makes a difference for me when I teach cases like *Plessy*, *Brown*, and *Grutter* in a classroom where the students are truly aware of and understand the realities and complexities of the issues posed, either from their own experiences or those of the individuals enrolled with them. I doubt, however, that this is the type of evidence the Court had in mind when it accepted the diversity rationale. More to the point, it is certainly not proof positive that the diversity I value has in fact itself had a positive impact on the students in question, which is after all what ultimately matters.

Affirmative action is, I suspect, both a necessary and appropriate public policy in a society in which inequality of opportunity remains a pervasive reality. This assumes, of course, that by affirmative action we mean that our institutions, and in particular our colleges and universities, take positive steps to afford all individuals equal opportunities. Unfortunately, affirmative action as it is now commonly practiced has been transformed into something quite different. Moreover, it has accumulated considerable negative baggage as pervasive public support for the fair and equal treatment of individuals collides with the realization that all too often affirmative action involves granting preferences predicated solely on group membership.

The challenge for those shaping a new generation of affirmative action programs in the wake of *Grutter* and *Gratz* will be to articulate clearly an appropriate vision of what it means to be diverse. In particular, to the extent that an institution believes it necessary to use affirmative action as a means toward that end, it must adhere strictly to professed values, forms, and procedures, regardless of consequences. As part of that process, universities in particular must place themselves in a position in which they can maintain credibly that the debate about affirmative action is in fact a debate about the nature and value of diversity as an educational or social construct. If they are able to do so, they will likely prevail when the inevitable legal challenges are mounted. If, on the other hand, institutions act as many have in the past, *Grutter* and *Gratz* will in effect pose temptations best avoided.

The debate about diversity and affirmative action must continue to be a debate about education and opportunity, rather than about institutional prestige, political comfort, or any of the myriad other realities that have distorted and destroyed what was once an appropriate impulse. That dialogue will, I suspect, continue to be at least as contentious as the debate that preceded and shaped *Grutter* and *Gratz*. Education and opportunity matter a great deal to the American people, and the passions triggered by a reformulated dialogue on diversity and critical mass will certainly run just as deep.

There will, however, be one very important difference. At least for the time being, the quest for diversity and the active consideration of race in those efforts has the Court's imprimatur. That matters, and will continue to matter, provided our decision makers do not squander the opportunities they have been given. The sorts of measures the Court has approved take race into account but simultaneously reach more broadly. We cannot and will not escape the shadow of group identity. But we can perhaps transform a debate that has to date been about racial politics into one that focuses on the needs of the nation and the opportunities it affords its citizens.

Social science studies have a role to play in these discussions. Properly conceived and appropriately implemented, they may well provide important evidence for the courts as they examine the inevitable legal challenges to affirmative action programs. Whether or not they will help resolve the public debate is another matter entirely. More to the point, whether or not the lessons actually learned through research will be heeded is an even more troubling question. For example, I doubt very much that if new studies begin to show that a diverse learning environment does not in fact have an appreciable, positive effect on learning that the institutions practicing affirmative action will abandon it. It is in this respect that I noted earlier that the embrace of social science is a double-edged sword. For just as there was no amount of social science evidence that would have changed the votes of Justices Scalia and Thomas in *Grutter* and *Gratz*, there is also no amount of social science evidence that will persuade diversity's most ardent supporters—which includes virtually every college and university in this nation—from embracing that cause.

The most important challenges posed by *Grutter* and *Gratz* are ultimately social and political rather than educational: the need for this nation to finally and effectively guarantee to each of its citizens meaningful opportunities for a safe, healthy, and fulfilling life. In the interim, people of good will continue to debate what these decisions mean and how we should respond to them.

References

American Association of University Professors (1984). Affirmative action in higher education: A report by the council committee on discrimination. In *AAUP policy documents and reports* (pp. 82–89). Washington, D.C.: AAUP.

Arnone, M. (2003, December 12). Texas A&M will not consider race in admissions decisions, its president says. *The Chronicle of Higher Education*, p. 17.

Becker, L. C. (1993). Affirmative action and faculty appointments. In S. M. Cahn (Ed.), *Affirmative action and the university: A philosophical inquiry* (pp. 93–121). Philadelphia: Temple University Press.

Bowen, W. G., & Bok, D. (1998). *The shape of the river: Long-term consequences of considering race in college and university admissions*. Princeton, NJ: Princeton University Press.

Carnegie Council on Policy Studies in Higher Education (1975). *Making affirmative action work in higher education: An analysis of institutional and federal policies with recommendations*. San Francisco: Jossey-Bass.

CBS News Poll, January 5–8, 2006. Race and ethnicity, at http://www.pollingreport.com/race.htm (accessed April 8, 2006).

Cohen, C. (2003). Preface One. In C. Cohen & J. P. Sterba, *Affirmative action and racial preference: A debate* (pp. ix–x). New York: Oxford University Press.

Edwards, H. T., & Zaretsky, B. L. (1975). Preferential remedies for employment discrimination. *Michigan Law Review*, 74(1), 1–47.

Elliott, J. (1994, May 23). UT responds to lawsuit with policy changes. *Texas Lawyer*, p. 10.

Farber, D. A. (1994). The outmoded debate over affirmative action. *California Law Review*, 82(4), 893–934.

Fisher, L., & Devins, N. (1993). The political dynamics of constitutional law. St. Paul, MN: West.

Glazer, N. (1975). *Affirmative discrimination: Ethnic inequality and public policy*. Cambridge, MA: Harvard University Press.

Graham, H. D. (1990). *Civil rights era: Origins and development of national policy, 1960–1972*. New York: Oxford University Press.

Green, P. (1981). Affirmative action and the individualist principle. *Social Policy, 11*(5), 14–20.

Harvard Law Review (1971). Developments in the law, employment discrimination and Title VII of the Civil Rights Act of 1964. *Harvard Law Review, 84*(5), 1109–1316.

Hughes, G. (1968). Reparations for Blacks? *New York University Law Review, 43*(6), 1063–1074.

Johnson, L. B. (1966). Commencement address at Howard university, "to fulfill these rights." In *Public papers of the presidents of the United States*, II 1965, pp. 635–640.

Joint Statement of Constitutional Law Scholars (2003). *Reaffirming diversity: A legal analysis of the university of michigan affirmative action cases*. Cambridge, MA: The Harvard Civil Rights Project.

Killenbeck, M. R. (1999). Pushing things up to their first principles: Reflections on the values of affirmative action. *California Law Review, 87*(6), 1299–1407.

Killenbeck, M. R. (2004). *Affirmative action and diversity: The beginning of the end? Or the end of the beginning?* Princeton, NJ: Educational Testing Service.

Leonard, J. S. (1990, Autumn). The impact of affirmative action regulations and equal employment law on black employment. *Journal of Economic Perspectives, 4*(4), 47–63.

Mangan, K. S. (2006, March 17). Foes of affirmative action seek revocation of ABA's accrediting power. *The Chronicle of Higher Education*, p. 30.

National Association for College Admission Counseling. (2003). *Diversity and college admission in 2003: A survey report*. Alexandria, VA: National Association for College Admission Counseling.

Posner, R. (1998). Against constitutional theory. *New York University Law Review, 73*(1), 1–22.

Sander, R. H. (2005). A systemic analysis of affirmative action in American law schools. *Stanford Law Review, 57*(2), 367–483.

Sandler, B. (1975). Backlash in academe: A critique of the Lester report. *Teachers College Record, 76*(3), 401–419.

Scalia, A. (1979). The disease as cure: "In order to get beyond racism, we must first take account of race." *Washington University Law Quarterly, 1979* (1), 147–157.

Schmidt, P. (2006, October 27). A referendum on race preferences divides Michigan. *The Chronicle of Higher Education*, p. 21.

Sher, G. (1987). *Desert*. Princeton, NJ: Princeton University Press.

Silberman, L. H. (1977, August 11). The road to racial quotas. *The Wall Street Journal*, p. 14.

Steele, C. M., & Green, S. G. (1976). Affirmative action and academic hiring: A case study of value conflicts. *The Journal of Higher Education, 47*(4), 413–435.

Swisher, C. B. (1958). *The supreme court in modern role*. New York: New York University Press.

Syverud, K. D. (1999). Expert Report of Kent Syverud. In J. Payton (Ed.), *The compelling need for diversity in higher education: Expert reports prepared for Gratz and Grutter*. Washington, DC: Wilmer, Cutler & Pickering.

Taylor, H., Jr. (1995, June 11). Quoted in N. Lemann, Taking affirmative action apart. *The New York Times Magazine*, pp. 36–43.

Tierney, J. (2006, March 25). On campus, a good man is hard to find. *The New York Times*, p. 15.

United States Commission on Civil Rights (1970). *Federal civil rights enforcement.* Washington, DC: US Government Printing Office.

Verhovek, S. H. (1997, November 6). Referendum in Houston shows complexity of preferences issue. *The New York Times*, p. A1.

Welch, S., & Gruhl, J. (1998). *Affirmative action and minority enrollments in medical and law schools.* Ann Arbor: University of Michigan Press.

Young, W. M. (1964). *To be equal.* New York: McGraw-Hill.

Legal Citations

Adarand Constructors, Inc. v. Pena, 515 U.S. 200 (1995).

Association of American Law Schools (2002). Brief Amicus Curiae of the Association of American Law Schools in Support of Respondents, *Grutter v. Bollinger*, 539 U.S. 306 (2003) (No. 02-241).

Board of Curators of the University of Missouri v. Horowitz, 435 U.S. 78 (1978).

Bowers v. Hardwick, 478 U.S. 186 (1986).

Brown v. Board of Education of Topeka, 347 U.S. 483 (1954).

City of Richmond v. J. A. Croson Company, 488 U.S. 469 (1989).

Executive Order 10925 (1961, March 8). *Federal Register 26*(44), 1977–1979.

Gratz v. Bollinger, 539 U.S. 244 (2003).

Grutter v. Bollinger, 288 F.3d 732 (6th Cir. 2002).

Grutter v. Bollinger, 539 U.S. 306 (2003).

Hopwood v. Texas, 78 F.3d 932, 948 (5th Cir. 1996), *reh'g denied*, 84 F.3d 720 (5th Cir. 1996), *cert. denied*, 518 U.S. 1033 (1996).

Johnson v. Board of Regents of the University of Georgia, 263 F.3d 1234 (11th Cir. 2001).

Lawrence v. Texas, 539 U.S. 558 (2003).

McFarland v. Jefferson County Public Schools, 416 F.3d 513 (6th Cir. 2005), *cert. granted, sub nom. Meredith v. Jefferson County Board of Education*, 126 S. Ct. 2351 (2006).

National Labor Relations Act, Pub. L. No. 74-98, § 10(c), 49 Stat. 449, 454 (1935) (codified at 29 U.S.C. § 160(c) (1994)).

National Labor Relations Board v. Fansteel Metallurgical Corporation, 306 U.S. 240 (1939).

Parents Involved in Community Schools v. Seattle School District, No. 1, 426 F.3d 1162 (9th Cir. 2004) (en banc), *cert. granted*, 126 S. Ct. 2351 (2006).

Petit v. City of Chicago, 352 F.3d 1111 (7th Cir. 2004), *cert. denied*, 541 U.S. 1074 (2004).

Plessy v. Ferguson, 163 U.S. 537 (1896).

Regents of the University of California v. Bakke, 438 U.S. 265 (1978).

Republic Steel Corporation v. National Labor Relations Board, 311 U.S. 7 (1940).

Revised Order No. 4 (1971, December 4). Affirmative action programs. *Federal Register, 36*(234), 23, 152–157.

Smith v. University of Washington Law School, 233 F.3d 1188 (9th Cir. 2000), *cert. denied*, 532 U.S. 1051 (2001), *on remand*, 392 F.3d 367 (9th Cir. 2004), *cert. denied*, 126 S. Ct. 334 (2005).

Turner v. Safley, 482 U.S. 78 (1987).

University of Michigan. Brief for Respondents University of Michigan, *Grutter v. Bollinger*, 539 U.S. 306 (2003) (No. 02-241) (2002).

Wygant v. Jackson Board of Education, 476 U.S. 267 (1986).

6
The University of Michigan Cases: Social Scientific Studies of Diversity and Fairness

Faye J. Crosby and Amy E. Smith

In 1997, the then-president of the University of Michigan, Lee Bollinger, was named as a defendant in two lawsuits brought in federal district court. The College of Literature, Science and Arts had denied admission to Jennifer Gratz and Patrick Hammacher, two White residents of Michigan. The applicants claimed that the University's race-sensitive admissions policy had deprived them of their constitutional and statutory rights. Meanwhile, the University of Michigan Law School had denied admission to another White applicant, Barbara Grutter, and she too claimed reverse discrimination.

How could the University defend itself? American jurisprudence is built around the concept of *stare decisis*: Precedent matters. It is helpful to an organization to be able to argue that its behaviors conform to and promote principles that the Court has explicitly endorsed in prior rulings. In American courts of law, as in the court of public opinion, a successful defense also requires that the defendant construct a cogent and coherent story about its behaviors and intentions. Increasingly, compelling stories must show that they are consistent not only with prevailing moral values but also with accepted social scientific data. Ever since the Supreme Court acknowledged in *Brown v. Board of Education* that social scientific studies have a legitimate role to play in its reasoning, lawyers have increasingly, and with varying degrees of success, called on social scientists to provide expert testimony. Social scientific data have made their way into public debates about policy and about law as well (Smith & Crosby, in press).

Three questions thus faced the University of Michigan as it constructed a defense of race-sensitive admissions policies. First, could it articulate a coherent story to describe both its intentions and its actions? Second, could it link that story to established legal principles? Third, could it bring forward social scientific data to support its claims and could it refute social scientific data put forward by the other side?

At least two different avenues lay open to the University as it set about to find answers and to construct a defense (Lehman, 2004; Stohr, 2004). It could decide to follow the road that led to the 1954 *Brown* victory for civil rights, emphasizing that, in view of the present consequences of historical discrimination, affirmative steps needed to be taken if one were to achieve the equality mandated by the Equal Protection Clause of the 14th Amendment. Justice Brennan's dissent in *The Regents of the University of California v. Bakke* suggested the viability of such a route (Dale, 2004). Alternately, the University could decide to center its argument on diversity, reminding the Court of the pronouncement of Justice Powell, who wrote the majority opinion in *Bakke*, that the state has a compelling interest in fostering diversity among the student bodies of its universities.

Lee Bollinger and others at the University of Michigan felt that its chances of victory were greater if the University pinned its colors to the diversity argument (Stohr, 2004). But while the University's briefs and oral arguments gave only minimal attention to any justification of affirmative action other than diversity, some of the many *amicae* briefs filed in support of the University filled in the gaps. In the public debates about the Michigan cases and about affirmative action more generally, issues of fairness have loomed large. Some opponents of the policy have pointed out that it is counterproductive to sacrifice fairness, in even the short run, to achieve diversity.

In this chapter, we examine the social scientific evidence pertaining to race-based admissions. First, we look briefly at the question of whether race-based admissions policies help initially to diversify student bodies and ultimately to diversify managerial or professional cadres. We then turn directly to the putative educational benefits of diversity, looking not only at the evidence that social scientists had produced by the time the cases went to court but at subsequent evidence as well. In a nutshell, the evidence shows that both students of color and White students have much to gain by studying and working in ethnically diverse groups. Indeed, so great are the benefits that some have thought to extend the diversity justification to other aspects of public life, and the evidence suggests that such an application may be justified. While the first two sections of our chapter substantiate the benefits of race-sensitive admissions policies and of diversity in academe, the third section centers around the costs of race-sensitive admissions policies used to produce diversity. Here we take very seriously criticisms leveled against the University both by the plaintiffs in the cases and by commentators in the public. We scrutinize three criticisms in detail: that race-based policies are unfair, that they harm their intended beneficiaries by diminishing their self-esteem, and that they foster intergroup animosity. Again, our conclusion is that the weight of the social scientific evidence shows that affirmative action generally and race-sensitive admissions policies specifically function well and that the gains of affirmative action are greater than the losses. We end the chapter with a brief reflection on the use of social scientific data.

Consequences of Race-Sensitive Admissions Policies for Diversity

Since affirmative action was put into place in the 1960s, much has changed in American higher education. And much has stayed the same. The percentages of African Americans and Latinos to graduate from high school, to attend college, and to graduate from college have increased dramatically. So too, however, have the percentages of Whites, with the result that over the last 40 years, there has been no closing of the ethnic gap in educational attainment (Renner & Moore, 2004), at least at the level of graduation from schools and colleges (Jackson, 2003).

While the position of people of color relative to White people has not changed as much as one might hope throughout academe, targeted efforts have yielded results (Crosby & Clayton, 2004). In 1998, William Bowen, former president of Princeton University, and Derek Bok, former president of Harvard University, published the first study to document the positive effects of race-sensitive admissions. Analyses presented in Bowen and Bok's landmark study, *The shape of the river*, showed that for 28 select colleges and universities, race-sensitive admissions had doubled the number of African American students (Bowen & Bok, 1998).

Drawing on data from the High School and Beyond survey, a 10-year longitudinal study of Americans who graduated from high school in 1982, Kane (1998) found that in 80% of the colleges and universities, the acceptance rate of African Americans and Latinos was not greater than the acceptance rate of Whites, primarily because most colleges accept virtually all applicants. When the colleges are more selective, admitting students with combined average SAT I and SAT II scores of 1100 or better, the picture changes. Among selective universities and colleges, African Americans enjoyed an advantage equivalent to 400 points (out of 1600).

While the consensus among social scientists has been that race-sensitive admissions policies have produced increases in the number of ethnic minority students attending selective colleges and universities (Crosby, 2004a), some skeptics have sounded a warning bell. Based on comparisons of all California and Texas SAT-takers with the administrative data from eight University of California campuses over a period of 7 years, Card and Krueger (2004) noted the very high correlation between the sending of SAT scores and the act of submitting a college application. Working from this determination, Card and Krueger (2004) presented data that showed where ethnic minority students in California and Texas sent their SAT scores during the years 1994, 1995, and 1996 (before the elimination of affirmative action) and during the years 1999, 2000, and 2001. They found little reliable change in applicant behavior. Although Card and Krueger do not provide a baseline comparison looking at the behavior of majority students, their analyses do challenge the claim that ending affirmative action would have a chilling effect on minority applications.

Other critics of affirmative action have sounded stronger warnings. Stephen and Abigail Thernstrom (1997) proposed that affirmative action policies have actually boomeranged as underqualified people of color find themselves unable to retain the positions they have achieved. In the popular press, too, opponents of affirmative action opine that the policy cheats ethnic minorities by admitting them to schools and jobs where they cannot compete (Zelnick, 1996).

Recently the skeptics' point of view has garnered a great deal of attention as a result of a provocative article published by Richard Sander (2004) in *The Stanford Law Review*. Sander contended that affirmative action in law school admissions, although once quite useful, has come to have a negative effect on the number of African Americans who become lawyers. His contention rested on his a set of connected analyses of the records of more than 27,000 students who matriculated in law school in 1991. For each student, Sander calculated a score on an eligibility index, composed of the student's LSAT score (multiplied by .6) and her or his undergraduate grade point average (GPA) (multiplied by .4). The first analysis then showed that African Americans attended higher-prestige law schools than did Whites with comparable scores on the eligibility index. The second analysis demonstrated that scores on the eligibility index accounted for grades in law school, and the third analysis suggested that grades in law school predicted graduation from law school and passage of the bar exam. Stringing together the different analyses, Sander concluded that African Americans would be well served to attended less prestigious law schools than they now attend (owing to the affirmative action bump) in which they would presumably obtain higher grades and would thus be less likely to drop out and more likely to eventually pass the bar.

Sander not only presented his analytically derived conclusions; he also offered some speculations about the mind-set of African American law students. Sander opined that the underprepared African American law students felt discouraged and unable to keep up with their classmates. Disengagement would then occur.

Sander's conclusions have not gone unchallenged. Like any econometric analysis, Sander's analyses depend on a set of assumptions about the data and about relationships among variables. Some rebuttals have pointed out technical or methodological issues. Ayres and Brooks (2005), for example, delve into two significant methodological problems in Sander's analyses. First, while the data clearly show a different relationship between eligibility scores and law school grades among Whites and African Americans, Sander's interpretations rest on the assumption that the relationship between the two variables is the same in the two populations. Second, Sander "interprets away the strong evidence that, holding entering credentials constant, students have a higher probability of becoming lawyers when they attend higher quality tiers" (p. 1853). Whether one finds the quality of the law school or the entering characteristics to be stronger predictors of bar passage depends on the way one sets up the parameters of the analysis; but under all circumstances, the quality of the law school accounts for some or much of the variance in bar passage rates. Similarly, Chambers, Clydesdale, Kidder, and Lempert (2005) demonstrate how the results of Sander's analysis depend on assumptions about the generalizability of data from a particular atypical year (1991) and point out that Sander lumps together errors of over- and underestimation in some of his analyses. Like Ayers and Brooks, Chambers et al. note the statistical problems that arise from how Sander downplays the importance of the quality of the law school in predicting bar passage.

Some of the problems with Sander's interpretations have to do with what may be erroneous assumptions about social reality. Chambers et al. (2005) question how reasonable it is to assume, as Sander clearly does, that African Americans would apply to and matriculate in law school (rather than pursuing alternative professions) if the applicants had to resign themselves to attending lower tier schools. Wilkins (2005) elaborates on several other assumptions made by Sander about social realities that seem ill conceived or short sighted. Nowhere, for example, does Sander acknowledge the considerable help given to African American graduates of lower tier schools by African American graduates of higher tier schools. Elimination of affirmative action would, Wilkins argues, have a very deleterious trickle-down effect. Also suspect is Sander's assumption that African Americans who have started law school but have not passed the bar (which, both Sander and critics agree, is about 40% of all African American matriculants) have wasted their time, when in fact the value of a J.D. degree for African Americans is about $20,000 per annum in additional earnings.

Does graduation from a higher-tier law school produce greater earnings that graduation from a lower-tier law school, either for students of color or for majority students? The implication of Wilkins' analysis is that the prestige of the law school affects earnings. Sander would be more skeptical. Consistent with Sander's point of view, Dale and Krueger (1999) discovered in an analysis of the longitudinal College and Beyond data set concerning students who graduated from high school in 1972 that the rated selectiveness of a person's undergraduate institution did not predict earnings in later life. Students who had attended more highly rated schools than other students with the same SAT scores did not later earn more money.

It is likely that the controversy over the effectiveness of race-sensitive admissions will continue to produce both heat and light. Scholars are bound to wish to reanalyze the data set that formed the bases of Sander's conclusions. For the moment, even though all do not agree with the conclusion, there is a great deal of evidence to suggest that race-sensitive admissions policies have contributed to increasing the numbers of ethnic minority students in American universities and colleges.

Consequences of Diversity in Academe

If one plank in the University's defense consisted of showing that race-sensitive admissions policies were needed to ensure diverse student bodies, another related plank required the University to demonstrate that a diverse student body is more valuable to students and to society than a monolithic one. Central to the demonstration was the work of Patricia Gurin, who was a professor and administrator at the University and who prepared expert testimony for the trials. Perhaps predictably, Gurin's work was roundly criticized by the conservative National Association of Scholars (Rothman, Lipset, & Nevitte, 2003); but several bodies of experts, including the American Psychological Association, have found that the criticisms were themselves flawed and that Gurin's work withstands critical scrutiny (Brief Amicus of AER, 2003; Brief Amicus of APA, 2003; see also Barton, 2003; Gurin, 2004).

In both the expert witness testimony and later reprises of the work, Gurin first outlined the reasons why, in theory, one might expect diversity to have positive outcomes for students, especially for students in late adolescence and early adulthood, and then described the empirical research that tested the theory (Gurin, 1999; Gurin, Dey, Hurtado, & Gurin, 2002).

Gurin's theoretical rationale for seeing diversity as beneficial, especially in young adulthood, rested on the work of many other psychologists. Central to Gurin's conceptualization is the contrast between the sort of thinking in which people usually engage and more focused thinking, described by dual processing models (see, e.g., Bargh, 1997). People's customary form of thinking has been documented by many psychologists to be "mindless" (Langer, 1978), "automatic," or "preconscious" thinking (Bargh, 1997), based on scripts and past experience. In contrast is the kind of thinking characterized by alertness and increased mental activity, sometimes called "minded" or "conscious" thinking. Research has shown that conscious, minded thinking results in better learning, increased development of new ideas, and new ways of processing information (Langer, 1978).

Engaging in mindful, as opposed to mindless, thinking may be especially important at certain developmental stages. This aspect of the diversity argument is grounded in Erikson's (1956) concept of identity and is consistent with Piaget's (1971) concept of discontinuous intellectual growth. Erikson proposed that late adolescence is a time for the formulation of a person's adult identity, and that the identity formation process is enhanced when young adults have the opportunity to experiment with life within different and diverse environments. The college years, furthermore, are a prime time for people to establish a "relationship to the socio-political world" (Stewart & Healy, 1989). In a series of studies examining the impact of diversity and peer influence on students from Bennington College over a period of 50 years, Theodore Newcomb (1943; Newcomb, Koenig, Flacks, & Warwick, 1967) demonstrated that it was beneficial for young people in a safe college environment to encounter ideas and information different from those they had experienced at home and throughout childhood. The beneficial effects for students exposed to an environment most different from their own, especially engaged and flexible thinking, persisted throughout adulthood. Through exposure to social situations, political ideas, and environments different from their own experiences (exposure, in other words, to diversity), students and their assumptions were challenged, and students were forced to engage in conscious thinking. Exposure to diverse ideas and novel situations, therefore, resulted in the types of thinking, described in the preceding text, that increase learning outcomes and depth of analysis. These changes presumably result because individuals, when exposed to unique situations that challenge their existing schemas, are forced to engage in active thinking processes rather than rely on heuristics or scripts.

The conditions that produce focused rather than mindless thinking have been systematically demonstrated by researchers to include those in which an individual is faced with a "novel situation" (Langer, 1978) or a "complex social structure" (Coser, 1975). These are precisely the types of environments created when universities bring together students from different backgrounds. Gurin's (1999) conclusion is that, as a result of this exposure, "[s]tudents learn more and think in deeper, more complex ways in a diverse educational environment" (p. 104).

Gurin undertook a series of studies before, during, and after the trials that have provided empirical support for the assertion that diversity benefits students of color and White students as well. In a highly informative and elegantly written chapter in a book published subsequent to the court rulings, Gurin (2004) describes the nature and findings of three separate lines of research. All three studies had been described in her expert testimony, but in less complete form.

The first line involved data collected from 11,383 students attending 184 colleges and universities around the country who were first contacted in 1984 when they were first-year students, and then were contacted at the end of college and again 5 years after graduation. The study assessed interactional diversity, meaning the extent to which students interacted informally with students of other ethnicities, and classroom diversity, measured by a single item (enrollment in an ethnic studies class). Although classroom diversity had inconsistent effects (probably owing to the use of a single measure), interactional diversity produced consistent results. The more contact students had had with other students from different ethnic groups, the more intellectually engaged they were and the greatest were the self-assessed gains in critical thinking, problem solving, listening skills, and general academic ability (Gurin, 2004; Gurin, et al., 2002). The results were robust, existing even when one adjusted for the students' intellectual engagement at the start of college.

The second line of research included information from the Michigan Student Study (MSS) involving 1,582 students who filled out long questionnaires when they entered college in 1990 and in subsequent years. By looking at the change in scores from the first to the final year of college, Gurin and colleagues were able to track changes. As with the national data, so with the MSS data: students with the most intergroup contact had the highest level of intellectual engagement by the end of college and were the most satisfied with the intellectual quality and challenge of Michigan curriculum (Gurin, 2004; Gurin et al., 2002).

Embedded in the second study was a third, very focused, study of 174 students. Eighty-seven of the students had taken the initial course in Michigan's Program on Intergroup Relations (IGR) in which they confronted the issues of multiculturalism; the other 87 students in the study were matched to the first set in terms of gender, ethnicity, and other demographic factors. Students who had engaged in the course differed from the comparisons in terms of how much they deepened their interest in civic engagement over the 4 years of college—what Gurin and associates called "democracy outcomes" (Lopez, Gurin, & Nagda, 1998).

How reliable are the studies conducted by Gurin and colleagues? Around the time that the Court was to hear oral arguments in the Michigan cases, a group of conservative scholars published a study that they portrayed as demolishing Gurin's line of research (Rothman et al., 2003). The conservative study showed that there was a negative relationship between the percentage of students of color at a school and student satisfaction with the school. The conservative study did not, of course, undermine Gurin's conclusions because Rothman et al. did not control for the "quality" of the schools and did not, therefore, try to compare schools simply in terms of how integrated or segregated they were. Meanwhile, several scholars, across a number of different samples and using a variety of different measures, confirmed the general conclusion that diversity enhances student engagement, learning, and satisfaction. Antonio et al. (2004), for example, reported positive effects in an experimental study of racial diversity on cognitive outcomes such as integrative complexity in an experimental setting. Chang, Astin, and Kim (2004) presented a longitudinal study supporting the positive effects of cross-racial interaction on the intellectual, social, and civic development of White students. Orfield and Whitla (2001) found higher academic success rates for students of color matriculating from "integrated educational backgrounds" into elite law schools.

Extensions Beyond Academe

The University of Michigan's decision to frame their defense around the compelling need for diversity involved some risk. A major legal risk was that the justices of the Supreme Court would decide, as had the justices of the Fifth Circuit Court of Appeals in *Hopwood,* that Powell's opinion in *Bakke* about the compelling need for diversity was simply his own opinion, not joined by others, and that it did not therefore carry the weight of law. Had the justices made such a decision, there would have been no legal precedent for the concept that the state has a compelling need to diversify.

Another risk of the strategy was the apparent awkwardness of extending the diversity argument beyond academe to employment. In his opinion, partially concurring and partially dissenting, in the *Grutter* case, Justice Scalia mocked the state's interest in diversity by derisively applying the concept to public employment jobs. Claiming that "cross-racial education" is a "lesson of life rather than law," Justice Scalia went on:

If [cross-racial understanding is] properly considered an 'educational benefit' at all, it is surely not one that is either uniquely relevant to law school or uniquely "teachable" in a formal educational setting. And therefore: If it is appropriate for the University of Michigan Law School to use racial discrimination for the purpose of putting together a "critical mass" that will convey generic lessons in socialization and good citizenship, surely it is no less appropriate—indeed, particularly appropriate—for the civil service system of the State of Michigan to do so. There, also, those exposed to "critical masses" of certain races will presumably become better Americans, better Michiganders, better civil servants (*Grutter v. Bollinger,* 2003, at 32)

Justice Scalia's sarcastic remark put into high relief the question that all the time had lain beneath the surface of Michigan's defense: Could one extend the diversity argument to public service jobs like police, fire fighters, and public school teachers? Within the year, the question came into play in the case of *Petit v. City of Chicago* (2003), in which a three-judge panel of the Seventh Circuit found that the affirmative action plan of the Chicago Police Department withstood legal challenge. The plan was justified on the grounds of diversity where the Court concluded that a diverse force at the rank of sergeant would help ethnic minority citizens develop a sense of trust in police authorities (Dale, 2004, p. 62).

Expert testimony in the case of *John M. Kohlbek and Michael Pritchard v. the City of Omaha* (2004), cited by the district court, emphasized the role of trust as a reason why the state has a compelling interest in fostering diversity among fire fighters and perhaps in all civil service occupations that have significant amounts of contact with members of the public (Crosby, 2004b). In the Omaha case, the court noted that the issue of trust plays out at both the institutional and the personal level. At the personal level, research has shown that all individuals are calmed by the presence of familiar others. The United States is still a largely segregated society in terms of residential patterns and schooling (Sugrue, 1999), and members of ethnic minority groups may therefore find White people to be less familiar than people of color. Given that calm members of the public can function more effectively (by, for example, cooperating fully with instructions) than agitated ones, it would seem important to have members of different ethnic groups working in American communities. Especially important is instilling public trust through contact with familiar others in tense, emotional, or emergency situations, such as those that the members of the police, fire, or emergency medical crews encounter regularly.

Issues of trust go beyond personal contact. Research conducted by social and organizational psychologists has demonstrated that people are very aware of the degree to which high status groups are "open" or "closed"(Wright, Taylor, & Moghaddam, 2001; Wright & Tropp, 2002). Individual members of ethnic minority groups in the general population are thus likely to respond differently to a corps of fire fighters or police officers that is entirely or almost exclusively White than to a corps that includes a critical mass of individuals who are themselves members of minority groups. People who believe, because of what they see with their own eyes, that members of their own ethnic community can enter and excel in high-status and visible occupations are likely to conclude that fairness prevails. As Tyler's research on procedural justice, conducted in a variety of settings, has demonstrated, perceptions of fairness result in increased trust in and attachment to government and its agencies and institutions (Tyler & Blader, 2000; Tyler & Huo, 2002).

Costs of Diversity

Perhaps because Bowen and Bok (1998) and the educators at Michigan (e.g., Gurin, Nagda, & Lopez, 2004) have successfully justified race-sensitive admissions policies on the basis of diversity, critics of the policy have wondered aloud about whether the benefits of diversity are worth the costs in other terms. Although the courts have mentioned these studies only in passing, three questions have loomed large in the court of public opinion. First, some have asked if diversity is bought at the price of fairness. Second, others question whether affirmative action by its very nature erodes the self-confidence of its intended beneficiaries, stripping them of the chance to feel pride in their own accomplishments. Finally, opponents of affirmative action have questioned whether affirmative action policies engender animosity against the direct beneficiaries among those who are not the direct beneficiaries.

Fairness

A substantial amount of social scientific research has shown that Americans generally strive to maintain the illusion that their worlds are fair or just (Lerner, 1980). North Americans, it seems, care about fairness, and especially about the kind of fairness that is called "meritocracy." Further, the more people care about meritocracy, the more strongly they feel about affirmative action (Son Hing, Bobocel, & Zanna, 2002)—sometimes in a positive and sometimes in a negative direction, depending on how they conceptualize affirmative action and also how they conceive of the policy (Crosby, 2004a).

Some of the most outspoken commentators have argued that affirmative action violates cherished values concerning justice or fairness. "Civil rights legislation," according to Perloff and Bryant (2000) "is supposed to be color blind. . . . It is repugnant in the view of many to achieve nondiscriminatory benefits and a level playing field for one race by unjustly discriminating against another race" (p. 102). Philosopher Lou Marinoff (2000) voices the concerns of many when he complains that it is unjust "preferentially to employ certain people (e.g., females of color) on the basis of criteria irrelevant to the position (i.e., skin pigmentation and sex chromosomes) and preferentially to exclude certain other people (e.g., while males) from employment on the basis of criteria irrelevant to the position (i.e., skin pigmentation and sex chromosomes)" (p. 24).

Nor are public intellectuals alone in questioning the fairness of affirmative action (Chesler & Peet, 2002). How, ask students, can it be fair to admit to a public university applicants whose test scores and grades are lower than the test scores and grades of other applicants simply because the former have darker skin tones than the latter? How, ask employed people, can it be fair to give a job to a woman rather than a man when the man ranks higher than the woman does on the qualifying tests? How, ask parents, can it be fair to make offspring pay for the prejudices of their parents and forbearers? In terms of both distributive and procedural justice, race-sensitive admissions policies and other forms of affirmative action seem to fly in the face of justice (Zuriff, 2004). At least, at first glance they do.

Several social scientists have asked people to look well beyond the first glance (Crosby, Iyer, Clayton, & Downing, 2003). Scrutiny reveals that some of the criticisms of affirmative action are really just caricatures of the policy, and inaccurate ones at that. Consider the denunciation of affirmative action and other diversity-promoting policies that have appeared in the specialty journal *Rehabilitation Education*. Questioning the "appropriateness of a federal policy. . . that offers special preferences to individuals based on their race, ethnicity, or gender," the authors note: "We strongly support the objective of vigorously avoiding discriminatory practices and policies . . . however, we have reservations regarding the notion that cultural diversity should be considered as the transcending force that takes precedence over every other professional issue" (Thomas & Weinrach, 1998, p. 68).

How misleading it is to suggest that affirmative action requires that race, ethnicity, and gender take precedence over other factors. Affirmative action does not require that race, ethnicity, or gender be treated as the most important characteristic of a person; rather, affirmative action in general, and race-sensitive admissions policies in particular, simply requires that people's race, ethnicity, or gender be considered as relevant factors among many factors.

Sometimes those who get the particulars of the policy correct still make several unfounded assumptions about what is or is not fair. Upset by what they see as a violation of the rule "treat same the same," many critics of affirmative action assume that equity is the only rule of fairness. Yet from both a conceptual (Deutsch, 1975) and an empirical (Prentice & Crosby, 1987) point of view, we know now that equity is not the only justice principle. Where early justice models recognized only an "equity" approach, research has since shown that in some situations, particularly those involving family and friends, rather than more distant business relations, what is "fair" is an equality or need-based distribution.

Not only do such critics incorrectly presume that everyone feels that equity is a universally agreed upon rule of distributive justice; they also falsely assume that people can easily agree on what the dimensions of similarity are or should be. For this reason, the critics of affirmative action rarely move beyond general platitudes to specify what they mean by the concept of sameness. Yet, a minute of reflection shows how problematic it is to remain imprecise about the exact dimensions of similarity. As Crosby et al. (2003) have noted, while it might seem fair to say that when we are running a race, we should wear the same shoes, the impression changes immediately if the dictate results in a huge person and a tiny person wearing shoes of the same size. Sameness along one dimension (shoe size) results in difference along another (how well the shoes fit the feet). In short, a call to treat everyone the same may sound reasonable—but only until one reflects on the difficulty of figuring out in what exactly it means to treat everyone "the same."

Moving back to reality from the world of analogies, it is clear that the concept of "sameness" or "similarity" is a complicated one. We may need to expend extra effort to make a first-generation student feel as comfortable in college as a legacy student does. We may need to devote extra resources to making women students feel the same sense of belonging in a math classroom as men students tend to feel. When the critics of affirmative action lambaste the policy for affording special privilege to some and the proponents defend the policy as a simple corrective or leveling of the playing field, the two sides of the debate may have in mind different dimensions of comparison: the critics feel that when people are not treated identically, they are not being treated the same. The proponents, in contrast, feel that being treated comparably is more important than being treated identically.

Another presumption among those who see affirmative action as operating counter to the American ideals of fair competition and meritocracy is the assumption that the markers of qualification, the tests that supposedly indicate who is well qualified and who is not, are themselves accurate, precise, and uncontaminated by circumstances. If test scores and grades are not accurate measures of people's capabilities, then it is improper to use them when making decisions about whom to admit to school. Similarly, to the extent that screening tests fail to predict people's performance on the job, their use is suspect.

The point about the validity of tests can be communicated with an exaggerated example. Imagine that University X wishes to create a world-class water polo team. To achieve their goal, the university institutes generous water polo fellowships, and they create a test to screen applicants to the team. People who pass the test receive a spot on the team, regardless of their ethnic, social, or academic background; and when more people pass the test than there are spots on the team, those with the highest scores receive positions first. On the face of it, the system sounds fair, does it not? But the picture surely changes when it becomes known that the qualifying test is a spelling bee.

The example may sound extreme, but it corresponds in many ways to the well known case of *Griggs et al. v. Duke Power Co. (1971)*. Until July, 1965, the Duke Power Company in Draper, North Carolina, had overtly discriminated against African American employees, assigning them to the dirtiest and most labor-intensive jobs. When overt discrimination became illegal as a result of the Civil Rights Act of 1964, the Duke Power Company began using a registered professional aptitude test and a high school diploma as a gating mechanism for any employee who wished to transfer to indoor work. The trouble arose for the company when the plaintiffs in the case were able to demonstrate that the high school diploma was not necessary for the jobs in question (Whites had previously taken those jobs with no diploma) and that the diploma requirement had the effect of excluding virtually all of the African American employees. The Court found that the power company had violated the rights of its African American employees.

The Court's decision in *Griggs* inaugurated a period during which American federal courts accepted disparate impact as proof of discrimination. Previously, to prove discrimination one had to prove intentional disparate treatment. Although we are now again in a conservative period in which the Courts prefer discussions of intentions to statistical proofs, it is still true that employers are forbidden from using irrelevant tests as gating mechanism for jobs when the tests are known to disfavor women or ethnic minorities (Sackett, Schmitt, Ellingson, & Kabin, 2001).

Social scientists have devoted a great deal of effort to studying the issue of predictive tests in education and employment generally, and they have looked specifically at the question: What about tests that are neither totally inaccurate nor totally accurate in their predictions of future performance? What about tests that let the school or employer know future likely performance—but only within a broad range?

When qualifying tests provide general, but not specific, predictions of future performance, it is inappropriate to insist on making overly fine-grained distinctions. If, in other words, one cannot say that a person with a score of 630 will generally do better than a person with a score of 629 (even though one can say that a person with a score of 630 will generally do better than a person with a score of 520 or 420), then it is wrong to consider that the score of 630 differs in any functional sense from a score of 629. Similarly, if there is no reliable difference in the target performance of those who score 630 and those of who score

620, one needs to treat the two scores as functional equivalents. Treating scores as functionally equivalent is a process known as "banding."

Banding occurs in many situations. Whenever we "round up" or "round down," we are banding. Whenever we consider that all scores about a 90 constitute an A and all scores between 80 and 89 constitute a B, we are banding.

Several types of banding have been proposed as ways to keep our universities, especially our public universities, diverse in their student bodies. At the University of California, with its more than 150,000 undergraduate students, educators have been very interested in the issue of banding because careful analysis has revealed that the SATs are only generally, and not precisely, predictive of success at the university. Indeed, one internal study has shown that a difference of 200 points on SAT II scores tends to result in only one third of a grade of difference in students' GPAs (Geiser & Studley, 2001). Thus, even on the SAT II, which are known to be better predictors of college grades than the SAT I, a 200-point difference on the test means the difference only between a B+ and a B average (Crosby et al., 2003).

One form of banding considers that all people who are above a certain threshold merit entry to the university. A popular alternative is to slice the applicant pool into three general categories: those who are almost certain to succeed; those who are almost certain to fail; and those in the middle. Difficulty arises when the number of meritorious applicants exceeds the number of university places available (Bowen & Rudenstine, 2003). In such a situation, several fair solutions exist. We might conduct a lottery, letting chance select who shall attend and who shall not (Tomasson, 1996). Or we might select among qualified applicants those who have a special talent or are likely to make a special contribution (Bowen & Rudenstine, 2003). We might also give a slight preference to applicants among the band of qualified applicants who belong to groups that are or have been subject to discrimination—either to "make whole" those who have suffered or because we think that people who make progress against all odds possess talents beyond those measured by a single score on a test.

Extrapolating from our earlier discussion of Sander's article, it is clear that one way to see whether the pro-affirmative action theorizing turns out to be reasonable is to examine what happens when we utilize admissions policies in which ethnicity is considered a "plus factor" among qualified applicants. If banding works in practice, as it would seem to in theory, then admitted students of color with relatively low scores in the band of qualified applicants should accomplish as much in college and beyond college as do admitted students with relatively high scores.

Several tests have now been conducted testing the empirical results of race-sensitive admissions policies of the type permitted by banding (Vars & Bowen, 1998). The first major study was the one published by Bowen and Bok (1998) and mentioned in the preceding text. Bowen and Bok conducted extensive and extended analyses of a voluminous data set from students who had matriculated in 28 selective colleges and universities in 1951, 1976, and 1989. They tracked these students over a number of years as the students progressed through college and often through graduate or professional school into professional life.

In Bowen and Bok's data set some African American students were tagged as presumptive "affirmative action admits" because their paper credentials were less impressive at the time of admission than was true for the other students. Bowen and Bok found that the presumptive affirmative action admits were as likely as others to graduate from college, to be accepted into professional or graduate school programs, to graduate from those programs, and to enter a profession. There were some reliable differences between groups: the "presumptive affirmative action admits" earned lower grades than others; White alumni had higher earnings than anyone else; and African American alumni gave especially elevated levels of community service. Yet, in most other ways, the groups were indistinguishable from each other.

Bowen and Bok's work was profoundly important for the University of Michigan as it constructed its legal defense. Bowen and Bok's work served, further, as a model for an impressive study undertaken at the law school of the University of Michigan. In an article entitled "The river runs through law school," Lempert, Chambers, and Adams (2000a, 2000b) reported on their survey of more than 1000 graduates, randomly selected, from the classes of 1970 through 1996 of the University of Michigan Law School. Lempert et al. found that LSAT scores and undergraduate GPA did predict the grades of both White students and students of color in law school. They also found that ethnic differences in LSAT scores and undergraduate GPAs did not translate into ethnic differences in terms of passing the bar, current income, or reported satisfaction.

What accounts for the differences in the findings of Lempert et al. (2000a, 2000b) and Sander (2004)? One difference concerns the samples. Lempert et al. looked at individuals who attended one law school over time, while Sander looked at individuals attending many law schools who all matriculated in a given year. Perhaps more important was the difference in methodology. Lempert et al. based their findings on the actual, self-reported experiences of their participants while Sander's conclusions were based on a series of related, but separate, statistical analyses of a large data set.

Additional studies (Brown, Charnsangavej, Keough, Newman, & Rentfrow, 2000; Geiser & Studley, 2001; Van Laar & Levin, 2000) have confirmed that average differences in college GPAs of White students and students of color are smaller than average differences between White applicants and applicants of color in scores on the entrance indicators. If competitive schools like the University of Michigan, the University of California, or the University of Texas were to rely exclusively on rankings in the entrance indicators, virtually all African American and Latino applicants would fail to gain acceptance, even though many of those eliminated would be able to perform well at college. At a macro level, societal imbalances resulting from such "selective system bias" (Jencks, 1998) would be very unfair indeed.

In sum, social scientific research has much to contribute concerning the issue of whether race-sensitive admissions policies and other forms of affirmative action achieve diversity at the cost of fairness. Despite the misinformed schemas of affirmative action that people hold, race-sensitive policies and other related forms of affirmative action seek not to establish, but rather to eliminate privilege.

Of course, the privileges that affirmative action seeks to eliminate are often so ingrained that they have become invisible in the system. One disconcerting, but ultimately healthful, consequence of affirmative action, suggest some commentators (Crosby, 1994) is that it makes clear systems of privilege that may otherwise remain obscure.

Self esteem

One of the most persistent criticisms of race-sensitive admissions policies and other forms of affirmative action is the way they create an "enlargement of self doubt" (Steele, 1990, p. 116). No one, it seems, wants to think of him- or herself as an "affirmative action baby" (Carter, 1991). The suspicion that one's gender or ethnicity has played a role in being admitted to school or in being given a job is surely demoralizing (Eastland, 1997).

Laboratory evidence has clearly shown the pernicious effects on people who are told that they have been selected by virtue of their demographic characteristics instead of being chosen by virtue of their talents or merits (Heilman, Simon, & Repper, 1987). For example, in one study, when researchers told women that they had been awarded a favorable position because there were not enough women subjects signing up for the experiment, the women devalued their skills in a post-experimental test. Men did not suffer from the same syndrome; no matter what the researchers told them, the men continued to value their skills.

Before jumping to the conclusion that preferential treatment is always harmful to self-esteem, however, we should pause to take note of other laboratory findings. A number of studies have shown that it is a relatively easy matter to curtail or eliminate the negative effects of preferential selection on self-appraisal and on behavior. For example, women who are told that their gender was one reason for their selection do not fall into self-derogation if they are also told that they have performed well on the qualifying test (Heilman, Lucas, & Kaplow, 1990). Similarly, while women who are uncertain of their talents are adversely affected when they think that others believe them to have been preferentially selected, knowledge of the beliefs of others has no negative effect on women who are secure in the knowledge of their own talents (Heilman & Alcott, 2001). A number of other researchers have demonstrated how very circumscribed the deleterious effects of preferential selection are: only under very specialized conditions does it harm a person to know that her or his demographic characteristics have influenced her or his selection (Crosby, 2004a, pp. 150–155). On the basis of laboratory studies, it seems that affirmative action can "enlarge self doubt" when, and only when, the beneficiaries are not secure in their self-evaluations in the first place. Otherwise, no ill effects occur.

Consistent with the conclusion from laboratory studies are the results of several surveys of ethnic minority college students. African and American and Latino college students are not blind to the reality of prejudice. They know that White students and faculty may underestimate them. They know that White students and faculty may assume that people of color have been admitted to college as the result of preferential selection. However, such knowledge has little detrimental effect and does not undercut the minority students' approval of affirmative action provided that the students begin with adequate self-confidence (Elizondo & Crosby, 2004; Ponterotto, Martinez, & Hayden, 1986; Schmermund, Sellers, Mueller, & Crosby, 2001; Truax, Wood, Wright, Cordova, & Crosby, 1998). Nor is the sort of self-doubt of which Shelby Steele and Carter speak visible among women and people of color who have been hired in organizations with strong affirmative action programs (Ayers, 1992; Parker, Baltes, & Christiansen, 1997; Taylor, 1994; Tougas, Joly, Beaton, & St-Pierre, 1996).

Animosity

Writing in *Hopwood v. Texas* (1996), the Fifth Circuit Court observed: "Diversity fosters, rather than minimizes, the use of race. It treats minorities as a group, rather than as individuals. It may further remedial purposes but, just as likely, may promote improper racial stereotypes, thus fueling racial hostility" (p. 945).

Some researchers have looked for signs that affirmative action has produced intergroup animosity by looking at surveys of students and workers. Large-scale surveys have shown that White students and students of color find it rewarding, not irritating, to have contact with students from other ethnic groups than their own and that alumni and alumnae are of the opinion that intergroup contact contributed to their education (Bowen & Bok, 1998; Gurin, 2004; Orfield & Whitla, 2001; Whitla et al., 2003). Similarly, surveys of workers have shown that dominant groups generally do not feel animosity toward disadvantaged groups who are benefited by appropriate affirmative action policies but, instead, exhibit positive attitudes (Konrad & Linnehan, 1995a, 1995b; Parker et al., 1997)

Researchers have also looked specifically at the effects of preferential treatment on intergroup feelings by conducting controlled studies. Among the most carefully done are the studies of Madeline Heilman and associates, who have looked at the question of how categorical preferences produce intergroup animosity in a laboratory situation. In a set of four experiments, male participants were brought into the lab with a female confederate posing as another research participant. In all instances, the woman was awarded the job of supervisor and in all instances, the experimenter claimed that the woman's gender was part of the reason she was selected. How did the men react? When the woman had scored as well or better than themselves on the skill-determining test, the men did not derogate the woman or think her incompetent (Heilman, Block, & Strathatos, 1997; Heilman, McCullough, & Gilbert, 1996), but they were nonetheless somewhat unwilling to perform other services for the experimenter (Heilman, Battle, Keller, & Lee, 1998, study 3). Additional studies by Heilman and colleagues demonstrate that under some conditions men who seem to harbor a sort of latent sexism are willing to find ways to derogate the performance of women (Crosby, 2004a, pp. 134–139); but generally the deleterious effects of "preferential treatment" are limited to extreme cases in which someone who is unqualified is given benefit simply on the basis of characteristics acquired at birth.

Parting Thoughts on the Search for Unity

Bringing together the two major justifications for race-sensitive admissions policies and other forms of affirmative action—diversity and fairness—is a task that may help the American public embrace affirmative action more fully than we currently do. One result of the effort may also be to sharpen or deepen our thinking about issues of merit and meritocracy. As Crosby et al. (2003) note at the end of their *American Psychologist* article:

Questions of affirmative action in both employment and education have illuminated an observation of fundamental importance: organizations need a variety of different talents. It is unlikely that any one person would be the most outstanding individual on all dimensions of talent. While it may be psychologically satisfying to recognize and reward outstanding achievements of individuals, groups, teams, organizations and societies may function best if they include and make use of many different types of talent. Thus, in the end, the merit of the group may depend on the diversity of talented individuals within it. (p. 115)

Also important is another form of unity. Not only should we bring together considerations of diversity and considerations of fairness in our discussions of race-sensitive admissions. We should also strive to bring into closer alignment social science and the law (Cordes, 2004; Green, 2004; Laycock, 2004). The tensions between the two traditions have existed for a long time. Many justices, including prominently Justice Scalia, have expressed confusion with and frustration over arcane methodologies. Certainly, debates over how to analyze data sets and how to interpret statistical analyses may convince those outside of the social sciences that subjectivity has a large role to play in the supposedly objective social sciences. For their part, any social scientists—those on both sides of the issues–have expressed frustration at the Court's only sporadic acceptance of social scientific evidence (e.g., Crump, 2004; Cunningham, Loury & Skrentny, 2002; Heriot, 2003). The best and most extensive evidence will be of limited usefulness if the legal system fails or refuses to recognize it in making its determinations.

The fields of psychology and law communicate in two very different languages, neither of which is fully comprehensible to the general public. However, we must continue the struggle for effective communication. Only by working together can we find good solutions to the complex problems of diversity and fairness that face our evolving democracy.

References

Antonio, A. L., Chang, M. J., Hakuta, K., Kenny, D. A., Levin, S., & Milem, J. F. (2004). Effects of racial diversity on complex thinking in college students. *Psychological Science, 15*(8), 507–510.

Ayers, L. R. (1992). Perceptions of affirmative action among its beneficiaries. *Social Justice Research, 5*, 223–238.

Ayres, I., & Brooks, R. (2005). Does affirmative action reduce the number of Black lawyers? *Stanford Law Review, 57*, 1807–1854.

Bargh, J. A. (1997). The automaticity of everyday life. In R. S. Wyer, Jr. (Ed.), *The automaticity of everyday life: Advances in social cognition* (Vol. 10, pp. 1–61). Mahwah, NJ: Erlbaum.

Barton, A. H. (2003). A note on the Rothman, Liposet, and Nevitte paper. *International Journal of Public Opinion Research, 15*, 381–388.

Bowen, W. G., & Bok, D. (1998). *The shape of the river: Long-term consequences of considering race in college and university admissions.* Princeton, NJ: Princeton University Press

Bowen, W. G., & Rudenstine, N. L. (2003, February 7). Race-sensitive admissions: Back to basics. *The Chronicle of Higher Education,* B7–B10.

Brown, R. P., Charnsangavej, T., Keough, K. A., Newman, M. L., & Rentfrow, P. J. (2000). Putting the "affirm" into affirmative action: Preferential selection and academic performance. *Journal of Personality and Social Psychology, 79*, 736–747.

Card, D., & Krueger, A. B. (2004). *Would the elimination of affirmative action affect highly qualified minority applicants Evidence from California and Texas.* National Bureau of Economic Research Working Paper 10366. Available at: http://www.nber.org/papers/w10366.

Carter, S. L. (1991). *Reflections of an affirmative action baby.* New York: Basic Books.

Chambers, D. L., Clydesdale, T. T., Kidder, W. C., & Lempert, R. O. (2005). The real impact of eliminating affirmative action in American law schools: An empirical critique of Richard Sander's study. *Stanford Law Review, 57*, 1855–1898.

Chang, M. J., Astin, A. W., & Kim, D. (2004). Cross-racial interaction among undergraduates: Some causes and consequences. *Research in Higher Education, 45*(5), 529–553.

Chesler, M., & Peet, M. (2002). White student views of affirmative action on campus. *The Diversity Factor, 10*(2), 21–27.

Cordes, M. W. (2004). Affirmative action after *Grutter* and *Gratz. Northern Illinois University Law Review, 24*, 691–751.

Coser, R. (1975). The complexity of roles as a seedbed of individual autonomy. In L. A. Coser (Ed.) *The idea of social structure: Papers in honor of Robert K. Merton* (pp. 85–102). New York: Harcourt Brace Jovanovich.

Crosby, F. (1994). Understanding affirmative action. *Basic and Applied Social Psychology, 15*, 13–41.

Crosby, F. J. (2004a). *Affirmative action is dead; long live affirmative action.* New Haven: Yale University Press.

Crosby, F. J. (2004b). Expert witness testimony. *John M. Kohlbek and Michael Pritchard v. The City of Omaha, Nebraska, a Municipal Corporation* in the United States District Court for the District of Nebraska Case No. 8:03CV68.

Crosby, F. J., & Clayton, S. (2004). Affirmative action and the search for educational equity. *Analyses of Social Issues and Public Policy, 4*, 243–249.

Crosby, F. J., Iyer, A., Clayton, S., & Downing, R. A. (2003). Affirmative action; Psychological data and the policy debates. *American Psychologist, 58*, 93–115.

Crump, D. (2004). The narrow tailoring issue in the affirmative action cases: Reconsidering the Supreme Court's approval in Gratz and Grutter of race-based decision-making by individualized discretion. *Florida Law Review, 56*(3), 483–539.

Cunningham, C. D., Loury, G. C., & Skrentny, J. D. (2002). Passing strict scrutiny: Using social science to design affirmative action programs. *The Georgetown Law Journal, 90*, 835–885.

Dale, C. V. (2004, December 15). *Affirmative action revisited: A legal history and prospectus.* Washington, DC: Congressional Research Service, The Library of Congress.

Dale, S. B., & Krueger, A. B. (1999). *Estimating the payoff to attending a more selective college on application of selection on observables and unobservables.* National Bureau of Economic Research Working Paper 7322. Available at: http://www.nber.org/papers/w7322.

Deutsch, M. (1975). Equity, equality, and need: What determines which value will be used as the basis of distributive justice? *Journal of Social Issues, 31*(3), 137–149.

Eastland, T. (1997). *Ending affirmative action: The case for colorblind justice.* New York: Basic Books.

Elizondo, E., & Crosby, F. J. (2004). Attitudes toward affirmative action as a function of the strength of ethnic identity among Latino college students. *Journal of Applied Social Psychology, 34*, 1773–1796.

Erikson, E. L. H. (1956). The problem of ego identity. *Journal of the American Psychoanalytic Association, 4*, 56–121.

Geiser, S., & Studley, R. (2001). *UC and the SAT: Predictive validity and differential impact of the SAT I and SAT II at the University of California.* Retrieved February 28, 2005 from http://www.ucop.edu/sas/research/researchandplanning/.

Green, D. O. (2004). Justice and diversity: Michigan's response to Gratz, Grutter, and the affirmative action debate. *Urban Education, 39*, 374–393.

Gurin, P. (1999). Expert report of Patricia Gurin, *Gratz, et al. v. Bollinger, et al.,* No. 97-75321 (E.D. Mich). In *The Compelling Need for Diversity in Higher Education.* Retrieved January 22, 2003 from the University of Michigan Admissions Website: http://www.umich.edu/~urel/admissions/legal/expert/gurintoc/html.

Gurin, P. (2004). The educational value of diversity. In P. Gurin, J. S. Lehman, & E. Lewis (Eds.), *Defending diversity: Affirmative action at the University of Michigan* (pp. 97–188). Ann Arbor, MI: University of Michigan Press.

Gurin, P., Dey, E. L., Hurtado, S., & Gurin, G. (2002). Diversity and higher education: Theory and impact on educational outcomes. *Harvard Educational Review, 72*, 330–366.

Gurin, P., Nagda, B. R. A., & Lopez, G. E. (2004). The benefits of diversity in education for democratic citizenship. *Journal of Social Issues, 60*, 17–34.

Heilman, M. E., & Alcott, V. B. (2001). What I think you think of me: Women's reactions to being viewed as beneficiaries of preferential selection. *Journal of Applied Psychology, 86*, 574–582.

Heilman, M. E., Battle, W. S., Keller, C. E., & Lee, R. A. (1998). Type of affirmative action policy: A determinant of reactions to sex-based preferential selection? *Journal of Applied Psychology, 83*, 190–205.

Heilman, M. E., Block, C. J., & Stathatos, P. (1997). The affirmative action stigma of incompetence: Effects of performance information ambiguity. *Academy of Management Journal, 40*, 603–625.

Heilman, M. E., Lucas, J. A., & Kaplow, S. R. (1990). Self-derogating consequences of sex-based preferential selection: The moderating role of initial self-confidence. *Organizational Behavior and Human Decision Processes 46*, 202–216.

Heilman, M. E., McCullough, W. F., & Gilbert, D. (1996). The other side of affirmative action: Reactions of nonbeneficiaries to sex-based preferential selection. *Journal of Applied Psychology, 81*, 346–357.

Heilman, M. E., Simon, M. C., & Repper, D. P. (1987). Intentionally favored, unintentionally harmed? Impact of sex-based preferential selection on self-perceptions and self-evaluations. *Journal of Applied Psychology, 72*, 62–68.

Heriot, G. L. (2003). Strict scrutiny, public opinion, and affirmative action on campus: Should the courts find a narrowly tailored solution to a compelling need in a policy most Americans oppose? *Harvard Journal on Legislation, 40*, 217–233.

Jackson, J. (2003). Toward administrative diversity: An analysis of the African-American male educational pipeline. *Journal of Men's Studies, 12*, 43–60.

Jencks, C. (1998). Racial bias in testing. In C. Jencks & M. Phillips (Eds.), *The Black-White test score gap* (pp. 55–85). Washington, DC: Brookings Institute.

Kane, T. J. (1998). Racial and ethnic preferences in college admissions. In C. Jencks & M. Phillips (Eds.), *The black-white test score gap* (pp. 431–456) Washington, DC: Brookings Institute.

Konrad, A. M., & Linnehan, F. (1995a). Formalized HRM structures: Coordinating equal employment opportunity or concealing organizational practices? *Academy of Management Journal, 38*, 787–820.

Konrad, A. M., & Linnehan, F. (1995b). Race and sex differences in line managers' reactions to equal employment opportunity and affirmative action interventions. *Group and Organizational Management, 20*, 409–439.

Langer, E. J. (1978). Rethinking the role of thought in social interaction. In J. Harvey, W. Ickes, & R. Kidd (Eds.), *New directions in attribution research* (Vol. 2, pp. 36–58. Hillsdale, NJ: Lawrence Erlbaum.

Laycock, D. (2004). The broader case for affirmative action: Desegregation, academic excellence, and future leadership. *Tulane Law Review, 78*, 1767–1843.

Lehman, J. S. (2004). The evolving language of diversity and integration in discussions of affirmative action from *Bakke* to *Grutter*. In P. Gurin, J. S. Lehman, & E. Lewis (Eds.), *Defending diversity: Affirmative action at the University of Michigan* (pp. 61–96). Ann Arbor, MI: University of Michigan Press.

Lempert, R. O., Chambers, D. L., & Adams, T. K. (2000a). Michigan's minority graduates in practice: The river runs through law school. *Law and Social Inquiry, 25*, 395–505.

Lempert, R. O., Chambers, D. L., & Adams, T. K. (2000b). Law school affirmative action: An empirical study of Michigan's minority graduates in practice: Answers to methodological queries. *Law and Social Inquiry, 25*, 585–597.

Lerner, M. (1980). *The belief in a just world: A fundamental delusion*. New York: Plenum.

Lopez, G. E., Gurin, P., & Nagda, B. A. (1998). Education and understanding structural causes for group inequalities. *Political Psychology, 19*, 305–329.

Marinoff, L. (2000). Equal opportunity versus equity. *Sexuality and Culture: An Interdisciplinary Quarterly, 4*, 23–43.

Newcomb, T. L. (1943). *Personality and social change: Attitude formation in a student community*. New York: Dryden Press.

Newcomb, T. L., Koenig, K. E., Flacks, R., & Warwick, D. P. (1967). *Persistence and change: Bennington College and its students after 25 years*. New York: John Wiley & Sons.

Orfield, G., & Whitla, D. (2001). Diversity and legal education: Student experiences in leading law schools. In G. Orfield & M. Kurlaender (Eds.), *Diversity challenged: Evidence on the impact of affirmative action* (pp. 143–174). Cambridge, MA: Harvard University Press.

Parker, C. P., Baltes, B. B., & Christiansen, N. D. (1997). Support for affirmative action, justice perceptions, and work attitudes: A study of gender and racial-ethnic group differences. *Journal of Applied Psychology. 82*, 376–389.

Perloff, R., & Bryant, F. B. (2000). Identifying and measuring diversity's payoffs: Light at the end of the affirmative action tunnel. *Psychology, Public Policy, and Law, 6*, 101–111.

Piaget, J. (1971). The theory of stages in cognitive development. In D. R. Green, M. P. Ford, & G. B. Flamer (Eds.), *Measurement and Piaget* (pp. 1–11). New York: McGraw-Hill.

Ponterotto, J. G., Martinez, F. M., & Hayden, D. C. (1986). Student affirmative action programs: A help or hindrance to development of minority graduate students. *Journal of College Student Personnel, 27*, 318–325.

Prentice, D., & Crosby, F. (1987). The importance of context for assessing deservingness. In J. C. Masters & W. P. Smith (Eds.), *Social comparison, social justice and relative deprivation: Theoretical, empirical, and policy perspectives* (pp. 165–182). Hillsdale, NJ: Lawrence Erlbaum.

Renner, K. E., & Moore, T. (2004). The more things change, the more they stay the same: The elusive search for racial equity in higher education. *Analyses of Social Issues and Public Policy, 4*, 227–241.

Rothman, S., Lipset, S. M., & Nevitte, N. (2003). Does enrollment diversity improve university education? *International Journal of Public Opinion Research, 15*, 8–26.

Sackett, P. R., Schmitt, N., Ellingson, J. E., & Kabin, M. B. (2001). High-stakes testing in employment, credentialing, and higher education: Prospects in a post-affirmative action world. *American Psychologist, 56*, 302–318.

Sander, R. H. (2004). A systemic analysis of affirmative action in American law schools. *Stanford Law Review, 57*, 367–483.

Schmermund, A., Sellers, R., Mueller, B., & Crosby, F. (2001). Attitudes toward affirmative action as a function of racial identity among African American college students. *Political Psychology, 22*, 759–774.

Smith, A. E., & Crosby, F. J. (In press). From Kansas to Michigan: The path from desegregation to diversity. In G. Adams, N. Branscomb, & M. Biernat (Eds.), *Brown at 50*. Washington, DC: Psychological Press.

Son Hing, L. S., Bobocel, D. R., & Zanna, M. P. (2002). Meritocracy and opposition to affirmative action: Making concessions in the face of discrimination. *Journal of Personality and Social Psychology, 83*, 493–509.

Steele, S. (1990). *The content of our character: a new vision of race in America*. New York: Harper Perennial.

Stewart, A. J. & Healy, J. M. (1989). Linking individual development and social change. *American Psychologist, 44*, 30–42.

Stohr, G. (2004). *A black and white case: How affirmative action survived its greatest legal challenge*. Princeton, NJ: Bloomberg Press.

Sugrue, T. (1999) Expert report of T. Sugrue, *Gratz, et al. v. Bollinger, et al.*, No. 97-75321 (E.D. Mich). In *The compelling need for diversity in higher education*. Retrieved on February 28, 2005 from http://www.umich.edu/~urel/admission/legal/expert/sugrutoc.html.

Taylor, M. C. (1994). Impact of affirmative action on beneficiary groups: Evidence from the 1990 General Social Survey. *Basic and Applied Social Psychology, 15*, 143–178.

Thernstrom, S., & Thernstrom, A.M. (1997). *America in black and white: One nation indivisible*. New York: Simon & Schuster.

Thomas, K. R., & Weinrach, S.G. (1998). Multiculturalism, cultural diversity, and affirmative action goals: A reconsideration. *Rehabilitation Education, 12*, 65–75.

Tomasson, R. F. (1996). Against affirmative action. In R. F. Tomasson, F. J. Crosby, & S. D. Herzberger (Eds.), *Affirmative action: The pros and cons of policy and practice* (pp. 112–267). Washington, DC: The American University Press.

Tougas, F., Joly, S., Beaton, A. M., & St.-Pierre, L. (1996). Reactions of beneficiaries to preferential treatment: A reality check. *Human Relations, 49*, 453–464.

Truax, K., Wood, A., Wright, E., Cordova, D. I., & Crosby, F. J. (1998). Undermined? Affirmative action from the targets' point of view. In J .K. Swim & C. Strangor (Eds.), *Prejudice: The target's perspective* (pp. 171–188). New York: Academic Press.

Tyler, T. A., & Blader, S. L. (2000). *Cooperation in groups: Procedural justice, social identity, and behavioral engagement*. Philadelphia: Psychology Press.

Tyler, T. R., & Huo, Y. J. (2002). *Trust in the law: Encouraging public cooperation with the police and courts.* New York: Russell Sage.

Van Laar, C., & Levin, S. (2000, June). Persona, and social identity in stereotype threat: Is affirmative action stigmatizing?. Paper presented at the biannual meeting of the Society for the Psychological Study of Social Issues, Minneapolis, MN.

Vars, F. E., & Bowen, W. G. (1998). Scholastic aptitude test scores, race, and academic performance in selective colleges and universities. In C. Jencks & M. Phillips (Eds.), *The Black-White test score gap* (pp. 457–479). Washington, DC: Brookings Institution.

Whitla, D. K., Orfield, G., Silen, W., Teperow, C., Howard, C., & Reede, J. (2003). Educational benefits of diversity in medical school: A survey of students. *Academic Medicine, 78,* 460–466.

Wilkins, D. B. (2005). A systematic response to systemic disadvantage: A response to Sander. *Stanford Law Review, 57,* 1915–1961.

Wright, S. C., Taylor, D. M., & Moghaddam, F. M. (2001). Responding to membership in a disadvantaged group: From acceptance to collective protest. In H. Hogg & D. Abrams (Eds.), *Intergroup relations: Essential readings* (pp. 337–351). Philadelphia: Psychology Press.

Wright, S. C., & Tropp, L. R. (2002). Collective action is response to disadvantage: Intergroup perceptions, social identification, and social change. In I. Walker & H. Smith (Eds.), *Relative deprivation: Specification, development, and integration* (pp. 200–236). New York: Cambridge University Press.

Zelnick, B. (1996). Backfire: *A reporter's look at affirmative action.* Washington: Regnery.

Zuriff, G. E. (2004). Is affirmative action fair? *American Psychologist, 59,* 124–125.

Legal Citations

Brief Amicus Curiae of the American Psychological Association in Support of Respondents, *Grutter v. Bollinger,* 539 U.S. 306, 123 S. Ct. 2325 (No. 2-241) and *Gratz v. Bollinger,* 529 U.S. 244, 123 S. Ct. 2411 (No. 2-516) (2003).

Brief of the American Educational Research Association, the Association of American Colleges and Universities, and the American Association for Higher Education as Amici Curiae in Support of Respondents, *Grutter v. Bollinger,* 539 U.S. 306, 123 S.Ct. 2325 (No. 2-241) (2003).

Gratz v. Bollinger, 122 F. Supp. 2d 811 (E.D. Mich. 2000).

Gratz v. Bollinger, 539 U.S. 244, 123 S. Ct. 2411 (2003).

Griggs v. Duke Power Co., 401 U.S. 42 (1971).

Grutter v. Bollinger, 137 F. Supp. 2d 821 (E.D. Mich. 2001).

Grutter v. Bollinger, 288 F. 3d. 732 (6th Cir. 2002).

Grutter v. Bollinger, 529 U.S. 306, 123 S. Ct. 2325 (2003).

Hopwood v. Texas, 78 F.3d 932 (5th Cir. 1996).

Kohlbek v. The City of Omaha, Nebraska, United States District Court for the District of Nebraska Case No. 8:03CV68, D. Ct. Order of March 30, 2004.

Petit v. City of Chicago, 352 F.3d 1111 (7th Cir. 2003)

Regents of the University of California v. Bakke, 438 U.S. 265 (1978).

7
Social Science in the Courts: The View from Michigan

Steven L. Willborn

The University of Michigan cases[1] are interesting and provocative case studies on the role of social science in the law, but I think they cut in quite a different direction than suggested by Professors Killenbeck and Crosby in their chapters. Professors Killenbeck and Crosby both argue that social science was quite central to the decisions. I think that social science was relegated to a very minor role. Moreover, on balance, I think this minor role is probably good both for the law and for social science.

The most important contribution to affirmative action jurisprudence made by the University of Michigan cases is the holding in *Grutter v. Bollinger* (2003) that diversity is a compelling interest that can justify the use of race in making university admissions decisions.[2] Justice Powell had said as much in *Regents of the University of California v. Bakke* (1978) decades earlier, but in an opinion that only he joined and that was controlling only because the Court was so fractured.[3] Before *Grutter*, the lower courts had split on how much weight to place on his decision.[4] The Court in *Grutter* decided not to rely on Justice Powell's decision as a major justification for its decision. The Court said it would not be "useful" to analyze *Bakke* closely to try to determine the precedential value of Powell's decision. Instead, the Court decided to endorse his position, not because of precedent, but instead based on a new and fresh analysis.[5]

The Court was very clear about the principal reason for its decision that diversity was a compelling interest: deference to the judgment of the university.

---

[1] Gratz v. Bollinger, 539 U.S. 244 (2003); Grutter v. Bollinger, 539 U.S. 306 (2003).

[2] *Grutter*, 539 U.S. at 327–333. *Gratz* accepted this holding in *Grutter* without discussion, 539 U.S. at 268, but proceeded to find that the admissions program there failed to meet constitutional standards because it was not sufficiently narrowly tailored. 539 U.S. at 269-76.

[3] Regents of University of California v. Bakke, 438 U.S. 265, 311–315 (1978).

[4] *Grutter*, 539 U.S. at 325.

[5] Id.

"The Law School's educational judgment that . . . diversity is essential to its educational mission is one to which we defer."[6] The Court emphasizes that this sort of judgment is one that "lies primarily within the expertise of the university"[7] and that deference was especially appropriate because universities occupy a "special niche in our constitutional tradition."[8]

The Court did not simply announce deference to the University's decision and end its analysis. It provided other reasons. But all were secondary to the primary reason, deference, which began[9] and ended the Court's analysis.[10] All the other reasons were cited to substantiate, bolster, or inform the Court's decision to defer to the University. "The Law School's assessment that diversity will, in fact, yield educational benefits is *substantiated* by respondents and their *amici*."[11] "The Law School's claim of a compelling interest is further *bolstered* by its *amici*, who point to the educational benefits that flow from student body diversity."[12]

The Court's specific treatment of the social science evidence reinforces its secondary role in the case. First, the Court's discussion of the benefits of diversity focused primarily on a variety of anecdotal reports from law school professors,[13] other individuals, the military, major corporations, and the Association of American Law Schools.[14] Second, the Court pointedly did not cite Professor Gurin's study, the main academic study focusing on the importance of diversity at the University of Michigan specifically. Third, in the single paragraph in which the Court did cite social science research, the description was very brief and perfunctory.[15] Fourth, the Court made no attempt to respond to contrary social science evidence cited by Justice Thomas in his dissent.[16] At best, this is a very cautious use of social science evidence.

The Court's cautious use of social science evidence in *Grutter* was not accidental. Instead, it reflects a general judicial hesitancy in using social science

---

[6] Id. at 328.

[7] Id.

[8] Id. at 329.

[9] "The Law School's educational judgment that such diversity is essential to its educational mission is one to which we defer." Id. at 328.

[10] "The Law School has determined, based on its experience and expertise, that a 'critical mass' of underrepresented minorities is necessary to further its compelling interest in securing the educational benefits of a diverse student body." Id. at 333.

[11] Id. at 328 (emphasis added to first italicized word).

[12] Id. at 330 (emphasis added to first italicized word).

[13] The Court quoted four excerpts from the District Court's decision in the case. 539 U.S. at 330. For two of the excerpts, the District Court supported them with the testimony of "[s]everal law professors." *Grutter v. Bollinger*, 137 F. Supp. 2d 821, 849 (E.D. Mich. 2001).

[14] *Grutter*, 539 U.S. at 330–332.

[15] The Court included only one short quote from a brief referring to the studies, and did not include any discussion whatsoever of the methodologies of the studies, their specific findings, or their strengths and weaknesses. Id. at 330.

[16] Id. at 364–366 (Thomas, J., dissenting).

evidence to craft legal rules.[17] One reason for this hesitancy is that social science evidence provides a weak and relatively unstable foundation for legal rules. This was quickly recognized, both academically and very practically, after the most celebrated use of social science evidence in a constitutional case. In *Brown v. Board of Education of Topeka* (1954),[18] the Court relied on social science studies to find that school segregation harmed Black children and, hence, to overrule *Plessy v. Ferguson* (1896).[19] A leading scholar quickly warned that it was dangerous to base such important rights on a foundation as "flimsy . . . as some of the scientific demonstrations" cited in the case.[20] As if to demonstrate the point, a Georgia district court later made its own factual determination that segregation did not cause psychological harm and, based on that finding, upheld the constitutionality of a segregated school system.[21] That Court was immediately reversed, with the Court of Appeals emphasizing that no lower court could review the factual basis of the Supreme Court's decision.[22]

The way in which the Court structured the *Grutter* decision avoids this problem. The result in *Grutter* does not depend on social science evidence finding that diversity contributes to a better education. The Court says that while there is such evidence, it merely provides support for the main reason for the decision: deferral to the University's judgment. It is telling that Justice Thomas, in dissent, claimed that the majority "relie[d] heavily on social science evidence"[23] and even more telling that the majority felt no need to respond to his statement. Justice

---

[17] It is important to note that I am talking here about the use of social science evidence by the courts to craft legal rules, and in particular to interpret the Constitution. See Kenneth Culp Davis, *An Approach to Problems of Evidence in the Administrative Process*, 55 Harv. L. Rev. 364, 402 (1942)(special rules should apply when courts are considering legislative or constitutional facts, rather than adjudicative facts). The reasons discussed here do not apply to other uses of social science evidence in the law, for example, when courts make factual determinations concerning only individual parties or when the legislature relies on social science evidence to craft legislation.

[18] 347 U.S. 483 (1954).

[19] 163 U.S. 537 (1896). *Plessy* had denied that separate-but-equal facilities had any detrimental effect on Black children:

"We consider the underlying fallacy of the [Black] plaintiff's argument to consist in the assumption that the enforced separation of the two races stamps the colored race with a badge of inferiority. If this be so, it is not by reason of anything found in the act, but solely because the colored race chooses to put that construction upon it." Id. at 551.

Brown relied on contemporary social science studies to find the opposite: "Whatever may have been the extent of psychological knowledge at the time of Plessy v. Ferguson, [the finding that segregation harms Black children] is amply supported by modern authority." 347 U.S. at 494. The Court's famous footnote 11 cited seven studies to support this finding. Id. at 494 n. 11.

[20] Edmond Cahn, *Jurisprudence*, 30 N.Y.U. L. Rev. 150, 167 (1954). *See also* Charles L. Black, Jr., *The Lawfulness of the Segregation Decisions*, 69 Yale L.J. 421, 426–427 (1960).

[21] Stell v. Savannah-Chatham County Board of Education, 220 F. Supp. 667 (S.D. Ga. 1963).

[22] Stell v. Savannah-Chatham County Board of Education, 333 F.2d 55 (5th Cir. 1963), *cert. denied sub nom.* Roberts v. Stell, 379 U.S. 933 (1964).

[23] *Grutter*, 539 U.S. at 364.

Thomas' statement, followed by citations to contrary authority, points to the instability that would be created if the social science studies had been a more central part of the majority's rationale; Justice Thomas recognized that this could be an opening to challenge the decision. The majority felt no need to reply to the statement because its decision had made clear that the evidence had played only a secondary role.

As a result, the battles after *Grutter* will not be about the presence or value of diversity. That issue is settled.[24] Universities, even those quite different from the University of Michigan, need not commission studies to demonstrate the value of diversity in their particular circumstances. Thus, an influential monograph advising universities about how to structure their admissions programs to ensure compliance with the Michigan decisions does not advise them that they need to take any steps to ensure that diversity would be accepted as a compelling interest; that necessary element was tacitly treated as settled. The advice all focused on how to ensure that their programs were sufficiently narrowly tailored.[25]

Nor is it at all likely that anyone will successfully challenge an affirmative action plan by presenting social science evidence that diversity does *not* enhance educational outcomes in a particular setting. Thus, in an important post-*Grutter* case involving the University of Washington, the plaintiffs did not even present a challenge to the diversity justification for using race as a factor in making law school admissions decisions. Instead, the plaintiffs devoted all their efforts to the claim that the University's program was not sufficiently narrowly tailored.[26] Unless there is truly compelling evidence, the holding of *Grutter* is that the courts must defer to the educational judgment of universities on that issue.[27]

---

[24] Or, at least, it is settled for universities that express the appropriate belief in the value of diversity, which for practical purposes is *all* universities. *See* Killenbeck (this volume). There is, of course, still room for debate about the value of diversity in other contexts, even other contexts within universities. For example, would the Court be equally willing to accept that diverse *teachers* contribute to a better education?

[25] Lawrence White, Understanding the Principles of Affirmative Action Law (2005). This monograph has been presented at several national conferences, including the annual meeting of the Law School Admissions Council and professional conferences at Arizona State University and the University of Arizona.

[26] Smith v. University of Washington, 392 F.3d 367 (9th Cir. 2004)(upholding the University's program).

[27] Some very interesting permutations are possible on the deferral issue. The Court emphasizes that deferral is appropriate because of the special role and status of universities. But what if the decision is made by the state, rather than the university? Is it still entitled to strong deference? What if the state and the university disagree on the value of diversity and, hence, on the extent to which the university should consider race in making admissions decisions? Are private universities, proprietary institutions, community colleges, and every other type of educational institution entitled to the same deference as the University of Michigan? What other types of institutions might also be entitled to this type of deference? The military? Police departments? Local school boards? *See* Petit v. City of Chicago, 352 F.3d 1111 (7th Cir. 2003)(court defers to city's judgment that a diverse police force is a compelling interest).; McFarland v. Jefferson County Public Schools, 330 F. Supp.3d 834 (W.D. Ky. 2004) (court defers to local school board's judgment that diversity in a public school is a compelling interest).

In limiting its reliance on social science evidence in *Grutter*, the Court was probably also influenced by its own limitations in assessing such evidence. If the holding had been based directly on the social science, the Court would have had to weigh that evidence and explain why it relied on certain studies and not others. But the courts are quite ill suited to arbitrate disputes between social scientists. They are only very rarely trained in social science methodologies, their procedures tend to frame social scientists as partisans for one side or the other, and they operate within a system where stories and anecdotes predominate over numbers and experiments.

The experience under *Daubert v. Merrell Dow Pharmaceuticals*[28] tends to confirm these doubts about judicial capabilities. *Daubert* changed the rules for admissibility of expert testimony in a way that called on courts to scrutinize such testimony more closely and using more scientific standards. The most recent scholarship finds that *Daubert*'s move to closer judicial scrutiny of expert evidence had no effect on scientific admissibility determinations.[29] Although prior scholars reaching the same result found this "surprising," I do not.[30] The most parsimonious explanation is that courts simply are not up to the task of applying the newer, more scientific standards.

The current controversy surrounding the provocative study of affirmative action by Professor Sander provides another good case in point.[31] Professor Sander's article provoked several studies and articles in response, to which he replied, eliciting more responses.[32] Much is still in dispute. But a point that defies rebuttal is that the vast majority of judges would be quite unable to make reliable judgments about the merits of Professor Sander's study, or its alternatives.

The structure of the *Grutter* decision permits judges to avoid the difficult task of evaluating the scientific merit of social science studies. If one vote had changed in *Grutter*, Justice Thomas' studies against the value of diversity may well have been in the majority opinion and Justice O'Connor's studies in favor of diversity may have been in the dissent. But this certainly would not have been

---

[28] 509 U.S. 579 (1993).

[29] Edward K. Cheng & Albert H. Yoon, *Does Frye or Daubert Matter? A Study of Scientific Admissibility Standards*, 91 Va. L. Rev. 471 (2005).

[30] Jennifer L. Groscup et al., *The Effects of Daubert on the Admissibility of Expert Testimony in State and Federal Criminal Cases*, 8 Psychol., Pub. Poly & L. 309, 345–348, 364 (2002).

[31] Richard H. Sander, *A Systemic Analysis of Affirmative Action in American Law Schools*, 57 Stan. L. Rev. 367 (2004).

[32] See, for example, David L. Chambers et al., *The Real Impact of Eliminating Affirmative Action in American Law Schools: An Empirical Critique of Richard Sander's Study*, 57 Stan. L. Rev. 1855 (2005); David B. Wilkins, *A Systemic Response to Systemic Disadvantage*, 57 Stan. L. Rev. 1915 (2005); Ian Ayres & Richard Brooks, *Does Affirmative Action Reduce the Number of Black Lawyers?*, 57 Stan. L. Rev. 1807 (2005); Daniel E. Ho, Comment, *Why Affirmative Action Does Not Cause Black Students to Fail the Bar*, 114 Yale L.J. 1997 (2005); Richard H. Sander, *A Reply to Critics*, 57 Stan. L. Rev. 1963 (2005); Richard H. Sander, *Mismeasuring the Mismatch: A Response to Ho*, 114 Yale L.J. 2005 (2005); Daniel E. Ho, *Affirmative Action's Affirmative Actions: A Reply to Sander*, 114 Yale L.J. 2011 (2005).

because of a careful judicial evaluation of the scientific merit of the studies. Instead, it would have occurred, rightly or wrongly, because judges treat social science evidence like they treat other evidence: as imperfect approximations of the truth, presented by partisans, which they draw upon to construct a reasoned opinion. Thus, *Grutter* does not hold that it was appropriate for the University of Michigan to consider race in making admissions decisions because studies demonstrate that diversity produces important educational benefits. Instead, the case holds that the Court is willing to defer to the educational judgment of the University. The studies are relevant only because they demonstrate that the University's judgment was reasonable. Because social science plays only a minimal, back-up role in the case, the Court finesses the issue of scientific merit.[33]

The reasons the Court was reluctant to accord great weight to social science evidence in *Grutter* are not at all unique to that case. In virtually all cases, courts have a strong interest in the stability of their decisions and in avoiding the need to explore the scientific merit of studies. *Grutter*, then, should be viewed, not as a case dealing only with how social science evidence should be used in cases involving affirmative action, but rather as a recent example of how cautious the courts are likely to be in *all* cases involving this type of evidence to craft rules.

For example, the Court was equally cautious in *Roper v. Simmons*,[34] a case in a completely different substantive area, but one also noted for its use of social science evidence. Although *Roper* cites social science to support its decision that capital punishment for minors violates the Constitution, the Court was careful to protect the stability of its decision and to avoid detailed debate about scientific methods. The Court signals this clearly at the very beginning of the relevant discussion: "[A]s any parent knows and as the scientific and sociological studies . . . tend to confirm [minors are immature, irresponsible, and act impetuously]."[35] Thus, the primary base of the decision is common knowledge (what every parent knows). The studies were merely backup that *tend to* confirm what we all know. Second, for all but one of the three points citing social science evidence, the first and primary citation was to a case. Thus, in the preceding example, the first citation was to *Johnson v. Texas*,[36] in which the Court made the statement about immaturity without providing any social science evidence in support. In *Roper*, the Court then added a secondary citation to social science. Finally, on the third point where social science was the primary source, the only citation was to a classic 1968 book.[37] Since the Court in *Roper* was overturning a decision made in 1989,[38] it would be hard to claim that the decision was driven by social science

---

[33] The Court's move was a classic one. By deferring to the University's decision, the Court shifted the burden of proof on social science heavily to those opposed to affirmative action. The social science evidence would be determinative only if it clearly and unambiguously undermined the University's decision.

[34] 543 U.S. 551 (2005).

[35] *Id.* at 569.

[36] 509 U.S. 350, 367 (1993).

[37] *Roper*, 543 U.S. at 570 (citing E. Erikson, Identity: Youth and Crisis (1968)).

[38] Stanford v. Kentucky, 492 U.S. 361 (1989).

that was well known at the time of both decisions, rather than by other changes in the Court and society.

At first glance, this tendency to treat social science evidence so cautiously would seem to be an unfortunate result for social scientists working on legal issues.[39] Social scientists would like to have their work taken seriously by the courts and the best measure of that would be direct causation: a social science finding results in a corresponding legal decision. *Grutter* and its kin obscures that causation. But causation can work in both directions and, viewed from the other direction, *Grutter* may benefit social science. A regime of direct causation would mean, not only that social science would have a direct effect on the law, but also that the law would have a much greater effect on social science. In *Grutter* itself, for example, there was no doubt whatsoever what Professor Gurin was expected to find in her studies designed specifically to support the litigation, and that is precisely what she found.[40] In her chapter, Professor Crosby cites studies finding that Whites exhibit only positive attitudes toward affirmative action and bear no animosity toward those favored by the policy.[41] These cannot be social scientists who were looking very hard for animosity.

Viewed in this way, *Grutter*'s approach to social science evidence may help to insulate researchers from these types of pressures.[42] Ironically, if the courts begin to perceive social science research as more neutral and unbiased, they may well begin to give it greater weight. Thus, one interpretation of *Grutter*'s approach to social science evidence is that it is seeking an equilibrium in which social scientists are encouraged to produce solid and unbiased research which, in turn, will permit courts to rely on it more heavily.

---

[39] I agree with Professor Killenbeck's implication that it does not matter whether we label the Court's use of social science evidence as primary or secondary. Killenback (this volume). But the actual use of the evidence, however labeled, *is* important. As I indicate in the preceding text, it matters to the stability of judicial decisions and to the capacity of judges to evaluate evidence and reach reasoned decisions. Professor Killenbeck hints at another interesting way in which actual use of the evidence may matter. Courts may be attempting to have it both ways by relying on social science evidence to make it appear that they are not simply imposing their own views, while at the same time carefully limiting use of the evidence. It would be interesting to explore how successful the courts are in this balancing act.

[40] *Expert Report of Patricia Gurin*, http://www.umich.edu/~urel/admissions/legal/expert/gurintoc.html; Patricia Gurin *et al., The Educational Value of Diversity*, in Defending Diversity: Affirmative Action at the University of Michigan (Patricia Gurin et al., eds., 2004). There has been a great deal of quiet skepticism about Professor Gurin's study from those who support and believe in its results, but have considerable doubt about its methods.

[41] Crosby (this volume). But see Madeline E. Heilman et al., *The other Side of Affirmative Action: Reactions of Non-Beneficiaries to Sex-Based Preferential Selection*, 81 J. Applied Psychol. 346 (1996) (males generally react negatively to preferential treatment of females).

[42] The threats to unbiased research, of course, extend far beyond the limited circumstances addressed by *Grutter* and can never be eliminated. Nevertheless, the ability to influence courts directly is an especially powerful temptation, and one to which the courts are likely to be especially attentive.

Unit III
Workplace Discrimination: Legal Developments and Empirical Research in Sexual Harassment

8
How Can We Make Our Research on Sexual Harassment More Useful in Legal Decision Making?

Barbara A. Gutek

Social scientists have contributed substantially to our understanding of sexual harassment, so much so that a legal scholar has recently recommended that judges use such research to develop "better legal standards that will actually reflect (or consciously choose not to reflect) how sexual harassment happens, is perceived, and affects workers" (Beiner, 2005, p. 3). But there is room for improvement, as law professor, Beiner, notes in her book, which is, among other things, a clear call to researchers to conduct studies that will be useful to the court. Many researchers, too, have argued that the research needs to be a more useful aide to the court's decision making (O'Connor & Vallabhajosula, 2004; Wiener & Gutek, 1999; Wiener & Hurt, 1999;).

How has the research on sexual harassment been used in court? In this chapter, I review areas of research that have been relevant to sexual harassment litigation with the goal of identifying areas where our research has been helpful and not so helpful. I also cover areas where research would be helpful in court even though such research has not been published. In doing so, I rely on my own experience as an expert witness, both for the plaintiff and the defendant.

I review the ways that sexual harassment is conceptualized and measured. This is important for litigation because ultimately our understanding of the predictors, correlates, and consequences of sexual harassment are based on our how we measure sexual harassment. The extent to which our measures depart from a legal measure affects our ability to talk about the antecedents and consequences of illegal sexual harassment.

After reviewing the ways sexual harassment is measured, I discuss the problems with our existing measures with respect to their utility in the legal context. I then tell why this issue matters in the legal context and suggest some changes so that the research is more useful in litigation. I contrast the area of defining and measuring sexual harassment with another area where the research is more useful in the courtroom—reporting or complaining about sexual harassment. I also discuss and an area where we lack the research to provide opinions based on research, namely what constitutes an effective sexual harassment policy.

Defining Sexual Harassment

Today, sexual harassment has both a legal and a broader lay definition and the two are confounded much of the time in the research literature. It has not always been that way. The journalist Lin Farley takes credit for coining the term *sexual harassment*; she wrote a book, *Sexual Shakedown* (1978), to bring attention to the phenomenon. The book describes many different kinds of incidents that Farley considered sexual harassment and provides the following definition of sexual harassment: "Sexual harassment is best described as unsolicited nonreciprocal male behavior that asserts a women's sex role over her function as a worker" (Farley, 1978, p. 15). In 1979, legal scholar Catharine MacKinnon wrote an influential book that provided a theoretical and a legal framework for understanding and dealing with sexual harassment in the United States. MacKinnon argued that sexual harassment was a form of sexual discrimination (i.e., denies women equal opportunity in the workplace) and therefore Title VII of the 1964 Civil Rights Act, which forbids discrimination on the basis of sex (among other social categories), should apply. A year after her book was published, the U.S. Equal Employment Opportunity Commission established guidelines on sexual harassment. Early empirical studies of the workplace and academia started appearing in print about the same time. Gutek, Nakamura, Gahart, Handschumacher, and Russell conducted the first study in 1978 and published it in 1980. Also in 1980, my colleague at UCLA, Charles Nakamura, and I received an grant from the National Institute of Mental Health to study sexual harassment, a project that resulted in several articles and my 1985 book, which has been cited by legal scholars and the California Supreme Court (*Farmers Insurance Group v. County of Santa Clara*, 1995), the New Jersey Supreme Court (*In the Matter of Seaman*, 1993; *Lehmann v. Toys 'R' Us*, 1993), and the First Circuit Court of Appeals (*Lipsett v. University of Puerto Rico*, 1988). In 1982, the *Journal of Social Issues* published an issue of the journal on sexual harassment (e.g., Brewer & Berk, 1982) and Benson and Thomson (1982) separately authored a published article from the earliest study of sexual harassment of students.

Sexual harassment increasingly became thought of as a legal concept as lawsuits alleging sexual harassment found their way to the courtroom and ultimately to the U.S. Supreme Court. The EEOC guidelines described two kinds of sexual harassment, *quid pro quo* harassment and hostile work environment harassment. Not surprisingly, the law on sexual harassment is still developing as the court struggles to define sexual harassment. For example, although *quid pro quo* harassment might seem to be straightforward, it turns out to also be complicated. For example, does the threat of a *quid pro quo* that is never carried out constitute illegal activity, or must one carry out the threat before breaking the law? Defining a hostile work environment is even more difficult and elusive. The courts are not all that clear about what constitutes hostile environment sexual harassment, but the behavior must be severe or pervasive. Still, even those words are not always helpful as reviews by Beiner (2005, chapter 1) and Goodman-Delahunty (1999), among others, show. Must the target of harassment show psychological or physical damage to prove that the behavior is severe, as some courts required? In 1993, in the *Harris* case, the U.S. Supreme Court said "no" to that (*Harris v. Forklift Systems, Inc.*, 1993). The context is key as evidenced 5 years after *Harris* when the U.S. Supreme Court said that one must "consider all the circumstances." (*Oncale v. Sundowner Offshore Services*, 1998; see Wiener & Winter, this volume). Further, the two most recent U.S. Supreme Court decisions, *Oncale* and *Burlington Industries, Inc. v. Ellerth* (1998), "eliminated the distinction between *quid pro quo* and hostile work environment claims. The Court determined that the distinction between the two forms of harassment was more academic than functional. Thus, elements of proof in a sexual harassment claim are those to establish a hostile work environment" (Foote & Goodman-Delahunty, 2005, p. 56).

These are hardly the only issues in sexual harassment law (see, e.g., Beiner, 2005; Foote & Goodman-Delahunty, 2005; O'Connor and Vallabhajosula, 2004), but they serve to highlight the difficulty researchers face if they try to measure sexual harassment in a manner that even roughly approximates the legal definition.

To avoid confusion with the legal concept of sexual harassment, in the early 1980s, my colleagues and I frequently used the term "social-sexual behaviors" to distinguish a set of behaviors that might be considered sexual harassment in that they were not work-related and they invoked a potentially inappropriate infusion of sex, sex roles, gender, or sexuality into the workplace (see, e.g., Gutek, 1985; Gutek et al., 1980). Such a set of behaviors typically included actions or activities that would be unlikely to satisfy the legal requirements for sexual harassment (but they would satisfy Farley's (1978) definition of sexual harassment that preceded the EEOC's guidelines). By including a broad range of behaviors, researchers could learn whether people's views of specific behaviors differed over time (or across samples). This approach would also allow researchers to see if social-sexual behaviors that are more or less likely to be illegal (depending in part on the development of the law) have common antecedents and consequences.

Although other researchers, notably Wiener and his colleagues (Wiener et al., 2002; Wiener & Hurt, 1997, 1999, 2000; Wiener, Winter, Rogers, & Arnot, 2004) also use the term, social-sexual behavior, more typically researchers claim to be studying and measuring sexual harassment, with no clear distinction between behaviors that are annoying or unwanted but not severe and pervasive enough to clearly meet the definition of unlawful sexual harassment (e.g., Fitzgerald et al., 1988; Fitzgerald, Swan, & Magley, 1997). This has caused confusion because a general audience increasingly aware that sexual harassment is illegal is likely to believe that the percent of the workforce that would have experienced any of a broad range of social-sexual behaviors at work is the same as those who have a reasonable legal claim of sexual harassment.

The message has not been lost on Americans. In fact, some think that behavior is illegal even though it is unlikely to be found illegal in a court of law. Several years ago, Robert Done and I explored this issue and found that a diverse sample of people rated a variety of social-sexual behaviors quite sexually harassing, according to their own definition (see Table 8.1). Unwanted physical touching and sexually explicit entertainment at work or company functions were rated

TABLE 8.1. Is this Behavior Sexual Harassment?

| | Is This Sexual Harassment? | |
| | Personal[a] | Legal[b] |
Item	Mean (SD)	Mean (SD)
Telling jokes with sexual meaning	3.30 (1.56)	3.61 (1.64)
Offensive gestures	4.31 (1.38)	4.41 (1.52)
Unwanted physical touching	5.61 (0.87)	5.60 (0.92)
Displaying sexually suggestive objects or pictures	4.91 (1.37)	4.82 (1.44)
Repeatedly asking a co-worker for a date or out after work, after they have indicated an unwillingness to go	4.97 (1.26)	4.86 (1.38)
Use of sexually explicit entertainment in the workplace or at company functions	5.13 (1.15)	5.12 (1.20)
Mean	4.70 (0.91)	4.74 (1.07)

Total $N = 152$, composed of undergraduate students ($N = 52$), MBA students ($N = 55$), and realtors ($N = 45$).
[a]Do you personally consider the following to be sexual harassment?
[b]Do you consider the following to meet the legal definition of sexual harassment?
Note: All items are 6-point scales, 1 = no, definitely not, 6 = yes, definitely.
Means for first item differ at $p < .01$; all others, ns.

more harassing than the other types of social-sexual behavior we asked about. In general, the scores for meeting their own definition of harassment and meeting a legal definition of harassment were similar, with the exception of "telling jokes with sexual meaning," where the rating scores for illegal behavior were significantly *higher* than were their own ratings. In other words, in general our sample of respondents thought the legal definition was broad and possibly broader than their own definition of the term.[1]

In general, people are likely to learn about sexual harassment from training programs and posted policies at work or from the media. The workplace policies and training programs tend to be given by lawyers who emphasize that sexual harassment is illegal. To protect the organization from lawsuits, companies may discourage or forbid behavior that would clearly not be sexual harassment in a court of law. Consultants urge companies to make their policy stricter than the law (e.g., Orlov & Roumell, 1999). They and managers generally prefer to err on the side of caution, to help ensure that employees will stay within legal limits. For example, employees may be told to not touch any other employee, including a pat on the back. The media tend to sensationalize sexual harassment, either focusing on particularly egregious behavior or what they consider trivial behavior that has nevertheless led to a legal allegation. In my experience, media sometimes treat sexual harassment as a topic of entertainment rather than an area of scientific inquiry or an area of the law. These trends together can lead people to think that illegal sexual harassment covers a broader range of behavior than it actually does.

---

[1] One defense attorney said that the first line of defense is to make sure that the jury understands the legal definition because most people think the law covers a lot more than it does.

Because of the confusion between the law's view of sexual harassment and any other definition of sexual harassment, Bowes-Sperry and Tata (1999) suggested that scholars explicitly state that a lay definition of sexual harassment does not necessarily imply that a law has been broken. However, using the same words to represent a variety of definitions is awkward. Further, if sexual harassment is a concept that is evolving in the law, how can researchers study it and measure it?

One seemingly simple solution is to decide to limit the use of the term, sexual harassment, to behavior that is most likely illegal and its meaning would change in parallel with developments in the law. This would mean that researchers use concepts like "social-sexual behavior," or perhaps "perceived sexual harassment," if that is what an instrument measures.

Measuring "Sexual Harassment"

Being able to opine in court about the organizational factors associated with the occurrence of sexual harassment or opine about the consequences of sexual harassment based on research results means that researchers have to measure sexual harassment. Among the behavioral scientists, psychologists in particular devote a considerable amount of time to devising ways of measuring complex psychological concepts. One identifies a psychologically meaningful construct (e.g., intelligence, self-esteem, job satisfaction, gender stereotyping) and applies a well-developed set of rules and procedures for devising a reliable and valid measure of that construct. When the concept of sexual harassment developed in the late 1970s and early 1980s, the possibility of developing a measure of this new construct became appealing.

However, as noted in the preceding, since sexual harassment is a legal concept, its definition changes as the law develops. Thus, the standard way of developing a measure for a psychological construct (defined and, in a sense, controlled by the social science community) runs into problems when researchers apply it to a legal concept that is and will continue to develop. Although the available measures may have been useful for researchers, they have some limitations for the legal context.

Researchers have attempted to measure social-sexual behavior since the late 1970s (Gutek et al., 1980) and to develop measures of sexual harassment since the late 1980s (Fitzgerald et al., 1988). Most of these measures assess specific behaviors that some might consider to be sexual harassment. In the late 1970s and early 1980s, understanding just what kind of experiences people had was important to the many people who had never encountered any sexual harassment, or if they did, thought theirs was a unique experience.

In attempting to measure social-sexual behaviors, my colleagues and I focused on the initiator's intentions as we thought these would affect the recipient's reactions. Thus, we asked questions about sexual comments that were "meant to be complimentary" or sexual comments that were "meant to be insulting or a 'put down'" (see Gutek, 1985, Appendix C). Among other questions, we also asked about touching that was "meant to be sexual" or "*not* meant to be sexual."

While the law may not be concerned with the perpetrator's intentions, I believe that perceived intentions are important to people. Moreover, the effect on the target (the focus of the law) undoubtedly depends on the target's interpretation of the perpetrator's intentions. Not only would recipients likely feel worse if they thought sexual comments were meant to be insulting rather than complimentary, but their reactions are likely to be different. Someone who made an offensive comment but didn't intend to be offensive (because of too much to drink at an office party, or insensitivity, or self-centeredness, or ignorance of the recipient's sensitivities) is not likely to be judged as harshly as someone who is perceived as intending to use sexual language and gestures to intimidate or threaten a co-worker or subordinate (see Wiener & Hurt, 1999 for data that support the differential effects of intent in harassment judgments). Whereas the behaviors might be ignored in the former instance (at least for a while, or if they were not repeated), the same behaviors, if they were meant to be insulting, might be more likely to lead to some action—perhaps talking with a friend or family member or someone at work, or even filing a formal complaint or quitting one's job.

The Sexual Experiences Questionnaire (SEQ), developed in the mid- to late-1980s, is the best known of the multi-item instruments that purportedly measures sexual harassment. Fitzgerald and her colleagues say the SEQ, first described in a 1988 article (Fitzgerald et al., 1988) measures "psychological" sexual harassment to distinguish it from illegal sexual harassment, adding further to confusion about what sexual harassment means. More specifically, the developers of the SEQ say that the " . . . advantage of our model is that it articulates the relation between the legal and psychological constructs without in any sense equating them" (Fitzgerald, Gelfand, & Drasgow, 1995, p. 438). In 1997, Fitzgerald et al. (1997, p. 15) defined psychological sexual harassment as ". . .unwanted sex-related behavior at work that is appraised by the recipient as offensive, exceeding her resources, or threatening her well-being." Not all items in the SEQ fit that definition of psychological sexual harassment.

Although the SEQ is well known by name, it is not clear how many people interested in the research on sexual harassment know that there are multiple versions or have seen a copy of some version of it. It appears that no version of the instrument appeared in a publication for at least 10 years after its introduction in the late 1980s (Fitzgerald et al., 1988).

My colleagues and I reviewed and critiqued the SEQ (Gutek, Murphy, & Douma, 2004). Each version contains a lead-in statement like "Have you ever been in a situation where . . . " (Barak, Pitterman, & Yitzhaki, 1995; Fitzgerald et al., 1988;) or "During the past two years while you have been employed, has any of your male supervisors or coworkers where you worked. . ." (Glomb et al., 1997). Respondents then read each of the items, each of which refers to a type of behavior, such as "Made you uncomfortable by staring at you (for example, at your breasts)," "Kept on asking you out even after you have said 'no,' " or "Told dirty stories or jokes." Respondents have a choice of three or five options such as *never*, *once*, and *more than once* (described in Fitzgerald et al., 1995, p. 427) or "a 5-point scale, ranging from 1 (*never*) to 5 (*most of the time*)" Fitzgerald et al.

(1997, p. 580). The authors designed most of the versions of the SEQ for women to complete, but there are also male versions.

Actually, "the SEQ" does not seem to exist. The many different SEQs together show inconsistencies in wording, time frame, and the like. The various SEQs lack the advantages of standardized measures such as the ability to assess changes over time or compare the amount of SEQ behavior across samples. The various versions also have weak psychometric properties; they define sexual harassment very broadly, extending well beyond a legal definition and the authors' own definition of psychological sexual harassment. It is not clear what or whose definition of sexual harassment the SEQ assesses.

A much simpler approach to measuring sexual harassment is to simply ask, "Have you ever been sexually harassed?" This "global item" approach is rarely used with a few exceptions. Most notably, the Navy Equal Opportunity/Sexual Harassment survey (NEOSH), "one of the most widely distributed surveys that has not been modified with each administration" (Culbertson & Rodgers, 1997, p. 1958) that was first administered in 1989 (Rosenfeld, Culbertson, Booth-Kewley, & Magnusson, 1992), measures sexual harassment with two items. "During the past year, have you ever been sexually harassed while on duty?" and "During the past year, have you ever been sexually harassed on base or ship while off duty?"

Global items are used infrequently because some researchers contend that these measures would result in an underreporting of the phenomenon (see Cortina, Swan, Fitzgerald, & Waldo, 1998; Fitzgerald et al., 1997), as workers seem reluctant to acknowledge that they have been sexually harassed (Barak, Fisher, & Houston, 1992; Chan, Tang, & Chan, 1999; Jaschik & Fretz, 1992; Schneider, 1982; Stockdale & Vaux, 1993; Stockdale, Vaux, & Cashin, 1995). In addition, asking respondents if they have been sexually harassed may require an unrealistic cognitive performance, as respondents would have to determine first what constitutes sexual harassment and then determine if they had experienced any behavior that met those criteria.

Thus, some researchers have proposed that a single question asking respondents if they have been sexually harassed should be considered an indicator of acknowledging or labeling sexual harassment. Indeed researchers have used these items as indicators of labeling (e.g., Adams-Roy & Barling, 1998; Cortina et al., 1998; Magley, Hulin, Fitzgerald, & DeNardo, 1999; Stockdale et al., 1995), rather than as measures of sexual harassment, per se.

In addition, in some studies involving the Sexual Experiences Questionnaire (SEQ), the single item asking the respondent if she has been sexually harassed has been used as a criterion by which to validate a multi-item measure (e.g., Fitzgerald et al., 1988). Thus, a single-item asking the respondent if she or he has been sexually harassed has played multiple roles. It has been used as an indicator (1) of sexual harassment, either alone or along with other items, (2) that the respondent has labeled his/her experience as one of sexual harassment, or (3) of the validity of a much longer set of questions inquiring about specific behaviors that the respondent has experienced. Clearly, it makes little sense to make the same question perform so many different functions! Of the three uses, treating the single-item self-report measure as an indicator of the validity of a larger set of self-report questions stretches credulity. If, in fact, the researchers who developed and used the SEQ view the single item as the valid measure, and if the researchers' goal is to assess the amount of sexual harassment, then why would they bother to ask the longer set of questions?

It is not clear, however, that one item will do the job. Kidder, LaFleur, and Wells (1995) found that it was often only on reflection that women labeled their experiences as sexually harassing. A single item probably will not do the job as a good reliable and valid measure of sexual harassment. Perhaps the best use of the single item is as a measure of labeling, that is, the fact that the respondent has experienced something that she/he considers sexual harassment. However, a single item might underestimate the amount of sexual harassment if people are reluctant to admit being the recipient of illegal behavior.

It is possible to get around the concern that people might be reluctant to label their own experience sexual harassment. In a very early study, my colleagues and I (Gutek, 1985; Gutek, Cohen, & Konrad, 1990) asked respondents whether they considered various kinds of social-sexual behavior to be sexual harassment separately from asking them if they had experienced any of the same set of social-sexual behaviors. Then we considered respondents to be harassed if they (1) considered a kind of behavior to be sexual harassment and (2) they experienced that kind of behavior. Although it is not a perfect measure, that approach has two advantages: it avoids the cognitive load burden of having to deal with definition and one's own experience at the same time and it reduces the bias caused by whatever reluctance one might have to assert that one had been a target of illegal behavior. A disadvantage is that one might generally consider a behavior to be sexual harassment but not experience that behavior as harassing—or vice versa. Another potential disadvantage for less severe harassment is that respondents might forget some experiences; it is unlikely anyone would forget a really severe incident.

Measures of the Work Environment

As an alternate approach to using measures of social-sexual behavior to approximate the amount of illegal sexual harassment in legal proceedings, researchers can assess the work environment directly. Several measures were designed to indicate the extent to which the work environment—and by extension, the managers of that work environment—tolerates sexual harassment. In theory, such measures might be useful in research done to support legal action because whether management knew or should have known is an element that helps to determine an organization's legal liability.

These measures describe the work environment as perceived by the respondent rather than try to assess the experiences of individual women or men. I think the best such measure is one developed by Lott, Reilly, and Howard (1982; Reilly,

Lott, & Gallogly, 1986). Their 10-item measure, the Tolerance for Sexual Harassment Inventory (TSHI), yields three factors, labeled "flirtations are natural," "provocative behavior," and "feminist beliefs." The TSHI measures the respondent's beliefs about men and women (e.g., "An attractive woman has to expect sexual advances and should learn how to handle them."), not organizational norms.

Hulin, Fitzgerald, and Drasgow (1996) describe the development of their measure, the Organizational Tolerance for Sexual Harassment Inventory (OTSHI), using a sample of employees at a regulated utility company. In this 18-item measure that focuses on the respondent's view of the organization's tolerance for harassment, respondents read a scenario and then answer questions about what they think would happen if the behavior described in the scenario occurred at their own workplace. The OTSHI contains three subscales corresponding to the three kinds of questions asked about each scenario: risk of reporting, likelihood of being taken seriously, and probability of sanctions. Fitzgerald, Drasgow, Hulin, Gelfand, and Magley (1997) subsequently used this instrument in a structural equation model involving employees at the same company. A disadvantage is that it is a projective measure (the respondent tells what she thinks the company would do in response to various scenarios) and therefore may say more about the respondent than about the work environment.

Developed as part of the Navy's study (NEOSH), Culbertson and Rodgers' (1997) report on a questionnaire that uses nine items to measure sexual harassment climate perceptions. Their scale measures respondents' perceptions of the extent to which sexual harassment occurs, if it is a problem, if anything is being done to stop it, and if respondents know what actions and words are considered sexual harassment.

Finally, Gutek et al. (1990) used eight items to measure perceptions of the extent to which the work environment is sexualized. Examples of items were: "How many men (women) dress to be attractive to women (men) at work? Would you say most, some, hardly any, or no men (women) do this?" and "Where you work, how much social pressure is there for men (women) to flirt with women (men)? A lot, some, or none?"

Each of these measures might provide some useful information about the extent to which employees believe the work environment supports offensive behavior or encourages workers to treat each other in a potentially illegal manner.

Why Good Measurement Matters: Using Measures in Litigation to Estimate the Amount of Sexual Harassment

In a class action, the premise is that a whole class of people in a large organization or organizational unit has been subjected to illegal behavior. More is at stake in a class action than an individual action, but a class action is more efficient than numerous individual actions if one firm has generated multiple plaintiffs with the same complaint (Landy, 2005).

How does one know that a whole class of workers experiences sexual harassment? Several people from the same company might file a complaint with the EEOC or a law firm. However, even if their complaints have merit, do they represent the tip of the iceberg or isolated incidents? To answer these questions, one might surmise that it would be helpful to be able to give an instrument measuring sexual harassment to the class of plaintiffs (or potential plaintiffs) in order to determine the amount of sexual harassment over the time frame covered by the (pending) lawsuit.

To find out what people have experienced, at various times the Equal Employment Opportunity Commission (EEOC) has either conducted a survey or engaged an expert to conduct such a survey to collect data in a systematic way and analyze it in a systematic way. In some of those cases, consultants have administered the SEQ and the results of the survey were used to provide an expert opinion on the amount of illegal sexual harassment in the company or agency based on the percentage of female employees (current and/or former) who reported SEQ behaviors. In one of those cases (*Equal Employment Opportunity Commission v. Dial Corporation*, 2002), I was retained by the defendant firm, the Dial Corporation, to evaluate the survey given which included a version of the SEQ. The judge concluded that the "survey materials [SEQ] are too flawed to be useful in assisting the fact finder in this case" (*EEOC v. Dial*, 2002, p. 14). It is important to note that in the Dial case, the SEQ was used specifically (but not exclusively) to support opinions about the amount of sexual harassment at the Dial plant. Yet, the published research using the various versions of the SEQ tends to focus on predictors and correlates of scores on the SEQ, linking SEQ scores to various aspects of the work environment. The published research using the SEQ does not discuss whether or not any particular sample has yielded a high or low level of sexual harassment. In fact, the current state of the research on the SEQ does not allow one to draw any conclusions about whether any particular sample has yielded a particularly high or low rate of sexual harassment.

If the various versions of the SEQ are not appropriate for use in court, is there some other instrument that is? To my knowledge, no single, well-documented measure published in a peer-reviewed journal currently exists. Although Lengnick-Hall (1995) advised researchers to use the legal definition in their research, up to now, they have not done so, for a variety of good reasons: (1) the legal definition changes as the law develops, so the legal definition is a moving target; (2) laws vary from country to country; (3) targets may experience negative consequences of sexual harassment without having the harassment rise to meet a legal definition; and (4) there is no reason to believe that we can learn about sexual harassment only by measuring it to conform to its legal definition. Despite these potential problems, my colleagues and I have been working on just such a measure.[2]

---

[2] Gutek, B. A., Stockdale, M., Done, R., & Swindler, S. (n.d.) The experiences of sexual harassment scale: A five-item measure of sexual harassment based on a legal definition, unpublished manuscript.

The law expects juries to take into account "all the circumstances." Therefore, a list of behaviors will not do the trick. Further, a list of behaviors has another disadvantage when it is used in legal proceedings to assess the amount of sexual harassment. Let us say that a reliable measure based on a set of questions each assessing some specific kind of social-sexual behavior had been developed and it was given to various random samples of employed women (or men and women) so that it was possible to come up with reliable estimates (means and standard deviations) across samples. It would not make sense to consider any score above zero to constitute illegal behavior. How much higher would a firm have to score before it would be guilty of illegal sexual harassment? Could an "average" company, that is, one whose scores are within normal range, say one standard deviation, of the mean, be guilty of illegal behavior?

Our work therefore has abandoned the "list" approach that has dominated the measurement of sexual harassment and social-sexual behavior more broadly. Instead, our work focuses on the EEOC's definition, which, by virtue of the fact that it acts as a guide to the court on its interpretation of individual cases, may be broad enough to encompass future changes. Although we think our new measure will fill a need, it will not be a panacea.

In sum, although it might sound like a nice idea to use a measure of "sexual harassment" to determine if a class of workers is subject to illegal behavior in a given firm, in reality such a task is far from easy and is complex. It involves more than coming up with a measure that meets traditional standards of psychometric measurement. I have suggested two different approaches. One is to develop a measure of sexual harassment that approximates the legal definition. The second is to use (or refine) a measure of the work environment that will provide useful information on the extent to which the work environment, and by extension the organization's managers, condone or tolerate a sexualized, discriminatory, or hostile work environment.

Research that Is Useful in the Courtroom: Complaining About Harassment

In contrast to measuring sexual harassment, there are areas that have been more useful in a court of law and that do not directly involve the complexities of defining and measuring illegal sexual harassment. As Beiner (2005, chapter 5) pointed out, the court often expects employees to complain. Failure to file a complaint makes the plaintiff less credible because filing a complaint demonstrates that the behavior was "unwelcome," and that the respondent considered the behavior severe enough to do something about it. Plaintiffs may lose and courts may sometimes dismiss cases on summary judgment because the plaintiff did not complain or did not complain soon enough (see Wiener & Hurt, 1999, for a detailed discussion of this issue). Not only the law, but also people more generally, expect a formal or informal complaint from someone who has been sexually harassed. A person who never complains, or does not complain until the boss fires her or she quits her job, leaves her behavior open to interpretation. If the harassment was so bad, why wouldn't she complain about it right away? Did she wait to complain after she left the company because she is angry about her boss firing her or because she was harassed? A study of 81 cases filed in Illinois over a 2-year period found that notifying management before filing a formal complaint increased the probability of a favorable outcome for the plaintiff alleging sexual harassment (Terpstra & Baker, 1992).

In contrast to the common sense view that anyone who is sexually harassed would naturally complain about it to someone in charge, the body of research suggests that is not the case. Many surveys, starting with the earliest ones (Gutek et al., 1980; U.S. Merit Systems Protection Board, 1981) have asked respondents whether they talked to anyone or filed a complaint of sexual harassment as a result of experiencing social-sexual behaviors. Most people do not complain about behavior they consider trivial but many do not complain even when the behavior is not trivial. Further, they provide good reasons why they do not (e.g., the supervisor is the harasser, fear of retaliation, belief that she/he should deal with the problem person, belief that their supervisors think she/he should handle the situation, or concern about hurting the perpetrator). This "underreporting" is robust, and is widely found; the results hold up across samples and the idiosyncrasies of individual studies (see Fitzgerald, Swan, & Fischer, 1995; Gutek & Koss, 1993; Livingston, 1982). Because most studies do not assess illegal sexual harassment, we do not know the true extent of underreporting of illegal behavior. However, the small percentages who do complain, and the reasons they give for not complaining, provide convincing evidence that many people who are illegally harassed do not complain. Further, available research suggests that complaining does not necessarily or even usually lead to a positive outcome for the complainant, confirming some of the concerns of people who chose not to report their harassing experiences. For example, only 32% of targets in the U.S. Merit Systems Protection Board (1994) study who filed grievances or complaints with the government found that it made things better, 47% found that it made things worse. Realistic concern about negative consequences provides another reason why people who are illegally harassed do not complain.

Thus, having an expert discuss the research findings with respect to complaining can be very helpful to the cause of the person alleging sexual harassment. It may be important for a jury to appreciate the fact that there are good reasons why someone who is subject to illegal sexual harassment would not talk about the harassment to others at work or file a formal complaint with an appropriate unit such as human resources.

As a result, people's usual behavior is a problem for the law. The law encourages or even requires workers to notify their employer if they are victims of unwelcome social-sexual behavior. Complaining about this unwelcome conduct is especially important if the company has a sexual harassment policy (see, e.g., *Madray v. Publix Super Markets, Inc.*, 1998). A requirement that people complain when many do not complain reduces the effectiveness of the law in preventing and redressing the harm suffered by targets of sexual harassment.

To make matters worse, the law seems to allow for only a narrow window when workers "should" complain. Beiner (2005, chapter 5) noted that if the plaintiff complains before the behavior reaches some threshold of severity, the case may be dismissed because the alleged behavior was determined to be trivial. If they wait too long, the case may also be dismissed because the plaintiff failed to complain in a timely manner, especially if the employer has an anti-harassment policy in place. (See, e.g., *Caridad v. Metro North Commuter Railroad,* 1999, in which the plaintiff did not report the harassment for 3 months; *Watkins v. Professional Services Bureau,* 1999, in which the plaintiff did not report the harassment for about 4 months, both of which were dismissed.)[3]

Research that Could Be Useful in the Courtroom: Research on Sexual Harassment Policies

Developments in the courtroom point to interesting areas where it would be very useful to have research available, but so far very little has been published. Here I will focus on sexual harassment policies. As noted in the preceding text, courts have given a lot of attention to whether or not the defendant company has a sexual harassment policy in place. It seems that the mere presence of some kind of sexual harassment policy both requires the complaining party to promptly complain and exonerates the employer of the behavior of its managers and employees if the alleged victim fails to complain at the appropriate time.

What many companies now do is to have a consultant or an in-house legal staff review their sexual harassment policy, making sure that it is up-to-date on legal developments. In the process, the written manifestation of the sexual harassment policy may follow trends in the law, such as the "zero tolerance" movement. Some sexual harassment policies make a point of asserting that the organization has "zero-tolerance" for sexual harassment, a phrase that has not been defined (Stockdale, Bisom-Rapp, O'Connor, & Gutek, 2004). How does having a policy forbidding sexual harassment differ from a "zero tolerance" policy that forbids sex harassment? Zero tolerance may mean, for example, that the company will not tolerate even the hint of sexual talk or conduct, and/or that it will mete out severe punishment to anyone found guilty of sexual harassment. It may also be a symbolic word, intended to signal that the company is serious about sexual harassment. In the absence of research showing whether having a zero tolerance policy versus a plain old policy makes any difference in amount of harassment, likelihood of reporting harassment or any other meaningful indicator of validity, organizations can appear virtuous by having a zero tolerance policy without making any substantial change. Further, those organizations seeking the best advice to ensure a harassment-free work environment for their employees may adopt practices that do not necessarily further their goal.

---

[3] Beiner,(2005, chapter 5) reviewed these cases.

Companies are likely to include the sexual harassment policy in the package of materials given to new employees. Employers ask new employees to read and sign the policy and turn it in along with their other hiring materials. The employer places the new employees' signed statements into their personnel files proving that they saw and read the policy. There may be training for some or all employees and the employer may document the names of those who attend or who have viewed a training video.

Yet, is there any evidence that these procedures mean that the employer is serious about sexual harassment—or more serious than an employer who does not have such procedures? Or is that employer just more knowledgeable about the law than an employer without a sexual harassment policy? This emphasis on policy might simply be an example of form over substance; it is possible to go through the motions without really addressing the problem, if indeed a problem exists. It is possible to have few problems without having a formal policy drawn up by someone who is current on sexual harassment law.

More importantly, does any of the legal discussion about policies have anything to do with employees' behavior? Does the mere existence of a sexual harassment policy change anything for the employee—except the obligation to report the harassment? That is, is there any justification for the view that all of the reasons harassed employees give why they do not complain, would no longer apply just because the employer has a sexual harassment policy that satisfies legal obligations? I think the answer is "no." If an employee's supervisor is threatening the employee's job security because that employee refuses to have sex with the supervisor, the mere presence of a sexual harassment policy—which the supervisor is blithely violating—is unlikely to reassure any employee. And that employee is not likely to complain because behavior trumps any written policy. As Wiener and Gutek (1999, pp. 507–508) noted, "legal parameters. . . must to some extent depend on assumptions about how people behave. . ." When they fail to do so, people are likely to pay attention to the behavior. My own feeling is, therefore, that a policy, per se, means relatively little; it is the behavior of employees and management that matters. If managers serve as models of good behavior and if they do not tolerate an abusive work environment, and there is some mechanism for complaining about sexual harassment in the event it does happen, then I think that any reasonable policy will suffice. Nevertheless, the law emphasizes the policy and in my experience that leads to detailed examination of a company's sexual harassment policy in many lawsuits. Unfortunately, we have little published research focusing directly on whether having a policy really does matter. Lack of research does not mean lack of expert opinion; in fact, it may mean more varied opinions because no research is required to test any sensible opinion offered by someone with expertise. Such expertise may include experience in writing a sexual harassment policy or providing sexual harassment training, or serving in some HR capacity or being an attorney who has handled sexual harassment allegations. We have no idea if any of the recommendations given by consultants about elements of a good sexual harassment policy make any difference at all.

We need research on the nature, quality, and implementation of sexual harassment policies that will be useful to the courts. In the case of policies, we know little about which specific features of a policy make any kind of difference (in knowledge, likelihood of reporting a harassing behavior). I have seen expert reports arguing that to be effective, a policy must have a list of potentially harassing behaviors, or it must have a clause forbidding retaliation against someone who complains. However, if employees who think they may have been sexually harassed read their company's policy, is it likely that they will even notice if there is no list of potentially harassing behaviors, for example? Unfortunately, it is difficult to publish such research because it is typically not very theoretical, even though it would be useful.

Conclusion

In this chapter, I have discussed the applicability of our research on sexual harassment to the courtroom. If we expect the courts to make use of our research to make legal judgments about social sexual behavior, we must provide them with rigorously conducted studies. I am heartened by the fact that there is now more such research available. Not all research on sexual harassment or social-sexual behavior need be applicable to the courtroom, of course. There is room for research on measuring social-sexual behavior and testing theories that advance science that is not for use in the courtroom. Nevertheless, I agree with Wiener and Hurt (1999) who argued that social science has paid too little attention to the law in this area. They advocate more research designed to be used in the courtroom, an area they call social-analytic jurisprudence. In addition, we need to make sure our research really fits the law if we are going to use our research in the courtroom.

Besides being useful in the courtroom, research can show where the law makes unreasonable demands on people, a point emphasized by Beiner (2004). At the urging of industry, justifiably eager to find a reliable way to defend themselves in sexual harassment cases, the courts have provided employers with a set of guidelines: Have a sexual harassment policy, provide training, and provide a way for people to complain about harassment. If employees do not use those mechanisms put in place to help them, they can lose their right to their day in court—even though they may face substantial risk to their career or psychological well-being by complaining.

References

Adams-Roy, J., & Barling, J. (1998). Predicting the decision to confront or report sexual harassment. *Journal of Organizational Behavior, 19*, 329–336.

Barak, A., Fisher, W. A., & Houston, S. (1992). Individual difference correlates of the experience of sexual harassment among female university students. *Journal of Applied Social Psychology, 22*, 17–37.

Barak, A., Pitterman, Y., & Yitzhaki, R. (1995). An empirical test of the role of power differential in originating sexual harassment. *Basic and Applied Social Psychology, 17*, 497–518.

Beiner, T. (2005). *Gender myths v. working realities: Using social science to reformulate sexual harassment law*. New York: New York University Press.

Benson, D. J., & Thomson, G. E. (1982). Sexual harassment on a university campus: The confluence of authority relations, sexual interest, and gender stratification. *Social Problems, 29*, 236–251.

Bowes-Sperry, L., & Tata, J. (1999). A multiperspective framework of sexual harassment. In G. Powell (Ed.), *Handbook of gender and work* (pp. 263–280). Thousand Oaks, CA: Sage.

Brewer, M. B., & Berk, R. A. (Eds.) (1982). Beyond nine to five: Sexual harassment on the job. *Journal of Social Issues*, 38(4 entire issue).

Chan, D. K. S., Tang, C. S. K., & Chan, W. (1999). Sexual harassment: A preliminary analysis of its effects on Hong Kong Chinese women in the workplace and academia. *Psychology of Women Quarterly, 23*, 661–672.

Cortina, L. M., Swan, S., Fitzgerald, L. F., & Waldo, C. (1998). Sexual harassment and assault: Chilling the climate for women in academia. *Psychology of Women Quarterly, 22*, 419–441.

Culbertson, A. L., & Rodgers, W. (1997). Improving managerial effectiveness in the workplace: The case of sexual harassment of Navy women. *Journal of Applied Social Psychology, 27*, 1953–1971.

Farley, L. (1978). *Sexual shakedown: The sexual harassment of women on the job*. New York: McGraw-Hill.

Fitzgerald, L. F., Drasgow, F., Hulin, C. L., Gelfand, M. J., & Magley, V. J. (1997). Antecedents and consequences of sexual harassment in organizations: A test of an integrated model. *Journal of Applied Psychology, 82*, 578–589.

Fitzgerald, L. F., Gelfand, M. J., & Drasgow, F. (1995). Measuring sexual harassment: Theoretical and psychometric advances. *Basic and Applied Social Psychology, 17*, 425–445.

Fitzgerald, L. F., Shullman, S. L., Bailey, N., Richards, M., Swecker, J., Gold, Y., Ormerod, A. J., & Weitzman, L. (1988). The incidence and dimensions of sexual harassment in academia and the workplace. *Journal of Vocational Behavior, 32*, 152–175.

Fitzgerald, L., Swan, S., & Fischer, K. (1995). Why didn't she report him? The psychological and legal implications of women's responses to sexual harassment. *Journal of Social Issues, 51*, 117–138.

Fitzgerald, L. F., Swan, S., & Magley, V. J. (1997). But was it really sexual harassment? Legal, behavioral, and psychological definitions of the workplace victimization of women. In W. O'Donohue (Ed.), *Sexual harassment: Theory, research, treatment* (pp. 5–28). Boston: Allyn & Bacon.

Foote, W. E., & Goodman-Delahunty, J. (2005). *Evaluating sexual harassment: Psychological, social, and legal considerations in forensic examinations*. Washington, DC: American Psychological Association.

Glomb, T. M., Richman, W. L., Hulin, C. L., Drasgow, F., Schneider, K. T., & Fitzgerald, L. F. (1997). Ambient sexual harassment: An integrated model of antecedents and consequences. *Organizational Behavior and Human Decision Processes, 71*, 309–328.

Goodman-Delahunty, J. (1999) Pragmatic support for the reasonable victim standard in hostile workplace sexual harassment cases. *Psychology, Public Policy, and Law, 5*(3), 519–555.

Gutek, B. A. (1985). *Sex and the workplace*. San Francisco: Jossey-Bass.

Gutek, B. A., Cohen, A. G., & Konrad, A. M. (1990). Predicting social-sexual behavior at work: A contact hypothesis. *Academy of Management Journal, 33*(3), 560–577.

Gutek, B. A., & Koss, M. P. (1993). Changed women and changed organizations: Consequences of and coping with sexual harassment. *Journal of Vocational Behavior, 42*, 28–48.

Gutek, B. A., & Morasch, B. (1982). Sex-ratios, sex-role spillover, and sexual harassment at work. *Journal of Social Issues, 38*, 55–74.

Gutek, B. A., Murphy, R. O., & Douma, B. (2004). A review and critique of the Sexual Experiences Questionnaire (SEQ), *Law and Human Behavior, 28*(4), 457–482.

Gutek, B. A., Nakamura, C., Gahart, M., Handschumacher, I., & Russell, D. (1980). Sexuality and the workplace. *Basic and Applied Social Psychology, 1*, 255–265.

Hulin, C. L., Fitzgerald, L. F., & Drasgow, F. (1996). Organizational influences on sexual harassment. In M. S. Stockdale (Ed.), *Sexual harassment in the workplace* (pp. 127–150). Newbury Park, CA: Sage.

Jaschik, M., & Fretz, B. (1992). Women's perceptions and labeling of harassment. *Sex Roles, 27*, 19–23.

Kidder, L. H., Lafleur, R. A., & Wells, C. V. (1995). Recalling harassment: Reconstructing experience. *Journal of Social Issues, 51*(1), 53–68.

Landy, F. (2005). Phases of employment litigation. In F. Landy (ed.) *Employment discrimination litigation: Behavioral, quantitative, and legal perspectives* (pp. 3–19). San Francisco: Jossey-Bass.

Lengnick-Hall, M. L. (1995). Sexual harassment research: A methodological critique. *Personnel Psychology, 48*, 841–864.

Livingston, J. A. (1982). Responses to sexual harassment on the job: Legal, organizational, and individual actions. *Journal of Social Issues, 38*(4), 5–22.

Lott, B., Reilly, M. E., & Howard, D. (1982). Sexual assault and harassment: A campus community case study. *Signs, 8*, 296–318.

MacKinnon, C. (1979). *Sexual harassment of working women: A case of sex discrimination.* New Haven, CT: Yale University Press.

Magley, V. J., Hulin, C. L., Fitzgerald, L. F., & DeNardo, M. (1999). Outcomes of self-labeling sexual harassment. *Journal of Applied Psychology, 84*, 390–402.

O'Connor, M. O., & Vallabhajosula, B. (2004). Sexual harassment in the workplace: A legal and psychological framework. In B. J. Cling (Ed.) *Sex, violence and women: A Psychology and Law Perspective* (pp. 115–147). New York: Guilford Press.

Orlov, D., & Roumell, M. T. (1999). *What every manager needs to know about sexual harassment.* New York: AMACOM.

Reilly, M. E., Lott, B., & Gallogly, S. M. (1986). Sexual harassment of college students. *Sex Roles, 15*, 333–358.

Rosenfeld, P., Culbertson, A. L., Booth-Kewley, S., & Magnusson, P. (1992). *The Navy Equal Opportunity/Sexual Harassment Survey. Part I: Assessment of Equal Opportunity Climate.* (NPRDC TR 92-17). San Diego: Navy Personnel Research and Development Center.

Schneider, B. E. (1982). Consciousness about sexual harassment among heterosexual and lesbian women workers. *Journal of Social Issues, 38*, 75–98.

Stockdale, M. S., & Vaux, A. (1993). What sexual harassment experiences lead respondents to acknowledge being sexually harassed? A secondary analysis of a university survey. *Journal of Vocational Behavior, 43*, 221–234.

Stockdale, M. S., Vaux, A., & Cashin, J. (1995). Acknowledging sexual harassment: A test of alternative models. *Basic and Applied Social Psychology, 17*, 469–496.

Stockdale, M., Bisom-Rapp, S., O'Connor, M., & Gutek, B. A. (2004). Coming to terms with zero-tolerance sexual harassment policies. *Journal of Forensic Psychology Practice*, *4*(1), 65–78.

Terpstra, D. E., & Baker, D. D. (1992). Outcomes of federal court decisions on sexual harassment. *Academy of Management Journal, 35*, 181–190.

United States Merit System Protection Board, *Sexual Harassment in the Federal Workplace* (1981, 1987, 1988, 1994). Washington, DC: U.S. Government Printing Office.

Wiener, R. L., & Gutek, B. A. (1999). Advances in sexual harassment research, theory, and policy. *Psychology, Public Policy, and Law, 5*(3), 507–518.

Wiener, R. L., Hackney, A., Kadela, K., Rauch, S., Seib, H., Warren, L., & Hurt, L.E. (2002). The fit and implementation of sexual harassment law to workplace evaluations. *Journal of Applied Psychology, 87*, 747–764.

Wiener, R. L., & Hurt, L. E. (1997). Social sexual conduct at work: How do workers know when it is harassment and when it is not? *California Western Law Review, 34*, 53–99.

Wiener, R. L., & Hurt, L. E. (1999). An interdisciplinary approach to understanding social sexual conduct at work. In R. Wiener & B. Gutek (Eds). *Advances in Sexual Harassment Research, Theory and Policy*. Special edition of *Psychology, Public Policy, and Law*, *5*, 556–595.

Wiener, R. L., & Hurt, L. E. (2000). How do people evaluate social-sexual conduct: A psycholegal model. *Journal of Applied Psychology, 87*, 75–85.

Wiener, R. L., Winter, R., Rogers, M., & Arnot, L. (2004). The effects of prior workplace behavior on subsequent sexual harassment judgments. *Law and Human Behavior, 28*(1), 47–67

Wiener, R. L., & Winter, R. J. (2007). Totality of circumstances in sexual harassment decisions: A decision-making model, this volume.

Legal Citations

Burlington Industries, Inc. v. Ellerth, 524 US 742 (1998).

Caridad v. Metro North Commuter Railroad,191 F.3d 283 (5th Cir. 1999).

Equal Employment Opportunity Commission v. Dial Corporation, WL 31061088, N. D. Ill. (Sept. 17, 2002).

Equal Employment Opportunity Commission (EEOC) v. Dial Corporation, Northern District, Ill., No. 99 C 3356 (Nov. 17, 2002).

Farmers Insurance Group v. County of Santa Clara,11 Cal. 4th 992, 1030, 906 P.2d 445, 459 (1993).

Harris v. Forklift Systems, Inc., 510 U.S. 17 (1993).

In the Matter of Seaman,133, N.J. 67, 90, 627 A.2d 106 (1993).

Lehman v. Toys 'R' Us, 133 N.J. 587, 614, 626, A.2d 445, 459 (1993).

Lipsett v. University of Puerto Rico, 864 F.2d 881, 889, n.19 (1st Cir. 1988).

Madray v. Publix Super Markets, Inc., 30 F.Supp.2d 1371 (S.D. Fla. 1998).

Oncale v. Sundowner Offshore Services, 111 S. Cty. 998 (1998).

Watkins v. Professional Services Bureau, Ltd., WL 1032614 (4th Cir. 1999).

9
Totality of Circumstances in Sexual Harassment Decisions: A Decision-Making Model

Richard L. Wiener and Ryan J. Winter

> "...we can say that whether an environment is "hostile" or "abusive" can be determined only by looking at all the circumstances. These may include the frequency of the discriminatory conduct; its severity; whether it is physically threatening or humiliating, or a mere offensive utterance; and whether it unreasonably interferes with an employee's work performance."
>
> —*Harris v. Forklift Systems, Inc.*, 1993, p. 19.

The Totality of the Circumstances in the Law

Writing the majority opinion in *Harris v. Forklift Systems, Inc.* (1993), Justice O'Connor emphasized the circumstances surrounding an employee's complaint in determining whether it reaches a violation of Title VII. The Supreme Court rejected the proposition that a hostile work environment requires a showing of a particular outcome, in this case psychological harm, in favor of careful consideration of the entirety of the work environment. The truth is that hostile work environment claims are as diverse as the complaints and organizations in which they arise. Simple, or for that matter, complex rules that draw bright lines of law around the boundaries of hostile work environment harassment are doomed to failure. The Supreme Court in *Harris* reiterated (see *Meritor Savings Bank v. Vinson*, 1986, p. 67) that the best that could be done was to look to the circumstances surrounding an allegation and craft a test that acknowledged the almost limitless variability in unwelcome sexual conduct at work that could contribute to a hostile work environment. The Supreme Court has repeated this basic logic in years following *Harris* and *Meritor* and required a demonstration of hostile work environment harassment to consider all the circumstances in *Faragher v. Boca Raton* (1998, p. 787), *Oncale v. Sundowner Offshore Services, Inc.* (1998, p. 81), and most recently in *Pennsylvania State Police v. Suders* (2004, p. 2350). This chapter begins to ask the question, "How do decision makers make judgments about sexual harassment that takes into consideration the totality of the circumstances?"

The fact patterns that make up typical social sexual conduct complaints at work do indeed vary so extensively from case to case that it is difficult for a decision maker to find the threshold for discriminatory conduct. Consider the exceptional facts in the *Harris* case, itself. Charles Hardy was the supervisor of Teresa Harris, a manager at an equipment rental company (*Harris*, 1993). According to Harris, Hardy made insulting comments to her about work deficits that he attributed to her being a woman, but still made unwelcome sexual propositions toward her. At one point, Hardy threw objects down in front of Harris and asked her to pick them up as he looked on. Harris eventually left the company and sued Forklift for a Title VII violation of her civil rights.

Cases of hostile work environment harassment do not always involve supervisory relationships; very often, the actionable complaints involve co-workers not separated by a power differential. For example, in *Rabidue v. Osceola Refining Co.* (1986), Ms. Rabidue was an administrative assistant responsible for purchasing supplies, monitoring government regulations, assigning other employees work assignments, and contacting regular customers. Her work brought her into contact with Douglas Henry, who was a supervisor for the company's computing division, and with whom Rabidue needed to coordinate some of her work efforts to complete her assigned tasks. According to Rabidue, Henry made vulgar and crude remarks toward her and all the women at Osceola, creating a work environment that she and the other women found difficult to bear. Rabidue also complained that other men at work displayed regularly pictures of naked and scantily clothed women. The circumstances in this case, unlike Harris, involved relationships among co-workers without a power differential and without any one-sided sexual contact interest.

Other case fact patterns include both power differentials and egregious exhibitions of unwelcome sexual contact. In *Faragher v. City of Boca Raton* (1998), Beth Ann Faragher worked as a lifeguard at the beach under the supervision of Bill Terry and David Silverman, both of whom repeatedly touched her (and other women) in offensive and uninvited ways. Apparently, the culture of life guarding on the beach promoted a sexualized environment among the college student workers. On at least one occasion, Terry put his hands around Faragher and touched her in sexual ways. At another time, Silverman tackled Faragher, and remarked that he would have liked to have sexual relations with her if it were not for a physical attribute that he found unappealing. Faragher complained to another supervisor, Robert Gordon, to whom other women had also complained, but who had failed to report the women's grievances. Eventually Faragher filed a Title VII complaint against the city.

Context in the Psychology of Sexual Harassment Decision-Making

These fact patterns are indeed very different with regard to power differentials of the workers, severity of the complained after conduct, response of the complainant, conduct of supervisors, and conduct of co-workers. Each case demonstrates a unique set of circumstances, which must be weighed as part of the totality of the circumstances to determine whether hostile work environment sexual harassment indeed transpired. The difficulty in understanding how workers, jurors, students, and others reach these decisions is still more complicated than the comparison of these knotty fact patterns might suggest. The typical workers likely have experiences with other examples of social sexual conduct at work, so that prior experience with those cases could act to stimulate attitudes and beliefs about ongoing or future cases. Judging the totality of the circumstances is not a simple matter of considering the events that transpired in a single workplace interaction in isolation of other events. In fact, judgments about the totality of the circumstances very likely involve the totality of the work experiences of the students, workers, jurors, litigators, and judges who make those judgments. In the language of social psychology, the fact that workers experience multiple exposures to situations like those described in the cases mentioned earlier can result in priming effects or, alternatively, contrast effects. Priming results when separate but related psychological constructs become activated through prior independent tasks and influence subsequent social judgments (Higgins, Rholes, & Jones, 1977), attitudes (Bargh, Chaiken, & Govender, 1992), stereotypes (Blair & Banajia, 1996; Lepore & Brown, 1997), and behavior (Bargh, Chen, & Burrows, 1996; Dijksterhuis, Spears, & Postmes, 1998). Here the separate evaluations of sexual harassment claims are conceptually related, but factually and temporarily separated.

The influence of prior experience with similar events but different in degree can produce comparison effects exactly the opposite of those expected under priming. For example, Stapel and colleagues (e.g., Stapel & Koomen, 1997; Stapel, Koomen, & Van Der Pligt, 1997; Stapel & Winkielman, 1998) report some situations when extreme stimuli, which were intended as primes, led to contrast effects because observers compared the initial exemplars to the "to be judged" instances of the category and found the "to be judged" instances less extreme than the first examples. Less extreme exemplars led to assimilation effects because observers use the primes as a foundation for evaluating ambiguous novel stimuli. However, when prior experience is conceptually related but very different in quantity to the "to be judged" stimuli, the "to be judged" stimuli may look more or less serious depending on their relationship to the prior experience. In prior research with sexual harassment judgments using written scenarios, we found evidence for both priming effects and contrast effects when we asked college students to make multiple judgments of hostile work environment cases (Wiener, Winter, Rogers, & Arnot, 2004).

As observed in the preceding text, the variability in the kinds of actions that can lead to hostile work environment harassment is vast. Further, the likelihood that workers are exposed to multiple workplace-related situations (i.e., different fact patterns within the same work environment) and multiple workplace independent fact patterns (i.e., different fact patterns across different work environments), argues for psychological research that models the complexity of the work environment and the complexity of the experience of workers exposed to multiple complaints. Justice O'Connor was clearly not concerned with the psychological mechanisms that govern how decision makers evaluate workplace environments when she stated, ". . .we can say that whether an environment is 'hostile' or 'abusive' can be determined only by looking at all the circumstances." (*Harris*, 1993, p. 19). However, we suggest that a totality of the circumstances judgment will involve the differential experiences of workers in current and past environments.

Older research in psychology studying how workers decide what constitutes sexual harassment in their daily work environments (e.g., Baker, Terpstra, & Cutler, 1990; Burgess & Borgida, 1997; Gutek, Morasch, & Cohen, 1982; Gutek et al., 1999; Hartnett, Robinson, & Singh, 1989; Jones, Remland, & Brunner, 1987; Kovera, McAuliff, & Hebert, 1999; Powell, 1986; Saal, Johnson, & Weber, 1989; Terpstra & Baker, 1986; Thomann & Wiener, 1987; Valentine-French & Radtke, 1989; Wayne, Riordan, & Thomas,, 2001; Wiener, Hurt, Russell, Mannen, & Gasper, 1997; Wiener, Watts, Goldkamp, & Gasper, 1995) fell short of modeling the Court's intuitive understanding of the complexity of hostile and abusive work environments. Most of the early studies that strived to understand the way in which workers, jurors, students, and others determined whether social sexual conduct was harassing followed a uniform format. Participants read single vignettes usually in the form of written summaries of case facts and evaluated the facts to determine whether the complainants had or had not been the victim of sexual harassment. Sometimes the judgments that workers made reflected the elements of hostile work environment law and sometimes they did not. Seldom did researchers make an effort to capture the totality of the circumstances either at work or in the minds of the evaluators. Even less frequently did researchers examine how experienced workers reach judgments about sexual harassment in complex environments as they attribute blame, causality, and responsibility to workers, coworkers, and supervisors.

The social science literature continues to grow with the presentation of single scenarios in which researchers ask respondents to make judgments about the likelihood that these situations constitute hostile work environment sexual harassment complaints. These studies rarely ask respondents to compare situations across or within work environments. For example, in a recent study that examined the impact of dissolved workplace relationships on reactions to a sexual harassment complaint Pierce, Broberg, McClure, and Aguinis (2004) presented a written scenario in which two employees were involved for 3 years in an office romance that they mutually agreed to end. Nonetheless, several weeks later the woman complained that the man continued to rub her neck and shoulders, as well as tell her unwelcome sexual jokes. While the results provide an interesting test of a moral model of judgment and decision making, one can only wonder about the impact of the evaluators' prior experiences, encounters, and resulting idiosyncratic judgment biases in these types of evaluations.

In an important study of cultural differences in responses to sexual harassment complaints, Sigal et al. (2005) had participants from a number of different countries review a single written scenario in which a female student accused a male professor of touching her nonsexually, but doing so frequently, and making comments about her physical appearance. The results of this type of research are undeniably informative and the extension of judgment models across international boundaries is an important contribution to the literature. Still, one can only ponder the effects of prior experiences and wonder whether such experience acts differently in different cultures.

To be sure, not all research looking at sexual harassment judgments presents single scenarios and asks for harassment-related judgments. For example, Stockdale, O'Connor, Gutek, and Greer (2002) presented to research participants a series of vignettes including a short written scenario, the scenario accompanied by still photographs, and a 1 hour and 20 minute broadcast video to examine the effects of prior victimization and judgments of sexual harassment. A female worker in each of the scenarios complained about a work environment in which she encountered sexually explicit materials and sexual jokes repeatedly told in her presence and in the presence of other workers. In later work, Stockdale, Berry, Schneider, and Cao (2004) again tried to model the comparative decision-making process when they investigated the role of intra- and intergender status on judgments of sexual harassment complaints made by men. Here participants judged two different scenarios that manipulated whether a male worker was the target of unwelcome sexual advances (an approach-based scenario) or the victim of vulgar and derogatory name calling focusing on the complainant's sexual fantasies (an insult-based scenario). Further, as discussed in more detail below, Wiener and colleagues (Wiener & Hurt, 1997, 2000; Wiener et al., 1995, 1997, 2002,) have conducted several studies that employ multiple scenarios in an attempt to capture the complexities of the work environment and the judgment strategies of evaluators.

A Judgment Model for Evaluating Social Sexual Conduct

Wiener and colleagues' studies present independent scenarios with the intended purpose of examining how exposure to one set of sexual harassment complaints will influence judgments in subsequent evaluations. Presenting more than one scenario to the same participants allows the first case to prime attitudes and beliefs about the "to be judged complaints," or to act as a baseline against which evaluators compare new and independent social sexual conduct. In this manner, it is possible to examine both priming and contrast effects as workers evaluate the totality of the circumstances. This work has evolved (Wiener & Hurt, 1997, 2000; Wiener et al., 1995, 1997, 2002, 2004) into a model of decision making in cases of sexual harassment, which accommodates contextual differences in the work environment, as well as, judgment differences in the minds of the decision makers. The model uses the law of hostile work environment sexual harassment as a normative theory and builds on it a psychological perspective on how people are likely to make these types of decisions.

Federal Law

Federal statute prohibits employee discrimination with respect to compensation, terms, conditions, or privileges of employment because of race, color, religion, sex, or national origin (Title VII of the Civil Rights Act of 1964 as amended in 1991). Case law forbids employers to exact sexual contact in exchange for compensation or advancement (i.e., *quid pro quo* harassment, *Henson v. City of Dundee*, 1982; and *Miller v. Bank of America*, 1979) or to subject workers to intimidating, hostile, or offensive working environments because of their sex (i.e., *hostile work environment harassment, Harris v. Forklift Systems, Inc.*, 1992 and *Meritor Savings Bank v. Vinson*, 1986). In *Meritor* (1986), the Supreme Court held that hostile work environment theory requires that plaintiffs experienced *unwelcome* social-sexual misconduct because of their sex. Further, the misconduct must have been "sufficiently severe or pervasive to alter the conditions of employment and create an abusive working environment" (*Meritor*, 1986, p. 60). Normally, the law requires a pattern of offensive behaviors unless the conduct is exceptionally severe (e.g., assault).

Recent social psychological theory suggests that people may evaluate some allegations of sexual harassment with little cognitive effort (Wiener & Hurt, 1999, 2000; Wiener et al., 2002). Accordingly, workers reach a preliminary judgment based upon well-rehearsed and easily retrievable attitude structures. These attitude structures can come from existing dispositional properties possessed by the individual, experience with prior cases, or some combination of both. Prior research (Wiener & Hurt, 1999, 2000; Wiener et al., 2002) demonstrated that at least two attitude structures, hostile sexism (i.e., women are aggressive and must be kept in their place through gender dominance) and benevolent sexism (i.e., woman are weak and should be protected from overbearing men) (Glicke & Fiske, 1996) influence perceptions of hostile work environment harassment. Further, Wiener et al.(2004) demonstrated that college students who read written scenarios and who judged and thought about an aggressive complainant in one case, were less willing to find evidence of sexual harassment in that case than those not exposed to an aggressive complainant. On the other hand, women exposed to a submissive complainant in the first case were more likely to find sex-based discrimination in a subsequent independent case than were those who were not exposed to a submissive complainant. Wiener et al. (2004) interpret the latter findings as an example of women blaming victims of harassment after exposure to a submissive complainant who accepted bad treatment at work.

Summing up the expectations of the model, if initial categorizations of people or conduct trigger a hostile attitude toward the complainant, then the offensive behavior that the worker complains about will fall below an internal offensiveness threshold and people perceive it as not harassing with little cognitive activity. On the other hand, if observers activate a benevolent attitude toward the complainant, then the offensive conduct will fall above an internal threshold and people will perceive it as harassing, again with little cognitive activity. This process is "partially automatic" in that a consciously recognized event (prior exposure) launches an unintended and biased judgment (i.e., overt actions in the workplace trigger hostile or benevolent attitudes toward the complainant), which unfolds outside the individual's conscious control (Bargh, 1994; Wegner & Bargh, 1998). This initial judgment is likely to be heavily influenced by the context in which the decision takes place (i.e., by the totality of the circumstances of the harassment complaint).

If conflicting belief structures are triggered (i.e., hostile and benevolent attitudes – ambivalent sexism; Glick & Fiske, 1996) or if the perceiver is held accountable for the final judgment, the perceiver engages in an effortful, second process to correct the biases and reach a more thoughtful conclusion. Here, evaluators apply some set of parameters to reach a conscious and carefully thought out judgment. If people understand the legal elements (i.e., unwelcomeness, severity, and pervasiveness) and are asked to apply them, judgments about those factors act as criteria that signal completion of the task and thus trigger conscious control of the process (Chen & Bargh, 1997; Wegner & Bargh, 1998). However, if people make these judgments without a decisional guideline (legal or otherwise), then the final judgment likely remains partially automatic, relying little on systematic effortful processing. Based on earlier findings, we hypothesize that this effortful thought process uses a self-referencing test (i.e., perceivers measure the conduct against their own standards of unwelcomeness, severity, and pervasiveness) to determine whether ambiguous social sexual conduct at work is harassing. Because people use themselves as reference points to reach these decisions, the process produces unintended gender effects. Gender is a salient and ubiquitous referral point, which colors judgments of harassment. Figure 9.1 presents the outline of the model adjusting it for the elements of hostile work environment harassment articulated in the case law.

Several empirical investigations offer support for the primary propositions of this model. For example, in one study full-time workers viewed tapes of equal employment opportunity officers interviewing workers involved in two harassment cases (Wiener & Hurt, 2000) and rated the complained after conduct on several elements of sexual harassment law (e.g., unwelcomeness, severity, and pervasiveness). Participants who applied the reasonable person (as compared to the reasonable woman) legal standard and those high (as opposed to low) in hostile sexism found less evidence of sexual harassment, regardless of gender (Wiener & Hurt, 2000). Notably, legal standard offset the effects of hostile sexism; the difference in harassment judgments between high and low hostile sexists disappeared under the more specific reasonable woman standard, but was pronounced in the more abstract reasonable person condition.

In Wiener and Hurt (2000), the main effect for gender was significant across cases but especially strong in the moderately severe, as opposed to relatively benign, fact pattern, that is, the one most likely to trigger effortful and reflective thought. However, in this and other studies (Wiener and Hurt, 2000; Wiener et al., 1997, 2002) the gender effect dropped out when self-referencing was statistically controlled with respondents' ratings of how they would have perceived the conduct had they been the complainant. Similar efforts at eliminating gender differences with measures of social identification measures were unsuccessful (Wiener et al., 1997). These studies explain gender differences in sexual harassment judgments as the result of women being more sensitive to gender discrimination because, compared to men, they experience it more at work. Stockdale et al. (2004) find additional support for the self-referencing effect in a study examining judgments of harassment when men are the complainants.

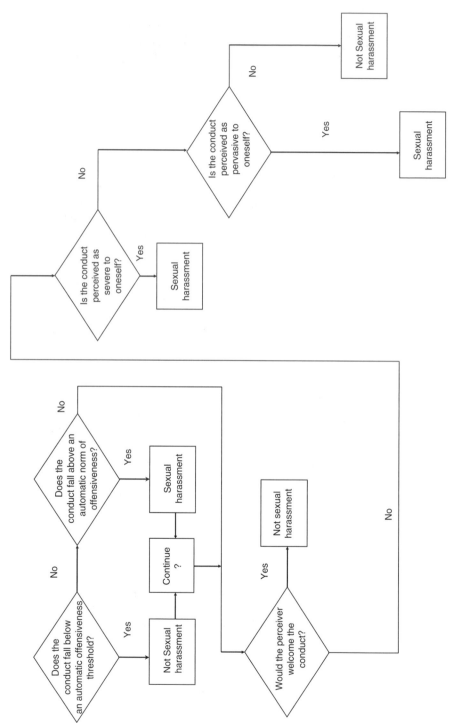

FIGURE 9.1. Sexual harassment judgment model.

Judgments of Reenacted Sexual Harassment Complaints

This model accommodates the laws' requirement that judgments about sexual harassment take into consideration the context in which the actions occur (*Harris*, 1993; Wiener and Hurt, 2000; Wiener et al., 2002). Because abusive environments include multiple episodes of offensive behavior, extant claims likely influence workers' judgments of subsequent actions. In the present study, we first hypothesized that aggressive (or submissive) complainants will act as primes and trigger hostile (or benevolent) attitudes in evaluators and influence subsequent judgments about those complainants. Specifically, observers will find less evidence of harassment with aggressive complainants. In prior research, Wiener and Hurt (2000; Wiener et al., 2002) showed that measured hostile sexism predicts harassment judgments, when viewers evaluate video representations of conflict resolution interviews. In more recent work, Wiener et al. (2004) demonstrated priming and contrast effects in undergraduate respondents reading written scenarios. The current study tests the causal connections between hostile and benevolent primes (i.e., aggressive and submissive complainants) and harassment judgments among full-time workers viewing video tapes of reenacted social sexual conduct at work.

Second, we anticipate that the activation of these attitudes in one case will spill over into a second, independent case to influence the manner in which observers judge social-sexual complaints, even though the actors, facts, and indeed theory of the second case may be very different. In keeping with our model, we expect that this process is largely uncontrolled and semi-automatic. Indeed, effects of different types of complainants (i.e., aggressive, submissive, ambiguous, or neutral) in an initial case spilling over into judgments in a subsequent case best evidence a priming effect as it is discussed in the social psychological literature (i.e., constructs activated through an initial task shaping subsequent independent social judgments). We predicted that aggressive (or submissive) complainants will act as primes, trigger hostile (or benevolent) attitudes in evaluators, and influence subsequent judgments about complainants in independent cases with new complainants. That is, observers will find less evidence of sexual harassment for neutral complainants when they have encountered prior aggressive complainants as compared to when they encounter submissive, neutral, or ambiguous initial complainants.

Finally, following the work of Wiener and Hurt (2000), we expected that the biasing effects of the priming complainants in (e.g., hostility and benevolence) would be offset under the reasonable woman legal standard relative to the reasonable person standard. It will be remembered that Wiener and Hurt found effects for measured hostile sexism for workers utilizing the reasonable person standard, but not for those employing the reasonable woman perspective. This was an exploratory prediction because some prior work has shown inconsistent results for the effects of legal standard in studies that used written scenarios (Wiener et al., 1995, 1997) and sometimes weaker but significant effects in studies of jury decision-making (Gutek et al., 1999).

Method

Research Participants

Participants were 145 male and 168 female full-time workers ($N = 314$, 1 person did not indicate his or her gender) recruited from the New York City metropolitan area through newspaper advertisements and community flyers distributed at local businesses. One-hundred-twenty-six (40%) were European Americans, 78 (25%) were African American, 58 (11%) were Hispanic, 35 (5%) were Asian, and 58 (18%) either failed to report their ethnic background or reported an ethnic background other than the ones indicated above.

Overview of the Procedure

Participants watched two short sexual harassment videotapes that recreated the work environments and reenacted the complained after events that made up two Title VII cases. The first video (hereafter the priming case) varied the introductory scene so that participants viewed a complainant who behaved in an aggressive, submissive, ambiguous (aggressive and submissive), or neutral manner. The initial conduct of the complainant in the second video (hereafter the target case) was always neutral in tone.

After viewing each videotape, participants evaluated the main characters in the scenario and determined whether the complained after social sexual conduct constituted sexual harassment, using the "severity or pervasiveness" test, as well as a general indicator of gender based discrimination. Half of the participants made their sexual harassment determination using the Reasonable Person Standard while remaining participants used the Reasonable Woman Standard. Finally, participants completed the Ambivalent Sexism Inventory (Glicke & Fiske, 1996) and demographic questionnaires.

Cases

We hired a production crew and professional actors to reenact scripts that we modeled after the fact patterns in two Title VII cases: *Faragher v. City of Boca Rotan* (1998) and *Rabidue v. Osceola Refining Co.* (1986). We based the scripts on the essential facts in both cases but modified the facts slightly in the interests of efficiency, the need for experimental control, and the demands of the New York winter. In our Faragher case, Ms. Faragher, was a college student who worked part time as a lifeguard for a local indoor swimming pool, rather than for a city beach club. Faragher claimed that two of her supervisors created a hostile work environment by repeatedly subjecting her and other female lifeguards to "uninvited and offensive touching," and making lewd remarks, speaking about women in "offensive terms" (*Faragher*, p. 780). In the second case, our Ms. Rabidue, an executive assistant, complained about a male co-worker who made crude and extremely vulgar comments about her and other women. The alleged perpetrator treated women with little respect, often downplaying their abilities to complete their assignments successfully. Ms. Rabidue claimed that some of the male employees displayed pictures of nude or scantily clad women in the workplace.

Vignettes

To minimize the unlikely possibility that participants would recognize the cases, we renamed the scenarios (The *Rabidue v. Osceola Refining Co.* case became *Reynolds v. River City Refining Co.,* and the *Faragher v. City of Boca Rotan* case became *Farell v. City of Clearwater*). Participants watched both the Farell and Reynolds videotapes in counterbalanced order. Thus, Farell was the priming case and Reynolds was the target case for half of the participants while Reynolds was the priming case and Farell was the target case for remaining participants. Each videotape ranged from 23 to 25 minutes in length, followed by 3 minutes of legal definitions and instructions.

After a brief introduction to the characters and the work environment, each vignette presented one of four opening scenes in which the complainant acted in an aggressive, submissive, ambiguous, or neutral manner. The case presentation manipulated the behavioral tone of the complainant by altering the actor's voice tone, non-verbal behaviors, and emotional reactions. We instructed the actors to play the scene differently according the four experimental conditions. For example, in the Reynolds priming case, the priming sequence showed Ms. Reynolds complaining to her boss about her work frustrations. In the aggressive condition, the complainant made belligerent demands, nearly shouting at her boss (not the alleged harasser) with a look of anger in her face. The actress was told to portray an aggressive complainant. In the submissive condition, the complainant could barely make eye contact. She looked at her feet and the floor as she sheepishly reported her complaints, but in a muffled tone. The actress was told to portray a submissive complainant in this scene. Those participants in the *Reynolds-Ambiguous* condition viewed an opening scene in which the performer acted alternatively with aggressive and submissive behavior styles. (We split these scenes into two different video workdays and showed them in counterbalanced order. That is, some participants watched the complainant act aggressively in the opening scene on the first day and submissively on the second day. Remaining participants saw the complainant behave submissively and then aggressively. In the ambiguous conditions, the two scenes across the two days were presented contiguously in the video.) In the neutral condition, the complainant acted in a business-like manner in the opening scene making moderate eye contact, speaking in a businesslike voice, and displaying a typical workday expression. The actress was told to portray a neutral, typical workday. The content of the verbal complaints were nearly identical across the priming conditions.[1]

---

[1] The ambiguous conditions in both priming videos were slightly different from the other conditions because the sessions depicted two separate workdays (one with an aggressive presentation and one with a submissive presentation). However, the actual verbal content of the scenes across the 2 days was identical to the content in the single day presentations. In the 2-day scenes (i.e., ambiguous conditions), the complainant left the scene on the first day before she was finished and came back the next day to complete her comments.

Similarly, participants who saw the Farell videotape first viewed the opening scene(s) during which the complainant acted in an aggressive, submissive, ambiguous, or neutral manner when she greeted a fellow lifeguard (again, not the alleged harasser) who was late relieving her at the conclusion of her shift. As with the Reynolds prime, the case presentation manipulated the behavioral tone of the complainant through adaptations of the actor's voice tone, nonverbal behaviors, and emotional reactions. Participants in the *Farell-Ambiguous* condition saw both hostile and submissive complainant behaviors (once again split between successive workdays and presented in counterbalanced order) while those in the neutral condition saw the complaint behave in a business-like manner.

Legal Instructions

At the conclusion of each video, a male and female narrator presented participants with legal definitions and instructions to use to determine whether sexual harassment had occurred in the vignette. Written instructions were also provided on the questionnaires. Half of the participants received the reasonable person standard while the remaining participants received the reasonable woman standard. The narrators explained that, "hostile work environment sexual harassment results when an employee is subjected to unwelcome sexual conduct, which a reasonable [*person / woman*] would view as sufficiently severe or pervasive to alter the conditions of employment and create an abusive work environment." The narrators elaborated that, "The views of a reasonable [*person / woman*] are those that an [*objective / female*] worker would have in a similar environment under essentially like or similar conditions experienced by the complaining employee."[2] Finally, the narrators presented dictionary definitions of severe, pervasive, and abusive. In this manner, we provided guidelines for evaluating hostile workplace harassment that required participants to contemplate the criteria outlined in federal law. This language came directly from case law and publications from the Equal Employment Opportunity Commission.

Questionnaires

After viewing the priming case, participants applied the "severity or pervasiveness" test for that case. Using 9-point Likert scales, they rated on the following dependent measures: whether the sexual conduct was unwelcome, severity of the sexual conduct, pervasiveness of the sexual conduct, the likelihood that the plaintiff was subjected to hostile work environment sexual harassment, and the extent to which the conduct affected the complainant's work performance and psychological well-being. The next question (anchored on a 1 very unlikely to 9 very likely scale) asked participants for a rating of gender discrimination. It asked, "How likely was it that Suzanne Farell [Kathy Reynolds] was the victim of

---

[2] The full instructions and the full scripts are available from the first author.

sex-based discrimination at her work place?" The questionnaire next asked participants to evaluate several behavioral attributes for each of the main characters in the scenario anchored with 9-point scales (e.g., 1 = not at all aggressive to 9 = very aggressive). The adjectives that represented the behavioral attributes were aggressive, meek, competent, likable, passive, forceful, hostile, and kind. These items served as manipulation checks for the priming complainant's conduct in the opening video scenes.[3]

Participants next viewed the second video, the target vignette during which the complainant always acted in a neutral manner in the opening scene. After this case, participants answered the same questions as they answered for the first case but with the other complainant as the object of the Likert measures and with the behavioral attribute questions (aggressive, meek, and so on) pertaining to the characters in the target video.

Next, participants completed the Ambivalent Sexism Inventory (ASI; Glick and Fiske, 1996), which measures hostile and benevolent sexism with 22 self-report items for which respondents rate their agreement on 6-point Likert scales ranging from 0 – disagree strongly to 5 = agree strongly. Examples of hostile and benevolent sexism items are, respectively, "Most women interpret innocent remarks or acts as being sexist," and "Women should be cherished and protected by men." Prior work by Glicke and Fiske (1996) demonstrated the ASI to be a psychometrically sound instrument and work by Wiener and Hurt (2000) and Wiener et al. (2004) demonstrated that the constructs work well in predicting judgments of sexual harassment. In the current study internal consistency scores for both hostile and benevolent sexism were more than adequate (coefficient α for hostile sexism = .84, N = 314 and for benevolent sexism α = .83, N – 314). Finally, participants completed a demographic survey.

Results

Overview

We report the results of our context analyses in three separate sections. First, we report manipulation check data to test if presentation of the prime complainants in the first video's opening scenes did alter the attitudes of the workers toward the complainants in the videos. Second, we report the results of path analysis that examines the effects of judgments in the first case on judgments in the second case. Finally, we report an analysis that examines the effects of the complainant's

---

[3] Next, participants answered the severity and pervasiveness test from their own perspective (the self-referencing item). They were told, "Put yourself in the place of Suzanne Farell [Kathy Reynolds] and respond to the following statements as if you were Suzanne Farell [Kathy Reynolds]." "If you had been treated like Suzanne Farell [Kathy Reynolds], how likely is it that you would have been the victim of hostile work environment sexual harassment?" These questions were not analyzed for this chapter. A similar set of questions were asked for the Reynolds case and they were not analyzed for this chapter.

initial conduct on the judgments of harassment in the initial (priming case) and in the follow-up (target) case.

Manipulation Checks

Figure 9.2 shows the effects of the complainants' initial conduct across the significant aggressive complainant attribute evaluations and Figure 9.3 shows the same for the significant submissive complainant traits evaluations. A 4 (initial scene: aggressive vs. submissive vs. ambiguous vs. neutral) by 2 case (*Farell v. Reynolds*) between subjects MANOVA with ratings of aggressiveness, meekness, competency, likeability, passiveness, forcefulness, hostility, and kindness of the complainants in the priming case serving as dependent measures yielded a

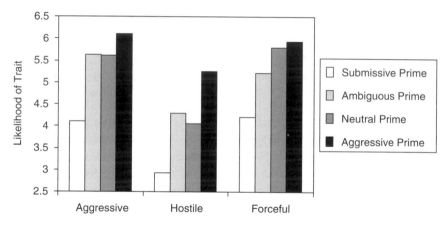

FIGURE 9.2. Manipulation checks for aggressive character traits.

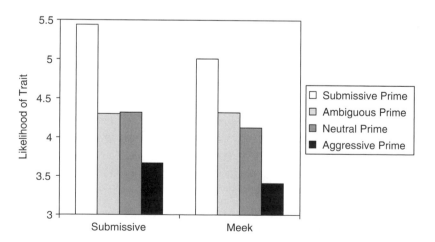

FIGURE 9.3. Manipulation checks for submissive character traits.

significant main effect for case, Mult. F (8, 289) = 16.27, $p < .001$, $r^2 = .311$, prime condition, Mult F (24, 873) = 3.40, $p < .001$, $r^2 = .09$, and a nonsignificant effect for interaction of case by prime condition, Mult. F (24, 873) = 1.21, ns, $r^2 = .03$. Main effects of case were not of central interest for the priming manipulation under the hypotheses under investigation and we therefore did not consider them further. Most importantly, the absence of an interaction between case and prime indicates that the priming manipulations were equally successful for both cases. Univariate follow-up F-tests for the priming effects on the manipulation check ratings produced significant test values, F's (3, 306) = (13.10, 14.96, 11.63, 8.27, 7.31, respectively), $p < .05$, for aggressive, hostile, forceful, submissive, and meek. The F-values for competence, $F(3, 306) = 2.62$, likable, $F(3, 306) = 1.85$ and kind, F (3, 303) = 1.70, failed to reach significance.

Post hoc tests between means using the least significant difference (LSD) method showed that the differences between the aggressive and submissive complainant conditions were significant on all behavioral attributes with significant F-tests. For the aggressive, submissive, and forceful behavioral attributes, the aggressive prime condition was not different from the ambivalent or neutral condition and neither was the submissive prime condition different from the ambivalent or neutral condition. However, for hostile and meek, the aggressive priming conditions were different from the ambivalent and neutral conditions as was the submissive priming condition. Overall, we concluded that our attempts to prime aggressive and submissive attitudes to complainants in both cases were successful. Adding to that conclusion was the distribution of scores for the ambiguous and neutral primes, which fell midway between the aggressive and submissive complainants.

Path Analyses

We conducted a series of multiple linear regressions to create path models to describe the manner in which gender, legal standard, hostile sexism, and benevolent sexism in the first case predicted judgments of sexual harassment in the first and second cases. First, we created a scale of hostile sexism aggregating the 11 items (reversed scored when necessary) from the Ambivalent Sexism Inventory that measured hostile sexism ($\alpha = .84$), and did the same with the 11 items from the benevolent sexism scale (reverse scored when necessary) ($\alpha = .83$). Next, we aggregated the seven measures of harassment judgments for our Reynolds case (i.e., unwelcomeness, severity, pervasiveness, negative work impact, negative psychological impact, likelihood of harassment, and likelihood of gender based discrimination; coefficient $\alpha = .91$) and aggregated the same variables for the Farell case ($\alpha = .90$). We labeled each scale "overall judgment of sexual harassment" with a higher score indicating a stronger inference of hostile work environment harassment and a lower score a weaker inference.

The first regression equation treated the overall judgment of sexual harassment in the second, target case as a criterion variable and main effects for legal standard (dummy coded 0 = reasonable person, 1 = reasonable woman), hostilesexism, benevolent sexism, gender, prime (i.e., three dummy coded variables comparing aggressive, submissive, and ambiguous to neutral primes), and the overall judgment of harassment in the first case as predictor variables. Follow-up analysis treated each significant predictor, which resulted from that first equation as a criterion with the other factors in the process as predictor variables. Figure 9.4 presents the results for the judgment of harassment in Reynolds as the target case. (The path coefficients in Figs. 9.4 and 9.5 are statistically significant standardized beta weights the resulted from the regression analyses.) It shows that the judgment of harassment in Reynolds was a positive function of the judgment of harassment in Farell and legal standard. Those who worked under the reasonable woman standard and those who found evidence for harassment in Farell as a priming case were more likely to find evidence of harassment in Reynolds as the target case. Further, workers scoring high in hostile sexism were least likely to find the complainant in Farell (as a priming case) the victim of hostile work environment sexual harassment.[4] Note that the main effects for the prime conditions in Farell did not impact either the overall Farell judgment or the overall Reynolds judgment.

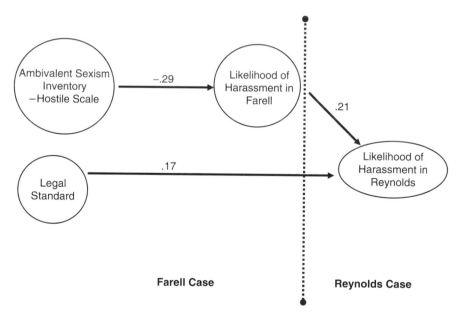

FIGURE 9.4. Path analysis with Reynolds as the target case.

---

[4] For the first regression equation, with overall judgment of harassment in Reynolds as the target criterion, both overall judgment of harassment in Farell (beta = .21, $p < .01$) and legal standard (beta = .17, $p < .05$) predicted the judgment in Reynolds, $F(2, 148) = 5.78$, $p < .05$, $R^2 = .060$). For the second regression equation, with overall judgment of harassment in Farell as the prime criterion, only hostile sexism (beta = $-.29$, $p < .001$) predicted the judgment in Farell, $F(1, 149) = 14.49$, $p < .01$, $R^2 = .082$).

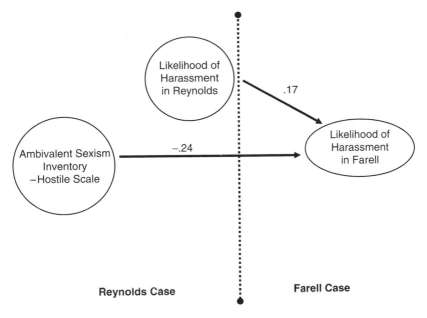

FIGURE 9.5. Path analysis with Farell as the target case.

Figure 9.5 presents the results for the overall judgment of harassment in Farell as the target case. It shows that the judgment of harassment in Farell was a positive function of the judgment of harassment in Reynolds and, once again, hostile sexism. Those who scored low in hostile sexism and those who found evidence for harassment in Reynolds as a priming case were more likely to find evidence of harassment in Farell as the target case.[5]

Prime Analyses

The path analyses failed to demonstrate priming or contrast effects in the Farell or Reynolds case for either initial or subsequent case judgments. However, a more refined analysis looking for interactions between the priming factor and gender or legal standard might produce priming effects, for one or the other case, acting as a target or a prime with members of one gender, or the other, in one legal standard condition, or the other. Using the composite overall judgment of harassment scale, we conducted a 4 (Prime: Aggressive vs. Submissive vs. Ambiguous vs. Neutral) × 2 (Legal Standard: reasonable person vs. reasonable woman) × 2 (Gender) × 2 (Case Order: Reynolds first vs. Farell first) × 2 (Case: Reynolds vs. Farell) mixed model Analysis of Variance with repeated measures only on the last

---

[5] For the regression equation, with overall judgment of harassment in Farell acting as the target criterion, both judgment of harassment in Reynolds as the priming case (beta = .17, $p < .05$) and hostile sexism (beta = $-.24$, $p < .01$) predicted the judgment in Farell, $F(2, 151) = 7.27$, $p < .01$, $R^2 = .086$.

factor. There was a significant main effect for case such that the overall harassment inference was stronger in the Farell case (M = 7.34) than in the Reynolds case (M = 6.76), $F(1,281)$ = 24.16, $p < .001$. The higher score in the Farell case suggests participants were more certain about sexual harassment in that case and less certain with the Reynolds fact pattern. Therefore, we expected that the Reynolds case would be more subject to priming effects. As is often found in sexual harassment studies, female workers (M = 7.22) found more evidence of harassment across both cases, than did male workers (M = 6.87), F (1, 281) = 5.68, $p < .05$.

Most interesting for the purposes of this analysis, the results showed a Case × Prime × Gender interaction, $F(3, 281)$ = 4.12, $p < .01$, and follow-up simple effects found a significant case × prime interaction for males only, $F(3,141)$ = 2.88, $p < .05$. Further simple effects isolated the priming effects for males in the Reynolds case regardless of whether it was judged first as the priming case or second as the target case, $F(3, 141)$ = 3.31, $p < .025$. Figure 9.6 illustrates the results. When male workers first observed an aggressive or ambiguous Ms. Reynolds, (as opposed to a neutral toned Ms. Reynolds) they made weaker inferences that Ms. Reynolds was sexually harassed; further, when they observed an aggressive or ambiguous Ms. Farell in the priming case, they also judged Ms. Reynolds less likely to be the victim of harassment. Apparently, the hostility that male workers harbored for the aggressive Ms. Farell carried over, primed hostility toward Ms. Reynolds in the second independent case, and weakened their inferences of harassment.

Now, it will be remembered that the ambiguous condition participants saw either a hostile complainant followed the next day in our video by a submissive complainant or they watched the opposite order of presentation, the submissive complainant followed by a hostile complainant. To help explain the difference between the ambiguous condition and the neutral condition, we broke the ambiguous condition into two, one with the hostile prime followed by the submissive prime

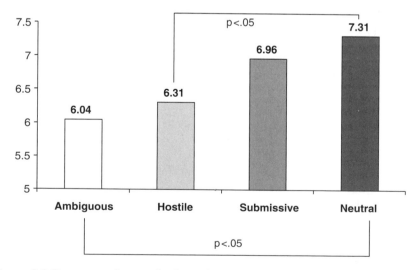

FIGURE 9.6. Duncan post hoc test for four prime effects of males' evaluations in Reynolds.

and a second with the submissive prime followed by the hostile prime. Following a significant omnibus main effect for the resulting 5 conditions with an ANOVA, F (4, 135) = 3.26, p < .05), we conducted LSD post-hoc tests between the five conditions. As shown in Fig. 9.7, men who first observed a hostile complainant in either the Farell or Reynolds case followed by a submissive prime were least likely to judge Ms. Reynolds a victim of hostile work environment harassment. Males with the hostile/submissive priming sequence made significantly lower harassment judgments than the submissive primed male workers or the neutral male workers. Once again, those men exposed to the pure hostile complainant prime were also significantly less likely to infer hostile work environment sexual harassment. Thus, with regard to the Reynolds judgment, the data support the conclusion that men who first observed a hostile complainant were less likely to find evidence of harassment for that complainant and for a subsequent independent complaint. The fact that this is especially true for those who saw a second scene with a submissive complainant suggests that initial hostile scene was augmented with contrast effects that made the first hostile scene look even more hostile.

What Have We Learned?

Context in Sexual Harassment Allegations.

This chapter tells a story about the role of context in legal judgment. It began with what might appear as a plain and well settled point of law, which the Supreme Court announced and reiterated in several of its older (*Meritor Savings Bank v. Vinson*, 1986; *Harris v. Forklift Systems, Inc.*, 1993) and more recent cases (*Faragher v. Boca Raton*, 1999; *Oncale v. Sundowner Offshore Services, Inc.*, 1998;

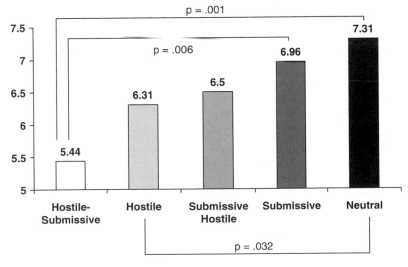

FIGURE 9.7. LSD post hoc test for five prime effects of male's evaluations in Reynolds.

Pennsylvania State Police v. Suders, 2004). Recognizing both the diversity and complexity of the behaviors that can contribute to an abusive work environment, the Court predicated the "severe or pervasive" test of hostile work environment sexual harassment on the totality of the circumstances rather than on bright line indicators of abusive workplaces. While this test may not offer definitive guidance to determine what is and is not sexual harassment, it does give meaning to Title VII prohibitions as they apply to the context-dependent area of workplace discrimination. This chapter explains how empirical research can help us understand what constitutes a hostile work environment by examining in some detail a model of the judgment process that people use to determine when social sexual conduct results in a hostile work environment. If nothing else, we hope to have shown that the extent to which empirical work will be relevant to judgments of social sexual conduct in the everyday workplace depends on the extent to which our experimental paradigms take seriously the totality of the circumstances. It has been difficult for psychological research to take into account the totality of the circumstances even in some of the most recent efforts at developing models of moral decision making in failed workplace romances (Pierce et al., 2004), and even in studies of the role of cultural differences in judgments of sexual harassment (Sigal et al., 2005). The contributions of these and other recent studies that expanded the domain of research exploring the judgment processes by which people evaluate allegations of harassment (Stockdale et al., 2002, 2004) are vital to the advancement of our knowledge in this area. Still, the problem of the totality of the circumstances requires an approach that allows, and even encourages, the prior experience of full-time workers to influence their judgments of realistic complaints that have surfaced in workplace environments.

We suggested that isolated incidences of social sexual conduct are rare and that workers are much more likely to be exposed to multiple workplace-related situations (i.e., different fact patterns within the same work environment) and multiple workplace-independent situations (i.e., different fact patterns across different work environments). We offered a judgment model of sexual harassment that allows for the effects of prior exposures to social sexual conduct at work to influence current judgments, either as individual differences in extant beliefs (e.g., measured hostile sexism) or as situational triggers of attitudinal responses (i.e., through priming or contrast effects). There are undoubtedly other situational factors that may produce automatic or "partially automatic" (Bargh, 1994; Wegner & Bargh, 1998) ripples in sexual harassment judgments and there are very likely to be different decision outcomes that result from these triggers. However, our experiment demonstrated individual difference effects, priming effects, and possibly contrasts effects that need to feature prominently in any explanation of how people evaluate the totality of the circumstances in allegations of hostile work environment harassment.

Summary of Our Findings

Our data showed the importance of examining the effects of multiple harassment judgments using realistic stimuli. First, we found that people who made strong inferences of sexual harassment in one case were likely to make strong inferences in a second independent fact pattern, independent of the order in which they evaluated the cases. Full-time workers who made stronger inferences of sexual harassment in our Reynolds case were more likely to make stronger inferences of harassment in our Farell case and vice versa, regardless of which case they evaluated first. This study did not manipulate the strength of the evidence in the initial case; instead, it manipulated the complainant's behavioral tone in the opening scenes of the videotaped scenario. As the result of this design choice, we were unable to determine whether the prior judgment process itself influenced subsequent judgments, the evaluation of the evidence in the specific case influenced those judgments, or there was a general tendency of people to be more or less sensitive to harassment judgments. What is clear, however, is that these cases are independent and that the order in which the cases were presented did not influence the way in which one set of judgments influenced the second set. These data suggest to us that future attempts to understand the totality of the circumstances would do well to consider prior exposures to social sexual conduct at work. It may serve our interests to use more than one fact pattern, rather than focusing on a single instance of social sexual conduct carefully described without the richness of the environment in which it occurred.

Replicating prior research (Wiener and Hurt, 2000; Wiener et al., 2002, 2004) we found strong effects for measured hostile sexism on judgments of sexual harassment. Workers scoring high in hostile sexism against women made weaker harassment inferences with regard to Ms. Farell, our lifeguard who claimed that she was the victim of a hostile work environment. Interestingly, while the effect of hostile sexism did not come out in our Reynolds fact pattern, those who scored high on hostile sexism made equally weak judgments of harassment with that fact pattern, regardless of whether they evaluated another case before or after they viewed the Reynolds reenactment. Hostile sexism reached across two case judgments to predict how people evaluate the totality of the circumstances in our Farell fact pattern.

Once again, the path analysis that takes into account the effects of prior judgments on subsequent judgments replicates prior results (Wiener and Hurt, 2000; Wiener et al., 2002), which demonstrated that those operating under the reasonable woman legal standard made stronger inferences of sexual harassment, at least in some cases. However, in our path analysis results, legal standard appeared to have this effect only in our Reynolds case, and only then when it came as the second judgment. At first, this result seems inconsistent with prior findings. However, on closer investigation we find that in all the opening scenes in the second case, the complainant acted neutral in behavioral tone. This neutral tone is similar to the conditions in earlier research (Wiener and Hurt, Wiener et al., 2002) that did not manipulate behavioral tone and that found legal standard effects. No other study that we know of manipulated complainant behavioral tone and hostile work environment legal standard. The other three conditions in this experiment that did not produce legal standard effects either presented our Farell case, a new fact pattern that we have not used in prior research, or used Reynolds, but included behavioral tone manipulations that have not yet allowed the effects of legal standard. Participants in earlier research that demonstrated stronger inferences of harassment under the reasonable woman condition did so when evaluating a fact pattern modeled after *Ellison v. Brady* (1991), also depicted with a complainant who was neither hostile nor submissive. As we discuss later, participants found more evidence of harassment in our Farell video, relative to our Reynolds video. The lack of a legal standard effect for the Farell case may be the result of the strong inference of sexual harassment that those participants reached in the Farell video.

Most importantly, this research examined directly the manipulated effects of complainant behavioral tone on the inferences of harassment across two independent fact patterns. We were able to influence the manner in which workers evaluated "to be judged" complainants by presenting hostile complainants in a prior case with an independent set of facts, actors, and context. Simply put, workers exposed to a hostile, as opposed to a submissive, complainant across two different fact patterns found the complainant more aggressive, hostile, and forceful, while finding her less submissive and meek. When we examined the effects of behavioral tone of the complainant on judgments in both cases, we found several interesting findings. First, we found two main effects, namely, that workers made stronger inferences of harassment in our Farell case than in our Reynolds video and women, compared to men, made stronger inferences of harassment across both cases. Second, we found that in the case with the more equivocal inferences, namely, the Reynolds case, male workers, but not females, were influenced by the complainants behavioral tone in the first case. This was true regardless of whether the complainant with the manipulated behavioral tone was Reynolds or Farell. In other words, when men saw either hostile complainant they made weaker inferences of harassment in the Reynolds video regardless of whether the hostile complainant they had encountered was Ms. Reynolds or Ms. Farell. We interpret this as a priming effect, especially when viewers of a hostile Ms. Farell in one case found less evidence that Ms. Reynolds was a victim of sexual harassment in a second independent case. Here, one psychological construct, hostile attitudes toward a complainant, was activated through a prior independent task, evaluation of an nonharassing scene, and influenced a subsequent inference of sexual harassment based upon Title VII law (c.f., Bargh et al., 1992, 1996; Blair & Banajia, 1996; Dijksterhuis et al., 1998; Higgins et al., 1977; Lepore & Brown, 1997).

The fact that ambiguous (hostile and submissive) complainants also triggered weaker inferences of sexual harassment in men, but only when the hostile scene was followed by a submissive scene, is evidence of contrast effects triggered by prior experience with sexual harassment complainants. More specifically, the effect of a hostile complainant scene was stronger when a submissive complainant followed it. While the hostile complainant condition produced a weaker inference than the submissive complainant, this difference was statistically significant only when the hostile complainant was followed by a submissive complainant. When the order reversed and a hostile complainant followed a submissive complainant, the effect of the ambiguous prime dropped out. We interpret this finding as a type of contrast effect. When observers compared an initial exemplar, here a hostile scene, to a comparison stimulus, here a submissive scene, the first scene had a stronger effect on the inferences workers drew about the "to be judged" instances of alleged hostile work environment sexual harassment. Admittedly this is a different form of contrast than Stapel and colleagues identify (see Stapel & Koomen, 1997; Stapel et al. 1997; Stapel & Winkielman, 1998) in which the effects of the prime depend directly on the extremity of the "to be judged" stimuli rather than on subsequent behavior. Nonetheless, it is clear from the overall pattern of our data that the effects of complainant behavior tone could be altered by its contrast with subsequent behavioral episodes. These processes show subtle but important effects in how workers evaluate the totality of the circumstances in harassment cases.

We have only begun to scratch the surface in understanding how prior experience with social sexual conduct at work influences the way in which workers evaluate the totality of the circumstances in sexual harassment judgments. Much more work needs to be done before we reach conclusions about the way in which people evaluate contextualized allegations of harassment. However, several points are clear from our current work on this topic. First, to be legally relevant and psychologically interesting research on sexual harassment should begin with models that can accommodate the influence of prior experience with social sexual conduct at work. Second, research projects should make every effort to include multiple workplace-related and/or multiple workplace-independent exemplars of harassment allegations. Third, the richer the judged stimuli, the more relevant will be the findings of the research to law and legal process. Fourth, research about judgments of sexual harassment would do well to include both individual difference measures and situational manipulations of psychological constructs that influence social judgments of legally relevant factors.

In the end, we offer this chapter as another step in our efforts to take seriously the law's view of sexual harassment as the product of a complex work environment in which a judgment of the totality of the circumstances is controlling. Our work shows that it is difficult to model the way in which workers judge the circumstances surrounding allegations of harassment, but it also shows that simplifying the environment to include single instances of simple fact patterns extracted from context will not produce realistic descriptions of how the law influences judgments in everyday life. To study legal judgments in everyday life, it is necessary to model those judgments in ways that include the parameters that are indigenous to our daily environments, and therefore pivotal to the rules of law.

References

Baker, D. D., Terpstra, D. E., & Cutler, B. D. (1990). Perceptions of sexual harassment: A re-examination of gender differences. *Journal of Psychology: Interdisciplinary & Applied, 124*, 409–416.

Bargh, J. A. (1994). The four horseman of automaticity: Awareness, intention, efficiency, and control in social cognition. In R. S. Wyer & T. K. Srull (Eds.), *The handbook of social cognition, 1*, 1–40. Hillsdale, NJ: Lawrence Erlbaum.

Bargh, J. A., Chaiken, S., & Govender, R. (1992). The generality of the automatic attitude activation effect. *Journal of Personality and Social Psychology, 62*, 893–912.

Bargh, J. A., Chen, M. & Burrows, L. (1996). Automaticity of social behavior: Direct effects of trait construct and stereotype activation on action. *Journal of Personality and Social Psychology, 71,* 230–244.

Blair, I. V., & Banajia, M. (1996). Automatic and controlled processes in stereotype priming. *Journal of Personality and Social Psychology, 70,* 1142–1163.

Burgess, D., & Borgida, E. (1997). Refining sex-role spillover theory: The role of gender subtypes and harasser attributions. *Social Cognition, 15,* 291–311.

Chen, M., & Bargh, J. A. (1997). Nonconscious behavioral confirmation processes: The self-fulfilling consequences of automatic steretype activation. *Journal of Experimental Social Psychology, 33,* 541–560.

Dijksterhuis, A, Spears, R., & Postmes, T. (1998) Seeing one thing and doing another: Contrast effects in automatic behavior. *Journal of Personality & Social Psychology, 75,* 862–871.

Glick, P., & Fiske, S. T. (1996). The ambivalent sexism inventory: Differentiating hostile and benevolent sexism. *Journal of Personality and Social Psychology, 70,* 491–512.

Gutek, B. A., Morasch, B., & Cohen, A. G. (1982). Interpreting social-sexual behavior in a work setting. *Journal of Vocational Behavior, 22,* 30–48.

Gutek, B. A., & O'Connor, M. A. (1995). The empirical basis for the reasonable woman standard. *Journal of Social Issues, 51,* 151–166.

Gutek, B. A., O'Connor, M. A., Melancon, R., Stockdale, M. Geer, T. M.,& Done, R. S. (1999). Utility of the reasonable woman legal standard in hostile environment sexual harassment cases: A multi-method, multi-study examination. *Psychology, Public Policy, and Law, 5,* 596–629.

Hartnett, J. J., Robinson, D., & Singh, B. (1989). Perceptions of males and females toward sexual harassment and acquiescence. *Journal of Social Behavior and Personality, 4,* 291–298.

Higgins, E. T., Rholes, W. S., & Jones, C.R. (1977). Category accessibility and impression formation. *Journal of Experimental Social Psychology, 54,* 181–192

Jones, E. E., Remland, M. S., & Brunner, C. C. (1987). Effects of employment relationship, response of recipient, and sex of rater on perceptions of sexual harassment. *Perceptual and Motor Skills, 65,* 55–63.

Kovera, M. B., McAuliffe, B. D., & Hebert, K. S. (1999). Reasoning about scientific evidence: Effects of juror gender and evidence quality on juror decisions in a hostile work environment case. *Journal of Applied Psychology, 84,* 362–375.

Lepore, L., & Brown, R. (1997). Category and stereotype activation: Is prejudice inevitable? *Journal of Personality and Social Psychology, 72,* 275–287.

Pierce, C. A., Broberg, B. J., McClure, J. R., & Aguinis, H. (2004). Responding to sexual harassment complaints: Effects of a dissolved workplace romance on decision-making standards. Organizational Behavior and Human Decision Processes, *95*(1), 66–82.

Powell, G. N. (1986). Effects of sex role identity and sex on definitions of sexual harassment. *Sex Roles, 18,* 405–417.

Saal, F. E., Johnson, C. B., & Weber, N. (1989). Friendly or sexy? It may depend on whom you ask. *Psychology of Women Quarterly, 13,* 263–276.

Sigal, J., Gibbs, M. S., & Goodrich, C. (2005). Cross-cultural reactions to academic sexual harassment: Effects of individualist vs. collectivist culture and gender of participants. *Sex Roles, 52,* 201–215.

Stapel, D. A., & Koomen, W. (1997). Using primed exemplars during impression formation: Interpretation or comparison? *European Journal of Social Psychology, 27,* 357–367.

Stapel, D. A., Koomen, W., & Van Der Pligt, J. (1997). Categories of category accessibility: The impact of trait concept versus exemplar priming on person judgments. *Journal of Experimental Social Psychology, 33*, 47–76.

Stapel, D., & Winkielman, P. (1998). Assimilation and contrast as a function of context-target similarity, distinctness, and dimensional relevance. *Personality and Social Psychology Bulletin, 24*, 634–646.

Stockdale, M. S., Berry, C. G., Schneider, R. W., & Cao, F. (2004). Perceptions of the sexual harassment of men. *Psychology of Men and Masculinity, 5*(2), 158–167.

Stockdale, M. S., O'Connor, M., Gutek, B. A., & Greer, T. (2002). The relationship between prior sexual abuse and reactions to sexual harassment: Literature review and empirical study. *Psychology, Public Policy, and Law, 8*(1), 64–95.

Terpstra, D. E., & Baker, D. D. (1986). A framework for the study of sexual harassment. *Basic and Applied Social Psychology, 7*, 17–34.

Thomann D. A., & Wiener, R. L. (1987). Physical and psychological causality as determinants of culpability in sexual harassment cases. *Sex Roles, 17*, 573–591.

Valentine-French, S., & Radtke, H. L. (1989). Attributions of responsibility for an incident of sexual harassment in a university setting. *Sex Roles, 21*, 545–555.

Wayne, J. H., Riordan, C. M., and Thomas, K. M. (2001). Is all sexual harassment viewed the same? Mock juror decisions in same- and cross-gender cases. *Journal of Applied Psychology, 86*, 179–187.

Wegner, D. M., & Bargh, J. A. (1998). Control and automaticity in social life. In D. T. Gilbert, S. T. Fiske, and G. Lindzey (Eds.), *The handbook of social psychology: Vol. 1* (4th ed., pp. 446-496). Boston: McGraw-Hill.

Wiener, R. L., Hackney, A., Kadela, K., Rauch, S., Seib, H., Warren, L. & Hurt, L. E. (2002). The fit and implementation of sexual harassment law to workplace evaluations. *Journal of Applied Psychology, 87*, 747–764.

Wiener, R. L., & Hurt, L. E. (1997). Social sexual conduct at work: How do workers know when it is harassment and when it is not? *California Western Law Review, 34*, 53–99.

Wiener, R. L., & Hurt, L. E. (1999). An interdisciplinary approach to understanding social sexual conduct at work. In R. Wiener & B. Gutek (Eds.), *Advances in sexual harassment research, theory, and policy*. Special Edition of *Psychology, Public Policy, and Law, 5*, 556–595.

Wiener, R. L., & Hurt, L. E. (2000). How do people evaluate social-sexual conduct: A psycholegal model. *Journal of Applied Psychology, 85*, 75–85.

Wiener, R. L., Hurt, L. E., Russell, B. L., Mannen, R. K., & Gasper, C. (1997). Perceptions of sexual harassment: The effects of gender, legal standard, and ambivalent sexism. *Law and Human Behavior, 21*, 71–93.

Wiener, R. L., Watts, B. A., Goldkamp, K. H., & Gasper, C. (1995). Social analytic investigation of hostile work environments: A test of the reasonable woman standard. *Law and Human Behavior, 19*, 263–281.

Wiener, R. L., Winter, R., Rogers, M., & Arnot, L. (2004). The effects of prior workplace behavior on subsequent sexual harassment judgments. *Law and Human Behavior, 28*, 47–67.

Legal Citations

Ellison v. Brady, 924 F.2d 872 (9th Cir. 1991).
Faragher v. City of Boca Raton, 118 S.Ct. 2275, (1998).

Harris v. Forklift Systems, Inc., 114 S.Ct. 367 (1993).
Henson v. City of Dundee, 682 F.2d 211 (9th Cir. 1979).
Meritor Savings Bank v. Vinson, 477 U.S. 57, (1986).
Miller v. Bank of America, 600 F.2d 211, (9th Cir. 1979).
Oncale v. Sundowner Offshore Services, Inc., 523 U.S. 75 (1998).
Pennsylvania State Police v. Suders, 124 S.Ct. 2342, (2004).
Rabidue v. Osceola Refining Co., 805 F.2d 611 (6th Cir.1986).
Title VII of the Civil Rights Act of 1964, 42 U.S.C. Sec. 2000c-(a)(1) (1964).

10
What Can Researchers Tell the Courts, and What Can the Courts Tell Researchers About Sexual Harassment?

Brian H. Bornstein and Meera Adya

The chapters by Gutek and by Wiener and Winter (this volume) highlight what is possibly the most vexing component of sexual harassment jurisprudence, namely, how does the law of sexual harassment influence psychological research on the topic, and vice versa? As Gutek points out, it is difficult to determine exactly what the law is, because it is continually evolving. Both authors make the excellent point that the broader concept of "social-sexual behaviors" in the workplace—in contrast to the narrower legal concept of sexual harassment—affords a wealth of interesting psychological research topics, in areas such as person perception, attitudes, stereotypes, etc. Indeed, as we discuss in the text that follows, the concept of a continuum of "social-sexual behaviors" seems to be a promising guide for future research. However, to ensure that psychological research is still relevant in its applications such that it can influence the courts, public policy, and companies' policies, it is essential that it address relevant real-world and legal scenarios (Wiener & Hurt, 2000; Wiener et al., 2002;).

In this chapter, we use the preceding chapters as a springboard to address several issues that have implications for how researchers should conduct studies of sexual harassment, and for the legal and policy implications of that research. First, we consider the diverse meanings of sexual harassment—that is, how the law and the public construe the term—and discuss some of the intended and unintended effects of sexual harassment policies. Second, we look at how the "totality of the circumstances" test applies to sexual harassment. Third, we consider some of the difficulties inherent in measuring sexual harassment and similar behaviors. We conclude with recommendations for what researchers and the courts can both do in addressing this vexing issue together.

The Meanings of Sexual Harassment and Sexual Harassment Policies

The problem with attempting to distinguish between sexual harassment in its narrow legal sense and in its broader social, or popular sense, is that the term has become so well known and so widely used that people make assumptions about what constitutes sexual harassment that may or may not be well founded in the law. In support of this view, Gutek cites research showing that people consider certain behaviors—such as a pat on the back—to be potentially harassing, when the behaviors generally would not meet the current legal standard for harassment.

Of course, to know what kind of a problem this is, we need clear guidance from the legal system as to what it is trying to achieve with its jurisprudence. Is it the case that the definition is to be normative; that is, that sexual harassment is a pervasive problem when "reasonable persons" would have difficulty in the work environment in question? If so, are the judgments that people make about scenarios, which represent *legal* social sexual behaviors, merely incorrect, because the current law would not find these behaviors harassing; or are they informative, because the law is inapt and fails to recognize that most people would find such circumstances hostile? The answer to this question has implications for how one uses the law's definitions to change personal definitions. As Gutek notes, legal definitions have been shifting, but personal definitions have not been keeping pace.

There are a number of consequences of overgeneralizing the concept of sexual harassment. One consequence, as Gutek points out, is that workplace policies are overinclusive, barring various behaviors that are legally acceptable. A second, perhaps more insidious consequence, is the chilling effect on non-harassing behaviors that are harmless and may even be desirable. For example, we know of several colleagues who refrain from making that pat on the back, or complimenting a colleague on his or her attire or haircut, out of fear that such gestures might be unwelcome. On the one hand, one might adhere to a "better safe than sorry" philosophy and view this as a good thing; on the other hand, it makes the workplace a colder, more sterile environment with less camaraderie. Research shows that employees who have a high sense of teamwork and camaraderie are more satisfied with their jobs and more involved (e.g., Daily & Bishop, 2003). Thus, going too far in avoiding potentially harassing behavior carries some potential costs. Is the tradeoff worth it? We are definitely not advocating the elimination of laws and company policies against sexual harassment; but such policies carry costs that both organizations and courts need to acknowledge. Moreover, as Gutek points out, there is surprisingly little research on whether a company's having a policy against sexual harassment really matters. Research examining discrimination in the workplace and the effectiveness of nondiscrimination policies, general diversity training initiatives, and specific-issue related initiatives (e.g., gay/lesbian diversity training as opposed to generic diversity training) have been shown to be efficacious and to positively impact a range of employee behaviors (Griffith & Hebl, 2002), which suggests that sexual harassment policies should be efficacious as well. Nonetheless, the adoption of policies should be driven by data and not intuition (Saks, 1989).

If a company has a policy barring sexual harassment, new employees have to read and sign it. Is there any evidence that this reduces the incidence of sexual harassment? From a deterrence perspective, one would imagine that the answer to this question is "yes." As with the threat of other kinds of criminal and civil penalties, one would expect that the threat of punishment for engaging in harassing behavior would deter potential harassers. However, that requires a degree of insight into the antecedents and consequences of one's behavior that most harassers might simply lack. Just as many criminals do not engage in an explicit cost–benefit analysis before committing a crime (e.g., Exum, 2002; Nagin & Pogarsky, 2004), harassers might not either. And even if they did, any deterrent effect would still depend on their awareness that their behavior constituted harassment. It seems possible that one reason why sexual harassment is so difficult to eradicate is because most harassers fail to perceive their behavior as unwelcome or inappropriate, rather than the result of inadequate deterrents. A worker who persistently asks a co-worker out on a date, or who prominently displays a pinup calendar, might not construe his behavior as harassing—though he might learn from informal feedback that it is inappropriate—in which case the threat of penalties would have little effect. At the risk of sounding naïve, we imagine that a perpetrator who knows that co-workers would perceive some act as unwelcome would be much less likely to engage in said act.

Of course, companies' sexual harassment policies are designed not only to change employees' behavior, but also (cynics would say primarily) to avoid liability by satisfying the implicit legal requirement of having a policy to "address" the potential problem. Having a policy may serve more purposes than satisfying legal requirements. It is not merely the legal judgment of wrongdoing that an organization wishes to avoid, but the economic liability that accompanies it. In other words, organizations are concerned about economic implications. If sexual harassment becomes an expensive problem, organizations will pay more heed to it. Indeed, there is evidence that it can be economically inefficient to ignore the problem: lower productivity, absenteeism, and turnover are known costs that rise when workers experience harassing environments (e.g., in a 1998 study of the U.S. Army, the cost of sexual harassment was estimated to be greater than $250,000,000; Faley, Knapp, Kustis, & Dubois, 1999). As these costs rise, they parallel the deterrence incentive that legal liability creates, resulting in a potentially synergistic force for change.

The perpetrator's awareness (or lack thereof) of how his actions might be perceived raises the issue of intent. Intent is always relevant under state tort law, which comes into play in some harassment cases, and it also factors into punitive damages, which sometimes attach under federal sexual harassment law. We agree with Gutek that although the perpetrator's intentions are legally irrelevant under current law—either the reasonable person or reasonable woman standard—they nonetheless influence the recipient's reaction. For example, an off-color joke told with the intention to be humorous would likely elicit a less severe reaction than the same joke told with the intention to demean or intimidate. In that sense, then, the perpetrator's intention could legitimately factor into the "totality of the circumstances" in adjudging sexual harassment (*Harris v. Forklift Systems, Inc.*, 1993).

Another way in which intent might factor into the totality of the circumstances examination is in the consideration of why else company policies may fail. Perhaps deterrents do not work because of a lack of enforcement (or perceived lack of enforcement)—that is, a harasser who expects that his or her victim will not complain, and that the administration will not do anything about a complaint, is unlikely to alter his or her behavioral pattern. This could pertain to the totality of circumstances in a given case pattern. In other words, the fact that a victim is unlikely to complain, or the fact that a company has a pattern of disregarding complaints, become relevant if such facts account for why a harasser chose a certain victim and purposefully did not edit his or her behavior.

Circumstances that Comprise the Totality

A totality of the circumstances test implies some sort of balancing, similar to a cost–benefit analysis. So, for example, one severe incident (e.g., an assault) might trump several milder incidents (e.g., dirty jokes); but should all circumstances be weighed equally? Should the perpetrator's and recipient's relationship history count just as much in deciding whether harassment occurred as the impact on employee performance? Models from decision-making research, such as multi-attribute utility theory (MAUT; e.g., Keeney, 1988), prescribe how to quantify and weigh attributes relevant to a decision. Courts appear not to have explicitly taken this approach in applying a balancing test, although one could argue that such weighing of circumstances (as opposed, say, to mere tallying) is strongly implied.

Moreover, it is likely that different evaluators would weigh potentially relevant factors differently. In a sense, all the decision makers are making the same judgment—whether or not sexual harassment has occurred—but the tasks involve different decisions. Harassers are deciding whether to act in a potentially objectionable manner; victims are deciding whether to report the harassment; companies are deciding whether the behavior constitutes harassment and what to do about it; and jurors/judges are deciding whether the behavior warrants sanctions. The harasser's judgment affects the decision to behave in a questionable way, and his or her cost–benefit analysis may include whether or not the victim is likely to report, as well as the organization's likelihood to act upon the report. The victim's cost–benefit analysis may include whether or not the organization will support a claim or complaint and how onerous it is to tolerate the hostile work environment. An organization (i.e., a top executive acting on behalf of the organization) is likely to engage in a cost–benefit analysis that is largely economically based; as delineated earlier, costs rise when liability is imposed by courts or when victims become more likely to be absent, low in productivity, and experience psychological and medical problems. Finally, a jury's or court's judgment affects the decision to find the defendant liable for sexual harassment, along with any compensatory and/or punitive action. This judgment could also include the public policy ramifications of labeling certain behavior legally unacceptable.

As mentioned earlier, context matters, and each decision maker sees context differently. A long line of social psychological research on "actor-observer" differences suggests that people engage in different cognitive processes when making a decision for the self versus another individual (e.g., Cunningham, Starr, & Kanouse, 1979; Malle & Knobe, 1997). Wiener and Winter's "self-referencing" questions get at this issue partially, and also implicate judgmental processes based on false consensus (i.e., the assumption that most ordinary people would act similarly to oneself (see Ross, Greene, & House, 1977). Future research in this area should examine both types of decisions, as they are both relevant to the ultimate determination of whether sexual harassment has occurred. The other two chapters in this section do a nice job of illustrating the complementary, yet distinct decisions: Gutek identifies some of the various factors that go into making a claim and describes how research on making complaints is useful in court. Gutek noted that companies, jurors, and courts often punish victims for their delay or failure to report harassing behavior. When victims fail to report an incident (not necessarily an illegitimate decision considering that those who report have been shown to have lower perceptions of justice than those who are harassed but do not report; Adams-Roy & Barling, 1998) because of the negative consequences of a report followed by organizational or legal inaction, they are focused on context. When companies, jurors, and courts punish victims for the delayed reporting, they are focusing on the victim (e.g., perhaps the victim did not suffer much or at all) rather than the context. In addressing this phenomenon, it might be instructive to consider literature on whistle-blowing (e.g., Lee, Heilmann, & Near, 2004). Wiener and Winter, on the other hand, examine a task that is more akin to jurors' evaluation of whether certain behavior constitutes sexual harassment.

In doing so, Wiener and Winter call attention to the importance of considering the multiplicity of "circumstances" that are potentially relevant to determining whether sexual harassment has occurred. In addition to the more obvious circumstances identified in case law, such as the frequency and pervasiveness of discriminatory conduct, the conduct's severity, and the impact on the employee's work performance (*Harris v. Forklift Systems, Inc.*, 1993), they show how people's judgments can be influenced by their attitudes (especially regarding sexism), gender, prior experience (e.g., exposure to instances of harassment), and individual sensitivity to harassment. All of these factors contribute to the "context" within which one evaluates a particular incident of possible harassment, and could legitimately be considered among the circumstances contributing to the totality. One of the main contributions of Wiener and Winter's research is that it expands the scope of inquiry to encompass more circumstances than those that are traditionally considered.

This contribution is more valuable than merely the expansion of the number of variables that researchers consider. Wiener and Winter propose a model of decision making about sexual harassment scenarios; theoretical models necessitate the consideration and integration of not just specific research on a topic, but corollary research as well. As an example, we alluded earlier to a long line of social psychological research on actor-observer differences and the false consensus effect. To the degree that we see the same effects in sexual harassment scenarios, we have much more research to draw upon when moving forward empirically and when offering guidance to the courts. A similarly helpful theoretical and empirical development would be for both researchers and courts to consider the broad continuum of social-sexual behaviors. Although Caselaw has the potential to lead to a narrow band of behaviors being labeled as illegal, it has rarely drawn bright line distinctions around actionable and acceptable workplace conduct, in part because of the role that context plays in workplace discrimination. On the other hand, understanding the full spectrum of social-sexual behaviors and the varying ways in which harassers, victims, organizations (vis-à-vis their policies), and legal actors (i.e., policy makers such as the E.E.O.C., jurors, and judges) draw boundary lines can be informative—particularly when the court aims to map behavior onto "reasonableness."

The other main contributions of this study are methodological. The study (as well as other studies by Wiener and colleagues; e.g., Wiener et al., 2002; Wiener & Hurt, 2000) employs realistic materials, multiple sample cases, and a diverse set of participants. Psychological research in many domains, such as jury decision making and eyewitness testimony, has been criticized, by both courts and researchers, for lacking external validity (for recent reviews of these critiques, see Bornstein & McCabe, 2005 [on jury research]; Penrod & Bornstein, 2007 [on eyewitness research]). For courts and policy makers to pay attention to research findings, it is essential that the research be high in both internal and external validity. More research such as that done by Wiener and Winter would help allay these concerns.

Unfortunately, as the study's findings make clear, increasing external validity has both an upside and a downside. The finding that the priming effects differed for their two cases highlights the importance of using multiple cases in research, rather than just generalizing from a single case. It shows that, as in most areas of life, the pattern of effects for sexual harassment judgments is subtle and complex. This sort of case specificity has been observed in other areas of psycholegal research (e.g., Greene & Bornstein, 2003), and it is useful to know that it occurs in this domain as well. The downside of case specificity is that it makes it hard to draw general conclusions. The results indicate that the legal standard matters, but only some of the time; that hostile sexism can have a direct or indirect effect on people's judgments; and that priming occurs, but only for men, and only for some cases. These qualifications limit the policy implications that can be drawn from the study. Ironically, then, research of a type that is most likely to be taken seriously by the courts and policy makers—by virtue of its high degree of verisimilitude—might end up not being taken seriously because of the messy pattern of results. However, it is important to note that empirical results that look messy at first blush can often be integrated into a theoretical model that more cleanly explains initially disparate findings. The model as a whole, informed by convergent and programmatic research, can then guide organizational and legal decision makers better. Thus, while models that do not consider the complexity of the task may more easily lead to parsimonious conclusions, that parsimony may be purchased at a high cost—the cost of legal relevancy.

Measuring Sexual Harassment

Both of these chapters point to the difficulty of measuring the experience of sexual harassment accurately. We could find no evidence to dispute Gutek's claim that "no single, well-documented measure [of sexual harassment] published in a peer-reviewed journal currently exists." She cites several reasons for this dearth of reliable and valid instruments to measure the construct: the changing legal definition within and across jurisdictions, the slippery border between illegal social-sexual behavior (i.e., sexual harassment) and more general inappropriate/unwanted social-sexual behavior (as discussed above), and the difficulty of establishing a threshold for when behavior crosses the threshold from the latter to the former. To these, we would add possible reporting biases that occur when inquiring about any sensitive topic (e.g., sexual abuse, crime victimization and perpetration history, mental illness), which could lead some individuals to underreport the relevant behaviors, while others might overreport. Nonetheless, there are reliable instruments for assessing these other sorts of sensitive topics, so what makes sexual harassment so difficult to assess?

One answer, of course, is the law of sexual harassment itself. Because the law involves both a subjective component (i.e., the victim's perspective of what is abusive) and an objective component (i.e., the reasonable person's or woman's perspective), it is difficult to measure harassment as a psychological construct. Beyond the legal component, we propose three possible answers to the question of why harassment is difficult to assess. First, behaviors that constitute sexual harassment have for so long been an ingrained, accepted element of the workplace. This is not to say that it was ever considered acceptable to require sex acts to gain a promotion (though at times, and in certain industries, it undoubtedly was tolerated); but subtler behaviors of the "hostile work environment" sort, such as jokes, innuendo-laden banter, and sexist displays (e.g., posters, calendars), went unchallenged for generations. In comparison, other sensitive topics that people might be reluctant to admit to—such as perpetration or victimization of child sexual abuse—have never had the patina of popular permissibility. This points to the need to understand better the organizational culture within which people operate. The integration of both genders within the workplace at the level we see today is a relatively recent phenomenon, and both men and women are still learning to navigate within this milieu and to edit their behavior accordingly.

Second, many kinds of social-sexual behavior that are inappropriate in the work setting are perfectly fine in other contexts. Comments that would be unwelcome at work might be harmless flirtation at a cocktail party (Gutek &

Morasch, 1982). According to this logic, much sexual harassment occurs because the perpetrators have failed in their discriminant learning; that is, "Behavior A is permissible (and maybe even rewarded) in Context X, but it is impermissible (and maybe even punished) in Context Y." Granted, a large number of nonhuman species learn to make these discriminations perfectly well; but where the behaviors themselves are complex, and the reinforcers/punishers temporally distant from the behaviors, learning proceeds at a slower pace (Domjan, 2006). Thus, we need more research to determine what the appropriate reinforcers and punishers are that will work well. Is it that a company policy outlining consequences for harassing behavior is a sufficient punisher/deterrent, or does successful deterrence require the actual experience of punishment? This narrows to the familiar concerns of defining reinforcers for this context (i.e., harassment in workplaces) and learning how to alter the contingencies to discourage harassing conduct.

A third reason for the difficulty of measuring sexual harassment is the legal standard itself. Whether it is a reasonable person or a reasonable woman, reasonable people differ, and individual sensitivities vary widely. The law's oft-used standard of "reasonableness" has been described as a "fiction" (cite) and, despite its claims of objectivity, is a shifting standard that varies across times, places, and individuals. It is to Wiener and Winter's credit that their research seeks to understand exactly how people understand and apply the different legal standards.

Concluding Thoughts and Recommendations

So, what can researchers tell the courts, and what can the courts tell researchers about sexual harassment? There are a great many things that researchers can tell the courts, many of which are highlighted in the preceding chapters: the prevalence of sexual harassment (admittedly difficult, as just described), the frequency and timing of claims, the effect of having a sexual harassment policy on the behaviors themselves and responses thereto, the role of attitudes and experiences, and the meaning of different legal standards. As with all social science research that seeks to influence public policy, this research must be not only methodologically but also legally sound. The research conducted by Wiener and Gutek and their colleagues are stellar examples of this kind of research.

The main thing that courts can tell researchers is what are the relevant legal assumptions and behaviors to investigate. Constructs such as "sexual harassment," "totality of the circumstances," and "reasonable person/woman" do not have unambiguous definitions. In the parlance of research methodology, they are variables that are very hard to operationalize, and they can change from one court decision to the next. It behooves researchers to keep abreast of the latest legal developments, so that they can conduct research on the topic that is pertinent and likely to receive a hearing. By doing so, researchers and the courts can better work together to understand, adjudicate, and ultimately reduce sexual harassment.

More generally and directly related to the main theme of this volume, legal decision-making research must be theoretically sophisticated, empirically rigorous, and legally relevant. This recommendation may be a tall order, but it has the greatest likelihood of successfully modeling legal judgments and thereby influencing law and policy.

References

Adams-Roy, J., & Barling, J. (1998). Predicting the decision to confront or report sexual harassment. *Journal of Organizational Behavior, 19*, 329–336.

Bornstein, B. H., & McCabe, S. G. (2005). Jurors of the absurd? The role of consequentiality in jury simulation research. *Florida State University Law Review, 32*, 443–467.

Cunningham, J. D., Starr, P. A., & Kanouse, D. E. (1979). Self as actor, active observer, and passive observer: Implications for causal attributions. *Journal of Personality and Social Psychology, 37*, 1146–1152.

Dailey, B. F., & Bishop, J. W. (2003). TQM workforce factors and employee involvement: The pivotal role of teamwork. *Journal of Managerial Issues, 15*, 393–412.

Domjan, M. (2006). *The principles of learning and behavior* (5th ed.). Belmont, CA: Thomson/Wadsworth.

Exum, M. L. (2002). The application and robustness of the rational choice perspective in the study of angry and intoxicated intentions to aggress. *Criminology, 40*, 933–966.

Faley, R. H., Knapp, D. E., Kustis, G., and Dubois, C. L. Z. (1999). Estimating the organizational costs of sexual harassment: The case of the U.S. army. *Journal of Business and Psychology, 13*, 461–483.

Greene, E., & Bornstein, B. H. (2003). *Determining damages: The psychology of jury awards*. Washington, DC: American Psychological Association.

Griffith, K. H., & Hebl, M. R. (2002). The disclosure dilemma for gay men and lesbians: "Coming out" at work. *Journal of Applied Psychology, 87*, 1191–1199.

Gutek, B. A., & Morasch, B. (1982). Sex-ratios, sex-role spillover, and sexual harassment at work. *Journal of Social Issues, 38*, 55–74.

Keeney, R. L. (1988). Value-focused thinking and the study of values. In D. E. Bell, H. Raiffa, & A. Tversky (Eds.), *Decision making: Descriptive, normative, and prescriptive interactions* (pp. 465–494). Cambridge, UK: Cambridge University Press.

Lee, J., Heilmann, S. G., & Near, J. P. (2004). Blowing the whistle on sexual harassment: Test of a model of predictors and outcomes. *Human Relations, 57*, 297–322.

Malle, B. F., & Knobe, J. (1997). Which behaviors do people explain? A basic actor-observer asymmetry. *Journal of Personality and Social Psychology, 72*, 288–304.

Nagin, D. S., & Pogarsky, G. (2004). Time and punishment: Delayed consequences and criminal behavior. *Journal of Quantitative Criminology, 20*, 295–317.

Penrod, S. D., & Bornstein, B. H. (2007). Methodological issues in eyewitness memory research. In M. Toglia, R. C. L. Lindsay, D. Ross, & Reed (Eds.), *Handbook of eyewitness psychology, 2*, 529–556. Mahwah, NJ: Erlbaum.

Ross, L., Greene, D., & House, P. (1977). The false consensus effect: An egocentric bias in social perception and attribution processes. *Journal of Experimental Social Psychology, 13*, 279–301.

Saks, M. J. (1989). Legal policy analysis and evaluation. *American Psychologist, 44*, 1110–1117.

Wiener, R. L., Hackney, A., Kadela, K., Rauch, S., Seib, H., Warren, L., & Hurt, L. E. (2002). The fit and implementation of sexual harassment law to workplace evaluations. *Journal of Applied Psychology, 87*, 747–764.

Wiener, R. L., & Hurt, L. E. (2000). How do people evaluate social sexual conduct at work? A psycholegal model. *Journal of Applied Psychology, 85*, 75–85.

Legal Citation

Harris v. Forklift Systems, Inc., 114 S. Ct. 367 (1993).

Unit IV
Hate Speech and Hate Crimes: Legal Developments and Empirical Research

11
The Hate Crime Project and Its Limitations: Evaluating the Societal Gains and Risks in Bias Crime Law Enforcement

Frederick M. Lawrence

The Hate Crimes Project in the United States, the expanded use of criminal legislation creating enhanced punishment for bias-motivated crimes, is now more than twenty-five years old. Before 1980, only the state of Connecticut criminalized bias-motivated violence as a particularized crime. Today, virtually every state expressly criminalizes bias crimes. Over this quarter century, states have employed different forms of bias crime laws, some focusing on the animus exhibited by the perpetrator of a crime against a member (actual or perceived) of a racial, ethnic, religious, or other included "group,"[1] others focusing on the perpetrator's discriminatory selection of his or her victim. Although numerous court challenges have been brought challenging bias crime laws, the constitutionality of these statutes has been largely resolved in favor of these laws, with limitations.[2]

Now is therefore a propitious time to begin to evaluate the societal gains and risks associated with bias crime law enforcement. This chapter sets out a framework from which to understand bias crime law, and then considers and addresses many of the issues raised by opponents of the bias crime program. Four issues in particular are considered. First, opponents have argued that the enhanced punishment of bias crime calls greater attention to racial and ethnic differences in society, therefore exacerbating, not helping, social divisions. Second, those opposed to expanded prosecution for bias-motivated crimes have argued that bias crime law enforcement unconstitutionally, or in any event unwisely, punishes thought and expression, not criminal acts. Third, bias crimes opponents have argued that the potential for selective enforcement of bias crime statutes exists, harming the

---

[1] This chapter uses "group" as the generic term for the categories encompassed by any particular bias crime statute. I discuss briefly below the legal and social implications of a legislative determination of the scope of bias crimes. See also Frederick M. Lawrence, *Punishing Hate: Bias Crimes Under American Law* 11–20 (1999).

[2] See Virginia v. Black, 538 U.S. 343 (2003) (upholding a construction of the Virginia cross-burning statute that limits its reach to cases of intended racial intimidation); Wisconsin v. Mitchell, 508 U.S. 476 (1993) (upholding Wisconsin penalty enhancement bias crime law.)

most disadvantaged members of society and ironically those whom bias crime laws are intended to help. Fourth, opponents question one of the prime justifications for the enhanced punishment of bias crimes—that these crimes cause a greater harm than similar crimes without bias motivation—claiming that the bias motivation of the perpetrator per se is not the cause of the harm. Bias crimes per se, the argument goes, should not receive enhanced punishment, rather only crimes, any crimes, that cause these great harms.

Finally, I offer some observations as to the most general challenge that may be asserted against bias crimes laws: the argument that these laws "don't work," that is, that these laws do not prevent or even appreciably reduce levels of bias in society, or even levels of bias crimes. I argue that in some ways there is no real answer to this question of whether bias crime laws "work" but I further argue, in the classic words of the late Alexander Bickel, that "no answer is what the wrong question begets."[3] Instead of asking questions about reduction of certain types of crime or even more so, certain types of social attitudes, we do better to ask whether bias crime laws punish that which society rightly condemns. Taking that path, we are led toward the implications of using bias crime law as a window into a society's self-perception as a multicultural society. The extent to which this will "end bigotry" in society will inevitably be an inquiry that is more aspirational than empirical.

The Nature of Bias Crimes[4]

Bias crimes are the criminal manifestation of prejudice. They may be distinguished from parallel crimes—crimes that are similar in every manner but for the absence of bias motivation—in terms of the mental state of the actor as well as the nature of the harm caused. A parallel crime may be motivated by any one of a number of factors whereas bias crimes are motivated by a specific, personal, and group-based reason: the victim's real or perceived membership in a particular group. Different bias crime laws cover different groups. In the United States, every bias crime law covers race and ethnicity in some form. Many also include religion, sexual orientation, gender, or other characteristics.[5]

Bias crimes thus attack the victim not only physically but also at the very core of his or her identity, causing a heightened sense of vulnerability beyond that normally found in crime victims. Perhaps most dramatically, victims of bias crimes directed against racial minorities experience the attack as a form of violence that

---

[3] Alexander Bickel, *The Least Dangerous Branch,* at 103 (1962).

[4] For a more detailed discussion of the nature of bias crimes, their cause, and their resulting harms, see Chapter 2 of Frederick M. Lawrence, *Punishing Hate: Bias Crimes Under American Law* 29–44 (1999).

[5] I have discussed elsewhere the legal and social implications of a legislative determination of the scope of bias crimes. See id. at 11–20.

manifests racial stigmatization and its resulting harms.[6] The stigmatized individual may experience clinical symptoms[7] and social symptoms.[8] The bias-motivated violence carries with it the clear message that the target and his or her group are of marginal value.[9] Stigmatization of bias crime victims is not limited to racially motivated bias crimes or to minority group victims. Group-motivated crimes generally cause heightened psychological harm to victims over and above that caused by parallel crimes.[10]

The impact of bias crimes reaches beyond the harm done to the immediate victim or victims of the criminal behavior. There is a more widespread impact on the "target community" that shares the Group characteristic of the victim and an even broader-based harm to the general society. Members of the target community do more than sympathize or even empathize with the immediate bias crime victim.[11] Members of the target community of a bias crime perceive that crime as if it were an attack on themselves directly. A cross burning or a swastika scrawling will not just call up similar feelings on the part of other Blacks and Jews, respectively. Rather, members of these target communities may experience reactions of actual threat and attack from this very event.[12]

Finally, the impact of bias crimes may spread well beyond the immediate victims and the target community to the general society. Such crimes violate not only society's general concern for the security of its members and their property but also the shared value of equality among its citizens and racial and religious harmony in a multicultural society.[13]

This societal harm is, of course, highly contextual. We could imagine a society in which racial motivation for a crime would implicate no greater value in society than the values violated by a criminal act motivated solely by the perpetrator's dislike of the victim's eye color. This notion of contextuality in turn helps us

---

[6] See, e.g., Gordon Allport, *Nature of Prejudice*, 148–149 (1954); Erving Goffman, *Stigma: Notes on the Management of Spoiled Identity*, 7–17, 130–135 (1963); Robert M. Page, *Stigma*, 1 (1984); Stevenson & Stewart, *A Developmental Study of Racial Awareness in Young Children*, 9 CHILD DEVELOPMENT, 399 (1958).

[7] See, e.g., Harburg et al., *Socio-Ecological Stress, Suppressed Hostility, Skin Color, and Black-White Male Blood Pressure: Detroit*, 35 PSYCHOSOMATIC MEDICINE, 276, 292–294 (1973); Kenneth Clark, *Dark Ghetto: Dilemmas of Social Power*, 82–90 (1965).

[8] See, e.g., Irwin Katz, *Stigma: A Social Psychological Analysis* (1981); Harry H. L. Kitano, *Race Relations*, 125–126 (1974); Kiev, *Psychiatric Disorders in Minority Groups*, PSYCHOLOGY AND RACE, 416, 420–424 (P. Watson, ed., 1973).

[9] Allport, *Nature of Prejudice*, 56–59 (discussing the degrees of prejudicial action from "antilocution," to discrimination, to violence).

[10] Lawrence, *Punishing Hate*, 39-41.

[11] See, e.g., Martha Minow, *Making All the Difference: Inclusion, Exclusion, and American Law*, 221 (1990) (stating the importance of empathy in combating discrimination in the United States).

[12] See, e.g., Robert Elias, *The Politics of Victimization*, 116 (1986); A. Karmen, *Crime Victims: An Introduction to Victimology*, 262–263 (2d ed., 1990); Jack Levin and Jack McDevitt, *Hate Crimes: The Rising Tide of Bigotry and Bloodshed*, 205, 220–221, 234 (1993).

[13] See Lawrence, *Punishing Hate*, at 43–44.

understand which categories should and should not be included in a bias crime law. The characteristics that ought to be included in a bias crime law are those that implicate societal fissure lines, divisions that run deep in the social history of a culture. In the United States, the strongest case is for race. Racial discrimination, the greatest American dilemma, has its roots in slavery, the greatest American tragedy.[14] Strong cases can also be made for the other classic bias crime categories, color, ethnicity, religion, and national origin. The very act of determining which groups will be included in a bias crime law is a legislative and thus social determination of social fissure lines.

The Risks in Bias Crime Enforcement

Bias Crime Law Enforcement Calls Greater Attention to Differences that Exist in Society, and Exacerbates, Rather than Helps to Heal, Societal Fissures.

Opponents are concerned that bias crime law enforcement leads to the exacerbation of racial tension and distracts from other means of addressing bigotry in society. Jacobs and Potter,[15] for example, assert that bias crime laws further polarize and are "likely to be divisive, conflict-generating, and socially and politically counterproductive."[16] They contend that these laws should be repealed and that generic criminal laws should be enforced "evenhandedly and without prejudice."[17]

The mere passage of bias crime laws leads to controversy. Each state must decide which groups will be protected. Groups not included are sent the message that they are less deserving of society's concern. For example, not all states include sexual orientation in their definition of bias crimes, sending the message that a bias-motivated crime committed against a gay person is less reprehensible than a crime that was racially motivated. Whether intentional or not, this implies that certain groups are more deserving of protection.[18]

The controversy spawned by bias crime laws, however, goes beyond this debate. Once a law has been passed, there are also disputes over which individual crimes should be labeled as bias crimes, compounded by the danger that once a crime is labeled as such it will further divide the community in which it occurred, leading to retaliatory crimes. The very existence of bias crime laws harms society both through false negative and false positive instances of law

---

[14] E.g., Andrew Hacker, *Two Nations, Black and White, Separate, Hostile, Unequal*, 4–6 (1992); Jennifer L. Hochschild, *Facing Up to the American Dream: Race, Class and the Soul of the Nation* (1996).

[15] James Jacobs & Kimberly Potter, *Hate Crimes: Criminal Law and Identity Politics* (1998).

[16] Id. at 153.

[17] Id. at 145

[18] See Lawrence, *Punishing Hate*, at 17–20; Jacobs & Potter, *Hate Crimes*, at 132–134.

enforcement. If the community perceives a crime as one of bias, but law enforcement does not label it as such, intergroup tensions will rise. Similarly, inaccurately labeling a non-bias–motivated crime as one of bias will lead to inflated statistics, also exacerbating intergroup tensions.[19]

In fact, Jacobs and Potter assert that the "very collection and reporting of hate crime statistics encourages Americans to think of the crime problem in terms of intergroup conflict."[20] Even when the number of bias crimes committed in a state is extremely low, such statistics can be blown out of proportion by politicians and the media, leading to the impression that the community is much more racially divided and rife with prejudice than is really the case.

Finally, critics have argued that bias crime laws can distract society from other means of addressing the problems of bigotry and discrimination in society. Having passed bias crime legislation, the legislature may perceive less need (or less political pressure) to explore legislative solutions to harm caused by bias-motivated conduct in employment, housing, education, and other areas.

Bias Crime Laws Punish Thought and Expression.

One of the classic criticisms of bias crime laws is that they will punish bigots for holding bigoted ideas, and punish speakers for expressing racist ideas or ideas that the listener perceives to be racist. Critics have argued that bias crime laws in general, and campus speech codes aimed at hate speech in particular, are aimed not at conduct that might be proscribed but at beliefs that are beyond the reach of regulation by the state or university.[21] Even supporters of bias crime laws accepted this criticism, in part. For example, in an argument for the enhanced punishment of bias crimes, I nonetheless argued against the criminalization of racist speech, asserting that the "expressive behavior" of racist speech could be distinguished from the *mens rea*–based criminal behavior of a bias crime.[22]

A risk of the bias crime project, therefore, is that law enforcement may overreach and indeed punish thoughts and beliefs. Some racist speech, as well as other forms of hate speech, is in fact protected speech. The First Amendment protects behavior that has as its prime motivation the intent to communicate or express a view. That this view is one of bigotry or asserted racial superiority is of no matter. Moreover, that the expression of such views may in some instances cause offense is also of no matter. Expression of views that are severely disturbing to

---

[19] Jacobs & Potter, *Hate Crimes*, at 130–132, 137–144.

[20] Jacobs & Potter, *Hate Crimes*, at 134.

[21] See, e.g., David E. Bernstein, *Defending the First Amendment from Antidiscrimination Laws*, 82 N.C. L. Rev. 223, 240-41 (2003); Susan Gellman, *Hate Speech and a New View of the First Amendment*, 24 Cap. U. L. Rev. 309 (1995); Robert A. Sedler, *The Unconstitutionality of Campus Bans on "Racist Speech:" The View from Without and from Within*, 53 U. Pitt. L. Rev. 631, 683 (1992); Susan Gellman, *Sticks and Stones Can Put You in Jail, but Can Words Increase Your Sentence? Constitutional and Policy Dilemmas of Ethnic Intimidation Laws*, 39 U.C.L.A. L. Rev. 333 (1991).

[22] See Frederick M. Lawrence, *The Hate Crimes/Hate Speech Paradox: Punishing Bias Crimes and Protecting Racist Speech*, 68 Notre Dame L. Rev. 673 (1993).

others does not constitute a criminal offense and cannot be criminalized constitutionally or, even were it is constitutional to do so, can be criminalized only with
strict limitations on the imposition of criminal sanctions.[23] Only where behavior
is accompanied by a culpability to do harm, that is, *mens rea*, does the behavior
cross the line into that which may be, both as a matter of constitutional law and
criminal law doctrine, proscribed.

Bias Crime Prosecutions Run the Risk of Disproportionate Enforcement, Hurting those Whom We Want to Help.[24]

The disproportionate enforcement critique of bias crime laws takes a variety of
forms, but the essence of the critique is the argument that members of minority
groups are more likely to be arrested, convicted, and punished as bias criminals
than are Whites. This argument could be understood either in a "false-positive"
or "false-negative" context. Were there no disproportionate enforcement, all bias
criminals—Whites and members of ethnic minorities—would be convicted
of bias crimes (no false negatives) and *only* bias criminals would be convicted of
bias crimes (no false positives). The disproportionate enforcement critique could
argue that White bias criminals are less likely to be punished as bias criminals
than are minority bias criminals. Alternatively, the critique could contend that
members of ethnic minority groups who are innocent of bias crimes (whether
or not guilty of the parallel offense) are more likely to be punished for having
committed a bias crime than are Whites.[25]

The concern with the racially disproportionate use of bias crime legislation has
been advanced by those who are highly critical of this legislation generally as
well as by those who tend to be more sympathetic to the bias crime project.

Professor James Jacobs, a noted critic of bias crime laws,[26] advanced the
disproportionate enforcement critique in an early treatment of this subject. He
raised the concern that ". . .new bias laws will be used more against minority

---

[23] See Joel Feinberg, *Offense to Others* 25-49 (1985).

[24] The description of the disproportionate enforcement of bias crimes laws is a condensed
version of Frederick M. Lawrence, *Enforcing Bias-Crime Laws Without Bias: Evaluating
the Disproportionate-Enforcement Critique*, LAW AND CONTEMP. PROB., Summer 2003, at
49 2003).

[25] The reverse argument, that bias crime laws will be disproportionately enforced against
White offenders, has generally not be asserted by academic critics of bias crime laws,
although it has received some attention in the popular press. See, e.g., Clarence Page, Op-
Ed, "Hate-Crime Laws Not for 'Whites Only,'" CHI. TRIBUNE, July 16, 2000, §1 at 17
(expressing doubt that bias crime laws are disproportionately enforced against Whites but
giving credence to the concern); John Leo, "When Rules Don't Count Double Standards
Are Accident; They Arise From a Theory," U. S. NEWS & WORLD REPORT, Aug. 7, 2000,
at 14 (arguing that bias crime enforcement is based on a "double standard" and will be disproportionate against Whites). This chapteraper deals directly with the disproportionate
enforcement critique concerned with over-enforcement *against* minority group members.
Many of the observations disputing the critique, however, apply equally to this "reverse"
argument.

[26] See, e.g., Jacobs & Potter, *Hate Crimes and Identity Politics*.

groups than against the white majority."[27] Similarly, Professor James Weinstein has written that ". . .hate crime laws promise to be difficult to administer, may well be counterproductive in that they might be used disproportionately against the very minority groups they were primarily designed to protect. . . ."[28]

Wisconsin Supreme Court Justice Shirley Abrahamson, author of a dissenting opinion in *Wisconsin v. Mitchell* that, anticipating the United States Supreme Court decision in that case would have upheld the Wisconsin bias crime statute, expressed a similar concern. Justice Abrahamson wrote, "[m]any persons also fear that hate crime laws will ultimately be used against the very groups they are designed to protect, and this case illustrates that phenomenon."[29] In her dissenting opinion, Justice Abrahamson took the unusual step of expressing her own view that "[h]ad I been in the legislature, I do not believe I would have supported [the penalty enhancement] statute because I do not think this statute will accomplish its goal. . . ."[30] She nonetheless found the statute to be a constitutional exercise of the legislature's power, a holding ultimately shared by the United States Supreme Court. In her subsequent writing on the subject, Justice Abrahamson raised the disproportionate enforcement critique: "[i]t appears that hate crime statutes may be disproportionately enforced against minority group members such as Todd Mitchell."[31]

The disproportionate enforcement critique has also been advanced by those who have otherwise expressed support, however muted, for the enterprise of identifying crimes of bias motivation and/or enhancing the punishment of those crimes on that basis. Professor Martha Minow, for example, in an essay balancing the arguments for and against criminal prohibitions on bias crimes and hate speech, raised the disproportionate enforcement critique.

Agents entrusted to enforce laws restricting hateful and subordinating speech rely upon their own perceptions about what precisely is hateful and subordinating—and those perceptions inevitably will be partial, and potentially even discriminatory against the least powerful or most vulnerable members of the society. . . . Thus, the case against hate speech and hate crime regulations rightly points out the dangers of selective enforcement, with a likely disparate impact on the weakest and the most minority members of society.[32]

To date, the disproportionate enforcement critique has relied less on specific empirical findings than on the general concern that providing additional tools to

---

[27] James Jacobs "Rethinking the War Against Hate Crimes: A New York City Perspective" in Crim. Just. Eth. 55, 60 (Summer/Fall 1992).

[28] James Weinstein "First Amendment Challenges to Hate Crime Legislation: Where's the Speech?" in Crim. Just. Eth. 6, 17 (Summer/Fall 1992).

[29] Shirley Abrahamson, et al., Words and Sentences, Penalty Enhancement For Hate Crimes," 16 U. Ark. Little Rock L.J. 515, 525 and n. 38 (1994). See 485 N.W.2d, 807, 818 (Wisc. 1992) (Abrahamson, J., dissenting), reversed, 508 U.S. 476 (1993).

[30] 485 N.W.2d at 818.

[31] Abrahamson, Words and Sentences, Penalty Enhancement For Hate Crimes, 16 U. Ark. Little Rock L.J. at 525–526.

[32] Martha Minow, "Regulating Hatred: Whose Speech, Whose Crimes, Whose Power?" in *Breaking The Cycles of Hatred: Memory, Law, and Repair* 31, 41 (2002).

the criminal justice system will tend to disadvantage those groups that are already politically disadvantaged in society. Understandably, where data are hard to come by, broad legal or sociological generalizations will fill the gap. The better approach, of course, would be for these data to be collected and studied.

The disproportionate enforcement critique is generally sympathetic with the goals that the advocates of bias crime enforcement articulate, and the critique is based on the concern that bias crime laws will hurt most those whom it tries to help most. This is true in its direct concern with disproportionate enforcement, arguing that bias crimes laws will be over-enforced *against* minorities, and thus under-enforced in cases of minority victims. It is also the case in the ironic concern with the *disproportionate* impact of *proportionate* enforcement.[33] The disproportionate enforcement critique, however, has lacked an empirical basis.[34]

The Justification for Punishing Bias Crimes Turns on the Harm Caused, Not the Bias Motivation. Thus Bias Crimes Per Se Should Not Receive Enhanced Punishment.

Critics of the bias crime project have on a fundamental level attacked the concern of bias crime laws with the motivation of the bias criminal rather than the harm caused by his or her criminal act. Dean Heidi Hurd and Professor Michael Moore, for example, have criticized the bias crime project for its focus on bias crimes per se rather than on injury to victims, regardless of the motivation of the actor.[35] In particular, Hurd and Moore assert that bias crime laws are unjustifiable because they punish the defendant not for the harm he caused, but for his or her bad character: the "enhanced penalty . . . is not for the underlying act, nor is it for the intentionality with which it is committed; it is for the hatred or prejudice that motivated the defendant to form and act on that intent."[36] It is argued that criminal law should not punish character because it is not immediately within the actor's control: one "cannot simply choose *not* to be a racist."[37] Further, the law has not, and should not, punish motivation. Because there is no support that bias or hatred are "morally worse mental states than greed, sadism, jealousy, and vengeance," we should not start punishing bias-motivation now. Even if the law did punish bias-motivation, there is no evidence that "bias [is] responsive to criminal sanctions in a way that greed, jealousy, sadism, and vengeance are not."[38]

---

[33] For an analysis of the distinction between the true disproportionate enforcement critique that is based on a concern with disproportionate enforcement, and a disproportionate effect critique that is based on a concern with proportionate enforcement leading to a disproportionate effect, see Lawrence, *Enforcing Bias-Crime Laws Without Bias*, LAW AND CONTEMP. PROB., Summer 2003, at 60–61.

[34] Id. at 55–60.

[35] Heidi Hurd and Michael S. Moore, *Punishing Hatred and Prejudice*, 56 STAN. L. REV. 1081 (2004).

[36] Id. at 11281129.

[37] Id. at 1130.

[38] Id. at 1131.

As will be discussed in greater detail below, this critique fails to address the rationale that bias crime law punishes the defendant's intent to cause the additional harm associated with a bias crime. Criminal law does not punish defendants only for the harm they cause. The severity of punishment also depends largely on the *mens rea*, or intent, of the actor. For example, there are varying degrees of homicide; the degree assigned to an act of homicide is largely dependent on the subjective intent of the actor—intentional homicide is murder, reckless homicide is manslaughter, and negligent homicide is a lower degree of homicide still.[39] This same principle can be carried over to bias crime: when an actor burns a cross on the lawn of a black family, he is not merely committing trespass and arson. The actor knows that his act may cause additional harm and indeed the actor desires to cause this additional harm. He thus has the intent to cause further harm, and should be punished accordingly. A defendant should not be punished for a bias crime simply because his "character" unconsciously motivates him to commit a crime against a protected group. The rationale behind bias crime law is punishing not character or motivation, but intent.

Addressing the Risks

The Criminal Law Cannot Escape Dealing With Issues of Differences in Society and Indeed Has a Crucial, Albeit Not All-encompassing, Role to Play in Addressing Bigotry in Society.

The criminal justice system is an awkward tool and blunt instrument for making fine social policy but will unavoidably wind up dealing with issues that are related to social policy.[40]

We should thus not look to bias crime laws as a solution to the overall problem of discrimination in society. At best, bias crime laws will address only a small aspect of the problem. We must avoid the risk of focusing too narrowly on bias *crimes* and thereby failing to observe the true breadth and depth of bigotry in our society. Bigotry and intragroup animus is a serious and multitiered social illness, and it would be facile in the extreme to expect bias crime laws to cure this condition completely or even to address all of its aspects. Some commentators have warned that bias crime laws will keep us from seeing the full dimensions of racism and other forms of bigotry and may distract us from noncriminal cures

---

[39] See, e.g., MODEL PENAL CODE § 210 (1985) (grades of criminal homicide determined by culpability of the accused). See detailed discussion below.

[40] See Susan B. Gellman and Frederick M. Lawrence, *Agreeing to Agree: A Proponent of Hate Crime Laws Reach for Agreement*, 41 HARV. J. ON LEGIS. 421 (2004). The arguments set out in the current chapter are solely those of the author, and not necessarily shared by Ms. Gellman.

such as civil antidiscrimination laws and education programs.[41] However, criminal law enforcement in any field cannot address all aspects of social pathology and should not be looked to for that purpose. Bias crime law is no exception to this general observation.

To say that bias crime laws are not the single answer to issues of bigotry in society, however, is not to deny a critical role for law enforcement in this arena. Bias crimes laws play a key part in the social recognition of the particular harms caused to the society by bias-motivated violence, and thereby the role of groups in a multicultural society. Bias crime laws locate the existence of "social fissure" lines in society, and recognize the greater harm that is represented by crimes that implicate these fissure lines.[42] It may well be that in doing so, the enforcement of bias crime laws does call greater attention to issues of bias and intergroup tension in society than would exist were law enforcement to focus exclusively on the parallel crime within a bias crime. In doing so, however, bias crime law does not create that which is not there. Rather, bias crime law observes and recognizes that which is there. Ultimately it is the society at large that evaluates the levels of harm caused by particular crimes and we properly expect those evaluations to be reflected in the criminal law and its sanctions. It is no overstatement to say that bias crime laws, as is true of all criminal laws, are meant only in part to protect individual victims; their primary purpose is to protect society more generally.

Enactment of bias crime legislation constitutes a societal condemnation of racism, religious intolerance, and other forms of bigotry that are covered by that law and, of perhaps greater significance here, a formal awareness of the role of these groups in society. If the criminal justice system does not punish bias crimes, or, if it expressly punishes them, but not more harshly than parallel crimes, there is also a message that the legislation expresses. The message here is that society, through its criminal law, is not cognizant of the additional harm caused by the bias-motivated crime. This message suggests a lack of formal awareness of the status and role of ethnic, racial, or other groups in the society. Simply put, it is impossible for the punishment choices made by the society *not* to express societal values.[43]

---

[41] See, e.g., Martha Minow, *Breaking the Cycles of Hatred: Memory, Law and Repair* 48 (2002) ("The agenda of regulating hatred whether through hate speech restrictions or hate crimes legislation has the unfortunate effect of focusing on the individual perpetrator but not the victims nor the social forces that assist and inform the perpetrator. Hate crimes prosecutions zero in on the one with the gun, not the one with the hate-filled talk radio show, the anti-women rap music, the neo-Nazi web-site, or the homophobic preacher.")

[42] Lawrence, *Punishing Hate*, at 12–14, 39–44, 58–63.

[43] See id. at 161–169. For a discussion of expressive punishment theory and of the role of social denunciation in punishment, see, e.g., Joel Feinberg, "The Expressive Function of Punishment," in Joel Feinberg, *Doing and Deserving* (1970), 95–118; Emile Durkheim, *The Division of Labor in Society* 44–52, 60–64 (W. D. Hall trans., Free Press 1984); Ronald J. Rychlak, "Society's Moral Right to Punish: A Further Exploration of the Denunciation Theory of Punishment," 65 TULANE L. REV. 299, 332–335 (1990). See also *Durkheim and the Law* 61–63 (Steven Lukes and A. Scull eds. 1983); Steven Lukes, *Emile Durkheim: His Life and Work*, 160–163 (Stanford ed. 1985); Robert Reiner, "Crime, law and deviance: The Durkheim legacy," in Steve Fenton, *Durkheim and Modern Sociology*, 176182 (1984). See generally, David Garland, *Punishment and Modern Society* (1990).

The understandable desire not to exacerbate racial and ethnic tensions through focusing on the bias element of a bias-motivated crime must therefore be placed along side the damage caused by ignoring the particularized harm caused precisely by the bias motivation. To call the burning of a cross on the lawn of an African American family an act of vandalism and vandalism alone, similar to a random prank by a neighborhood youth, is not merely to fail to capture accurately the full depth and context of the crime. It is to fail to acknowledge and validate the impact of the full crime on its victims, individual, group, and society. Indeed, it is more than a passive failure to validate harm; it is a powerful, and dangerous, statement rejecting the validity of those perceived harms. In the arena of bias-motivated violence, therefore, bias crime laws have a significant and inescapable role to play.

Although Thoughts and Expression May Not Be Punished, Criminal Intents and Effects May Be Punished. The Line Between the Two, If Not Always Easy to Draw, is Essential to Seek.

The balance that must be struck to protect free expression but permit the enhanced punishment of bias crimes is well illustrated through reference to the Supreme Court's 2003 decision in *Virginia v. Black*,[44] concerning Virginia's half-century-old cross-burning statute that provided in pertinent part as follows:

It shall be unlawful for any person or persons, with the intent of intimidating any person or group of persons, to burn, or cause to be burned, a cross on the property of another, a highway or other public place. Any such burning of a cross shall be prima facie evidence of an intent to intimidate a person or group of persons.[45]

Virginia v. Black arose out of two separate cases involving three defendants. Like textbook examples, the two cases represent the two poles of cross burnings—criminal domestic terrorism and constitutionally protected expression of White supremacy. Barry Black led a Ku Klux Klan rally on private property, at the conclusion of which a 25- to 30-foot cross was burned. At his trial, the jury was instructed that they were required to find an "intent to intimidate" and that "the burning of a cross by itself is sufficient evidence from which you may infer the required intent."[46] The cross burning for which Richard Elliott and Jonathan O'Mara were prosecuted was quite different. They attempted to burn a cross on the lawn of an African American, James Jubilee, who had recently moved next door, to "get back" at Jubilee.[47] At the trial, the jury was instructed that they could infer the requisite intent for the crime of cross burning from the act of burning the cross itself. The judge went on to instruct the jury that the Commonwealth was required to prove, among other things, that "the defendant had the intent of intimidating any person or group of persons."[48]

---

[44] Virginia v. Black, 538 U.S. 343 (2003).
[45] Va. Code. Ann. §18.2–423 (Michie 1991) (enacted in 1950). The prima facie provision was added to the statute in 1968.
[46] Virginia v. Black, 538 U.S. at 349.
[47] Id. at 350.
[48] Id.

All three defendants appealed to the Supreme Court of Virginia. That court struck down the cross-burning statute, relying heavily on *R.A.V. v. City of St. Paul*,[49] the 1992 case in which the Court struck down a cross-burning ordinance as a content-related proscription in violation of the First Amendment.[50] The United States Supreme Court granted certiorari on two related issues: whether the cross-burning statute violated the First Amendment as interpreted in *R.A.V.* (the *R.A.V.* issue), and whether the statutory presumption that cross burning itself is "prima facie evidence" of the defendant's intent to intimate was unconstitutionally over-broad (the overbreadth issue). In an opinion by Justice O'Connor, the majority of the Court upheld the statute on the *R.A.V.* issue. Although there was no majority opinion on the overbreadth issue, a majority of the Court was of the view that the statutory presumption was constitutionally invalid.[51]

A blueprint for a constitutional cross-burning statute emerges from a consideration of the Court's treatment of the two issues. The *R.A.V.* issue concerned the holding in that case that the St. Paul cross-burning ordinance was an unconstitutional content-based prohibition, proscribing only that conduct that will cause "anger, alarm or resentment in others on the basis of race, color, creed, religion or gender" and not on any other basis. The Court in *Black* upheld the Virginia statute as a law aimed at *all* cross burnings that are intended to intimidate, regardless of the race or ethnicity of the victim.[52] The overbreadth issue concerned the "prima facie evidence" clause of the cross-burning statute. Intimidation would have to be proved, not presumed, unless it is an easily rebuttable presumption.[53] The decision in *Black* thus represents a significant refinement to the holding in *R.A.V.*, and one that is ultimately supportive of a view of the hate crime project that is consistent with concerns of free expression, both constitutional and philosophical.

The balance between protecting speech and enforcing bias crimes may be illustrated by considering the specific facts at issue in *Black*. Wholly consistent with the values of free expression, Virginia might punish Richard Elliott and Jonathan O'Mara, and these same values preclude Virginia from punishing Barry Black. Moreover, Virginia could prosecute Elliott and O'Mara for a bias-motivated crime of cross-burning. Virginia could punish Elliot and O'Mara not only for intending to terrorize Jubilee but also for doing so with a further intent ("motivation" if you like) to terrorize Jubilee because of his race and to cause fear and harm to other African Americans.[54] They would receive an enhanced punishment for committing a crime with a heightened level of intent, one that is intended to cause a great and more pervasive level of harm.

---

[49] R.A.V. v. City of St. Paul, 505 U.S. 377 (1992).

[50] 262 Va. 764, 553 S.E. 2d 738 (2001).

[51] See Virginia v. Black, 538 U.S. at 364–367 (O'Connor, J., plurality); 538 U.S. at 384–387 (Souter, J., concurring in judgment and dissenting in part).

[52] Id. 362–363.

[53] Id. at 366 (O'Connor, J.); id. at 385 (Souter, J.); id. at 368–371 (Scalia, J., concurring in part, concurring in the judgment in part, and dissenting in part).

[54] See Lawrence, *Punishing Hate*, at 106–109.

The Disproportionate Enforcement Critique Cannot Overcome the Burden that it Must Bear in its Opposition to Bias Crime Law Enforcement.

Bias crime legislation in America expresses precisely the values that many of the disproportionate enforcement critics espouse: the law ought to protect all citizens, including, and perhaps particularly, minority citizens, and society should not use the criminal justice system in a manner that harms members of minority groups. The disproportionate enforcement critique primarily follows the general argument that agents of the criminal justice system enforce its prohibitions in a discriminatory manner such that they treat members of ethnic minority groups unequally and unfairly both as perpetrators and as victims. To a certain extent, this reliance on a general argument of discriminatory criminal law enforcement instead of a more particularized argument of discriminatory bias crime law enforcement is understandable. For a number of systemic reasons, it is very difficult to obtain reliable data on the levels of bias crimes that are committed as would be necessary to support an assertion that bias crime laws are being enforced disproportionately.[55] Moreover, there is some basis for the proposition that bias crime laws are in fact not enforced disproportionately or, in any event, no more or less disproportionately than any other area of criminal law enforcement.[56] This leaves disproportionate enforcement critics to argue that *any* criminal law runs the risk of being enforced in a disproportionate manner that is adverse to minority groups and other disadvantaged members of society. Fair enough. But the general argument as to disproportionality in the criminal justice system would not seem to support an assertion to undo the criminal justice system generally. Yet this is essentially the argument that disproportionate enforcement critics have advanced, that a generalized concern with disproportionate enforcement of the criminal justice system should warrant a rejection of laws punishing bias-motivated crimes. It would be painfully ironic if the one place in which the general assertion were to be applied was one of the prime areas of the criminal law concerned with protecting the "right to be the same or different"[57] and recognizing the role of groups and subgroups in a multicultural society. Absent particular reason to believe that bias crime laws, more than other areas of the criminal law, are enforced in a racially discriminatory manner, an area of criminal law enforcement particularly concerned with the impact of bigotry and discrimination on its victims ought not be impeded, or worse yet, precluded.

The burden of the argument is on the disproportionate enforcement critics, and it is a burden that they cannot carry. Critics might better focus their efforts on the need to improve bias crime data than on a generalized nonempirical assault on the attempt to understand, recognize, investigate, and prosecute bias-motivated

---

[55] See Lawrence, *Enforcing Bias-Crime Laws Without Bias*, LAW AND CONTEMP. PROB., Summer 2003, at 55–60.
[56] Id. at 60–66.
[57] Allport, *The Nature of Prejudice*, at 518.

crimes. Indeed this is a point on which both critics and advocates of the bias crime project should be able to agree. Social scientists have a key role to play in providing evidence that would help support (or reject) the disproportionate enforcement critique of bias crime law.

The Role of Harm is Essential in Assessing Severity of the Crime and thus Severity of the Appropriate Criminal Sanction.

If a legislature determines that there is a greater harm caused when an assault is bias-motivated than when a similar assault is committed without bias, it is appropriate for that legislature to identify those crimes for enhanced punishment. I deliberately state this in the conditional form, that is, "*if* a legislature can determine harm, *then* there is a case for enhanced punishment." Too often, the legislative findings do not adequately support the case for greater harm. I have argued elsewhere that this case can be demonstrated and indeed has been made by social psychologists and sociologists.[58] Clearly, however, this is an area that would benefit from further research, both empirical and theoretical.

Harm, and the severity of harm, is thus critical to assessing the appropriate criminal sanction for a particular crime or group of crimes. The severity of a crime is a function of both the culpability of the action and the harm caused. Many commentators have analyzed the role of culpability in the assessment of the seriousness of a crime. It is not an overstatement to say that the entire thrust of the study and articulation of modern criminal law has been toward a focus on the state of mind or culpability of the accused. This focus does not mean that the results of the conduct are unimportant. Rather, justification of punishment under the criminal law, whether based on a retributive or consequentialist argument, follows directly from the actor's mental state.

In contrast to the doctrinally and theoretically well-developed understanding of the relationship between culpability and the level of punishment, the role of harm in assessing this relationship has been largely unexplored. This is surprising because the intuitive case for harm as a key component in assessing a crime's seriousness is at least as strong as it is for culpability. Holding either culpability or harm constant while varying the other demonstrates this point. The objective harm of a victim's death will be associated with the more serious crime of murder or the less serious crime of manslaughter solely on the basis of the actor's culpability.[59] However, intentional murder is a more serious crime than intentional assault because of the harm caused. Although the offender acts willfully in both instances, the murder victim is dead whereas the assault victim is only injured. The same point may be illustrated further down the homicide scale. Reckless conduct—that is, reckless risk creation—resulting in death constitutes the felony of manslaughter.[60] If the identical conduct with the identical culpability does not

---

[58] Lawrence, *Punishing Hate*, at 58–63.
[59] See, e.g., MODEL PENAL CODE § 210 (1985) (grades of criminal homicide determined by culpability of the accused).
[60] The Model Penal Code defines "criminal homicide" as purposely, knowingly, recklessly or negligently causing the death of another. MODEL PENAL CODE § 210.1(1). Criminal Homicide that is committed recklessly constitutes manslaughter. Ibid., § 210.3(1)(a).

result in death, however, the actor is guilty of a far lesser crime, often only a misdemeanor such as the Model Penal Code's "reckless endangerment."[61]

One further point with respect to the relationship between culpability and harm and their roles in understanding the severity of a crime completes the analysis. Not only do both the actor's culpability and the harm caused by his conduct play separate roles in comprising the severity of the crime, but also there is a mutual, interactive relationship between these two factors. An actor's culpability itself affects the level of harm caused. Consider the distinction between an intentional assault with a baseball bat and an unintended (and perhaps even non-negligent) accident in the midst of a game with a baseball bat; assume that the physical injury in the two cases in identical. It is not only true that there is a difference in culpability—the actor in the first case acted intentionally whereas the actor in the second case acted at worse negligently and perhaps reasonably albeit unfortunately. It is also true that the very harm to the two injured parties is different. Although the physical harm is the same, the emotional and psychological harm caused to the assault victim is likely to be far greater than that caused to the unfortunate baseball catcher who was hit in the head with a bat.

Bias crimes are a paradigmatic example of a category of criminal cases in which culpability and resulting harm have such a mutual, interactive relationship. Thus, the argument that enhanced criminal sentencing for bias crimes should turn on the harm caused in individual cases, not the categorical factor of the defendant's bias motivation, misses the mark. Certainly not every instance of a particular crime causes the precise harm as another instance of that same crime. This, however, calls for sentencing ranges and judicial discretion in imposing sentences within the range. The question is what the range should be for a particular crime. A legislature might rationally conclude that bias-motivated crimes cause a greater level of harm to the individual direct victim and the victim community than an otherwise similar but non-bias–motivated crime. In the end, it is reasonable, indeed it is necessary, for the sentencer to take into account the cause of this greater harm, the bias motivation, when assessing criminal punishment.

---

[61] See MODEL PENAL CODE § 211.2 (reckless risk of death is a misdemeanor). Several states have adopted this approach to the punishment of reckless endangerment. Compare, e.g., ALASKA STAT. § 11.41.250 (b)(2004) (making reckless endangerment a class A misdemeanor) with ALASKA STAT. § 11.41.120 (2004) (making manslaughter a class A felony); ARIZONA REV. STAT. ANN. § 13-1201 (2001) (making reckless endangerment class 1 misdemeanor or, if there was a substantial risk of imminent death, a class 6 felony) with ARIZONA REV. STAT. ANN. §13-1103 (West Supp. 2005) (making manslaughter a class 2 felony); CONN. GEN. STAT. § 53a-63 (West 2001) (making reckless endangerment class A misdemeanor) with CONN. GEN. STAT. § 53a-55 (West 2001) (making first-degree manslaughter a class B felony). Some states grade reckless endangerment as a felony, but in no jurisdiction is it graded as seriously as manslaughter. Compare, e.g., N.Y. PENAL LAW § 120.25 (McKinney 2004) (making first-degree reckless endangerment a class D felony) with N.Y. PENAL LAW §125.20 (McKinney 2004) (making first-degree manslaughter a class B felony); WIS. STAT. ANN. § 941.30 (West 2005) (making first-degree reckless endangerment a class D felony) with WIS. STAT. ANN. § 940.06 (West 2005) (making manslaughter a class C felony).

Conclusion

After twenty-five years of experience with the Hate Crimes Project in America, it is fair to ask whether bias crime laws are "working." Bias crime legislation must be more than merely symbolic expressions of legislative sympathy with a problem if it is to be a proper exercise of a legislative function. As that is the case, it is appropriate to ask what the measurable goals of a bias crime law are, so that we may also ask whether or not the laws are working to achieve those goals.

To a certain extent, the question of whether any criminal law is "working" turns on the underlying justification of criminal punishment upon which one relies. A consequentialist will presumably articulate a goal of crime reduction, and will accordingly attempt to measure bias crime levels in response to the enactment and implementation of a bias crime law. A retributivist will ask a different set of more overtly normative questions about whether or not bias criminals deserve greater punishment than those who commit parallel crimes.

Consequentialist justifications for bias crime laws are problematic. When it comes to bias crimes, data as to incidence levels are seriously flawed. Data compiled by local law enforcement agencies both for their own purposes and for reporting to the Department of Justice pursuant to the Federal Hate Crimes Statistics Act suffer from dramatic underreporting, and there are systemic reasons behind this underreporting.[62] Moreover, the better we understand the problem of bias-motivated violence, the more our numbers could go up, measuring less the levels of the problem than the levels of our awareness of the problem. These intractable problems, as least at the present time, in establishing reliable data conspire to make it very difficult to demonstrate whether bias crimes law enforcement has been an effective deterrent of bias crime; in all fairness it should be added that the same empirical difficulties make it difficult to assert that bias crime laws have failed to deter bias-motivated violence.

The best answer to the question of whether bias crime laws are "working" is perhaps to be found in an understanding that, at least for right now, we do not enact criminal laws only to reduce crime but also to punish criminal wrongs, and this punishment may or may not lead to a reduction in crime at any given time. We may best understand bias crimes from this perspective of a harms-based retributive punishment theory. So understood, the justification for bias crime laws does not require a largely futile effort to determine whether at any particular time levels of bias crimes are rising or falling, or whether we are just becoming more accurate at measuring what, undoubtedly for some time yet to come, will be very hard to measure.

The Hate Crime Project is in fact only one aspect of a broader development in American society and other nations as well, that is, a heightened recognition of the multiethnic nature of the society. It should be no surprise that the criminal law

---

[62] Lawrence, *Enforcing Bias Crimes Laws Without Bias: Evaluating the Disproportionate Enforcement Critique*, LAW AND CONTEMP. PROB., Summer 2003, at 55–60.

reflects this recognition. As theorists such as Emile Durkheim and, more recently, Joel Feinberg, have articulated, punishment represents societal condemnation of certain behavior.[63] Social cohesion thus emerges from the act of punishment. It is impossible for a society's punishment choices *not* to express its societal values. Through its choices concerning punishment, a society reveals in part the content of its values.

Criminal punishment, unique among official sanctions imposed by an authority, carries with it social disapproval, resentment and indignation. As summarized by the Royal Commission on Capital Punishment, "[T]he ultimate justification for any punishment is, not that it is a deterrent, but that it is the emphatic denunciation by the community of a crime."[64]

What happens when a legislature enacts a bias crime law and it is signed into law? This act of lawmaking constitutes a societal condemnation of racism, religious intolerance, and other forms of bigotry that are covered by that law and, of perhaps greater significance here, a formal awareness of the role of these groups in society. What happens if a criminal justice system does not expressly punish bias crimes, or, if it expressly punishes them, it does not punish them more harshly than parallel crimes? Here, too, there is a message expressed by the legislation. The message is that racial harmony and equality are not among the highest values held by the community. Perhaps more accurately, the message suggests a lack of formal awareness of the status and role of ethnic, racial, or other groups in the society. Simply put, it is impossible for the punishment choices made by the society *not* to express societal values.

Bias crime laws are thus a powerful reflection of societal attitudes of the multiethnic dimensions of that society. In a monochromatic society—in reality or as perceived by its legal system—we would expect a bias motivated assault to be punished identically to a parallel assault; the group bias motivation of the crime is rendered largely irrelevant in such a society and thus not part of that which is condemned. In a multiethnic society, however, we would expect bias motivated crimes to receive some special treatment by the criminal law, to reflect the harm caused by the motivation underlying the crime.

The treatment of bias crimes thus offers a significant window into the self-perception of a society. Further, this is not strictly or even primarily an American issue. The role of groups in Great Britain today, for example, is at a critical stage of evolution. The Parekh Report on *The Future of Multi-Ethnic Britain* speaks of Britain at the "crossroads," faced with the "recognition that England, Scotland, and Wales are multi-ethnic, multi-faith, multicultural, multi-community

---

[63] See, e.g., Emile Durkheim, *The Division of Labor in Society* 62–63 (W. D. Hall trans., Free Press 1984); Robert Reiner, *Crime, Law and Deviance: The Durkheim Legacy*, in Steve Fenton, *Durkheim and Modern Sociology*, 176–182 (1984); Joel Feinberg, *The Expressive Function in Punishment*, in Joel Feinberg, *Doing and Deserving*, 103–104 (1970).

[64] Royal Commission on Capital Punishment, Minutes of Evidence, Ninth Day, December 1, 1949, Memorandum submitted by the Rt. Hon. Lord Justice Denning (1950).

societies."[65] The fifty-five national states that comprise the Organization of Security and Cooperation in Europe have committed to develop practices throughout their various legal systems to address bias-motivated violence.[66] As nations continue to see themselves as multiethnic pluralistic states, violence motivated by group bias will continue to receive special attention from both the law enforcement community, and the various communities that together comprise the society. It is one means, and if not the only then certainly a significant means, by which societies answer the challenge presented by Gordon Allport when he asked whether America would continue to make progress toward tolerance and to stand as a "staunch defender of the right to be the same or different" from others in society, or whether a "fatal regression will set in."[67] This is our challenge still.

Acknowledgments. I thank Christine Chadwick for her research and editorial assistance and Deborah Norwood of the Jacob Burns Law Library at George Washington University Law School, for her editorial assistance.

---

[65] Runnymeade Trust Commission on the Future of Multi-Ethnic Britain, *Report on The Future of Multi-Ethnic Britain*, at 2 (2000) (The "Parekh Report").

[66] Recommendations adopted by the Organization of Security and Cooperation in Europe, Office for Democratic Institutions and Human Rights, Human Dimension Implementation Meeting at Warsaw, October 2004.

[67] Allport, at 518.

12
Implications of Automatic and Controlled Processes in Stereotyping for Hate Crime Perpetration and Litigation

Margaret Bull Kovera

In 1998, Matthew Shepard was a slightly built young man studying at the University of Wyoming who was active in politics and had a gift for learning foreign languages. He also was gay (Shepard, 2000). In an event that brought worldwide attention to the issue of hate crimes and legislation to punish them, two men picked up Shepard from a campus bar. Accounts vary about who approached whom, with some believing that the two men had told Matthew they were gay. No matter how the interaction began, it ended with the two men, Russell Henderson and Aaron McKinney, driving Matthew to a remote location, tying him to a fence, beating him, and leaving him to die from his injuries and the cold.

Almost immediately, perhaps because of his sexual orientation and the brutal nature of the attack, Matthew's murder was characterized as a hate crime. Six years after the attack, new details have come to light, raising questions about what truly motivated Henderson and McKinney to kill Matthew Shepard that night (ABC News, 2004). Friends of Matthew now report that he used illegal drugs. McKinney was a frequent drug user and dealer who had squandered an inheritance and was now broke with a new baby and a girlfriend to support. In new interviews, both Henderson and McKinney report that McKinney was determined to commit a robbery the evening of Matthew Shepard's murder so that he could support his methamphetamine habit and provide money for his family. When the original target of the robbery proved elusive, McKinney reported that he turned his attention to Shepard, judging him to be an acceptable alternative target because he was drunk (making him an easy target) and because his fine clothing suggested that he would be carrying a sizable amount of cash. When asked by a reporter to explain why the beating of Shepard was so severe if the motive was financial, McKinney claimed that he had ingested methamphetamines that night and that these drugs often caused him to rage. Additional evidence has also surfaced that McKinney himself had previously had sex with men, lending further evidence that McKinney may have been motivated by something other than hatred for homosexuality.

Although some, including a Laramie Police detective, now believe that robbery was the motive for the assault on Matthew Shepard, others, including Matthew's mother, continue to believe that McKinney and Henderson's hatred of gays motivated the attack. This controversy highlights some of the difficulties involved in determining whether to charge a suspect or convict a defendant of a hate or bias motivated crime. Although it may be clear whether a defendant had committed a crime, as it was in the Matthew Shepard case, it may be less clear whether hate or bias motivated the defendant to act, as many actions are multiply determined.

Psychologists have begun to research the causes and consequences of hate-motivated crimes and public perception of hate crime offenders and victims (Marcus-Newhall, Blake, & Baumann, 2002). For example, prejudiced perceivers do not distinguish between hate and non-bias crimes when rating victim or perpetrator culpability (Rayburn, Mendoza, & Davison, 2003). Reminding people of their mortality (i.e., mortality salience) increases their support of hate crime laws in the abstract but decreases their support of specific outgroup victims who threaten their world-view (Lieberman, Arndt, Personius, & Cook, 2001). And an exploration of the relationship between the incidence of hate crime in New York City and white unemployment rates found no evidence that increased frustration (i.e., higher white unemployment) led to increased aggression as measured by incidence of hate crimes (Green, Glaser, & Rich, 1998).

What is most remarkable about this nascent research on hate crime perpetration and litigation is that it has almost entirely ignored the tremendous body of social-psychological research on how cognitive representations of people who belong to groups other than our own (i.e., stereotypes) influence the way we think, feel, and behave toward these outgroup members. In an attempt to bridge the gap between this basic psychological theory and legal scholarship on hate crime legislation, I begin by reviewing the primary justifications for and criticisms of hate crime legislation as well as the limited psychological research that addresses issues surrounding hate crimes. Next, I review the psychological literature on automatic and controlled processes in stereotyping and prejudice and discuss the implications of this literature for the validity of these justifications and criticisms. Finally, I suggest possible avenues for future research on hate crimes that follow from our psychological understanding of how stereotypic processes can automatically influence judgments and behavior.

Hate or Bias-Motivated Crimes

According to the FBI, "Hate crimes are not separate, distinct crimes, but rather traditional offenses motivated by the offender's bias" (Federal Bureau of Investigation, 1999, p. 1). In other words, defendants who commit hate crimes select their crime victims because of the victim's membership in a particular racial, ethnic, religious, or other legally protected group. Decision makers can only infer whether a perpetrator is biased from the hateful actions of the perpetrator toward a member of a legally protected group.

Thus, an important component of adjudicating hate crimes is the determination of the perpetrator's motive (Lawrence, 2002). In many crimes, intent to commit a crime (e.g., the mental state related to the elements of the crime) is the only relevant mental state for determining whether a crime occurred; motive is irrelevant (e.g., a mental state that is not specifically related to the crime). In the context of hate crimes, however, motive is a critical issue for determining whether a hate crime has been committed. For example, suppose a perpetrator robs a store owned by an Arab American. When committing the robbery, it was the perpetrator's intent to steal money but what is his motive? Perhaps the perpetrator was motivated to get funds to buy drugs. In addition, or perhaps instead, the perpetrator may have been motivated to intimidate the store owner and other Arab Americans. Only in this latter scenario does the perpetrator's act of robbery become a hate crime. Thus, determination of a bias motivation is critical for a crime to be classified as a hate crime.

Justification for Hate Crime Legislation

Many states have enacted penalty enhancements for those perpetrators who are found guilty of committing crimes because of biased motivations and there are federal statutes specifying the conditions that must be met for a regular offense to also meet criteria for being bias motivated (Sullaway, 2004). Legislators and scholars have offered several justifications for the penalty enhancements found in hate crime legislation. Some have argued that it is important to punish hate-motivated crimes more severely to discourage the perpetrator and others from engaging in discriminatory behavior (Note, 1982). To date, there have been no studies to determine whether penalty enhancements for hate crimes have a deterrent effect, either specific (i.e., knowledge of enhanced penalties deters the perpetration of biased motivated crimes) or general (i.e., seeing others severely punished keeps others from committing biased motivation crimes; Gerstenfeld, 1992).

There is more evidence to support the second justification of enhanced penalties for hate crimes specifically that enhanced penalties recognize the additional harm presumed to be suffered by victims of hate crimes or by others who share group membership with the victim. Not only do police officers report that bias motivated crimes are more serious than their parallel non-bias crimes (McDevitt, Levin, & Bennett, 2002), but bias-motivated crimes are also more likely to have multiple offenders and to result in hospitalization than non-bias crimes (Levin & McDevitt, 1993). In addition to physical harm, targets of bias-motivated crimes suffer greater psychological harm from their victimization than do targets of parallel crimes. Controlling for the violence of the crime, gay men and lesbians who were targets of bias crimes suffered greater psychological distress than those who were targets of non-bias–motivated crimes (Herek, Gillis, & Cogan, 1999). For those who had been assaulted, the victims of bias-motivated crimes still exhibited greater depression, anxiety, and traumatic stress than victims of non-bias crimes, even 5 years after the attack (Herek et al., 1999). Victims of bias-motivated crimes are also more likely to exhibit avoidance behaviors (e.g., changing neighborhoods) after the crime than are victims of non-bias–motivated crimes (Weiss, Ehrlich, & Larcom, 1991–1992).

The impact of hate crimes on the wider community might also justify enhanced penalties for these crimes (Sullaway, 2004). Although crimes without bias motivation may strike fear in the heart of a community (e.g., a serial rapist), hate crime motivation may include the intention of terrorizing other members of the target's group and may result in harm to the group as a whole (Berk, 1990; Gerstenfeld, 1992). For example, at least one attack on a Jewish daycare center in which the perpetrator stated that he intended his acts to send a message to non-Whites (O'Neill, 2000) caused other Jewish organizations to enact costly security measures to protect their members. Further harm to the communities may result because hate crimes may be more likely to produce retaliatory crimes, as both analogue (Craig, 1999) and correlational (Green et al., 1998) studies suggest.

Objections to Hate Crime Laws

Despite these justifications for hate crime legislation, these laws are not without controversy. Indeed, critics offer several objections to enhanced penalties for bias-motivated crimes. A primary objection is that hate crime laws violate perpetrators' right to free expression guaranteed by the First Amendment, even if what is to be expressed is hate (Gerstenfeld, 1992). The First Amendment argument against hate crime laws is that slurs based on group membership are protected speech. If agents of the law determine bias motivation solely from the perpetrator's use of these protected slurs, then they have denied the defendant First Amendment protections. These arguments have proved generally unsuccessful as courts have held that hate crime legislation punishes conduct intended to do harm, not speech or mere behavioral expressions of thought (*State v. Beebe*, 1984; *State v. Hendrix*, 1991; *Wisconsin v. Mitchell*, 1993).

Critics of hate crime legislation also claim that these laws draw attention to group differences, exacerbating intergroup tensions (Gerstenfeld, 1992; Jacobs & Potter, 1998). Others have argued that there is no evidence to support this criticism. For example, Sullaway (2004) argues against this criticism by reporting data from California and national surveys of residents' perceptions of race relations. Relying primarily on the data from the California study, conducted between 1998 and 2000 (Hajnal & Baldassare, 2001), Sullaway argues that there is no evidence of increased tension due to the enactment of California's hate crime. Unfortunately, both surveys rely on residents' self-reports of racial tension and they may be motivated to deny racial tension for self-presentational reasons. Moreover, the California data do not allow for a time series analysis of changes since the enactment of the laws as the researchers collected the data after the laws went into effect, preventing a comparison of tension pre- and post-legislation.

Finally, both opponents and proponents of hate crime legislation have expressed concern about whether hate crime laws will be selectively enforced, leading to the increased prosecution of the groups the laws are intended to protect (Jacobs &

Porter, 1998; Lawrence, 2003). Because hate crime laws cannot eliminate prejudice or bias in the people who make decisions whether to charge or prosecute a hate crime, it is possible that majority group members who perpetrate bias crimes are less likely to be prosecuted than are perpetrators who are members of minority groups. Because stereotypes link aggression with minority group members, it is also possible that minority group members may be more likely to be prosecuted for hate crimes that they did not commit than are majority group members.

Do these objections to enhanced penalties for hate crimes find support in the psychological literature? Although researchers have examined factors that predict whether particular individuals will be likely to oppose hate crime legislation (Dunbar & Molina, 2004; Johnson & Byers, 2003), researchers have failed to examine whether the objections have any empirical support. As several of the objections implicate intergroup perceptions, attitudes, and behaviors, the social psychological literature on intergroup behavior is a reasonable place to turn for research that might shed light on the reasonableness of these objections and provide suggested paradigms for needed research on these issues. Although the official training manual for hate crime data collection provides an overview of the social psychology of prejudice (Federal Bureau of Investigation, 1996), that overview was dated and inaccurate even at the time it was written. Given the tremendous attention that stereotyping, prejudice, and discrimination have received from social psychologists in the intervening decade, it is time to revisit this literature for the insights it might provide for the understanding of hate crime perpetration and litigation.

A Social Psychological Analysis of Hate Crime Perpetration and Litigation

Despite its moniker, there is no requirement that the perpetrator experience hate while committing an act that meets the definition of a hate crime. What is required, however, is that the perpetrator selected a target based on the group membership of that target. This requirement implies deliberation, choice, and active cognitive processes in the selection of a target (Lawrence, 2002; Sullaway, 2004). However, is it possible that a perpetrator chooses a target in a way that is not deliberate and controlled, yet still uses group membership in the selection process? If so, would a perpetrator who selects a target through automatic application of stereotypes about outgroup members be guilty of a hate crime? Even the FBI's guide for collecting data on hate crime perpetration recognizes the difficulty of inferring a perpetrator's subjective motivation for committing a crime (Federal Bureau of Investigation, 1999). If determining motive is difficult, determining whether that motive arose out of automatic or controlled processes might prove impossible. How might legal decision makers discriminate between those perpetrators who targeted victims through deliberative processes and those who acted on automatically activated stereotypes and prejudice?

Automatic and Controlled Processes in Stereotyping, Prejudice, and Discrimination

> Look around and you will find
> No one's really color blind.
> Maybe it's a fact
> We all should face
> Everyone makes judgments
> Based on race.
>
> From the Broadway musical *Avenue Q*

In the 2004 Tony Award winning musical, *Avenue Q*, the characters Kate Monster, Princeton, and Gary Coleman sing an irreverent song "Everyone's a Little Bit Racist" based on a premise that has support from the social psychological literature: that even well-intentioned people who believe themselves to be egalitarian sometimes make unintentional judgments about others based on their race. Although the study of prejudice has a long history in social psychology (Allport, 1954), for the last two decades, social psychologists have focused their efforts on examinations of whether stereotypes are automatically activated and applied when making judgments about others, even by those who most would regard as low in prejudice (Dovidio, Glick, & Rudman, 2005). Under what conditions do people act on automatically activated stereotypes rather than engaging in controlled processing of group membership? Do these conditions affect whether people commit hate crimes or the choices that police officers and prosecutors make regarding the enforcement of these laws?

Social psychologists generally are interested in how variables influence thoughts, feelings, and behaviors. Perhaps because of these interests, they hold a tripartite view of attitudes, including outgroup bias, which differentiates between thoughts about group members (stereotypes), feelings toward a group or members of that group (prejudice) and disparate treatment of individuals based on their group membership (discrimination; Zanna & Rempel, 1988). Thus, discrimination is the behavioral manifestation of stereotypes (i.e., cognitive structures containing information about groups that are applied to individuals) and prejudice. The implication of this tripartite view is that these constructs are distinct but may overlap. That is, the tripartite view allows for the possibility that negative stereotypes groups may or may not result in negative affect (prejudice) or behavior (discrimination). Of interest for the discussion of hate crime legislation, is whether negative stereotypes that a perpetrator holds, although not consciously endorsed as true, may result in unintentional discrimination without the accompanying prejudice or deliberative choice of a target based on group membership that would justify enhanced penalties.

Automatic Stereotyping and Prejudice

Although it may seem unlikely that people who are low in prejudice (e.g., negative affect toward outgroups) would behave in discriminatory ways, evidence is mounting that there are situations in which this does occur. The earliest demonstration of this phenomenon occurred in a ground-breaking dissertation on automatic and controlled processes in stereotyping (Devine, 1989). In the first study, Caucasian participants listed the features of the societal stereotype of Blacks, describing the components of the cultural stereotype and not their own personal beliefs about the group. Participants then completed the Modern Racism Scale (McConahay, Hardee, & Batts, 1981), a purportedly nonreactive measure of prejudice. The most common themes in the verbal protocols provided by participants were those of aggressiveness, hostility, and criminality. What was surprising about these protocols is that their content did not differ as a function of the participants' level of prejudice; those high and low in prejudice were equally likely to report that the Black stereotype included hostility and criminality. Thus, stereotype knowledge was unrelated to negative affect for the stereotyped group.

If everyone has knowledge of cultural stereotypes, irrespective of whether they endorse those stereotypes, is it possible that this knowledge can result in discriminatory behavior even for people who are low in prejudice? The answer from Devine's second study is affirmative. In this study, Devine selected participants based on their pretest scores on the Modern Racism Scale to ensure equal numbers of those high and low in prejudice. She presented neutral and Black stereotypic primes to the parafoveal portion of participants' visual fields (i.e., in participants' peripheral vision) at speeds that did not allow participants to consciously recognize the primes. Devine varied whether participants viewed primes that were 80% neutral or 80% stereotypic. In a purportedly unrelated task, the participants read a paragraph about a man's day. The man engaged in several ambiguous behaviors that could be interpreted as aggressive or not (e.g., he refuses to pay rent until his apartment is painted; he demands money back from a cashier). Participants rated the man's hostility and a variety of other traits. Although participants' level of prejudice was unrelated to their ratings of the man, the content of the primes was predictive. Participants who viewed a greater percentage of the Black stereotype primes rated the man as being more hostile and aggressive than those who viewed a greater percentage of neutral primes. When the cultural stereotype was activated outside the participants' awareness, it resulted in discriminatory evaluations of a target, irrespective of the participants' prejudice. Priming the category of Blacks rather than the cultural stereotype associated with Blacks produces similarly negative evaluations of a man's ambiguous behavior (Lepore & Brown, 1997).

Finally, Devine demonstrated that there were conditions under which controlled processing of stereotypic information allowed individuals who were low in prejudice to overcome the activation of a cultural stereotype. Specifically, when participants listed their own thoughts about the racial group "Black Americans" (in contrast to the cultural stereotype reported in the first study), those who were highly prejudiced were more likely to report negative beliefs about the group than were people who were low in prejudice.

Since the publication of this groundbreaking research, others have obtained additional evidence of the automatic activation of stereotypes based on categories other than race and using different paradigms. For example, in one study, people viewed age primes (young vs. old) at speeds that prevented conscious awareness of the presentation, followed by positive or negative traits (Perdue & Gurtman, 1990). Then participants provided judgments of whether each trait was good or bad. Participants responded with their judgments faster (i.e., responding was facilitated) when the prime was consistent with the evaluative label of the trait (i.e., when positive traits were paired with young primes and negative traits were paired with old primes). The effects of the primes were the result of automatic processing because the participants could not consciously recognize the content of the primes.

Banaji and Hardin (1996) have also automatically activated gender stereotypes, showing gender consistency between gender-related primes (e.g., nurse, doctor, mother, father) and targets (gender related pronouns in Study 1 and gender related pronouns, neutral pronouns, or nonpronouns in Study 2). The primes produced faster response times when participants judged whether the target was a male or a female pronoun (Study 1) or a pronoun or nonpronoun (Study 2). Because of the short time lapse (300 ms) between presentation of the prime and the target, there was limited possibility for controlled processing of the relationship between prime and target, supporting the conclusion that gender stereotypes alter subsequent judgments through automatic processes. Other studies showed that gender stereotypes influence judgments about the ambiguous behaviors of targets, with male stereotype activation resulting in judgments of aggressive behavior and female stereotype activation resulting in judgments of dependent behavior, even when the participants have no explicit memories of the stereotypic primes (Banaji, Hardin, & Rothman, 1993).

After establishing the cognitive consequences of stereotypes for judgments of outgroup members, researchers turned to studying the effects of automatic stereotype activation on affect and behavior toward outgroups, finding similar patterns of results. Early research had shown that Whites have greater autonomic responses to Black targets as opposed to White targets (e.g., Rankin & Campbell, 1955; Vidulich & Krevanick, 1966), the particular response studied (i.e., skin conductance) provided information only about intensity of response but not about its valence (positive or negative). More recently, researchers have used functional magnetic resonance imaging to demonstrate greater activity in the area of the brain known as the amygdala (which is associated with negative affect and responses to threat) in response to faces of outgroup members (Hart et al., 2000). Among White participants, this greater activity in the amygdala in response to Black faces does not appear to be moderated by self-reported levels of prejudice but is associated with other measures of prejudice (Phelps et al., 2000). These measures include the startle eyeblink response to Black faces and the Implicit Association Test (IAT; Greenwald, McGhee, & Schwartz, 1998)—a measure of evaluative bias toward Black and White faces based on reaction times during a categorization task. Moreover, when researchers anger rather than sadden participants, their responses exhibit greater prejudice toward out-group members (DeSteno, Dasgupta, Bartlett, & Cajdric, 2004).

Studies are also showing that the automatic activation of constructs related to aggression may translate into aggressive behavior (Todorov & Bargh, 2002). Participants who viewed primes related to aggression (e.g., hostile, hurt, anger) presented parafoveally rated the behavior of an ambiguous target to be more aggressive than did participants who viewed neutral primes (e.g., water, long, number; Bargh & Pietromonaco, 1982). Children for who aggressive constructs are chronically accessible (i.e., the aggressive construct spontaneously comes to mind without specific situational priming) are more likely to perceive the ambiguous behavior of another child as having ambiguous intent (Dodge, 1980). Moreover, priming the construct of aggression by the subliminal presentation of African American faces (for whom aggression is part of the cultural stereotype) as opposed to Caucasian faces caused participants to react more aggressively to a frustrating experience (Bargh, Chen, & Burrows, 1996). Chen and Bargh (1997) replicated and extended this effect, showing that those who interact with other participants primed with the African American faces (but who were not primed themselves) acted with more hostility than those who interacted with participants primed with Caucasian faces. These results provide evidence that the activation of that aggressive construct not only influences the behavior of the person who was primed but spills over to affect those with whom that person interacts.

Predictors of Controlled Processing

There is now a large body of research demonstrating that stereotypes are automatically activated and that once activated, they influence people's judgments, affect, and behavior directed toward group members (Banaji & Hardin, 1996; Banaji et al., 1993; Devine, 1989; Hart et al., 2000; Perdue & Gurtman, 1990; Phelps et al., 2000). Stereotypes are activated not only upon the subliminal presentation of words associated with the cultural stereotype (Devine, 1989), but also on presentation of category label (e.g., Black; Lepore & Brown, 1997) or stereotypic facial features (Blair, Judd, & Fallman, 2004; Sczesny & Kühnen, 2004). The evidence for the automaticity of these effects lies in the facts that the stereotypic primes are presented outside participants awareness and that there is little time for controlled processing to override a stereotypically primed response. Indeed, systematic increases in the length of prime presentation from subliminally to supraliminally produce systematic decreases in the amount of prejudice exhibited by participants (Judd, Wittenbrink, & Park, 1999). Increasingly, research is also showing that there are a host of moderators of these automatic effects; the automatic activation of a stereotype does not require that the activated stereotype be applied (Brauer, Wasel, & Niedenthal, 2000). Under certain conditions, people exhibit evidence of controlled processing of group membership information and are able to counteract the effects of automatically activated stereotypes (Blair, 2002). Specifically, both motivation and cognition play a role in whether people will apply stereotypes when making judgments about outgroup members (Fiske, 2004).

There are several steps that people can take to avoid applying automatically activated stereotypes. The first step in controlling prejudice is to have an awareness of the need for counteracting automatically activated stereotypes (Devine, 1989; Devine & Monteith, 1993). One must also have the cognitive resources to avoid a discriminatory response. Although high cognitive load can prevent stereotypes from being activated altogether, if the stereotype is somehow activated, cognitive busyness or distraction with other tasks will make the application of that stereotype more likely (Gilbert & Hixson, 1991; Monteith & Voils, 1998). Finally, one must be motivated to avoid a discriminatory response. Several motivations may result in attempts to control the application of automatically activated stereotypes, including motivations to express one's nonprejudiced beliefs (Monteith, 1993), desire to adhere to situational norms disapproving of prejudice (Plant & Devine, 1998), and a motivation to create accurate impressions of others (Fiske & Neuberg, 1990).

People who are low in prejudice have a cross-situational motivation to avoid stereotyping and experience guilt when they do respond in a prejudiced manner (Monteith, 1993; Voils, Ashburn-Narado, & Monteith, 2002). Even those who are highly prejudiced experience some global discomfort when confronted with a discrepancy between what they would do and what they should do when they come into contact with either Blacks or gay men. However, those who are low or moderately prejudiced experience specific feelings of guilt and self-criticism in addition to global discomfort when confronted with the same discrepancy (Devine, Monteith, Zuwerink, & Elliot, 1991; Zuwerink, Devine, Monteith, & Cook, 1996). Moreover, the experience of this guilt and attention to the discrepancy between their attitudes and their discriminatory behavior causes those who are low in prejudice to inhibit further discriminatory behavior. For example, in one study, low prejudice participants who were told that they had provided survey responses that were more prejudiced than their general attitudes toward gays subsequently rated gay jokes to be less witty than did low prejudice participants who did not receive discrepancy feedback (Monteith, 1993). Once low prejudiced people have engaged in discrepant behavior (i.e., exhibited behavior that is more prejudiced than their attitudes would support), recognized the discrepancy, and inhibited the prejudiced response, situational cues will inhibit prejudiced responses in similar situations in the future (Monteith, Ashburn-Nardo, Voils, & Czopp, 2002).

Situational norms that communicate a disapproval of prejudiced responding may also propel people to engage in controlled processing to avoid discriminatory responding. Indeed, internal and external motivations to respond without prejudice exist, in varying degrees, for most people (Plant & Devine, 1998) and influence whether people inhibit discriminatory responses (Amodio, Harmon-Jones, & Devine, 2003; Devine, Plant, Amodio, Harmon-Jones, & Vance, 2002; Maddux, Barden, Brewer, & Petty, 2005). Some prejudices are socially accepted (e.g., prejudice against members of the Nazi party) whereas some are not (e.g., prejudice against Blacks) and this social acceptability influences whether people are willing to publicly express the prejudice (Crandall, Eshelman, & O'Brien, 2002). Moreover, situational priming of a nonprejudiced norm can reduce the expression of related discriminatory behavior (Monteith, Deneen, & Tooman, 1996).

The Need for Hate Crime Laws: A Psychological Perspective

The social psychological literature on the automatic and controlled processes involved in attitudes, feelings, and behaviors toward outgroup members raises important issues for hate crime perpetration and legislation. First, if a crime against a protected group results from automatically activated and applied stereotypes, will any law, including bias crime laws, reduce discriminatory behavior? Will such laws promote the controlled processing necessary to override the automatic application of stereotypes to decision making? Second, if a person commits a crime but targets a member of a protected group only because of automatically activated cultural stereotypes, can that person be held responsible for a hate crime? Does the person have the proper *mens rea* in this situation that would warrant the penalty enhancement? For example, although the perpetrator may have intended the criminal act, he or she may not have intended the discriminatory nature of the act.

These two issues, whether laws can control behavior that results from automatic processes and whether people are morally responsible for these behaviors, raise additional psychological questions. What factors determine whether people can control stereotype activation in hate crime situations? Moreover, if there are situations in which people can control the influence of automatically activated stereotypes on their behavior, can decision makers differentiate between situations that promote control of discriminatory behavior and those that do not?

To explore these issues and others, let us consider the implications of psychological research for the validity of each of the criticisms leveled at hate crime litigation. Is there research that specifically supports or contradicts these criticisms? If there is no preexisting research that is on point, what research do we need to evaluate the validity of these criticisms?

Implications of Psychology for First Amendment Criticism

Although one of the primary criticisms facing hate crime laws—that they abrogate people's First Amendment rights to free speech—is more of a philosophical than a psychological issue, research on the component structure of attitudes may provide a way of conceptualizing the differences between hate crimes and speech. As noted previously, the tripartite model of attitudes makes a distinction between affective, behavioral, and cognitive components of attitudes. Moreover, the research reviewed here suggests that people may hold negative beliefs about outgroup members (stereotypes), and experience negative affect toward those groups (prejudice) without engaging in discriminatory behavior. What hate crime laws seek to punish is not the possession of a stereotype, or even negative affect or prejudice toward outgroup members, but discriminatory behavior. And psychology clearly provides evidence that one can possess negative beliefs and affect without acting in a discriminatory fashion.

Courts have ruled that speech may be used as evidence of a biased motivation but that the speech is not the criminal act (*People v. Superior Court* [*Aishman*], 1995). If racial slurs accompany an assault, the slurs are not the crime but they are evidence of a possible biased motivation for the assault. If the slurs were the crime, it would be a clear violation of First Amendment rights. In contrast, decision makers use speech as evidence that the behavior (e.g., assault) is discriminatory because one infers from the slurs that the perpetrator chose the target based on group membership. Unfortunately, the psychological research does not tell us when slurs hurled in the context of assaults are evidence that the perpetrator consciously chose the target based on group membership (which would seem to be a requirement to be classified as a hate crime). It is indeed possible that in the heat of an argument people might be primed to use hateful language based on group membership because of automatically activated stereotypes.

Implications of Psychology for Heightened Divisiveness Criticism

Critics also question whether hate crime legislation will heighten divisiveness among groups. Again, there is no research that has specifically examined whether the enactment of hate crime legislation increases intergroup tensions or discriminatory behavior against the groups meant to be protected by the legislation. However, social psychological methods would be perfect for an investigation of the topic. For example, researchers could expose participants to reports of the punishment of a perpetrator, varying whether the target of the crime is an ingroup or outgroup member and varying whether the crime was a hate crime or a parallel crime. These manipulations would allow the determination of whether any subsequent increased hostility is a general increase toward everyone or just toward outgroup members as suggested by critics of the legislation. Moreover, varying whether the punishment is for a hate crime versus its parallel crime disentangles whether increased hostility is due to exposure to punishment generally or hate crime punishment in particular. If critics are correct about hate crime legislation heightening divisiveness, one would expect to find an interaction of these two variables with hostility increasing only when participants are exposed to hate crime punishment of outgroup members.

Several different methods could be used to measure whether this exposure to hate crime punishment increases hostility toward outgroup members. Drawing from priming research methods (Bargh & Pietromonaco, 1982; Devine, 1989), participants could rate the ambiguous behavior of an outgroup or an ingroup member to see whether those exposed to hate crime punishment are more likely to rate an outgroup member as hostile than an ingroup member. Alternatively, participants could rate the qualifications of an ingroup or an outgroup member for a job to see whether those exposed to hate crime legislation devalue the performance of outgroup members. Alternatively, researchers could provide participants with the opportunity to aggress toward an outgroup member in an actual interaction.

In sum, absence of evidence is not evidence of absence. That is, just because no one has demonstrated that hate crime legislation increases racial tension by examining community attitudes (Sullaway, 2004), it does not allow the conclusion that tensions have not increased, especially if no good tests of the hypothesis exist. If no good data exist on the level of racial tension pre- and post-enactment of hate crime legislation, these proposed studies based on experimental methods used to study stereotyping might provide better data than currently exists on this the heightened divisiveness criticism.

Implications of Psychology for Selective Prosecution Criticism

Certainly, research on stereotyping is relevant to the criticism that violations of hate crime laws are likely to be selectively prosecuted. Given the research providing evidence that the automatic activation of stereotypes without awareness for the need or the opportunity for controlled processing often leads to discriminatory behavior (Devine & Monteith, 1993), it is likely that stereotyping processes could lead to selective prosecution of hate crime offenders. Cultural stereotypes that link violence with particular racial and ethnic groups may result in the greater likelihood that prosecutors will charge perpetrators from these groups with hate crimes. The effect is most likely to result if those in the position to charge hate crime enhancements are unaware of the influence of automatically activated stereotypes on their decisions or if the heaviness of their case load prevents controlled processing of the case information. In contrast, if cultural stereotypes suggest that members of a particular group (e.g., gay men) are less prone to violence, stereotype activation without controlled processing may lead to under-prosecution of perpetrators from this group. Thus, stereotypes may lead to the overprosecution of those who are truly innocent of committing hate crimes or the underprosecution of those who are truly guilty. There are no data that directly address these issues of selective prosecution; rather for now we must rely on the generalizability of basic stereotyping research to the issue of selective prosecution of hate crimes. Of course, it would be preferable if researchers would collect the data required to test directly these hypotheses.

Selective Prosecution of the Innocent

According to FBI (1999) guidelines for reporting hate crimes, "bias is to be reported only if investigation reveals sufficient objective facts to lead a reasonable and prudent person to conclude that the offender's actions were motivated, in whole or in part, by bias" (p. 6). However, association of violent behavior with minority group members may encourage decision makers to prosecute minority group members who are innocent at greater rates than Whites. Moreover, stereotypes may cause law enforcers to interpret ambiguous stimuli in a manner consistent with their stereotypes.

Although there is no direct evidence that stereotypes will cause police or prosecutors to interpret the behavior of minority group members in a manner that is consistent with hate crime perpetration, evidence is mounting in other areas. Specifically, the activation of racial stereotypes influences decisions about whether a perpetrator is carrying a weapon. Priming with Black versus White faces affects the speed and accuracy of weapon identification, with speed and accuracy being greater when weapons are primed with Black faces (Payne, 2001). Priming with Black faces also facilitates recognition of degraded pictures of crime stimuli such as weapons (Eberhardt, Goff, Purdie, & Davies, 2004). In video simulations, participants made correct decisions to shoot armed targets and to not shoot unarmed targets more quickly when race and armed status is stereotype consistent (Correll, Park, Judd, & Wittenbrink, 2002; Plant, Peruche, & Butz, 2005). If these results generalize to other types of judgments made by police officers, it is possible that stereotyping could lead to the interpretation of minority groups members' behaviors as more hateful and aggressive and increase the likelihood that prosecutors will be more likely to charge them with hate crimes in comparison to White offenders.

> Everyone's a little bit racist -
> All right!. . .
> Bigotry has never been
> Exclusively white.

> From the Broadway musical *Avenue Q*

Selective Prosecution of the Guilty

Alternatively, people may have prototypes for hate crimes related to group membership that cause them to prosecute only a portion of those who are actually guilty of a hate crime. Research shows that people have preexisting beliefs about what features are necessary for finding someone guilty of a crime (Finkel & Groscup, 1997; Smith, 1991, 1993). Although there is no research that directly examines the prototypes that people hold about hate crimes, it is possible that prototypes include the rule that majority members typically commit hate crimes against minority group members. If so, it is possible that hate crimes that violate this expectancy (e.g., Black on White hate crimes) may be less likely to be reported or prosecuted and jurors may be less likely to find the defendants guilty when this type of hate crime is prosecuted. Vignette studies of hate crime decision making in which the researchers manipulated victim and perpetrator race support this prediction (Marcus-Newhall et al., 2002).

It is also possible that selective enforcement will not be the result of automatically activated stereotypes. People are more likely to report a crime as a hate crime if there is no other motive (e.g., money) for the crime (Boyd, Berk, & Hamner, 1996; Dunbar, Quinones, & Crevecoeur, 2005). The presence of another motive may then lead to a failure to prosecute those who are guilty of committing a hate crime because the target was chosen for bias-motivated reasons even though the crime would have been committed anyway. This outcome may not be completely unreasonable as multiple motivations for a behavior make any individual motive less likely to be the causal agent for the behavior (Kelley, 1973).

Some scholars have also argued that current events may change perceptions of whether a crime is bias motivated (Gerstenfeld, 2002). Is the murder of an Arab American during a robbery motivated by bias? Whether prosecutors charge it as a hate crime may depend on historical context (e.g., was the crime committed pre-or-post-9/11?). There is evidence that environmental events may spur the commission of hate crimes. The United States saw a dramatic increase in hate crimes against Arabs and Muslims after the attacks of 9/11 (Council on American-Islamic Relations, 2002; Nimer, 2001). Similarly, hate crimes against Muslims increased sixfold in London after the terrorist bombings of the subway system in the summer of 2005 (BBC News Online, 2005). Although hate crimes may wax and wane in response to external events, it is also possible that these external events will alter legal decision makers' evaluations of whether a particular situation constitutes a hate crime. What is as of yet unclear is whether these external events will serve to automatically activate stereotypes toward particular groups that will translate into aggression toward those groups or to activate controlled processing that will help people override their tendencies to apply the automatically activated stereotypes.

Conclusion

> Everyone's a little bit racist
> Sometimes.
> Doesn't mean we go
> Around committing hate crimes.
>
> From the Broadway musical *Avenue Q*

We have much to learn about what factors influence people to commit hate crimes and what features are deemed necessary for people to view a crime as bias motivated. Reporting data suggest that police officers deem the absence of another motive (e.g., fiduciary gain; revenge, provocation) as a requirement to categorize a crime as bias motivated (Dunbar et al., 2005). But we do not know whether the same features are required irrespective of the target or the type of crime. For example, it may be that stereotypes about the criminality of certain groups may influence perception and interpretation of the features required for charging a hate crime.

We are also lacking good information on whether bias-motivated crimes are selectively prosecuted. Does the automatic activation of certain stereotypes alter people's decisions about whether ambiguous behavior constitutes a hate crime? If so, are there interventions that will promote more even application of the law by promoting controlled processing? Or do prototypes lead to the failure to prosecute minority group members who commit hate crimes?

It is clear that the social psychological literature on automatic and controlled processes in stereotyping, prejudice, and discrimination has implications for the perpetration and litigation of hate crimes. The research shows that everyone is a little bit racist at times, depending on whether cultural stereotypes are automatically activated and whether there is the motivation and the opportunity to engage in controlled processing to counteract the stereotype once activated. And given the relative prevalence of the automatic activation of stereotypes and hate crimes, it is also clear that stereotype activation does not necessarily translate into hate crime commission or even other forms of discrimination. What is less clear is the role that automatic processing of group membership information does play in hate crime perpetration and litigation. Yet future studies of the role for automatic processes in this context will provide important information regarding the validity of critics' objections to the enactment of hate crime penalty enhancements.

References

ABCNews (November 26, 2004). New details emerge in Matthew Sheppard murder: Killers talk about crime that shocked the nation. Available at http://abcnews.go. com/2020/story?id=277685&page=1. Retrieved Oct. 24, 2005.

Allport, G. (1954). *The nature of prejudice*. Boston: Beacon Press.

Amodio, D. M., Harmon-Jones, E., & Devine, P. G. (2003). Individual differences in the activation and control of affective race bias as assessed by startle eyeblink response and self-report. *Journal of Personality and Social Psychology, 84*, 738–753.

Banaji, M. R., & Hardin, C. D. (1996). Automatic stereotyping. *Psychological Science, 7*, 136–141.

Banaji, M. R., Hardin, C. D., & Rothman, A. J. (1993). Implicit stereotyping in person judgment. *Journal of Personality and Social Psychology, 65*, 272–281.

Bargh, J. A., Chen, M., & Burrows, L. (1996). Automaticity of social behavior: Direct effects of trait construct and stereotype priming on action. *Journal of Personality and Social Psychology, 71*, 230–244.

Bargh, J. A., & Pietromonaco, P. (1982). Automatic information processing and social perception: The influence of trait information presented outside of conscious awareness on impression formation. *Journal of Personality and Social Psychology, 43*, 437–449.

BBC News Online (2005, August 4). Hate crimes soar after bombings. Available at http://news.bbc.co.uk/go/em/fr/-/1/hi/england/london/4740015.stm. (Retrieved October 23, 2005).

Berk, R. A. (1990). Thinking about hate-motivated crimes. *Journal of Interpersonal Violence, 5*, 334–349.

Blair, I. V. (2002). The malleability of automatic stereotypes and prejudice. *Personality and Social Psychology Review, 6*, 242–261.

Blair, I. V., Judd, C. M., & Fallman, J. L. (2004). The automaticity of race and Afrocentric facial features in social judgments. *Journal of Personality and Social Psychology, 87*, 763–778.

Boyd, E. A., Berk, R. A., & Hamner, K. M. (1996). "Motivated by hatred or prejudice": Categorization of hate-motivated crimes in two police divisions. *Law and Society Review, 30*, 819–850.

Brauer, M., Wasel, W., & Niedenthal, P. (2000). Implicit and explicit components of prejudice. *Review of General Psychology, 4*, 79–101.

Chen, M., & Bargh, J. A. (1997). Nonconscious behavioral confirmation processes: the self-fulfilling consequences of automatic stereotype activation. *Journal of Experimental Social Psychology, 33*, 541–560.

Correll, J., Park, P., Judd, C. M., & Wittenbrink, B. (2002). The police officer's dilemma: Using ethnicity to disambiguate potentially threatening individuals. *Journal of Personality and Social Psychology, 83*, 1314–1329.

Council on American-Islamic Relations. (2002). *Number of incidents by category since September 11, 2001* (Online). Available at http://www.cair-net.org/html/bycategory. htm. (Retrieved January 15, 2006).

Craig, K. M. (1999). Retaliation, fear, or rage: An investigation of African American and White reactions to racist hate crimes. *Journal of Interpersonal Violence, 14,* 138–151.

Crandall, C. S., Eshelman, A., & O'Brien, L. (2002). Social norms and the expression and suppression of prejudice: The struggle for internalization. *Journal of Personality and Social Psychology, 82,* 359–378.

DeSteno, D., Dasgupta, N., Bartlett, M. Y., & Cajdric, A. (2004). Prejudice from thin air: The effect of emotion on automatic intergroup attitudes. *Psychological Science, 15,* 319–324.

Devine, P. G. (1989). Stereotypes and prejudice: Their automatic and controlled components. *Journal of Personality and Social Psychology, 56,* 5–18.

Devine, P. G., Monteith, M. J., Zuwerink, J. R., & Elliot, A. J. (1991). Prejudice with and without compunction. *Journal of Personality and Social Psychology, 60,* 817–830.

Devine, P. G., & Monteith, M. J. (1993). The role of discrepancy associated affect in prejudice reduction. In D. M. Mackie & D. L. Hamilton (Eds.), *Affect, cognition, and sterotyping: Interactive processes in intergroup* perception (pp. 317–344). New York: Academic Press.

Devine, P. G., Plant, E. A., Amodio, D. M., Harmon-Jones, E., & Vance, S. L. (2002). The regulation of implicit and explicit race bias: The role of motivations to respond without prejudice. *Journal of Personality and Social Psychology, 82,* 835–848.

Dodge, K. A. (1980). Social cognition and children's aggressive behavior. *Child Development,* 51, 162–170.

Dovidio, J. F., Glick., P. S., & Rudman, L. A. (Eds). (2005). *On the nature of prejudice: Fifty years after Allport.* Malden, MA: Blackwell.

Dunbar, E., & Molina, A. (2004). Opposition to the legitimacy of hate crime laws: The role of argument acceptance, knowledge, individual differences, and peer influence. *Analyses of Social Issues and Public Policy, 4,* 91–113.

Dunbar, E., Quinones, J., & Crevecoeur, D. A. (2005). Assessment of hate crime offenders: The role of bias intent in examining violence risk. *Journal of Forensic Psychology Practice, 5,* 1–19.

Eberhardt, J. L., Goff, P. A., Purdie, V. J., & Davies, P. G. (2004). Seeing Black: Race, crime, and visual processing. *Journal of Personality and Social Psychology, 87,* 876–893.

Federal Bureau of Investigation (1996). *Training guide for hate crime data collection.* Washington, DC: Author.

Federal Bureau of Investigation. (1999). *Hate crime data collection guidelines, revised.* Washington, DC: Author.

Finkel, N. J., & Groscup, J. L. (1997). Crime prototypes, objective versus subjective culpability, and a commonsense balance. *Law and Human Behavior, 21,* 209–230.

Fiske, S. T. (2004). Intent and ordinary bias: Unintended thought and social motivation create casual prejudice. *Social Justice Research, 17,* 117–127.

Fiske, S. T., and Neuberg, S. L. (1990). A continuum of impression formation, from category-based to individuating processes: Influences of information and motivation on attention and interpretation. In M. P. Zanna (Ed.), *Advances in experimental social psychology* (Vol. 23, pp. 1–74). New York: Academic Press.

Gerstenfeld, P. B. (1992). Smile when you call me that!: The problems with punishing hate motivated behavior. *Behavioral Sciences and the Law, 10,* 259–285.

Gerstenfeld, P. B. (2002). A time to hate: Situational antecedents of intergroup bias. *Analyses of Social Issues and Public Policy, 2,* 61–67.

Gilbert, D. T., and Hixon, J. G. (1991). The trouble of thinking: Activation and application of stereotypic beliefs. *Journal of Personality and Social Psychology, 60,* 509–517.

Green, D. P., Glaser, J., & Rich, A. (1998). From lynching to gay bashing: The elusive connection between economic conditions and hate crime. *Journal of Personality and Social Psychology, 75,* 82–92.

Greenwald, A., McGhee, D., & Schwartz, J. (1998). Measuring individual differences in implicit cognition: The Implicit Association Test. *Journal of Personality and Social Psychology, 74,* 1464–1480.

Hajnal, Z., & Baldassare, M. (2001, January 4). *Finding common ground: Racial and ethnic attitudes in California.* Report by the Public Policy Institute of California, San Francisco.

Hart, A. J., Whalen, P. J., Shin, L. M., McInerney, S. C., Fischer, H., & Rauch, S. L. (2000). Differential response in the human amygdala to racial outgroup vs ingroup face stimuli. *NeuroReport, 11,* 2351–2355.

Herek, G., Gillis, R., & Cogan, J. (1999). Psychological sequelae of hate crime victimization among lesbian, gay, and bisexual adults. *Journal of Consulting and Clinical Psychology, 67,* 945–951.

Jacobs, J. B., & Potter, K. (1998). *Hate crimes: Criminal law and identity politics.* New York: Oxford University Press.

Johnson, S. D., & Byers, B. D. (2003). Attitudes toward hate crime laws. *Journal of Criminal Justice, 31,* 227–235.

Judd, C. M., Wittenbrink, B., & Park, P. (1999). Explicit and implicit racial prejudices. *Psychologie Française, 44,* 179–188.

Kelley, H. H. (1973). The processes of causal attribution. *American Psychologist, 28,* 107–128.

Lawrence, F. M. (2002). *Punishing hate: Bias crimes under American law.* Cambridge, MA: Harvard University Press.

Lawrence, F. M. (2003). Enforcing bias crime laws without bias: Evaluating the disproportionate-enforcement critique. *Law and Contemporary Problems, 66,* 49–69.

Lepore, L., & Brown, R. (1997). Category and stereotype activation: Is prejudice inevitable? *Journal of Personality and Social Psychology, 72,* 275–287.

Levin, J., & McDevitt, J. (1993). *Hate crimes: The rising tide of bigotry and bloodshed.* New York: Plenum Press.

Lieberman, J. D., Arndt, J., Personius, J., & Cook, A. (2001). Vicarious annihilation: The effect of mortality salience on perceptions of hate crimes. *Law and Human Behavior, 25,* 547–566.

Maddux, W. W., Barden, J., Brewer, M. B., & Petty, R. E. (2005). Saying no to negativity: The effects of context and motivation to control prejudice on automatic evaluative responses. *Journal of Experimental Social Psychology, 41,* 19–35.

Marcus-Newhall, A, Blake, L. P., & Baumann, J. (2002). Perceptions of hate crime perpetrators and victims as influenced by race, political orientation, and peer group. *American Behavioral Scientist, 46,* 108–135.

McConahay, J. B., Hardee, B. B., & Batts, V. (1981). Has racism declined? It depends upon who's asking and what is asked. *Journal of Conflict Resolution, 25,* 563–579.

McDevitt, J., Levin, J., & Bennett, S. (2002). Hate crime offenders: An expanded typology. *Journal of Social Issues, 58,* 303–318.

Monteith, M. J. (1993). Self-regulation of stereotypical responses: Implications for progress in prejudice reduction. *Journal of Personality and Social Psychology, 65,* 469–485.

Monteith, M. J., Asburn-Nardo, L., Voils, C. I., & Czopp, A. M. (2002). Putting the brakes on prejudice: On the development and operation of cues for control. *Journal of Personality and Social Psychology, 83,* 1029–1050.

Monteith, M. J., Deneen, N. E., & Tooman, G. D. (1996). The effect of social norm activation on the expression of opinions concerning gay men and Blacks. *Basic and Applied Social Psychology, 18,* 267–288.

Monteith, M. J., & Voils, C. I. (1998). Proneness to prejudiced responses: Toward understanding the authenticity of self-reported discrepancies. *Journal of Personality and Social Psychology, 75,* 901–916.

Nimer, M. (2001). *The status of Muslim civil rights in the United States: Accommodating diversity.* Washington, DC: Council on American-Islamic Relations.

Note. (1982). Racial and religious intimidation: An analysis of Oregon's 1981 law. *Willamette Law Review, 18,* 197.

O'Neil, A. W. (2000, September 19). Jury can hear Furrow's confession, judge rules. *Los Angeles Times,* B1.

Payne, B. K. (2001). Prejudice and perception: The role of automatic and controlled perceptions in misperceiving a weapon. *Journal of Personality and Social Psychology, 81,* 181–192.

Perdue, C. W., & Gurtman, M. B. (1990). Evidence for the automaticity of ageism. *Journal of Experimental Social Psychology, 26,* 199–216.

Phelps, E. A., O'Connor, K. J., Cunningham, W. A., Funayama, S., Gatenby, J. C., Gore, J. C., & Banaji, M. R. (2000). Performance on indirect measures of race evaluation predicts amygdala activation. *Journal of Cognitive Neuroscience, 12,* 729–738.

Plant, E. A., & Devine, P. G. (1998). Internal and external motivation to respond without prejudice. *Journal of Personality and Social Psychology, 75,* 811–832.

Plant, E. A., Peruche, B. M., & Butz., D. A. (2005). Eliminating automatic racial bias: Making race non-diagnostic for responses to criminal suspects. *Journal of Experimental Social Psychology, 41,* 141–156.

Rankin, R. E., & Campbell, D. T. (1955). Galvanic skin response to Negro and White experimenters. *Journal of Abnormal and Social Psychology, 51,* 30–33.

Rayburn, N. R., Mendoza, M., & Davison, G. C. (2003). Bystander perceptions of perpetrators and victims of hate crime: An investigation using the person perception paradigm. *Journal of Interpersonal Violence, 18,* 1055–1074.

Sczesny, S., & Kühnen, U. (2004). Meta-cognition about biological sex and gender-stereotypic physical appearance: Consequences for the assessment of leadership competence. *Personality and Social Psychology Bulletin, 30,* 13–21.

Shepard, D. (2000, April 30). My son Matt—murdered University of Wyoming student Matthew Shepard. *The Advocate.* Retrieved January 22, 2007, from http://www.findarticles.com/p/articles/mi_m1589/is_2000_April_30/ai_61692737.

Smith, V. L. (1991). Prototypes in the courtroom: Lay representations of legal concepts. *Journal of Personality and Social Psychology, 61,* 857–872.

Smith, V. L. (1993). When prior knowledge and law collide: Helping jurors use the law. *Law and Human Behavior, 17,* 507–536.

Sullaway, M. (2004). Psychological perspectives on hate crimes laws. *Psychology, Public Policy, and Law, 10,* 250–292.

Todorov, A., & Bargh, J. A. (2002). Automatic sources of aggression. *Aggression and Violent Behavior, 7,* 53–68.

Vidulich, R. N., & Krevanick, F. W. (1966). Racial attitudes and emotional response to visual representations of the Negro. *Journal of Social Psychology, 68,* 85–93.

Voils, C. I., Ashburn-Nardo, L., & Monteith, M. J. (2002). Evidence of prejudice-related conflict and associated affect beyond the college setting. *Group Processes & Intergroup Relations, 5,* 19–33.

Weiss, J. C., Ehrlich, H., & Larcom, B. (1991–1992). Ethnoviolence at work. *The Journal of Intergroup Relations, 18,* 28–29.

Zanna, M. P., & Rempel, J. K. (1988). Attitudes: A new look at an old concept. In D. Bar-Tal & A. W. Kruglanski (Eds.), *The social psychology of knowledge* (pp. 315–334). Cambridge, UK: Cambridge University Press.

Zuwerink, J. A., Devine, P. G., Monteith, M. J., & Cook, D. A. (1996). Prejudice towards Blacks: With and without compunction? *Basic and Applied Psychology, 18,* 131–150.

Legal Citations

People v. Superior Court (Aishman), 896 P. 2d 1387 (1995).
State v. Beebe, 67 Or. App. 738, 680 P.2d 11 (1984).
State v. Hendrix, 107 Or. App. 734, 813 P.2d 1115 (1991).
Wisconsin v. Mitchell, 508 U.S. 476 (1993).

13
Implicit Bias and Hate Crimes: A Psychological Framework and Critical Race Theory Analysis

Jennifer S. Hunt

On August 19, 1991, ongoing tensions between African Americans and Lubavitch Jews in Crown Heights, Brooklyn erupted into widespread rioting and violence after a Jewish driver killed a 7-year-old African American boy and seriously injured his cousin. The African American community was enraged by allegations that the police and ambulances gave preferential treatment to the Lubavitchers at the scene of the accident. During the riots, calls were made to "Kill the Jews." Subsequently, a Hasidic man, Yankel Rosenbaum, was surrounded by a group of African American men and stabbed to death by Lemrick Nelson. At trial, Nelson testified that he acted without premeditation and that he was drunk at the time of the stabbing (Conaway, 1996; Streissguth, 2003).

Another such incident occurred on December 19, 1986, when three African American men—Timothy Grimes, Michael Griffith, and Cedric Sandiford—stopped in the predominantly White neighborhood of Howard Beach, Queens after their car broke down. They were confronted by a group of White neighborhood youth who used racial epithets and told them to leave the area. Later that evening, Grimes, Griffith, and Sandiford were exiting a pizzeria when the youth returned, armed with baseball bats. They severely beat the three men and attempted to chase them away, shouting statements such as, "There's niggers in the boulevard. Let's kill 'em" (Levin & McDevitt, 1993, p. 5). While trying to escape his attackers, Michael Griffith ran onto a parkway and was killed by oncoming traffic (Perry, 2001; Streissguth, 2003).

The Crown Heights and Howard Beach incidents—which are similar in many ways, but very different in others—are only two of the thousands of racially motivated violent acts that have occurred in the United States (for reviews, see, e.g., Levin & McDevitt, 1993; Perry, 2001; Streissguth, 2003). Although racially motivated aggression has occurred since European settlers first arrived in the Americas, it was not until the late 1970s that such acts were given the label of "hate crimes" and treated as distinct entities (Streissguth, 2003). Since that time, hate crimes have been legally defined as criminal acts influenced by the victims' group membership and/or racial prejudice (Mennenger, 2005). The majority of states and the federal government have passed legislation intended to document, reduce, and punish hate crimes (Mennenger, 2005; Streissguth, 2003). In addition, social scientists from several disciplines have developed empirical research and theory aimed at identifying the causes and effects of hate crimes.

In this chapter, I build on the work of Margaret Bull Kovera (this volume) and Frederick Lawrence (this volume) by analyzing one potential contributor to hate crimes, implicit bias, from both psychological and legal perspectives. First, I review research on psychological processes that may contribute to hate crimes, as well as implicit prejudice and stereotyping. Based on that literature, I propose a framework for understanding when implicit bias is and is not likely to contribute to hate crime. Next, I discuss the legal implications of recognizing implicit bias as a potential contributor to aggressive acts, using a Critical Race Theory perspective to offer some observations about how the legal system might consider the role of psychological processes that do not involve conscious intent. Finally, I try to bring these analyses together, suggesting common threads and areas for future research.

Psychological Contributors to Hate Crime

The causes of hate crimes vary tremendously in scope and nature, from intrapsychic processes to societal and cultural values and conditions (Craig, 2002; Green, McFalls, & Smith, 2001). By definition, though, prejudice, or negative attitudes about members of particular social groups, is a key psychological process involved in hate crime. In addition to sheer dislike and negative feelings, prejudice frequently involves negative stereotypes, that is, generalized beliefs about the negative traits and characteristics of a particular group. Social psychological research shows that numerous low-status groups, such as ethnic minorities and gays and lesbians, are stereotypically associated with negative characteristics (e.g., Devine & Elliott, 1995; Fiske, Cuddy, Glick, & Xu, 2002; Madon, 1997; Niemann, Jennings, Rozelle, Baxter, & Sullivan, 1994). These beliefs may motivate and/or justify violent acts against members of stigmatized groups (e.g., Craig, 2002; Dovidio, Gaertner, & Pearson, 2005). As Perry (2001) explains, "Almost invariably, stereotypes are loaded with disparaging associations, suggesting inferiority, irresponsibility, immorality, and nonhumanness. . . Consequently, they provide both motive and rationale for injurious verbal and physical assaults on minority groups" (p. 63).

Unfortunately, prejudice and stereotypes are not aberrant or rare experiences; in fact, many psychologists argue that they are exceedingly common in our society. Because the United States is a largely segregated culture with historical and ongoing racial and ethnic oppression, most Americans cannot grow up without acquiring some negative feelings or beliefs about members of stigmatized groups (e.g., Crandall & Eshleman, 2003; Devine, 1989; Dovidio & Gaertner, 2004). However, an extremely small percentage of people possessing prejudice or stereotypes ever commit hate crimes; thus, simply having prejudiced attitudes or stereotypical beliefs cannot be considered sufficient to trigger violent acts.

Accordingly, several other factors appear to work in tandem with prejudice and stereotypes to trigger hate crimes. Some factors involve situational characteristics. For example, the experience of deindividuation, that is, lack of self-awareness and perceived accountability, may facilitate acting on negative attitudes or beliefs (Prentice-Dunn & Rogers, 1982). Situations involving groups or crowds may foster deindividuation, which is consistent with data showing that hate crimes—including the Howard Beach and Crown Heights incidents—often are committed by groups of perpetrators rather than individuals (Levin & McDevitt, 1993). Other factors that may precipitate hate crimes involve dispositional characteristics. Based on the Cognitive Neoassociationistic model of anger arousal, Berkowitz (2005) suggests that hate crimes are most likely to be committed by individuals who are both prejudiced and have dispositional tendencies toward anger. For such individuals, even minor cues related to a disliked group can provoke intense anger and/or fear, triggering aggressive behavior.

Another factor that may cause prejudice or stereotypes to be expressed through hate crime involves perceived threat to one's own group ("ingroup") from another group ("outgroup"). In-migration, or the entry of outgroup members (e.g., racial minorities) into a previously homogeneous domain, frequently is viewed as a threat and can provoke aggressive responses from prejudiced individuals (Glaser, Dixit, & Green, 2002; Green et al., 2001). For example, the tension leading up to the Crown Heights riots was in part due to the influx of Lubavitch Jews into the predominantly African American neighborhood (Conaway, 1996; Streissguth, 2003). Perceived competition for resources (e.g., jobs) between groups also may lead to aggression (Craig, 2002; Green et al., 2001; but see Green, Glaser, & Rich, 1998). In addition, hate crimes may be used as a means of enhancing the dominance and privileges of one's ingroup (Hamner, 1992; Perry, 2001). By aggressing against members of outgroups, perpetrators can symbolically distinguish between the groups, denigrate outgroup members, and reinforce the existing hierarchy. Such acts may further serve to increase perpetrators' positive views of their ingroups and, in turn, their self-esteem (Hamner, 1992; Tajfel & Turner, 1986).

The Role of Implicit Bias

Thus, by themselves or, more likely, in tandem with other factors, prejudice against and/or negative stereotypes about particular groups may lead to incidents of hate crime. The assumption in hate crime legislation is that perpetrators are aware of their negative attitudes and beliefs and, because of them, consciously intend to do harm to an individual based on group membership (F. M. Lawrence, 2002; Sullaway, 2004). Undoubtedly, these characteristics fit many instances of hate crime. For example, the perpetrators in the Howard Beach incident consciously decided to obtain baseball bats and chase the African American men out of their neighborhood. However, the intentions behind other potential hate crimes are not so clear-cut. For instance, in Crown Heights, Lemrick Nelson claimed that he stabbed Yankel Rosenbaum in the heat of the moment because of intoxication, not because of anti-Semitism.

The assumptions of awareness and intentionality in hate crime legislation also are at odds with research on prejudice and stereotypes conducted by social psychologists over the past two decades. Since the mid-1980s, an abundant body of research has demonstrated that prejudice and stereotypes are not always *explicit*, that is, outwardly expressed, deliberate, open to awareness, and subject to conscious control by an individual. Often, people possess *implicit* bias in the form of cognitive associations between particular groups and negative evaluations, feelings, or characteristics (for reviews, see, e.g., Blair, 2002; Bodenhausen & Macrae, 1998; Fazio & Olson, 2003; Fiske, 1998; Hunt, Borgida, Kelly, & Burgess, 2002). For example, many individuals implicitly associate African Americans with overall negativity (Fazio, Jackson, Dunton, & Williams, 1995; Gaertner & McLaughlin, 1983; Greenwald, McGhee, & Schwartz, 1998), as well as specific negative characteristics, such as hostility, lack of intelligence, and criminality (Devine, 1989; Lepore & Brown, 1997; Wittenbrink, Judd, & Park, 1997). Implicit bias is characterized by lack of awareness, intent, and conscious control; hence, many people may not know—or even vehemently deny—that they possess such biased associations.

Kovera (this volume) raises the provocative idea that implicit stereotypes may be related to hate crimes. Specifically, she suggests that automatically activated stereotypes may lead individuals to unconsciously select victims for hate crimes. In her view, implicit stereotyping may lead to unintentional discrimination and aggressive acts toward racial and ethnic minorities, even among low prejudice individuals, although motivation to behave in an unprejudiced manner and situational norms may mitigate those effects.

Kovera should be commended for suggesting these connections between implicit biases and hate crimes and for laying the groundwork for research that has the potential to contribute a great deal to our understanding of hate crime. My goal in this section of the chapter is to extend her general discussion of the possible relation between implicit bias and hate crime into a broader predictive framework for when implicit biases are—and are not—likely to contribute to hate crime. According to this framework, implicit biases may contribute to aggressive acts by coloring judgments and behavioral tendencies during interactions with members of stigmatized groups. In contrast to Kovera, I propose that implicit biases are likely to play a relatively circumscribed role in hate crime—specifically, that their primary influence involves exacerbating already negative encounters rather than instigating acts of aggression.

Implicit Prejudice and Stereotypes: A Brief Review

When people encounter members of stereotyped groups (or related cues, such as group labels or pictures), they often experience *cognitive activation*, that is, an increase in the accessibility of constructs and feelings associated with those groups. For example, encountering an African American man on a sidewalk may make thoughts of danger and feelings of fear more accessible. Likewise, constructs and feelings that are unassociated with a particular group may become less accessible, a process known as *cognitive inhibition*. For example, constructs related to wealth and scholastic achievement may become less accessible after meeting the man on the street. These dual processes of cognitive activation and inhibition may occur without intention or awareness, even in individuals who are low in explicit bias. However, they still may influence judgments or behavior, such as the decision to cross the street (Bodenhausen & Macrae, 1988).

Several studies have demonstrated that the accessibility of stereotypes and prejudice can have powerful effects on judgments and behavior. For example, in one study, participants received negative feedback from an evaluator. When the evaluator was African American, participants experienced heightened accessibility of negative stereotypes related to African Americans and made disparaging evaluations of the specific evaluator's skills, (Sinclair & Kunda, 1999). In another study, participants were subliminally primed with pictures of either African American or White individuals and then were induced to feel frustration. Participants who were primed with African American faces responded to the frustrating event in a more hostile manner than did participants primed with White faces (Bargh, Chen, & Burrows, 1996). This finding suggests that the participants' behavior was affected without their awareness by the automatic activation of the "hostile" stereotype for African Americans following the primes (for discussions of similar findings, see Fazio & Olson, 2003; Wheeler & Petty, 2001).

Perhaps most startlingly, recent research has explored the influence of race on judgments by both police officers and lay people to "shoot" or "don't shoot" individuals who may or may not be brandishing guns. In these studies, participants are shown a series of photographs of African American and White individuals who each are holding an object, either a gun or something else, such as a cell phone. Results consistently indicate that participants are faster to decide to shoot an African American than a White individual (Correll, Park, Judd, & Wittenbrink, 2002; Correll, Urland, & Ito, 2006; Greenwald, Oakes, & Hoffman, 2003; Plant & Peruche, 2005). This effect appears to reflect a tendency to misperceive objects held by African Americans as guns (Greenwald et al., 2003; Payne, 2001), as well as lower overall thresholds for deciding to shoot African American targets (Correll et al., 2002). Notably, participants' knowledge of the stereotype for African Americans, which includes characteristics such as aggressive and criminal (Devine & Elliott, 1995), is correlated with a bias toward shooting African American targets (Correll et al., 2006).

Thus, a considerable body of evidence shows that implicit prejudice and stereotypes can influence the manner in which individuals evaluate and behave toward members of stigmatized groups, even to the extent of promoting violent acts. However, personal and situational factors can affect stereotype activation, such that it is not an inevitable outcome of exposure to group-relevant cues (for reviews, see Blair, 2002; Bodenhausen & Macrae, 1998; Kunda & Spencer, 2003). For example, individuals who are low in prejudice often do not automatically activate stereotypes (Kawakami, Dion, & Dovidio, 1998; Lepore & Brown, 1997; Rudman & Kilianski, 2000; Wittenbrink et al., 1997; cf., Devine, 1989;

Kawakami & Dovidio, 2001). Likewise, motivation to control expressions of prejudice, either dispositional (e.g., Devine, Plant, Amodio, Harmon-Jones, & Vance, 2002; Dunton & Fazio, 1997; Moskowitz, Gollwitzer, Wasel, & Schaal, 1999) or situationally induced (Blair & Banaji, 1996; Pendry & Macrae, 1996; Sinclair & Kunda, 1999), can reduce or eliminate stereotype activation. In contrast, stereotype activation is increased when individuals feel threatened (Kunda, Davies, Adams, & Spencer, 2002; Sinclair & Kunda, 1999, 2000; Spencer, Fein, Wolfe, Fong, & Dunn, 1998) and when social norms support the expression of biased beliefs (Lowery, Hardin, & Sinclair, 2001). Cognitive busyness (i.e., devoting one's mental resources to another task) can prevent stereotypes from initially being activated yet increase the influence of stereotypes on judgments if they already are accessible (Gilbert & Hixon, 1991).

Although the exact relationship between implicit associations and explicit beliefs remains a subject of controversy (e.g., Blair, 2002; Fazio & Olson, 2003; Wilson, Lindsay, & Schooler, 2000), recent research suggests that they are not identical constructs. For example, a meta-analysis of 126 studies using the Implicit Associations Test found that explicit and implicit measures of stereotypes typically show similar patterns (e.g., consistent associations between groups and particular traits); however, the correlation between them tends to be modest (mean $r = .24$; Hofmann, Gawronski, Gschwendner, Le, & Schmitt, 2005). Also, implicit and explicit bias may predict different types of behavior, with explicit bias predicting overt and deliberate (i.e., thoughtful) acts and implicit bias predicting more subtle and spontaneous behaviors, such as nonverbal responses (Dovidio, Kawakami, & Gaertner, 2002).

In sum, people frequently have negative cognitive and affective associations with stigmatized groups that can influence a variety of judgments and behaviors, including decisions to shoot another person, without awareness or intention. However, both dispositional and situational characteristics can reduce stereotype activation. Further, implicit biases appear more likely to influence spontaneous and subtle behaviors than overt, controlled judgments.

A Framework for Understanding the Influence of Implicit Bias on Hate Crime

Given this body of research, how would we expect implicit prejudice and stereotypes to influence hate crimes? In this section, I propose a framework for understanding this issue. I begin with the assumption that implicit bias will influence judgments and behavior only in existing interactions with a member of a protected group.[1] Although there clearly are hate crimes where perpetrators "go looking" for someone from a particular group to harm (Levin & McDevitt, 1993; Perry, 2001; Streissguth, 2003), such deliberate acts are more likely to reflect

---

[1] Although hate crimes can involve the destruction of property, I restrict my analysis to crimes against the person, which seem more susceptible to the influence of implicit prejudice and stereotypes.

overt, explicit prejudice than implicit bias (Dovidio et al., 2002). Likewise, my framework focuses on "ordinary" individuals who (knowingly or unknowingly) possess some degree of implicit and/or explicit bias but are not true bigots. This focus reflects the assumption that true bigots are likely to feel justified in mistreating members of stigmatized groups simply on the basis of their explicit beliefs and feelings; as a result, implicit biases may not have substantial or distinctive effects on their behavior.

When an "ordinary" individual has an encounter with a member of a stigmatized group, the likelihood that implicit bias will trigger acts of aggression depends on characteristics of the actor as well as the situation. Personal characteristics may influence whether negative associations are activated and, if so, whether they lead to aggressive behavior. Individuals who are low in explicit prejudice or have chronic motivation to avoid bias are less likely to experience automatic stereotype activation (Devine et al., 2002; Dunton & Fazio, 1997; Kawakami et al, 1998; Lepore & Brown, 1997; Moskowitz et al., 1999; Rudman & Kilianski, 2000; Wittenbrink et al., 1997; cf., Devine, 1989; Kawakami & Dovidio, 2001). Likewise, individuals who have low levels of anger or aggressive tendencies should be less likely to act upon implicit biases even if they become cognitively accessible (Berkowitz, 2005). In contrast, people who chronically make hostile attributions for others' behavior should be more likely to act aggressively following stereotype activation (Orobio de Castro, Veerman, Koops, Bosch, & Monshouwer, 2002).

With respect to situational factors, if an encounter occurs under circumstances that, as a whole, facilitate controlled (deliberate) processing, individuals should be more likely to rely on explicit rather than implicit beliefs. Further, for most people, such situations lead to attempts to suppress prejudice and stereotypes and to avoid letting them impact behavior (Bodenhausen & Macrae, 1998). For example, when actors have adequate time and cognitive resources and are motivated to treat another person fairly due to accountability or social desirability concerns, they are likely to try to suppress their explicit biases and to be relatively uninfluenced by implicit biases (Blair & Banaji, 1996; Neuberg & Fiske, 1987; Pendry & Macrae, 1996). They also are likely to act in a deliberate manner, making thoughtful judgments and considering the consequences of potential outcomes. As a result, this type of situation generally will lead to non-biased behaviors and prevent negative encounters from escalating into hate crimes.[2]

In contrast, if an encounter with a member of a protected group takes place in a situation that promotes automatic (i.e., quick, often unconscious or unintentional) processing, individuals are more likely to be influenced by implicit prejudice and

---

[2] On the other hand, if an actor is engaging in thoughtful, deliberate processing and still decides to act on his or her biases, those behaviors would be clearly identifiable as intentional hate crimes. Although one potentially might argue that he or she suppressed their biases but still decided to act aggressively (e.g., "I would have beat up anyone who said that to me"), it seems likely that someone who was able to suppress prejudice or stereotypes also would be able to suppress aggressive tendencies.

stereotypes. If actors feel threatened (Sinclair & Kunda, 1999, 2000; Spencer et al., 1998), have constraints on time and/or cognitive resources (Blair, 2002; Blair & Banaji, 1996), or have been using substances like alcohol or drugs (Bartholow, Dicktow, & Sestir, 2006), their behavior may be strongly influenced by implicit biases, even though they may not be aware of it. Notably, simply being in an interaction with a member of a stigmatized group may deplete cognitive resources (due to the need to monitor one's behavior) or provoke anxiety (Richeson & Shelton, 2003; Stephan & Stephan, 1985). All of these situational characteristics are likely to promote relatively spontaneous behavior and increase the influence of implicit stereotypes and prejudice on judgments about and behaviors toward stigmatized targets. Such behaviors often may be subtle (Dovidio et al., 2002), such as slurs or "roughhousing" which do not meet legal definitions for criminal behavior. However, on some occasions, implicit biases may lead to hate crime by exacerbating a negative encounter that otherwise might not have turned violent.

The two hate crimes discussed throughout this chapter illustrate the situational distinction proposed by this model. In the Howard Beach incident, the perpetrators initially walked away from the African American men. Although there clearly was normative support for prejudice among their group, the men had adequate time and cognitive resources to suppress their racist attitudes if they so chose. Accordingly, it is easy to classify their decision to return to beat and chase the African American men as intentional and reflective of prejudicial beliefs—that is, a hate crime. On the other hand, the Crown Heights incident is harder to analyze. The entire African American community was threatened by the child's death and rumors of unfair treatment. Lemrick Nelson himself probably had limited cognitive resources due to being in a violent riot and being under the influence of alcohol. Thus, it is likely that any implicit biases Nelson had toward Jews influenced his behavior toward Yankel Rosenbaum. However, Nelson may well have been telling the truth when he claimed that the stabbing was not premeditated. Hence, even though anti-Semitism likely played a role in the incident, it does not meet the legal requirement of intentionality for hate crimes (and, in fact, a jury found that Nelson was not guilty of murder; Streissguth, 2003).

Once dispositional and/or situational characteristics facilitate implicit biases and spontaneous behaviors, at least four mechanisms may lead encounters to escalate into violence. First, actors may make stereotypical interpretations about ambiguous behaviors, leading them to perceive targets as hostile or threatening (Devine, 1989; Lepore & Brown, 1997; Sagar & Schofield, 1980). Such interpretations could be used to justify aggressive behavior (e.g., "getting him before he gets me"). Second, in negative encounters, implicit prejudice increases the likelihood that actors will categorize someone with ambiguous characteristics (e.g., light brown skin) as belonging to a stigmatized group (Hugenberg & Bodenhausen, 2004). Thus, implicit bias may increase the likelihood of responding to a given target in terms of (perceived) group membership. Both categorization and stereotypical interpretations also may contribute to the devaluing and dehumanization of minority targets (Dovidio et al., 2005). Third, actors may automatically activate behavioral tendencies related to target groups (e.g., Bargh et al., 1996; Chen & Bargh, 1997; Kawakami, Young, & Dovidio, 2002). As a result, encounters with members of groups stereotyped as hostile or aggressive (e.g., African Americans, skinheads) may automatically trigger hostile or aggressive behaviors (Bargh et al., 1996; Chen & Bargh, 1997). Fourth, individuals' thresholds for engaging in aggressive behavior may be lower when targets belong to stigmatized groups (Correll et al., 2002). For example, someone who might have "held back" from hitting a heterosexual target might aggress against a gay or lesbian target.

In sum, this framework proposes that implicit biases can contribute to hate crimes, but their influence is likely to be circumscribed. When situations facilitate controlled processing, implicit biases are not likely to influence aggressive behavior. In contrast, when situations facilitate automatic processing, implicit prejudice and stereotypes may contribute to hate crimes by causing hostile interpretations, increasing the likelihood that a target will be categorized in terms of a stigmatized group, activating aggressive behavioral tendencies, and/or lowering thresholds for aggressive behavior. Although the effects of implicit biases often may be subtle (including noncriminal acts such as hostile statements; Dovidio et al., 2002), in some situations, they may "tip the scale," causing an encounter to become violent when it otherwise would not have been. This outcome may be particularly likely in situations involving competition, threat, and supportive norms for prejudice (Dovidio et al., 2005). In addition to situational factors, individual differences related to prejudice and aggressiveness may increase the influence of implicit bias on behavior with members of protected groups.

The Role of Intention in Hate Crimes: A Critical Race Theory Analysis

Having proposed a framework for understanding the potential influence of implicit bias on hate crime, it is important to consider how this analysis comports with existing hate crime legislation and jurisprudence. Since 1964, hate crime legislation has been enacted by the federal government as well as the majority of the states (for reviews, see, e.g., F. M. Lawrence, 2002; Mennenger, 2005; Streissguth, 2003). Most federal hate crime statutes focus on acts that intentionally interfere with or violate the civil rights of protected groups. State statutes generally use one of three criteria to identify acts that constitute hate crimes: (1) racial animus (i.e., acts motivated by explicit prejudice against a particular group), (2) discriminatory victim selection (i.e., choosing a victim because of the group to which s/he belongs), or (3) causal role of group membership (i.e., committing a crime "because of" or "by reason of" the victim's group membership; Mennenger, 2005).

In addition to defining acts of hate, legislation and jurisprudence has addressed the punishment of hate crimes. Frequently, such legislation has enacted penalty enhancements, which are increased sanctions for hate crimes compared to parallel (i.e., comparable non-bias) crimes. For example, under California Penal Code

§422.75 (2001), sentences can be increased by one to four years when crimes are motivated by prejudice. To date, 42 states have adopted such statutes (F. M. Lawrence, 2002; Sullaway, 2004). Despite criticisms that penalty enhancements violate the free speech clause of the First Amendment, the U.S. Supreme Court in *Wisconsin v. Mitchell* (1993) has upheld these statutes as constitutional. In this case, the Court held that states are justified in giving harsher punishments for hate crimes because they result in greater levels of both individual and societal harm than do parallel crimes. It also held that penalty enhancements punish harmful behaviors, not biased beliefs, and therefore do not violate constitutional protections for personal beliefs and expression.

Hate crime legislation in general, and penalty enhancements in particular, have been highly controversial (e.g., F. M. Lawrence, 2002; Taslitz, 1999; Wang, 1997). In his chapter, Frederick Lawrence (this volume) did an excellent job identifying and refuting four common criticisms against hate crime statutes. First, Lawrence challenges the criticism that hate crime legislation is unconstitutional because it punishes people's beliefs by arguing (consistent with the *Mitchell* Court) that it is possible to distinguish between prejudiced beliefs and criminal behavior. Second, Lawrence rejects the view that hate crime statutes harm intergroup relations by exacerbating race and ethnic divisions in society and instead takes the position that such statutes serve an important societal role by formally condemning bias and intolerance. Third, he addresses the criticism that hate crime statutes will be disproportionately applied to perpetrators from minority groups, pointing out that this argument could be applied to all criminal legislation and questioning why the issue is raised primarily when legislation benefits minorities. Finally, Lawrence addresses the question of harm, arguing that hate crimes result in greater harm than do parallel crimes, increasing the culpability of perpetrators and therefore meriting harsher punishment. On the basis of these arguments, Lawrence concludes that hate crime legislation plays a beneficial role in promoting equality in our society.

Given the strength of these arguments, I will focus my legal analysis on a single issue that is specifically related to implicit bias. Hate crime legislation and jurisprudence requires a finding of intentionality; that is, the factfinder must determine whether the perpetrator intentionally decided to harm an individual due to his or her membership in a protected group (F. M. Lawrence, 2002; Sullaway, 2004). Assuming that implicit biases can contribute to hate crimes, a significant question arises. How should a judge or jury evaluate an aggressive act against a member of a protected class that is triggered by implicit bias and therefore may not have involved conscious intent or awareness (see Richter & Wiener, this volume)?[3] In other words, should actors be held legally responsible for behaviors resulting from implicit bias?

---

[3] Importantly, recent social cognition research indicates that goals can be automatically activated, suggesting that, in many cases, there may be intentional or motivated aspects of automatic stereotype activation (for a review, see Glaser & Kihlstrom, 2005). However, an analysis of how the courts might evaluate "unconscious motivation" is beyond the scope of this chapter.

How one answers this question depends on whether one is discussing criminal or civil law. Although most discussion of hate crime legislation involves criminal law, victims of alleged hate crimes can pursue civil litigation to try to obtain damages from their assailants. As discussed in this section, such civil litigation provides the most likely avenue for legal recognition of the influence of implicit bias on hate crime, and in fact, similar arguments have been raised in other areas of law by scholars in the Critical Race Theory movement.

Criteria for Determining Legal Responsibility

A central concept of criminal law is *mens rea* or criminal intent; individuals are not criminally blameworthy unless they intended to commit a particular act. In contrast, civil law focuses on redressing wrongs. Although intentionality often is required under civil law, the civil system recognizes some situations where people are wronged without conscious intent (e.g., strict liability cases in torts litigation). As a result, the civil system may be better equipped than the criminal system to consider how negative outcomes may result from implicit biases.

In fact, over the past 20 years, legal scholars who are part of the Critical Race Theory movement have argued that intentionality requirements in civil law can act as an impediment to achieving true racial equality. This argument first was raised in a seminal article by Charles R. Lawrence III (1987). Lawrence analyzed a case, *Washington v. Davis* (1976), in which the Supreme Court upheld the use of an entrance exam that disproportionately kept African American applicants from joining the Washington, DC police force. Although recognizing that use of the exam had a disparate impact on African Americans, the Court held that evidence of discriminatory intent was necessary to apply a strict scrutiny standard to facially neutral laws or policies. Lawrence challenged that conclusion, arguing that individuals in contemporary society frequently are influenced and motivated by "unconscious racism" rather than explicit prejudice. As a result, "By insisting that a blameworthy perpetrator be found before the existence of racial discrimination can be acknowledged, the Court creates an imaginary world where discrimination does not exist unless it was consciously intended" (C. R. Lawrence, 1987, pp. 324–325). He further asserted that, by not recognizing and redressing a common form of bias, "The intent requirement is a centerpiece in an ideology of equal opportunity that legitimizes the continued existence of racially and economically discriminatory conditions and rationalizes the superordinate status of privileged whites" (C. R. Lawrence, 1987, p. 387).

As an alternative to the intent requirement in antidiscrimination law, Lawrence (1987) suggested that factfinders engage in analyses of the "cultural meaning" of laws and policies that have disparate impacts across social groups. If those policies appear racial in nature (e.g., zoning restrictions that disproportionately prevent minorities from moving into an area), they probably reflect unconscious racism. As a result, Lawrence argued that they should merit strict liability, even absent a showing of intentional discrimination.

There clearly are limitations to Lawrence's (1987) analysis; most notably, his psychological analysis of unconscious racism was largely based on dated theory and research (e.g., Freudian constructs). However, by challenging the validity of the intent requirement and by suggesting that there may be alternative methods of discerning legal responsibility, his article sparked a great deal of important theorizing.

Since then, scholars have discussed the influence of implicit biases in a number of areas, including employment law (e.g., Krieger, 1995; Pollard, 1999), antidiscrimination law (e.g., Chamallas, 2001; Saujani, 2003), affirmative action (Krieger, 1998), criminal procedure (Johnson, 1988), and even federal communication law (Kang, 2005). In addition to extending Lawrence's legal analysis, these scholars have developed far more sophisticated analyses of the psychological research on implicit bias that was discussed earlier in this chapter. For example, Krieger (1995) outlined a "cognitive bias approach" to employment discrimination. In her article, she challenged the Title VII requirement that actionable employment discrimination requires intentional acts driven by explicit prejudice or stereotypes, arguing that such a requirement is more suited to identifying "old-fashioned" bias than contemporary acts of discrimination. Instead, Krieger proposed disentangling causation from intentionality. If a plaintiff could show that the actions of an employer were caused in part by his or her group membership, that causal relationship would serve to establish liability. In other words, "The critical inquiry would be whether the applicant or employee's group status 'made a difference' in the employer's action, not whether the decisionmaker intended that it make a difference" (Krieger, 1995, p. 1242).

Thus, Critical Race Theorists have developed a body of scholarship that challenges the requirement of establishing conscious intention in order to remedy discriminatory acts and policies. These arguments frequently are grounded in contemporary psychological research on implicit prejudice and stereotyping (although they also reflect broader societal concerns, such as ending oppression; see, e.g., Kang, 2005; Krieger, 1995). I propose that a similar argument could be applied to hate crime. As discussed earlier, under some circumstances, implicit prejudice and stereotypes may contribute to acts of aggression against members of protected groups that do not meet legal standards of intentionality. As a result, it is important to consider legislative and jurisprudential standards that would enable victims to pursue civil litigation when implicit bias and/or group membership appear to play a causal role in violent acts, even absent deliberate intent.

Clearly, this project needs to be undertaken with some degree of caution. Although Critical Race Theory has gained increasing currency among legal theorists, many of its ideas still are rejected by the courts. For example, even though some Supreme Court justices have mentioned the possibility of unconscious racism in their opinions, the Court as a whole has persisted in requiring evidence of intent in antidiscrimination cases (Saujani, 2003). Thus, it may be a challenging endeavor to convince courts and legislators to adopt standards that recognize the possible role of unintentional bias in hate crime. Further, despite calls for extending hate crime legislation beyond racial animus or discriminatory victim selection (e.g., Wang, 1997, 2000), developing fair and reliable methods for establishing the influence of implicit bias on aggressive acts may be quite difficult.

That said, considering ways of expanding civil law to address the potential influence of implicit bias on hate acts is likely to be a worthwhile endeavor that furthers the goal of equal treatment for people of all groups, a goal embraced by Critical Race Theorists as well as many proponents of hate crime legislation. One possible method for recognizing the potential contributions of implicit bias to hate crime might involve the use of a "mixed motive analysis" as set forth in *Price Waterhouse v. Hopkins* (1989). In that case, the Supreme Court held that workplace judgments involving legally permissible factors (e.g., job performance) still could be tainted by stereotypes about an employee's group, leading to legally impermissible discrimination. In other words, employment discrimination can occur even if decisions reflect more than one motive, so long as group membership is one factor influencing an employer's judgments. This kind of analysis is consistent with the proposed framework for hate crime, which suggests that implicit biases may contribute to aggressive acts by exacerbating negative encounters with members of protected groups. In such instances, aggressive behavior may be caused by a combination of non-biased motives (e.g., provocation by an insult) as well as implicit prejudice or stereotypes. A mixed motive analysis thus might conclude that the victim's group membership led the perpetrator to automatically activate stereotypes or prejudice, which in turn contributed to the decision to respond aggressively.

Admittedly, there are potential problems with suggesting a mixed motive analysis for civil claims related to hate crime. Even in *Price Waterhouse*, the standard was used to address conscious rather than implicit stereotyping. Also, to date, courts have not been receptive to a different form of mixed motive analysis in hate crime cases. Specifically, criminal courts have been reluctant to recognize cases where an alleged perpetrator was motivated by both the alleged victim's group and another factor, such as personal gain from a robbery (Chamallas, 2001; Wang, 2000). My goal is not to suggest that mixed motive analysis is the optimal strategy for recognizing implicit bias in civil litigation related to hate crimes, but rather to start others thinking so that a fully realized framework can be developed.

Evaluation by Factfinders

As noted by Saujani (2003), "The failure to endorse legal remediation of unconscious racism arises at least in part from the Court's skepticism about whether unconscious racism can actually be proved in a court of law" (p. 405). Thus, even if an adequate and acceptable jurisprudence for implicit influences on hate crime is developed, proving that implicit biases affected any given act is likely to pose a substantial challenge.

Unless a perpetrator openly admits that prejudice against a particular group influenced his or her behavior, inferences about motivation must be made (Sullaway, 2004). Given that individuals do not have introspective access to implicit biases—and may deny that they even have them—the need to infer that prejudice or stereotypes unintentionally contributed to an aggressive act is likely to be a major issue. Ultimately, there is unlikely to ever be solid proof that implicit biases affected a person's behavior in any given real-world situation.

However, there are several potential methods by which plaintiffs might suggest that implicit biases contributed to an aggressive act. For example, given that individuals high in explicit bias generally are more likely to exhibit implicit bias (Hofmann et al., 2005; Kawakami et al., 1998; Lepore & Brown, 1997; Rudman & Kilianski, 2000; Wittenbrink et al., 1997; cf., Devine, 1989; Kawakami & Dovidio, 2001), it may be reasonable to infer that an individual who explicitly expresses prejudice or stereotypes in one situation would be influenced by implicit biases in another situation.[4] Alternatively, by systematically identifying and ruling out possible motivations (e.g., provocation), factfinders may determine that prejudice or stereotypes—implicit or explicit—provide the most reasonable explanation for an act (Sullaway, 2004).

A third strategy that may have intuitive appeal involves (1) demonstrating that an individual has implicit prejudice or stereotypes, and (2) showing that the situation surrounding a potential hate act had features that might facilitate the use of implicit bias. Establishing both clauses could allow for an inference that implicit biases contributed to the behavior in question. However, there are potential shortcomings to this sort of strategy. From a legal perspective, this procedure may come uncomfortably close to punishing people for their thoughts and mental processes (i.e., for having implicit bias), which would violate the First Amendment. On the other hand, it is unclear whether drawing inferences from the fact that someone has implicit biases *and* was in a situation that would facilitate their use is more problematic than making the common assumption that someone who previously expressed racist views was motivated by those beliefs during a particular act (Sullaway, 2004). From a psychological perspective, there are concerns related to proving that an individual defendant holds implicit biases. Although some scholars (e.g., Saujani, 2003) have suggested administering measures from psychological research (e.g., the Implicit Associations Test; Greenwald et al., 1998) to discern whether decision makers have implicit prejudice or stereotypes, at this point, those measures have not been shown to have adequate predictive validity at the individual versus aggregate level to justify using them as the basis for civil penalties (e.g., Blanton & Jaccard, 2006; Greenwald, 2004). Thus, the ability to show that implicit biases may have contributed to a hate act will require advances in psychological science as well as jurisprudence.

Conclusion

In this chapter, I have tried to expand upon the work of Kovera (this volume) and Lawrence (this volume) by developing a framework for understanding when implicit prejudice and stereotypes are and are not likely to contribute to hate crimes as well as by discussing how unintentional bias might be recognized in civil litigation related to hate crime. In doing so, my intention has not been to

---

[4] In contrast, inferring that an individual who has never expressed explicit bias is not influenced by implicit bias is somewhat more tenuous.

suggest that implicit bias is more important than other factors known to influence hate behavior (e.g., perceived threat, explicit bias; Craig, 2002; Green et al., 2001). Hate crimes are complex behaviors requiring dynamic, multifactor theoretical explanations. In truth, implicit biases may be a relatively minor contributor to hate crime (see Fiske, 2002; Green et al., 1998). As suggested in this chapter, their most important influence may be to "tip the scales," exacerbating negative encounters that otherwise might not have resulted in aggression, particularly among individuals who are predisposed toward bias and aggressiveness.

However, it is my hope that proposing even this circumscribed role for implicit bias in hate crime leads others to investigate this issue. If implicit biases have the potential to contribute to hate crimes, it would behoove psychologists to study their influence and legal scholars to consider if and how they might be considered in hate crime legislation and jurisprudence. Although the framework presented in this chapter is grounded in social psychological research and theory, it clearly requires empirical testing. Likewise, it is important for legal scholars to critically assess the role of intent in civil litigation related to hate crimes.

These recommendations will not be easy to achieve, but the outcome is likely to justify those efforts. In the words of Charles Lawrence (1987), "When one finds that intentional racial discrimination is morally reprehensible but that unconscious racial stigmatization is not, one has made a value choice" (p. 384). It is incumbent on those who would not make this value choice to develop frameworks for the inclusion of both explicit and implicit biases in our understanding of and system for redressing hate crimes.

Acknowledgments. This chapter benefited greatly from comments from Rich Wiener, Brian Armenta, Evelyn Maeder, Kiernan McGorty, Samantha Schwartz, April Seifert, and Jessica Snowden. I also thank Jack Glaser for sharing his insights on hate crime.

References

Bargh, J. A., Chen, M., & Burrows, L. (1996). Automaticity of social behavior: Direct effects of trait construct and stereotype activation on action. *Journal of Personality and Social Psychology, 71*, 230–244.

Bartholow, B. D., Dicktow, C. L., & Sestir, M. A. (2006). Stereotype activation and control of race bias: Cognitive control of inhibition and its impairment by alcohol. *Journal of Personality and Social Psychology, 90*, 272–287.

Berkowitz, L. (2005). On hate and its determinants: Some affective and cognitive influences. In R.J. Sternberg (Ed.) *The psychology of hate* (pp. 155–183). Washington, D.C.: American Psychological Association.

Blair, I. V. (2002). The malleability of automatic stereotypes and prejudice. *Personality and Social Psychology Review, 6*, 242–261.

Blair, I. V., & Banaji, M. R. (1996). Automatic and controlled processes in stereotype priming. *Journal of Personality and Social Psychology, 70*, 1142–1163.

Blanton, H., & Jaccard, J. (2006). Arbitrary metrics in psychology. *American Psychologist, 61*, 27–41.

Bodenhausen, G. V., & Macrae, C. N. (1998). Stereotype activation and inhibition. In R. S. Wyer, Jr. (Ed.), *Advances in social cognition* (Vol. 11, pp. 1–52). Mahwah, NJ: Lawrence Erlbaum Associates.

Chamallas, M. (2001). Deepening the legal understanding of bias: On devaluation and biased prototypes. *Southern California Law Review, 74*, 747–806.

Chen, M., & Bargh, J. A. (1997). Nonconscious behavioral confirmation processes: The self-fulfilling consequences of automatic stereotype activation. *Journal of Experimental Social Psychology, 33*, 541–560.

Conaway, C. B. (1996, November). *Framing identity: The press in Crown Heights* (Research Paper R-16). Cambridge MA: The Joan Shorenstein Center on the Press, Politics, and Public Policy, John F. Kennedy School of Government, Harvard University.

Correll, J., Park, B., Judd, C. M., & Wittenbrink, B. (2002). The police officer's dilemma: Using ethnicity to disambiguate potentially threatening individuals. *Journal of Personality and Social Psychology, 83*, 1314–1329.

Correll, J., Urland, G. R., & Ito, T. A. (2006). Event-related potentials and the decision to shoot: The role of threat perception and cognitive control. *Journal of Experimental Social Psychology, 42*, 120–128.

Craig, K. M. (2002). Examining hate-motivated aggression: A review of the social psychological literature on hate crimes as a distinct form of aggression. *Aggression and Violent Behavior, 7*, 86–101.

Crandall, C. S., & Eshleman, A. (2003). A justification-suppression model of the expression and experience of prejudice. *Psychological Bulletin, 129*, 414–446.

Devine, P. G. (1989). Stereotypes and prejudice: Their automatic and controlled components. *Journal of Personality and Social Psychology, 56*, 5–18.

Devine, P. G., & Elliott, A. J. (1995). Are racial stereotypes really fading? The Princeton trilogy revisited. *Personality and Social Psychology Bulletin, 21*, 1139–1150.

Devine, P. G., Plant, E. A., Amodio, D. M., Harmon-Jones, E., & Vance, S. L. (2002). The regulation of explicit and implicit race bias: The role of motivations to respond without prejudice. *Journal of Personality and Social Psychology, 82*, 835–848.

Dovidio, J. F., & Gaertner, S. L. (2004). Aversive racism. In M. P. Zanna (Eds.), *Advances in experimental social psychology* (Vol. 36, pp. 1–52). San Diego: Elsevier.

Dovidio, J. F., Gaertner, S. L., & Pearson, A. R. (2005). On the nature of prejudice: The psychological foundations of hate. In R. J. Sternberg (Ed.) *The psychology of hate* (pp. 211–234). Washington, DC: American Psychological Association.

Dovidio, J. F., Kawakami, K., & Gaertner, S. E. (2002). Implicit and explicit prejudice and interracial interaction. *Journal of Personality and Social Psychology, 82*, 62–68.

Dunton, B. C., & Fazio, R. H. (1997). An individual difference measure of motivation to control prejudiced reactions. *Personality and Social Psychology Bulletin, 23*, 316–326.

Fazio, R. H., Jackson, J. R., Dunton, B. C., & Williams, C. J. (1995). Variability in automatic activation as an unobtrusive measure of racial attitudes: A bona fide pipeline? *Journal of Personality and Social Psychology, 69*, 1013–1027.

Fazio, R. H., & Olson, M. A. (2003). Implicit measures in social cognition research: Their meaning and uses. *Annual Review of Psychology, 54*, 297–327.

Fiske, S. T. (1998). Stereotyping, prejudice, and discrimination. In D. T. Gilbert, S. T. Fiske, & G. Lindzey (Eds.) *Handbook of social psychology* (4th ed., Vol. 2, pp. 357–411). New York: McGraw-Hill.

Fiske, S. T. (2002). What we know about bias and intergroup conflict, the problem of the century. *Current Directions in Psychological Science, 11*, 123–128.

Fiske, S. T., Cuddy, A. J. C., Glick, P., & Xu, J. (2002). A model of (often mixed) stereotype content: Competence and warmth respectively follow from perceived status and competition. *Journal of Personality and Social Psychology, 82*, 878–902.

Gaertner, S. L., & Dovidio, J. F. (1983). Racial stereotypes: Associations and ascriptions of positive and negative characteristics. *Social Psychology Quarterly, 46*, 23–30.

Gaertner, S. L., & McLaughlin, J. P. (1983). Racial sterotypes: Associations and ascriptions of positive and negative characteristics. *Social Psychology Quarterly, 46*, 23–30.

Gilbert, D. T., & Hixon, J. G. (1991). The trouble of thinking: Activation and application of stereotypic beliefs. *Journal of Personality and Social Psychology, 60*, 509–517.

Glaser, J., Dixit, J., & Green, D. P. (2002). Studying hate crime with the internet: What makes racists advocate racial violence? *Journal of Social Issues, 58*, 177–193.

Glaser, J., & Kihlstrom, J. F. (2005). Compensatory automaticity: Unconscious volition is not an oxymoron. In R. R. Hassin, J. S. Uleman, & J. A. Bargh (Eds.) *The new unconscious.* (pp. 171–195). New York: Oxford University Press.

Green, D. P., Glaser, J., & Rich, A. (1998). From lynching to gay bashing: The elusive connection between economic conditions and hate crime. *Journal of Personality and Social Psychology, 75*, 82–92.

Green, D. P., McFalls, L. H., & Smith, J. K. (2001). Hate crime: An emergent research agenda. *Annual Review of Sociology, 27*, 479–504.

Greenwald, A. G. (2004, January). *Revised top ten list of things wrong with the IAT.* Paper presented at the Society for Personality and Social Psychology conference, Austin TX.

Greenwald, A. G., McGhee, D., & Schwartz, J. L. K. (1998). Measuring individual differences in implicit cognition: The implicit associations test. *Journal of Personality and Social Psychology, 74*, 1464–1480.

Greenwald, A. G., Oakes, M. A., & Hoffman, H. G. (2003). Targets of discrimination: Effects of race on responses to weapon holders. *Journal of Experimental Social Psychology, 39*, 399–405.

Hamner, K. M. (1992). Gay-bashing: A social identity analysis of violence against lesbians and gay men. In G. M. Herek & K. T. Berrill (Eds.), *Hate crimes: Confronting violence against lesbians and gay men* (pp. 179–190). Thousand Oaks, CA: Sage.

Hofmann, W., Gawronski, B., Gschwendner, T., Le, H., & Schmitt, M. (2005). A meta-analysis on the correlation between the implicit association test and explicit self-report measures. *Personality and Social Psychology Bulletin, 31*, 1369–1385.

Hugenberg, K., & Bodenhausen, G. V. (2004). Ambiguity in social categorization: The role of prejudice and facial affect in race categorization. *Psychological Science, 15*, 342–345.

Hunt, J. S., Borgida, E., Kelly, K. M., & Burgess, D. (2002). Gender stereotyping. In D. L. Faigman, D. H. Kaye, M. J. Saks, & J. Sanders (Eds.), *Modern scientific evidence: The law and science of expert testimony* (2nd ed., Vol. 2, pp. 384–426). St. Paul, MN: West.

Johnson, S. L. (1988). Unconscious racism and the criminal law. *Cornell Law Review, 73*, 1016–1037.

Kang, J. (2005). Trojan horses of race. *Harvard Law Review, 118*, 1489–1593.

Kawakami, K., Dion, K. L., & Dovidio, J. F. (1998). Racial prejudice and stereotype activation. *Personality and Social Psychology Bulletin, 24*, 407–416.

Kawakami, K., & Dovidio, J. F. (2001). The reliability of implicit stereotyping. *Personality and Social Psychology Bulletin, 27*, 212–225.

Kawakami, K., Young, H., & Dovidio, J. F. (2002). Automatic stereotyping: Category, trait, and behavioral activations. *Personality and Social Psychology Bulletin, 28*, 3–15.

Krieger, L. H. (1995). The content of our categories: A cognitive bias approach to discrimination and equal employment opportunity. *Stanford Law Review, 47,* 1161–1248.

Krieger, L. H. (1998). Civil rights perestroika: Intergroup relations after affirmative action. *California Law Review, 86,* 1251–1333.

Kunda, Z., & Spencer, S. J. (2003). When do stereotypes come to mind and when do they color judgment? A goal-based theoretical framework for stereotype activation and application. *Psychological Bulletin, 129,* 522–544.

Kunda, Z., Davies, P. G., Adams, B. D., & Spencer, S. J. (2002). The dynamic time course of stereotype activation: Activation, dissipation, and resurrection. *Journal of Personality and Social Psychology, 82,* 283–299.

Lawrence, C. R. III (1987). The id, the ego, and equal protection: Reckoning with unconscious racism. *Stanford Law Review, 39,* 317–388.

Lawrence, F.M. (2002). *Punishing hate: Bias crimes under American law.* Cambridge MA: Harvard University Press.

Lepore, L., & Brown, R. (1997). Category and stereotype activation: Is prejudice inevitable? *Journal of Personality and Social Psychology, 72,* 275–287.

Levin, J., & McDevitt, J. (1993). *Hate crimes: The rising tide of bigotry and bloodshed.* New York: Plenum.

Lowery, B. D., Hardin, C. D., & Sinclair, S. (2001). Social influence effects on automatic racial prejudice. *Journal of Personality and Social Psychology, 81,* 842–855.

Madon, S. (1997). What do people believe about gay males? A study of stereotype content and strength. *Sex Roles, 37,* 663–685.

Mennenger, K. II. (2005). Hate crimes and liability for bias-motivated acts. *American Jurisprudence Proof of Facts 3d, 57,* 1–74.

Moskowitz, G. B., Gollwitzer, P. M., Wasel, W., & Schaal, B. (1999). Preconscious control of stereotype activation through chronic egalitarian goals. *Journal of Personality and Social Psychology, 77,* 167–184.

Neuberg, S. L., & Fiske, S. T. (1987). Motivational influences on impression formation: Outcome dependency, accuracy-driven attention, and individuating processes. *Journal of Personality and Social Psychology, 53,* 431–444.

Niemann, Y. F., Jennings, L., Rozelle, R. M., Baxter, J. C., & Sullivan E. (1994). Use of free responses and cluster analysis to determine stereotypes of eight groups. *Personality and Social Psychology Bulletin, 20,* 379–390.

Orobio de Castro, B., Veerman, J. W., Koops, W., Bosch, J. D., & Monshouwer, H. J. (2002). Hostile attribution of intent and aggressive behavior: A meta-analysis. *Child Development, 73,* 916–934.

Payne, B. K. (2001). Prejudice and perception: The role of automatic and controlled processes in misperceiving a weapon. *Journal of Personality and Social Psychology, 81,* 181–192.

Pendry, L. F., & Macrae, C. N. (1996). What the disinterested perceiver overlooks: Goal-directed social categorization. *Personality and Social Psychology Bulletin, 22,* 249–256.

Perry, B. (2001). *In the name of hate.* New York: Routledge.

Plant, A., & Peruche, B. M. (2005). The consequences of race for police officers' responses to criminal suspects. *Psychological Science, 16,* 180–183.

Pollard, D. A. (1999). Unconscious bias and self-critical analysis: The case for a qualified evidentiary equal employment opportunity privilege. *Washington Law Review, 74,* 913–1031.

Prentice-Dunn, S., & Rogers, W. (1982). Effects of public and private self-awareness on deindividuation and aggression. *Journal of Personality and Social Psychology, 43,* 503–513.

Richeson, J. A., & Shelton, J. N. (2003). When prejudice does not pay: Effects of interracial contact on executive function. *Psychological Science, 14,* 287–290.

Rudman, L. A., & Kilianski, S. E. (2000). Implicit and explicit attitudes toward female authority. *Personality and Social Psychology Bulletin, 26,* 1315–1328.

Sagar, H. A., & Schofield, J. W. (1980). Racial and behavioral cues in Black and White children's perceptions of ambiguously aggressive acts. *Journal of Personality and Social Psychology, 39,* 590–598.

Saujani, R. M. (2003). The implicit association test: A measure of unconscious racism in legislative decision-making. *Michigan Journal of Race and Law, 8,* 395–423.

Sinclair, L., & Kunda, Z. (1999). Reactions to a Black professional: Motivated inhibition and activation of conflicting stereotypes. *Journal of Personality and Social Psychology, 77,* 885–904.

Sinclair, L., & Kunda, Z. (2000). Motivated stereotyping of women: She's fine if she praised me but incompetent if she criticized me. *Personality and Social Psychology Bulletin, 26,* 1329–1342.

Spencer, S. J., Fein, S., Wolfe, C. T., Fong, C., & Dunn, M. A. (1998). Automatic activation of stereotypes: The role of self-image threat. *Personality and Social Psychology Bulletin, 24,* 1139–1152.

Stephan, W. G., & Stephan, C. W. (1985). Intergroup anxiety. *Journal of Social Issues, 41,* 157–175.

Streissguth, T. (2003). *Hate crimes.* New York: Facts on File, Inc.

Sullaway, M. (2004). Psychological perspective on hate crime laws. *Psychology, Public Policy, and Law, 10,* 250–292.

Tajfel, H., & Turner, J. C. (1986). The social identity theory of intergroup behavior. In S. Worchel & W. Austin (Eds.), Psychology of intergroup relations (pp. 7–24). Chicago: Nelson-Hall.

Taslitz, A. E. (1999). Condemning the racist personality: Why the critics of hate crimes legislation are wrong. *Boston College Law Review, 40,* 739–785.

Wang, L. (1997). The transforming power of "hate": Cognition theory and the harms of bias-related crime. *Southern California Law Review, 71,* 47–135.

Wang, L. (2000). Recognizing opportunistic bias crimes. *Boston University Law Review, 80,* 1399–1435.

Wheeler, S. C., & Petty, R. E. (2001). The effects of stereotype activation on behavior: A review of possible mechanisms. *Psychological Bulletin, 127,* 797–826.

Wilson, T. D., Lindsay, S., & Schooler, T. Y. (2000). A model of dual attitudes. *Psychological Review, 107,* 101–126.

Wittenbrink, B., Judd, C. M., & Park, B. (1997). Evidence for racial prejudice at the implicit level and its relationship with questionnaire measures. *Journal of Personality and Social Psychology, 72,* 262–274.

Legal Citations

Price Waterhouse v. Hopkins, 490 U.S. 228, 104 L.Ed.2d 268, 109 S.Ct. 1775 (1989).

Washington v. Davis, 426 U.S. 229 (1976).

Wisconsin v. Mitchell, 508 U.S. 476 (1993).

14
Psychology and Legal Decision Making: Where Should We Go From Here?

Erin M. Richter and Richard L. Wiener

Throughout this volume, leading scholars in both law and psychology have examined ways in which psychology intersects with the law across a multitude of topics. So often, it seems research in the psycho-legal domain focuses on criminal assessment, jury decision making, or eye witness identification, while other topics tend to fall to the wayside. The strength of this volume and the conference that gave rise to it is the creative way in which authors applied psychological reasoning to topics that often escape this type of analysis. Perhaps it is a more difficult task to link psychology to affirmative action than, say, to memory models and eyewitness identification, or even juror bias in decision making. Yet, this volume has demonstrated that the field of decision making within psychology has clear implications for multiple aspects of the legal and political fields. In this chapter, we return to the decision-making models discussed earlier in the volume, and more specifically examine their contributions to the topics of sexual harassment and hate crimes.

The lens model, as described by Hastie and Dawes (2001), and discussed by Wiener in the first chapter, offers one account of how decision makers may approach a problem of judgment. The lens model explains the balance of external cues and personal judgments made by the decision maker in the framework of the decision maker's view or "lens" of the world. This model seems especially appropriate for the topic of sexual harassment, where many decision makers may be bringing past personal experiences with them to the decision task. Here, a decision maker, who is perhaps an upper-level employee, an affirmative action officer, or even a juror views the external cues presented in the environment from his or her own perspective to arrive at a judgment. Depending on the view of the decision maker, various interpretations exist for each environmental cue, and the outcome or judgment may change depending on the interpretation of the cue.

Examine Figure 1, which portrays the lens model as applied to a judgment of whether or not social sexual conduct rises to the level of sexual harassment. On the left side exists the actual environment, or in this case, the amount of sexual harassment that is actually occurring. This, of course, is difficult to conceptualize

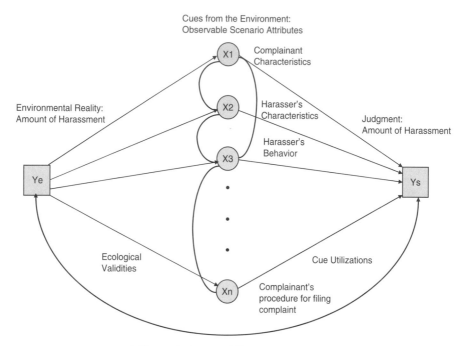

FIGURE 14.1. The lens model of sexual harassment.

because the harassment is naturally a subjective measurement. Nonetheless, we could conceive of this "reality" as the actual behavior of the employee accused of harassing another worker. Down the center columns, we see the environmental cues that are observable by the decision maker. In the instance of sexual harassment, examples of these cues are characteristics of the victim, characteristics of the harasser(s), descriptions of things said and done by the harasser(s), the number of harassment occurrences or date and manner of reporting by the victim, and even the reactions of other co-workers, and so forth. On the right side, we see the judgment made, in this case, the determination of whether or not the behavior in context gives rise to a judgment of whether sexual harassment occurred in the scenarios described by the victim.

In our view, the lens model does an excellent job of capturing the "totality of the circumstances" (Wiener, this volume; Gutek, this volume). For example, the model takes into account the viewer's personal assessment of the environmental cues, and realizes that each person's observations about the environmental cues may be different, depending on that person's demographic characteristics, worldview, or past experiences. As previous research has demonstrated, perceptions about sexual harassment differ by gender (Rotundo, Nguyen, & Sackett, 2001; Wiener, Winter, Rogers, & Arnot, 2004), so a woman may view more sexual harassment in a given situation than a man. Or, the lens may be affected by previous experiences with sexual harassment (Wiener et al., 2004; Wiener & Hurt, 2000) such that a person who has made prior judgments about harassment will be more likely (or sometimes less likely) to interpret the environmental cues as proof of harassment. The lens could also be different depending on the status or nature of the situation in which the decision maker is hearing about the case. An affirmative action officer or an upper-management company employee who is responding to the complaint, for instance, may take a very different view of the situation than a juror who is hearing about the harassment. An affirmative action officer and the company management will most likely have previous experiences dealing with sexual harassment situations and will have a protocol telling them how to respond and begin making the decision. These protocols may even be considered to be another environmental cue. The juror, however, will most likely not have had previous experience making decisions about sexual harassment situations (at least not as a juror), and thus will interpret the environmental cues differently. The lens may even be different depending on what type of standard (e.g., reasonable person or reasonable woman) the decision maker is using to make the decision (Wiener & Hurt, 2000).

The use of this model, while beneficial for its descriptive nature, serves to outline the struggle that policy makers and even researchers, as Gutek (this volume) points out, face when dealing with sexual harassment. The final judgment about what does and what does not constitute sexual harassment is as largely influenced by the decision maker's personal perceptions, perhaps even more so than by the official legal definitions for the types of sexual harassment. In her chapter, Gutek illustrates the fact that sexual harassment law is dynamic, and therefore difficult to conceptualize in research paradigms. Because the legal definitions of sexual harassment are continually changing, we have yet to create a consistent methodology for investigating sexual harassment in the laboratory. This obstacle, combined with the hindrances pointed out by Wiener and Winter (this volume) that sexual harassment scenarios are as varied as the number of complaints made about sexual harassment, exemplifies the true problem in sexual harassment policy development.

As discussed by Gutek (this volume), the general population believes the law forbids more sexually harassing behavior than it actually does. She also reported that, generally, people have expectations that the complainant will file a report about the harassment before filing suit. In addition, Wiener and Winter (this volume) emphasized the difficulty in determining how a decision maker chooses to interpret the "totality of the circumstances" standard he or she is asked to use when making decisions about sexual harassment scenarios, and suggest the decision maker use previous experiences with the social sexual conduct of others in the workplace to determine whether sexual harassment has occurred in the scenario before them. These are all variables that could affect the decision maker's judgment, and serve as cues for the decision maker in the lens model in Figure 1. The problem, of course, is that these variables do not remain consistent across cases, and therefore make it difficult to come up with a single legal standard that can standardize definitions of sexual harassment in the workplace.

The central point that decision-making models of sexual harassment point to is the fluidity of the problem. Sometimes social sexual conduct at work is unwelcome and sufficiently severe or pervasive to rise to the level of a hostile work environment and sometimes it does not rise to that level. As Wiener and Hurt (1999, 2000) point out, the determination depends to a large extent on the tolerance of individual workers and their own points of self-reference. Perhaps the best that can be done is to develop empirical methods for understanding what behaviors are unwelcome and offensive for which people in some (but not other) circumstances. The application of decision-making models such as the lens model to the problem points out this basic policy dilemma that the law simply relegates to the notion of the "the totality of the circumstances" and then proceeds to try to get beyond. The fluidity of the decision of what is and is not sexual harassment is an important topic for study in its own right with practical importance for specific cases that do and do not make their way to court.

Another developing area of law, where the psychology of decision making could certainly play a role, is hate crime legislation and hate crime policy. Lawrence (this volume) speaks of the importance of developing a federal hate crime statute, as individual states continue to pass their own hate crime laws. His analysis of how hate crime statutes are affecting both victims and offenders highlights the many places where psychology could offer help to legislators as they compose a federal statute.

Lawrence discusses the court case *Virginia v. Black* (2003), which upheld a Virginia statute that banned cross-burnings committed with the intent to intimidate. The statute, however, did not ban *all* cross-burnings, and would still allow cross-burnings committed for purposes other than the intimidation of another person. This distinction raises an interesting psychological question, namely, are we able to determine when a cross-burning is committed with the intent to intimidate or when it is committed for another purpose? Or, is it the case that most people would consider all cross-burnings intimidating in most contexts?

To examine this question, we presented participants with one of three versions of five different hate symbol scenarios. In one justification, the defendant displayed the hate symbol as part of an expression of political ideology. In another, the defendant displayed the symbol to show his solidarity to a particular group. In the final condition, the defendant gave no justification for displaying the symbol. This condition served as the control group. It is by default the intimidation condition because it allowed no other reason for the exhibition of the symbol. Participants read five scenarios involving four different hate symbols. There were two fact patterns about cross-burnings (one on private property at a KKK rally and one on a neighbor's lawn), one about a swastika, one about a confederate flag, and one about a skin fist. With the use of different symbols, we hoped to gain a better understanding of reactions to other hate symbols, some of which could be equally as intimidating as a cross-burning (the swastika) and some of which are lesser known (skin fist).

In general, our participants found the cross-burning committed on the neighbor's lawn to be the most intimidating, across all justification conditions.

Surprisingly, the cross-burning committed on private property was considered to be the least intimidating across all justification conditions. This suggests that our participants were convinced that there were differences in the offender's intent depending on the context in which he displayed the various hate symbols. However, judgments about guilt were not as clean. Though participants judged offenders who displayed the cross-burning on private property as less intimidating, they still found a majority of the defendants guilty of violating the state statute we presented to them, which was the Virginia statute upheld in *Virginia v. Black* (2003). In addition, for some scenarios, the political or group association justification, actually elevated ratings of intimidation and guilt certainty, suggesting that the model of decision making for these types of cases is not as clean as the Supreme Court expected (Wiener and Richter, under review).

How does one decide what is an act of intimidation? Applying the expected utility model discussed in Chapter 1 (Wiener, this volume), suggests the decision maker estimates the expected utility of each choice, and then selects the choice with the highest expected utility. The decision maker in our study had to decide whether the defendant in the described scenario was either guilty or not guilty of violating the statute that banned the display of hate symbols, when those symbols were intended to intimidate another. To make this decision, participants had to determine what the offender's intent was in displaying the scenario. Across the three justification conditions, the offenders provided different reasoning for displaying this symbol, but our results tended to show that participants still inferred intimidation as intent, even in justification conditions involving other intended messages, and assigned guilty verdicts to most cases, suggesting they assigned a higher utility rating to the guilty outcomes, in the expected utility model.

Figure 2 represents a decision-tree diagram for one of the fact patterns in the *Virginia v. Black* (2003) case. In this instance, the defendant burned a cross on the lawn of his African American neighbors after a dispute with them. Figure 2 displays possible utility values our participants might have assigned to the various outcomes they could choose in our study. The participants had two choices:

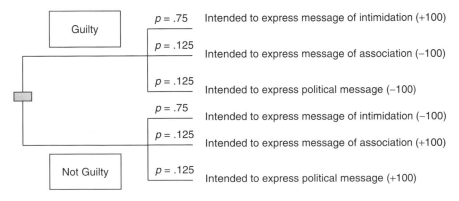

FIGURE 14.2. Decision tree for cross-burning on neighbor's lawn in control condition.

guilty or not guilty. The consequences for each choice are: (1) the offender intended to convey a message of intimidation to someone by displaying the symbol, (2) the offender intended to convey a particular political ideology by displaying the symbol, or (3) the offender intended to convey a message of solidarity with a particular group by displaying the symbol.

As suggested by Hastie and Dawes (2001), we can utilize a subjective scale to demonstrate the possible outcomes. Here a -100 (i.e., negative 100) represents the worst possible outcome and +100 represents the best possible outcome. Finding the defendant not guilty of violating the statute, in a case where he did intend to intimidate another by committing a cross-burning would result in the worst outcome, or a utility of −100. Finding the defendant not guilty in a case where they displayed the symbol for another purpose (political or group message) would represent a better outcome, or a utility score of +100. Similarly, finding the defendant guilty in a case where they did intend to intimidate another would also result in a positive outcome, or a score of +100. However, finding the defendant guilty when he or she intended to display another message would result in a negative outcome, and again, a utility score of −100. The chart also displays probability assessments for each outcome, which describe the likelihood that each outcome would occur. In our study, we would see these probability vary, depending upon the justification condition under which the participants made their decisions. Figure 2 represents a participant in the intimidation justification condition; therefore, the probability that the defendant intended to intimidate the victim is always high (.75).

Now examine Figure 3, which represents a decision tree for the same scenario, but in a different justification condition, here the political ideology condition. The outcomes and their utility values remain the same. It would be a negative outcome for the defendant to be found not guilty if he or she actually intended to intimidate another, and a positive outcome for the defendant to be found not guilty if he or she intended to convey a political message or a group association message. The difference, in this diagram, however, is that the probabilities for the outcomes change as the defendant's justification changes. In the political ideology condition, the defendant claims he displayed the message for a political reason, thus elevating the probability that a not guilty verdict for reasons of political intention would result in the best outcome. Figure 3 illustrates the decision process of a juror who must make a decision under these conditions. Future research that measures the utility outcomes and the subjective probabilities under a variety of other conditions would offer information to policy makers about the ways in which jurors are likely to evaluate different scenarios with hate symbol content.

Now examine Figure 4, which represents a decision tree for the group association condition, but with the other cross burning fact pattern in *Virginia v. Black* (2003), where the defendant had carried out a cross-burning on his own private property during a Ku Klux Klan rally. The state charged him with violating the Virginia statute because passersby could view the cross-burning from a road that ran close to his property. The jury convicted him but the Supreme Court later remanded his case because of a faulty jury instruction. In this diagram, we can

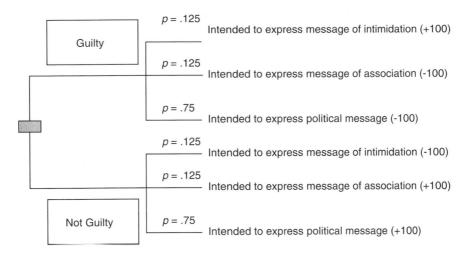

FIGURE 14.3. Decision-tree for cross-burning on neighbor's lawn in political condition.

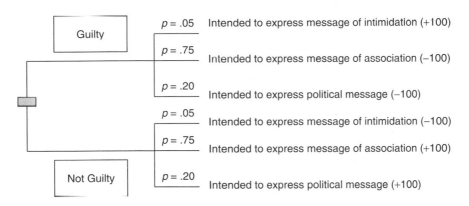

FIGURE 14.4. Decision tree for cross-burning on private property in group association condition.

see that the outcomes would stay the same, but the probabilities will change once again. In this instance, because the offender was committing the cross-burning on private property as part of a KKK rally, it would seem his primary message was not one of intimidation, but rather of group association. Again, it would be a negative outcome to find a defendant not guilty, if he did intend to intimidate someone, but, as previously stated, that does not seem to be true in this situation. Here, the likelihood that his message was one promoting group association should be elevated, resulting in a not guilty verdict because the defendant did not intend to intimidate a victim, if the juror were to calculate the expected utilities of each outcome. (Note that the subjective probabilities in Figure 4 reflect the fact that a rational decision maker should find both expressing group association and expressing political ideology as viable alternatives to victim intimidation to explain the defendant's intentions.)

The expected utility model clearly could serve as a useful tool for decision makers, if they were able to systematically think through each possible outcome available to them. The perplexing part of the problem, for policy makers, is that decisions may not always be made in this logical process. Consider, for example, Kovera's suggestion (this volume) that hate crime offenders could commit an automatic hate crime. That is, the reflex reaction for an offender, when confronted with a person of a minority racial group or minority sexual orientation group, might be to lash out at the other person. Kovera reasons that automatically activated stereotypes could lead to automatically activated responses against those evoking the stereotypes. If this theory is viable, it would make it almost impossible to determine what the offender's intent was in committing the crime. Of course, this scenario plays out more easily when imagining the beating of particular minority member and the yelling of racial slurs, as opposed to burning a cross on that minority member's lawn. In the cross-burning incidence, there are many necessary (probably conscious) steps to carrying out a cross-burning and this would suggest the process is deliberative and systematic, as opposed to automatic. Still, the juror making decisions in this type of case must estimate something like the subjective probabilities in Figures 2, 3, and 4 to reach a decision, if that juror follows the law. The important question for researchers and policy makers alike is, "How do jurors estimate the subjective probabilities for different intention outcomes in hate speech crime?" Viewing the hate speech problem from the expected utility point of view raises some very interesting and important empirical and policy oriented issues.

Though it would be difficult to imagine that a person should be punished for automatic thoughts, it is an interesting moral notion for policy makers to consider. As Kovera (this volume) mentioned, it is difficult to eliminate prejudice and stereotypes unless you are aware of them. One could argue that the elimination of prejudice in our country today is an important enough value that we should punish offenders who commit automatic hate crimes. This could serve as notice to those offenders and everyone that prejudice continues to exist in our world today, and that our society will no longer tolerate the prejudice. If people were going to be punished for their prejudicial actions, it may create more of an effort for members of society to actively pursue the elimination (or near elimination) of personal prejudices. However, this viewpoint ignores the very real problem that it would be improper for policy makers to punish offenders who commit hate crimes automatically because they are unable to control themselves. Much like pulling your hand away from a hot stove, a biased response that is automatically elicited would occur before the person even knows that it exists. A person could shout racial slurs during an assault or an argument without even realizing that they are doing it. As Kovera (this volume) suggests, this notion needs more study in psychological research before we can make a proper determination of whether it actually occurs in the real world. The point here is that regardless of how deliberate are the actions of defendants accused of committing hate crimes, others who evaluate their actions (i.e., member of the public, police, prosecuting attorneys, jurors, and judges) must determine their intentions. Researchers and policy makers interested in this process could benefit from applying the rational actor model because it translates attributions of intentions into subjective probabilities attached to specific outcomes. These can be measured, studied, and ultimately explained.

Throughout this chapter, we have tried to connect psychological decision theory concepts to legal problems and point out the implications for developing legal policy. In doing so, we hope to extend the current scope of psychology's value to the legal system by asking questions and solving problems that have not received a great deal of attention from psycho-legal scholars. We believe that both psychology and the law stand to gain a great deal from each other through projects like this volume and other enterprises that force the two disciplines to interact in new and creative ways.

References

Gutek, B. (2007). How can we make our research on sexual harassment more useful in legal decision-making? In R. L.Wiener, B. Bornstein, R. Schopp, & S. Willborn (Eds.), *Social consciousness in legal decision making: Psychological perspectives*, 151–170. New York: Springer.

Hastie, R. & Dawes, R. M. (2001). *Rational choice in an uncertain world*. Thousand Oaks, CA: Sage.

Kovera, M. B. (2007). Implications of automatic and controlled processes in stereotyping for hate crime perpetration and litigation. In R. L.Wiener, B. Bornstein, R. Schopp, & S. Willborn (Eds.), *Social consciousness in legal decision making: Psychological perspectives*, 227–246. New York: Springer.

Lawrence, F. M. (2007). The hate crime project and its limitations: Evaluating the societal gains and risk in bias crime law enforcement. In R. L.Wiener, B. Bornstein, R. Schopp, & S. Willborn (Eds.), *Social consciousness in legal decision making: Psychological perspectives*, 205–225. New York: Springer.

Rotundo, M., Nguyen, D., & Sackett, P. (2001). A meta-analytic review of gender differences in perceptions of sexual harassment. *Journal of Applied Psychology, 86*(5), 914–922.

Wiener, R. L. (2007). Law and everyday decision-making: rational, descriptive, and normative models. In R. L.Wiener, B. Bornstein, R. Schopp, & S. Willborn (Eds.), *Social consciousness in legal decision making: Psychological perspectives*, 1–30. New York: Springer.

Wiener, R. L., & Hurt, L. E. (1999). An interdisciplinary approach to understanding social sexual conduct at work. In R. Wiener & B. Gutek (Eds.), *Advances in sexual harassment research, theory, and policy. Psychology, Public Policy, and Law, 5,* 556–595.

Wiener, R. L., & Hurt, L. E. (2000). How do people evaluate social-sexual conduct: A psycholegal model. *Journal of Applied Psychology, 85,* 75–85.

Wiener, R. L., & Richter, E. M. (under review). Symbolic hate: Intention to intimidate, political ideology and group association.

Wiener, R. L. & Winter, R. (2007). Totality of circumstances in sexual harassment decisions: A decision making model. In R. L.Wiener, B. Bornstein, R. Schopp, &

S. Willborn (Eds.), *Social consciousness in legal decision making: Psychological perspectives*. New York: Springer.

Wiener, R. L., Winter, R., Rogers, M., & Arnot, L. (2004). The effects of prior workplace behavior on subsequent sexual harassment judgments. *Law and Human Behavior, 28*(1), 47–67.

Index